Introduction to Security Reduction

Fuchun Guo • Willy Susilo • Yi Mu

Introduction to Security Reduction

 Springer

Fuchun Guo
School of Computing
& Information Technology
University of Wollongong
Wollongong, New South Wales, Australia

Willy Susilo
School of Computing
& Information Technology
University of Wollongong
Wollongong, New South Wales, Australia

Yi Mu
School of Computing
& Information Technology
University of Wollongong
Wollongong, New South Wales, Australia

ISBN 978-3-030-06574-4   ISBN 978-3-319-93049-7   (eBook)
https://doi.org/10.1007/978-3-319-93049-7

Printed on acid-free paper

This Springer imprint is published by the registered company Springer International Publishing AG part of Springer Nature.
The registered company address is: Gewerbestrasse 11, 6330 Cham, Switzerland

To my lovely wife Yizhen,
two adorable sons John and Kevin,
and my kindly mother Suhua.
To the memory of my father Yongming.

–Fuchun Guo

To my wife Aurelia and our beloved son
Jayden, without whom this work will never be
accomplished.

–Willy Susilo

To my family!

–Yi Mu

Preface

Security reduction is a very popular approach for proving security in public-key cryptography. With security reduction, roughly speaking, we can show that breaking a proposed scheme is as difficult as solving a mathematical hard problem. However, how to program a correct security reduction using an adversary's adaptive attack is rather complicated. The reason is that there is no universal security reduction for all proposed schemes.

Security reductions given in cryptographic research papers are often hard for beginners to fully comprehend. To aid the beginners, some cryptography textbooks have illustrated how to correctly program security reductions with simpler examples. However, security reductions mentioned in research papers and previous textbooks are usually for specific schemes. The difference in security reductions for different schemes leads to confusion for the beginners. There is a need for a book that systematically introduces how to correctly program a security reduction for a cryptosystem, not for a specific scheme. With this in mind, we wrote this book, which we hope will help the reader understand how to correctly program a security reduction.

The contents of this book, especially the foundations of security reductions, are based on our understanding and experience. The reader might find that the explanations of concepts are slightly different from those in other sources, because we have added some "condiments" to help the reader understand these concepts. For example, in a security reduction, the adversary is not a black-box adversary but a malicious adversary who has unbounded computational power.

We thought this book would be completed within one year, but we underestimated its difficulty. It has taken more than four years to complete the writing of this book. There must still be errors that have not yet been found. We welcome any comments and suggestions.

University of Wollongong, Australia   *Fuchun Guo, Willy Susilo, and Yi Mu*
May 2018

Acknowledgements

We finally accomplished something which is meaningful and useful for our research society. Our primary goal is to make confusing concepts of security reductions vanish, and to provide a clear guide on how to program correct security reductions. Here, we would like to record some of our major milestones as well as to acknowledge several people who have helped us complete this book.

The time that we started to write this book can be traced back to the second half of 2013, after Dr. Fuchun Guo received his PhD degree in July of that year. At that time, being a research assistant, Fuchun was invited to co-supervise Professor Willy Susilo and Professor Yi Mu's PhD students at the University of Wollongong, Australia. Fuchun's primary task was to help Willy and Yi train PhD students with very little background in public-key cryptography. It is evident that there is a big gap between savvy researchers and PhD students just starting on their PhD journeys. Furthermore, we found it was really ineffective for our students to read papers by themselves to understand security proofs and some tricky methods in security reductions. How to quickly train our students remains an elusive problem as we have to repeat the interactions with each individual student day by day. We collected some basic but important knowledge that all our students must master in their studies to conduct research in public-key cryptography. Then we decided to write this book together to help our students. Hence, the original motivation of writing this book was to save our time in the training of our students. We do hope that this book will also benefit others who want to start their research careers in public-key cryptography, or others who want to study the techniques used in programming correct security reductions.

The first version of this book was completed in April 2015. In that version, Chapter 4 had only about 50 pages. That version was rather incomprehensible with a lot of logic and consistency problems. Then, we started to polish the book, which was completed in August 2017. It took 28 months to clarify many important concepts that are contained in this book. We patiently crafted Chapter 4 to ensure that all concepts and knowledge are presented clearly and are easy to understand. Originally, we either did not fully understand many concepts or did not clearly know how to explain them. A significant amount of time was used to think about how to explain each concept and exemplify it with a simple, yet clear, example. We were very passionate in completing this book without thinking about any time constraints. The external proofreading by our students was started in September 2017 and completed in March 2018. More than ten PhD students were involved in the proofreading. We believe this was an invaluable experience for us, which paints a very nice story to share and remember. This book would never have been completed without the hard work of our students.

At the early stage of this book writing, we received a lot of feedback from the process of training our students. This invaluable experience helped us see which concepts are hard for students to understand and how to clearly explain these. We are indebted to our colleagues and students: *Rongmao Chen, Jianchang Lai, Peng Jiang, Nan Li*, and *Yinhao Jiang*. They provided insightful feedback and thoughts when we trained them in public-key cryptography. We can now proudly say that these people have now completed their PhD studies and they have mastered the required skills as independent researchers in public-key cryptography, thanks to the information and training that are provided in this book.

When we completed the writing of this book, we decided to invite our PhD students to read it first. Without too much surprise, our students still found many confusing concepts and unclear knowledge points. They provided a lot of invaluable comments and advice that have been used to improve the quality of this book. In particular, more than 20 pages were added to Chapter 4 to improve the clarity of this important chapter. Specifically, we would like to thank these people: *Jianchang Lai, Zhen Zhao, Ge Wu, Peng Jiang, Zhongyuan Yao, Tong Wu*, and *Shengming Xu* for their helpful advice and feedback.

The first manuscript given to students for proofreading was full of typos and grammatical errors. We would like to thank the following people for their help in improving this book: *Jianchang Lai, Fatemeh Rezaeibagha, Zhen Zhao, Ge Wu, Peng Jiang, Xueqiao Liu, Zhongyuan Yao, Tong Wu, Shengming Xu, Binrui Zhu, Ke Wang, Yannan Li*, and *Yanwei Zhou*.

We would also like to thank all authors of published references that have been cited in this book, especially those authors whose schemes have been used as examples. We merely reorganized this knowledge and put it together with our understanding and our logic. We would also like to thank the Springer editor *Ronan Nugent* and the copy-editors of Springer, who gave us a lot of insightful comments and advice that have indeed improved the quality and clarity of this book.

Last but not least, we would like to thank our families who have always been very supportive. We spent so much time in editing and correcting this book, and without their patience, it would have been impossible to complete. Thank you.

Finally, we hope that the reader will find that this book is useful.

University of Wollongong, Australia   *Fuchun Guo, Willy Susilo, and Yi Mu*
May 2018

Contents

Chapter 1
Guide to This Book

The first step in constructing a provably secure cryptosystem in public-key cryptography is to clarify its cryptographic notion and formalize the definitions of the algorithm and its corresponding security model. A cryptographic notion helps the reader understand the definition of the algorithm, while the security model is essential for measuring the strength of a proposed scheme. Both a scheme construction and its security proof require knowledge of the corresponding cryptographic foundations. With this in mind, we arranged the book chapters in order to capture the working process of a provably secure scheme, as depicted in Figure 1.1.

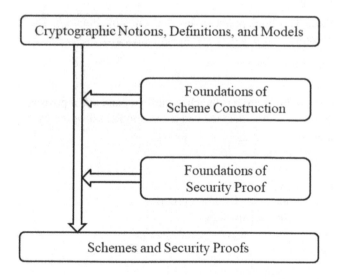

Fig. 1.1 Steps for constructing a provably secure scheme in public-key cryptography

There are two popular methods for security proofs in public-key cryptography, namely game-based proof and simulation-based proof. The former can also be classified into two categories, i.e., security reduction and game hopping. This book cov-

© Springer International Publishing AG, part of Springer Nature 2018
F. Guo et al., *Introduction to Security Reduction*,
https://doi.org/10.1007/978-3-319-93049-7_1

ers only security reduction, which starts with the assumption that there exists an adversary who can break the proposed scheme. In security proofs with security reduction, a concrete security reduction depends on the corresponding cryptosystem, the scheme, and the underlying hard problem. There is no universal approach to program the security reduction for all schemes. This book introduces security reductions for three specific cryptosystems: digital signatures, public-key encryption, and identity-based encryption. All examples and schemes given in this book are constructed over cyclic groups with or without a bilinear map.

The contents of each chapter are outlined as follows. Chapter 2 briefly revisits cryptographic notions, algorithms, and security models. This chapter can be skipped if the reader is familiar with the definitions. Chapter 3 introduces the foundations of group-based cryptography: we introduce finite fields, cyclic groups, bilinear pairing, and hash functions. Our introduction mainly focuses on efficiently computable operations and the group representation. We minimize the description of the preliminary knowledge of group-based cryptography. Chapter 4 is the most important chapter in this book. In this chapter, we classify and explain the fundamental concepts of security reduction and also summarize how in general to program a full security reduction for digital signatures and encryption. We take examples from group-based cryptography, when it is necessary to give examples to explain the concepts. The remaining chapters of this book are dedicated to the security proofs of some selected schemes in order to help the reader understand how to program the security reduction correctly. The security proof in each selected scheme corresponds to a useful reduction technique.

About Notation. This book prefers to use the following notation. The same notation may have different meanings in different applications.

For mathematical primitives:

- q, p: prime numbers.
- $\mathbb{F}_{q^n}$: the finite field where q is the characteristic, and n is a positive integer.
- k: the size of embedding degree in an extension field denoted by $\mathbb{F}_{(q^n)^k}$.
- $\mathbb{Z}_p$: the integer set $\{0, 1, 2, \cdots, p-1\}$.
- $\mathbb{Z}_p^*$: the integer set $\{1, 2, \cdots, p-1\}$.
- $\mathbb{H}$: a general group.
- $\mathbb{G}$: a cyclic group of prime order p.
- u, v: general elements in a field or a group.
- g, h: group elements of a cyclic group.
- w, x, y, z: integers in an integer set, such as $\mathbb{Z}_p$.
- e: a bilinear map.

For scheme constructions:

- λ: a security parameter.
- $(\mathbb{G}, g, p)$: a general cyclic group $\mathbb{G}$ of prime order p where g is a generator of $\mathbb{G}$.
- $|p|$: the bit length of the number p in the binary representation.
- $|g|$: the bit length of the group element g in the binary representation.

- $|\mathbb{G}|$: the number of group elements in the group $\mathbb{G}$.
- $\mathbb{PG} = (\mathbb{G}, \mathbb{G}_T, g, p, e)$: a pairing group composed of two groups $\mathbb{G}, \mathbb{G}_T$ of the same prime order p with a generator g of $\mathbb{G}$ and a bilinear map $e : \mathbb{G} \times \mathbb{G} \to \mathbb{G}_T$.
- $\{0, 1\}^*$: the space of all bit strings.
- $\{0, 1\}^n$: the space of all n-bit strings.
- α, β, γ: random integers in $\mathbb{Z}_p$ as secret keys.
- g, h, u, v: group elements.
- r, s: random numbers in $\mathbb{Z}_p$.
- n: a general positive number associated with the corresponding scenario.
- i, j: indexing numbers.
- m: a plaintext message.
- $\sigma_m = (\sigma_1, \sigma_2, \cdots, \sigma_n)$: a signature of m where σ_i denotes the i-th element.
- $CT = (C_1, C_2, \cdots, C_n)$: a ciphertext where C_i denotes the i-th element.
- (pk, sk): a key pair where pk is the public key and sk is the secret key.
- d_{ID}: a private key of identity ID in identity-based cryptography.

For hard problems:

- I: an instance of a mathematical hard problem.
- Z: the target to be decided in an instance of a decisional hard problem in which Z is either a true element or a false element.
- g, h, u, v: group elements.
- a, b, c: random and unknown exponents from $\mathbb{Z}_p$ in the problem instance I.
- $F(x), f(x), g(x)$: (random) polynomials in $\mathbb{Z}_p[x]$, namely polynomials in x where all coefficients are randomly chosen from $\mathbb{Z}_p$.
- F_i, G_i, f_i, a_i: the coefficients of x^i in polynomials.
- n, k, l: general positive integers associated with the corresponding scenario.

For security models and security proofs:

- $\mathscr{A}$: the adversary.
- $\mathscr{C}$: the challenger.
- $\mathscr{B}$: the simulator.
- ε: the advantage of breaking a scheme or solving a hard problem.
- t: the time cost of breaking a scheme.
- q: the number associated with the underlying hard problem.
- q_s: the number of signature queries.
- q_k: the number of private-key queries in identity-based cryptography.
- q_d: the number of decryption queries.
- q_H: the number of hash queries to random oracles.
- $c, coin$: a bit randomly chosen from $\{0, 1\}$.
- w, x, y, z: secret and random numbers chosen from $\mathbb{Z}_p$ by the simulator.
- T_s: the time cost of the security reduction.

A Note to Research Students. Security reduction requires very tricky analysis. Even if you can understand a security reduction from others, it may still be challenging for you to program a correct security reduction for your own scheme. A traditional Chinese proverb says

> *"Seeing once is better than hearing 100 times, but doing once is better than seeing 100 times."*

To best use this book, you can try to prove (Doing) the schemes provided in the book based on the knowledge in Chapter 4, prior to reading the security proofs given in the book (Seeing). You will understand more about which part is the most difficult for you and how security reductions can be programmed correctly. The reader can visit the authors' homepages to find supplementary resources for this book.

Chapter 2
Notions, Definitions, and Models

In this chapter, we briefly revisit important knowledge including the cryptographic notions, algorithms, and security models of digital signatures, public-key encryption, and identity-based encryption. For convenience in the presentation, we split the traditional key generation algorithm of digital signatures and public-key encryption into the system parameter generation algorithm and the key generation algorithm, where the system parameters can be shared by all users. Each cryptosystem in this book is composed of four algorithms.

2.1 Digital Signatures

A digital signature is a fundamental tool in cryptography that has been widely applied to authentication and non-repudiation. Take authentication as an example. A party, say Alice, wants to convince all other parties that a message m is published by her. To do so, Alice generates a public/secret key pair (pk, sk) and publishes the public key pk to all verifiers. To generate a signature σ_m on m, she digitally signs m with her secret key sk. Upon receiving (m, σ_m), any receiver who already knows pk can verify the signature σ_m and confirm the origin of the message m.

A digital signature scheme consists of the following four algorithms.

SysGen: The system parameter generation algorithm takes as input a security parameter λ. It returns the system parameters SP.

KeyGen: The key generation algorithm takes as input the system parameters SP. It returns a public/secret key pair (pk, sk).

Sign: The signing algorithm takes as input a message m from its message space, the secret key sk, and the system parameters SP. It returns a signature of m denoted by σ_m.

© Springer International Publishing AG, part of Springer Nature 2018
F. Guo et al., *Introduction to Security Reduction*,
https://doi.org/10.1007/978-3-319-93049-7_2

> **Verify:** The verification algorithm takes as input a message-signature pair (m, σ_m), the public key pk, and the system parameters SP. It returns "accept" if σ_m is a valid signature of m signed with sk; otherwise, it returns "reject."

Correctness. Given any (pk, sk, m, σ_m), if σ_m is a valid signature of m signed with sk, the verification algorithm on (m, σ_m, pk) will return "accept."

Security. Without the secret key sk, it is hard for any probabilistic polynomial-time (PPT) adversary to forge a valid signature σ_m on a new message m that can pass the signature verification.

In the security model of digital signatures, the security is modeled by a game played by a challenger and an adversary, where during the interaction between them the challenger generates a signature scheme and the adversary tries to break the scheme. That is, the challenger first generates a key pair (pk, sk), sends the public key pk to the adversary, and keeps the secret key. The adversary can then make signature queries on any messages adaptively chosen by the adversary itself. Finally, the adversary returns a forged signature of a new message that has not been queried. This security notion is called *existential unforgeability*.

The security model of existential unforgeability against chosen-message attacks (EU-CMA) can be described as follows.

Setup. Let SP be the system parameters. The challenger runs the key generation algorithm to generate a key pair (pk, sk) and sends pk to the adversary. The challenger keeps sk to respond to signature queries from the adversary.

Query. The adversary makes signature queries on messages that are adaptively chosen by the adversary itself. For a signature query on the message m_i, the challenger runs the signing algorithm to compute σ_{m_i} and then sends it to the adversary.

Forgery. The adversary returns a forged signature σ_{m^*} on some m^* and wins the game if

- σ_{m^*} is a valid signature of the message m^*.
- A signature of m^* has not been queried in the query phase.

The advantage ε of winning the game is the probability of returning a valid forged signature.

Definition 2.1.0.1 (EU-CMA) *A signature scheme is (t, q_s, ε)-secure in the EU-CMA security model if there exists no adversary who can win the above game in time t with advantage ε after it has made q_s signature queries.*

A stronger security model for digital signatures is defined as follows.

Definition 2.1.0.2 (SU-CMA) *A signature scheme is (t, q_s, ε)-secure in the security model of strong unforgeability against chosen-message attacks (SU-CMA) if there exists no adversary who can win the above game in time t with advantage ε after it has made q_s signature queries, where the forged signature can be on any message as long as it is different from all queried signatures.*

In the definition of (standard) digital signatures, the secret key sk does not need to be updated during the signature generation. We name this signature *stateless signature*. In contrast, if the secret key sk needs to be updated before the generation of each signature, we name it *stateful signature*. Stateful signature schemes will be introduced in Section 6.3 and Section 6.5 in this book.

2.2 Public-Key Encryption

Public-key encryption is another important tool in public-key cryptography, which has demonstrated many useful applications such as data confidentiality, key exchange, oblivious transfer, etc. Take data confidentiality as an example. A party, say Bob, wants to send a sensitive message m to another party, say Alice, though they do not share any secret key. Alice first generates a public/secret key pair (pk, sk) and publishes her public key pk to all senders. With pk, Bob can then encrypt the sensitive message m and sends the resulting ciphertext to Alice. Alice can in turn decrypt the ciphertext with the secret key sk and obtain the message m.

A public-key encryption scheme consists of the following four algorithms.

SysGen: The system parameter generation algorithm takes as input a security parameter λ. It returns the system parameters SP.

KeyGen: The key generation algorithm takes as input the system parameters SP. It returns a public/secret key pair (pk, sk).

Encrypt: The encryption algorithm takes as input a message m from its message space, the public key pk, and the system parameters SP. It returns a ciphertext $CT = E[SP, pk, m]$.

Decrypt: The decryption algorithm takes as input a ciphertext CT, the secret key sk, and the system parameters SP. It returns a message m or outputs $\perp$ to denote a failure.

Correctness. Given any (SP, pk, sk, m, CT), if $CT = E[SP, pk, m]$ is a ciphertext encrypted with pk on the message m, the decryption of CT with the secret key sk will return the message m.

Security. Without the secret key sk, it is hard for any PPT adversary to extract the message m from the given ciphertext $CT = E[SP, pk, m]$.

The indistinguishability security of public-key encryption is modeled by a game played by a challenger and an adversary. The challenger generates an encryption scheme, while the adversary tries to break the scheme. To start, the challenger generates a key pair (pk, sk), sends the public key pk to the adversary, and keeps the secret key sk. The adversary outputs two distinct messages m_0, m_1 from the same message space to be challenged. The challenger generates a challenge ciphertext

CT^* on a message m_c randomly chosen from $\{m_0, m_1\}$. If decryption queries are allowed, the adversary can make decryption queries on any ciphertexts that are adaptively chosen by the adversary itself with the restriction that no decryption query is allowed on CT^*. Finally, the adversary outputs a guess of the chosen message m_c in the challenge ciphertext CT^*.

Formally, the security model of indistinguishability against chosen-ciphertext attacks (IND-CCA) can be described as follows.

Setup. Let SP be the system parameters. The challenger runs the key generation algorithm to generate a key pair (pk, sk) and sends pk to the adversary. The challenger keeps sk to respond to decryption queries from the adversary.

Phase 1. The adversary makes decryption queries on ciphertexts that are adaptively chosen by the adversary itself. For a decryption query on the ciphertext CT_i, the challenger runs the decryption algorithm and then sends the decryption result to the adversary.

Challenge. The adversary outputs two distinct messages m_0, m_1 from the same message space, which are adaptively chosen by the adversary itself. The challenger randomly chooses $c \in \{0, 1\}$ and then computes a challenge ciphertext $CT^* = E[SP, pk, m_c]$, which is given to the adversary.

Phase 2. The challenger responds to decryption queries in the same way as in Phase 1 with the restriction that no decryption query is allowed on CT^*.

Guess. The adversary outputs a guess c' of c and wins the game if $c' = c$.

The advantage ε of the adversary in winning this game is defined as

$$\varepsilon = 2\left(\Pr[c' = c] - \frac{1}{2}\right).$$

Definition 2.2.0.1 (IND-CCA) *A public-key encryption scheme is (t, q_d, ε)-secure in the IND-CCA security model if there exists no adversary who can win the above game in time t with advantage ε after it has made q_d decryption queries.*

In general, we regard the IND-CCA model as the standard security model for the security of encryption. There is a weaker version of indistinguishability, i.e., indistinguishability against chosen-plaintext attacks (IND-CPA), which is also referred to as *semantic security*, defined as follows.

Definition 2.2.0.2 (IND-CPA) *A public-key encryption scheme is (t, ε)-secure in the security model of indistinguishability against chosen-plaintext attacks (IND-CPA) if the scheme is $(t, 0, \varepsilon)$-secure in the IND-CCA security model, where the adversary is not allowed to make any decryption query.*

In the description of security models, a random coin is chosen by the challenger to decide which message will be encrypted in the challenge phase. In this book, we denote the random coin by the symbol $c \in \{0, 1\}$ or by the symbol $coin \in \{0, 1\}$ if c has been used in the hardness assumption.

2.3 Identity-Based Encryption

Identity-based encryption (IBE) is motivated by a disadvantage of public-key encryption, which is that each public key looks like a random string and thus public-key encryption needs a certificate system. In the notion of IBE, there is a master key pair (mpk, msk) generated by a private-key generator (PKG). The master public key mpk is published to all users, and the master secret key msk is kept by the PKG. Suppose a party, say Bob, wants to send a sensitive message to another party, say Alice. Bob simply encrypts the message with the master public key mpk and Alice's identity ID, such as Alice's email address. Alice decrypts the ciphertext with her private key d_{ID}, which is computed by the PKG with the identity ID and the master secret key msk.

An IBE scheme only requires all encryptors to verify the validity of the master public key mpk. Therefore, they do not have to verify the public keys of the receivers since the public keys are the receivers' identity information. Only the receiver matching the identity information is able to receive its private key from the PKG and decrypt the corresponding ciphertext. IBE allows Bob to encrypt a message for Alice using her name as the identity; then Alice applies for the corresponding private key from the PKG. In this book, the decryption key is called the secret key in PKE; while the decryption key is called the private key in IBE.

An identity-based encryption scheme consists of the following four algorithms.

Setup: The setup algorithm takes as input a security parameter λ. It returns a master public/secret key pair (mpk, msk).

KeyGen: The key generation algorithm takes as input an identity ID and the master key pair (mpk, msk). It returns the private key d_{ID} of ID.

Encrypt: The encryption algorithm takes as input a message m from its message space, an identity ID, and the master public key mpk. It returns a ciphertext $CT = E[mpk, ID, m]$.

Decrypt: The decryption algorithm takes as input a ciphertext CT for ID, the private key d_{ID}, and the master public key mpk. It returns a message m or outputs $\perp$ to denote a failure.

Correctness. Given any $(mpk, msk, ID, d_{ID}, m, CT)$, if $CT = E[mpk, ID, m]$ is a ciphertext encrypted with ID on the message m, the decryption of CT with the private key d_{ID} will return the message m.

Security. Without the private key d_{ID}, it is hard for any PPT adversary to extract the message from the given ciphertext $CT = E[mpk, ID, m]$.

The indistinguishability security of identity-based encryption is modeled by a game played by a challenger and an adversary. The challenger generates an IBE scheme, while the adversary tries to break the scheme. To start, the challenger generates a master key pair (mpk, msk), sends the master public key mpk to the adversary, and keeps the master secret key msk. The adversary outputs two distinct messages m_0, m_1 and an identity ID^* to be challenged. The challenger generates a challenge ciphertext CT^* on a randomly chosen message from $\{m_0, m_1\}$ for ID^*. During the game, the adversary can adaptively make private-key queries on any identities other than the challenge identity and can make decryption queries on any ciphertexts other than the challenge ciphertext. In particular, the adversary can make a decryption query on (ID, CT) satisfying either $(ID = ID^*, CT \neq CT^*)$ or $(ID \neq ID^*, CT = CT^*)$. Finally, the adversary outputs a guess of the chosen message in the challenge ciphertext CT^*.

The security model of indistinguishability against chosen-ciphertext attacks (IND-ID-CCA) can be described as follows.

Setup. The challenger runs the setup algorithm to generate a master key pair (mpk, msk) and sends mpk to the adversary. The challenger keeps msk to respond to queries from the adversary.

Phase 1. The adversary makes private-key queries and decryption queries, where identities and ciphertexts are adaptively chosen by the adversary itself.

- For a private-key query on ID_i, the challenger runs the key generation algorithm on ID_i with the master secret key msk and then sends d_{ID_i} to the adversary.
- For a decryption query on (ID_i, CT_i), the challenger runs the decryption algorithm with the private key d_{ID_i} and then sends the decryption result to the adversary.

Challenge. The adversary outputs two distinct messages m_0, m_1 from the same message space and an identity ID^* to be challenged, where m_0, m_1, ID^* are all adaptively chosen by the adversary itself. We require that the private key of ID^* has not been queried in Phase 1. The challenger randomly chooses $c \in \{0, 1\}$ and then computes a challenge ciphertext $CT^* = E[mpk, ID^*, m_c]$, which is given to the adversary.

Phase 2. The challenger responds to private-key queries and decryption queries in the same way as in Phase 1 with the restriction that no private-key query is allowed on ID^* and no decryption decryption query is allowed on (ID^*, CT^*).

Guess. The adversary outputs a guess c' of c and wins the game if $c' = c$.

The advantage ε of the adversary in winning this game is defined as

$$\varepsilon = 2\left(\Pr[c' = c] - \frac{1}{2} \right).$$

Definition 2.3.0.1 (IND-ID-CCA) *An identity-based encryption scheme is $(t, q_k, q_d, \varepsilon)$-secure in the IND-ID-CCA security model if there exists no adversary who can win the above game in time t with advantage ε after it has made q_k private-key queries and q_d decryption queries.*

There are two weaker security models, defined as follows.

Definition 2.3.0.2 (IND-sID-CCA) *An identity-based encryption scheme is $(t, q_k, q_d, \varepsilon)$-secure in the selective-ID security model (IND-sID-CCA) if the encryption scheme is $(t, q_k, q_d, \varepsilon)$-secure in the IND-ID-CCA security model but the adversary must choose the challenge identity ID^* before the setup phase.*

Definition 2.3.0.3 (IND-ID-CPA) *An identity-based encryption scheme is (t, q_k, ε)-secure in the security model of indistinguishability against chosen-plaintext attacks (IND-ID-CPA) if the scheme is $(t, q_k, 0, \varepsilon)$-secure in the IND-ID-CCA security model, where the adversary is not allowed to make any decryption query.*

In Phase 1 and Phase 2 of the security model, the adversary can alternately make private-key queries and decryption queries. The total numbers of queries made by the adversary are q_k and q_d in the security model, but the adversary can adaptively decide the number of private-key queries denoted by q_1 and the number of decryption queries denoted by q_2 in Phase 1 by itself as long as $q_1 \leq q_k$ and $q_2 \leq q_d$.

2.4 Further Reading

In this section, we briefly introduce developments of security models for digital signatures, public-key encryption (PKE), and identity-based encryption (IBE).

Digital Signatures. Digital signatures were first introduced by Diffie and Hellman [34] and formally defined by Goldwasser, Micali, and Rivest [50], where the EU-CMA security model was first defined. One-time signature is a very special digital signature invented by Lamport [71] and is an important building block for cryptographic constructions.

Many security models for digital signatures have been proposed in the literature, where the security models of signatures are defined to model signature query and signature forgery. The notion of strong unforgeability (SU) was discussed in [13, 4]. If the adversary can query signatures but cannot decide which messages are to be signed, the security model is defined as known-message attacks [50] or random-message attacks [64]. If the adversary can choose the messages to be queried but must do so before seeing the public key, the security model is defined as weak chosen-message attacks [21], generic chosen-message attacks [50], or known-message attacks [64]. We refer the reader to the book [64] authored by Jonathan Katz for further reading on these models, the relations among them, and how to transfer a weaker model to a stronger model. Note that the EU-CMA model is not the strongest security model. Some security models (e.g., [12, 36, 59, 62]) have been defined to capture leakage-resistant security for digital signatures, and some security models (e.g., [82, 7, 8]) have been defined to consider the security under the multi-user setting.

Public-Key Encryption. The security model for public-key encryption is defined to model the decryption query and the security goal.

For the decryption query, we have the definitions of chosen-plaintext attacks (CPA) [49], chosen-ciphertext attacks (CCA) [11, 88], and non-adaptive chosen-ciphertext attacks (CCA1) [84]. In the CCA1 security model, the adversary is only allowed to make decryption queries prior to receiving the challenge ciphertext. For the security goal, we have the following four definitions.

- The definition of indistinguishability (IND) [49]: the adversary cannot distinguish the encrypted message in the challenge ciphertext.
- The definition of semantic security (SS) [49]: the adversary cannot compute the encrypted message from the ciphertext.
- The definition of non-malleability (NM) [37, 38]: given a challenge ciphertext, the adversary is unable to output another ciphertext such that the corresponding encrypted messages are "meaningfully related."
- The definition of plaintext awareness (PA) [15]: the adversary is unable to create a ciphertext without knowing the underlying message for encryption.

The notion of semantic security is proved [100] to be equal to indistinguishability, and non-malleability implies [11] indistinguishability under any type of attacks.

We refer the reader to the work [11] to see the relations among the security models mentioned above. There also exist stronger security models (e.g., [59, 36, 27, 35]) defined to capture leakage-resistant security for PKE. Some security models (e.g., [10, 60, 45, 46]) have been defined to consider the security under the multi-user setting.

Identity-Based Encryption. Identity-based cryptosystems were first introduced by Shamir [93]. The security models of IND-ID-CPA and IND-ID-CCA were defined in several works (e.g., [24, 25]). The security model of IND-sID-CCA was first defined in [27, 28, 20]. Similarly to PKE, there are some variants of the IBE security model such as IND-ID-CCA1, IND-sID-CCA1, NM-ID-CPA, NM-ID-CCA1, NM-ID-CCA, NM-sID-CPA, SS-ID-CPA, SS-ID-CCA1, SS-ID-CCA, and SS-sID-CPA. The work in [6] shows that non-malleability still implies indistinguishability under any type of attacks, and semantic security still equals indistinguishability for IBE. The stronger security models introduced in [103, 56] were proposed to capture leakage-resistant security for IBE.

Chapter 3
Foundations of Group-Based Cryptography

In this chapter, we introduce some mathematical primitives including finite fields, groups, and bilinear pairing that are the foundations of group-based cryptography. We also describe three types of hash functions that play an important role in the scheme constructions. We mainly focus on introducing the feasibility of basic operations and the size of binary representations.

3.1 Finite Fields

3.1.1 Definition

Definition 3.1.1.1 (Finite Field) *A finite field (Galois field), denoted by* $(\mathbb{F}, +, *)$, *is a set containing a finite number of elements with two binary operations "+" (addition) and "*" (multiplication) defined as follows.*

- $\forall u, v \in \mathbb{F}$, *we have* $u + v \in \mathbb{F}$ *and* $u * v \in \mathbb{F}$.
- $\forall u_1, u_2, u_3 \in \mathbb{F}$, $(u_1 + u_2) + u_3 = u_1 + (u_2 + u_3)$ *and* $(u_1 * u_2) * u_3 = u_1 * (u_2 * u_3)$.
- $\forall u, v \in \mathbb{F}$, *we have* $u + v = v + u$ *and* $u * v = v * u$.
- $\exists 0_{\mathbb{F}}, 1_{\mathbb{F}} \in \mathbb{F}$ *(identity elements),* $\forall u \in \mathbb{F}$, *we have* $u + 0_{\mathbb{F}} = u$ *and* $u * 1_{\mathbb{F}} = u$.
- $\forall u \in \mathbb{F}$, $\exists -u \in \mathbb{F}$ *such that* $u + (-u) = 0_{\mathbb{F}}$.
- $\forall u \in \mathbb{F}^*$, $\exists u^{-1} \in \mathbb{F}^*$ *such that* $u * u^{-1} = 1_{\mathbb{F}}$. *Here,* $\mathbb{F}^* = \mathbb{F} \backslash \{0_{\mathbb{F}}\}$.
- $\forall u_1, u_2, v \in \mathbb{F}$, *we have* $(u_1 + u_2) * v = u_1 * v + u_2 * v$.

We denote by the symbol $0_{\mathbb{F}} \in \mathbb{F}$ the identity element under the addition operation and by the symbol $1_{\mathbb{F}} \in \mathbb{F}$ the identity element under the multiplication operation. We denote by $-u$ the additive inverse of u and by u^{-1} the multiplicative inverse of u. Note that the binary operations defined in the finite field are different from the traditional arithmetical addition and multiplication.

A finite field, denoted by $(\mathbb{F}_{q^n}, +, *)$ in this book, is a specific field where n is a positive integer, and q is a prime number called the characteristic of $\mathbb{F}_{q^n}$. This finite

© Springer International Publishing AG, part of Springer Nature 2018
F. Guo et al., *Introduction to Security Reduction*,
https://doi.org/10.1007/978-3-319-93049-7_3

field has q^n elements. Each element in the finite field can be seen as an n-length vector, where each scalar in the vector is from the finite field $\mathbb{F}_q$. Therefore, the bit length of each element in this finite field is $n \cdot |q|$.

3.1.2 Field Operations

In a finite field, two binary operations are defined: addition and multiplication. They can be extended to subtraction and division through their inverses described as follows.

- The subtraction operation is defined from the addition. $\forall u, v \in \mathbb{F}$, we have

$$u - v = u + (-v),$$

  which calculates the addition of u and the additive inverse of v.
- The division operation is defined from the multiplication. $\forall u \in \mathbb{F}, v \in \mathbb{F}^*$, we have

$$u/v = u * v^{-1},$$

  which calculates the multiplication of u and the multiplicative inverse of v.

3.1.3 Field Choices

We introduce three common classes of finite fields, namely prime fields, binary fields, and extension fields.

- Prime Field $\mathbb{F}_q$ is a field of residue classes modulo q. There are q elements in this field represented as $\mathbb{Z}_q = \{0, 1, 2, \cdots, q-1\}$, and two operations: the modular addition and the modular multiplication. Furthermore,

$$-u = q - u \text{ and } u^{-1} = u^{q-2} \text{ mod } q.$$

- Binary Field $\mathbb{F}_{2^n}$ can be represented as a field of equivalence classes of polynomials whose degree is $n-1$ and whose coefficients are from $\mathbb{F}_2$:

$$\mathbb{F}_{2^n} = \left\{ a_{n-1}x^{n-1} + a_{n-2}x^{n-2} + \cdots + a_1 x + a_0 : a_i \in \mathbb{F}_2 \right\},$$

  where the corresponding element in this field is $a_{n-1}a_{n-2}\cdots a_1 a_0$. The addition in this field is calculated by applying XOR to each pair of two polynomial coefficients, while the multiplication in this field requires an operation of reduction modulo an irreducible binary polynomial $f(x)$ of degree n. Furthermore,

$$-u = u \text{ and } u^{-1} = u^{2^n-2} \text{mod} f(x).$$

- Extension Field $\mathbb{F}_{(q^{n_1})^{n_2}}$ is an extension field of the field $\mathbb{F}_{q^{n_1}}$. The integer n_2 is called the embedding degree. Similarly to the binary field, the representation can be described as

$$\mathbb{F}_{(q^{n_1})^{n_2}} = \left\{ a_{n_2-1}x^{n_2-1} + a_{n_2-2}x^{n_2-2} + \cdots + a_1 x + a_0 : \ a_i \in \mathbb{F}_{q^{n_1}} \right\},$$

where the corresponding element in this field is $a_{n_2-1}a_{n_2-2}\cdots a_1 a_0$. The addition in this field denotes the addition of polynomials with coefficient arithmetic performed in the field $\mathbb{F}_{q^{n_1}}$. The multiplication is performed by an operation of reduction modulo an irreducible polynomial $f(x)$ of degree n_2 in $\mathbb{F}_{q^{n_1}}[x]$. The computations of $-u$ and u^{-1} are much more complicated than for the previous two fields. We omit them in this book.

3.1.4 Computations over a Prime Field

Among three fields mentioned above, the prime field $\mathbb{F}_p$ is the most important field in group-based cryptography. This is due to the fact that the group order is usually a prime number. In the prime field $\mathbb{F}_p$, all elements are numbers in the set $\mathbb{Z}_p = \{0, 1, 2, \cdots, p-1\}$. All the following modular arithmetic operations over the prime field are efficiently computable. The detailed algorithms for conducting the corresponding computations are outside the scope of this book.

- **Modular Additive Inverse.** Given $y \in \mathbb{Z}_p$, compute

$$-y \bmod p.$$

- **Modular Multiplicative Inverse.** Given $z \in \mathbb{Z}_p^*$, compute

$$\frac{1}{z} = z^{-1} \bmod p.$$

- **Modular Addition.** Given $y, z \in \mathbb{Z}_p$, compute

$$y + z \bmod p.$$

- **Modular Subtraction.** Given $y, z \in \mathbb{Z}_p$, compute

$$y - z \bmod p.$$

- **Modular Multiplication.** Given $y, z \in \mathbb{Z}_p$, compute

$$y * z \bmod p.$$

- **Modular Division.** Given $y \in \mathbb{Z}_p$ and $z \in \mathbb{Z}_p^*$, compute

$$\frac{y}{z} \bmod p.$$

- **Modular Exponentiation.** Given $y, z \in \mathbb{Z}_p$, compute

$$y^z \bmod p.$$

The modular multiplicative inverse requires z to be a nonzero integer. However, in cryptography, we cannot avoid the case $z = 0$ during the calculation z^{-1}, although it happens with negligible probability. If this occurs, we define $1/0 = 0$ in this book for all hard problems and schemes.

3.2 Cyclic Groups

3.2.1 Definitions

Definition 3.2.1.1 (Abelian Group) *An abelian group, denoted by* $(\mathbb{H}, \cdot)$, *is a set of elements with one binary operation "$\cdot$" defined as follows.*

- $\forall u, v \in \mathbb{H}$, *we have* $u \cdot v \in \mathbb{H}$.
- $\forall u_1, u_2, u_3 \in \mathbb{H}$, *we have* $(u_1 \cdot u_2) \cdot u_3 = u_1 \cdot (u_2 \cdot u_3)$.
- $\forall u, v \in \mathbb{H}$, *we have* $u \cdot v = v \cdot u$.
- $\exists 1_{\mathbb{H}} \in \mathbb{H}$, $\forall u \in \mathbb{H}$, *we have* $u \cdot 1_{\mathbb{H}} = u$.
- $\forall u \in \mathbb{H}$, $\exists u^{-1} \in \mathbb{H}$, *such that* $u \cdot u^{-1} = 1_{\mathbb{H}}$.

We denote by $1_{\mathbb{H}}$ the identity element in this group. The only group operation can be extended to another operation called group division, i.e., given u, the aim is to compute u^{-1}. Note that the division u/v is equivalent to $u \cdot v^{-1}$.

Definition 3.2.1.2 (Cyclic Group) *An abelian group* $\mathbb{H}$ *is a cyclic group if there exists (at least) one generator, denoted by* h, *which can generate the group* $\mathbb{H}$:

$$\mathbb{H} = \left\{ h^1, h^2, \cdots, h^{|\mathbb{H}|} \right\} = \left\{ h^0, h^1, h^2, \cdots, h^{|\mathbb{H}|-1} \right\},$$

where $|\mathbb{H}|$ *denotes the group order of* $\mathbb{H}$ *and* $h^{|\mathbb{H}|} = h^0 = 1_{\mathbb{H}}$.

Definition 3.2.1.3 (Cyclic Subgroup of Prime Order) *A group* $\mathbb{G}$ *is a cyclic subgroup of prime order if it is a subgroup of a cyclic group* $\mathbb{H}$ *and* $|\mathbb{G}|$ *is a prime number, where*

- $|\mathbb{G}|$ *is a divisor of* $|\mathbb{H}|$;
- *There exists a generator* $g \in \mathbb{H}$, *which generates* $\mathbb{G}$.

3.2.2 Cyclic Groups of Prime Order

In group-based cryptography, we prefer to use a cyclic group $\mathbb{G}$ of prime order p due to the following reasons. Firstly, the cyclic group $\mathbb{G}$ is the smallest subgroup without confinement attacks [75]. Secondly, any integer in $\{1, 2, \cdots, p-1\}$ has a modular multiplicative inverse, which is very useful in the scheme constructions. For example, if g^x is a group element of $\mathbb{G}$ for any $x \in \{1, 2, \cdots, p-1\}$, then we have that $g^{\frac{1}{x}}$ is also a group element. Finally, any group element except $1_{\mathbb{G}}$ in $\mathbb{G}$ is a generator of this group. These three properties are desired for security and flexibility in the construction of public-key cryptosystems. In this book, a (cyclic) group refers to a cyclic group of prime order unless specified otherwise. Note that it is not necessary to construct all group-based cryptosystems from a group of prime order. For example, the ElGamal signature scheme can be constructed from any cyclic group.

To define a group for scheme constructions, we need to specify

- The space of the group, denoted by $\mathbb{G}$.
- The generator of the group, denoted by g.
- The order of the group, denoted by p.

That is, $(\mathbb{G}, g, p)$ are the basic components when defining a group in the scheme constructions. Notice that the group operation can be simplified or omitted depending on the choice of the group.

3.2.3 Group Exponentiations

Let $(\mathbb{G}, g, p)$ be a cyclic group and x be a positive integer. We denote by g^x the group exponentiation, where g^x is defined as

$$g^x = \underbrace{g \cdot g \cdots g \cdot g}_{x}.$$

The group exponentiation is composed of $x - 1$ copies of the group operations from the above definition. According to the definition of the group $(\mathbb{G}, g, p)$, we have

$$g^x = g^{x \bmod p}.$$

Therefore, when an integer x is chosen for the group exponentiation, we can assume that x is chosen from the set $\mathbb{Z}_p$ and call the integer x the exponent.

In public-key cryptography, x is an extremely large exponent whose length is at least 160 in the binary representation. Therefore, it is impractical to perform $x - 1$ copies of the group operations. Group exponentiation is frequently used in group-based cryptography. There exist other polynomial-time algorithms for the computation of group exponentiation. The simplest algorithm is the square-and-multiply algorithm, which is described as follows.

- Convert x into an n-bit binary string x:

$$x = x_{n-1} \cdots x_1 x_0 = \sum_{i=0}^{n-1} x_i 2^i.$$

- Let $g_i = g^{2^i}$. Compute $g_i = g_{i-1} \cdot g_{i-1}$ for all $i \in [1, n-1]$.
- Set X to be the subset of $\{0, 1, 2, \cdots, n-1\}$ where $j \in X$ if $x_j = 1$.
- Compute g^x by

$$\prod_{j \in X} g_j = \prod_{i=0}^{n-1} g_i^{x_i} = g^{\sum_{i=0}^{n-1} x_i 2^i} = g^x.$$

The group exponentiation costs at most $2n - 2$ group operations, which is linear in the bit length of x. The time complexity is $O(\log x)$, which is much faster than $O(x) = x - 1$ group operations.

Note that group exponentiation is just a common name for a cyclic group. It has different names in specific groups. For example, we call it modular exponentiation in a modular multiplicative group and point multiplication (or scalar multiplication) in an elliptic curve group, respectively. These groups will be introduced in Section 3.2.6 and Section 3.2.7, respectively.

3.2.4 Discrete Logarithms

The integer x satisfying $g^x = h$, where $g, h \in \mathbb{G}$ are not the identity element $1_{\mathbb{G}}$, is called the discrete logarithm to the base g of h. Computing x is known as the discrete logarithm (DL) problem.

The DL problem is the fundamental hard problem in group-based cryptography. There is no polynomial-time algorithm for solving the DL problem over a general cyclic group. The only relatively efficient algorithm (the Pollard Rho Algorithm) still requires $O(\sqrt{p})$ steps where p is the group order. For example, if the group order of $\mathbb{G}$ is as large as 2^{160}, solving the DL problem over the group $\mathbb{G}$ requires 2^{80} steps, which an adversary cannot run in polynomial time. Solving a problem with time complexity 2^l means that the problem has l-bit security. Note that the time complexity of solving the DL problem over a general cyclic group of order p is $O(\sqrt{p})$. However, for some specific groups, such as a cyclic group of order p constructed from a prime field, the time complexity of solving the DL problem over this group can be much less than $O(\sqrt{p})$.

Given a cyclic group $\mathbb{G}$, if $|\mathbb{G}|$ is not a prime number, for some group elements $g, h \in \mathbb{G}$, there exists either no discrete logarithm or more than one discrete logarithm. However, if $|\mathbb{G}|$ is a prime number, there must exist only one solution x in $\mathbb{Z}_p$. This is why we prefer to use a cyclic subgroup whose group order is a prime number.

3.2.5 Cyclic Groups from Finite Fields

The algebraic structure of an abelian group is simpler than that of a finite field. The reason is that the abelian group defines only one binary operation while the finite field defines two. The operation properties are identical, and thus we can immediately obtain an abelian group from a finite field. For example, $(\mathbb{F}_{q^n}, +)$ and $(\mathbb{F}_{q^n}^*, *)$ are both abelian groups. It seems that there is no need to explore other implementations of cyclic groups.

However, we do need to construct more advanced cyclic groups with a finite field for various reasons. For example, the Elliptic Curve Group was invented to reduce the size of group representation for the same security level. The operation "·" in the abelian group can be the same as or different from the operations "+, *" in the finite field. For example, the group operation in the Elliptic Curve Group is a curve operation over a finite field requiring both "+" and "*" operations.

3.2.6 Group Choice 1: Multiplicative Groups

The first group choice is a multiplicative group $(\mathbb{F}_{q^n}^*, *)$ from a finite field under the multiplication operation. The multiplicative group of a finite field is a cyclic group, where the finite field can be a prime field, a binary field or an extension field.

Here, we introduce the multiplicative group modulo q from a prime field $(\mathbb{F}_q^*, *)$. The group elements, group generator, group order, and group operation are described as follows.

- **Group Elements.** The space of the modulo multiplicative group is $\mathbb{Z}_q^* = \{1, 2, \cdots, q-1\}$. Therefore, each group element has $|q|$ bits in the binary representation.
- **Group Generator.** There exists a generator $h \in \mathbb{Z}_q^*$, which can generate the group $\mathbb{Z}_q^*$. However, not all elements of $\mathbb{Z}_q^*$ are generators. The group element h is a generator if and only if the minimum positive integer x satisfying $h^x \bmod q = 1$ is equal to $q - 1$.
- **Group Order.** The order of this group is $q - 1$. Since q is a prime number, $\mathbb{Z}_q^*$ is not a group of prime order for a large prime q (excluding $q = 3$).
- **Group Operation.** The group operation "·" in this group is integer multiplication modulo the prime number q. To be precise, let $u, v \in \mathbb{Z}_q^*$ and "×" be the mathematical multiplication operation. We have $u \cdot v = u \times v \bmod q$.

This modular multiplicative group is not a group of prime order. We can extract a subgroup $\mathbb{G}$ of prime order p from it if p divides $q - 1$, namely $p|(q-1)$. To find a generator g of $\mathbb{G}$, the simplest approach is to search from 2 to $q - 1$ and select the first u such that

$$u^{\frac{q-1}{p}} \neq 1 \bmod q.$$

The generator of $\mathbb{G}$ is $g = u^{\frac{q-1}{p}}$, where $g^p = 1 \bmod q$ and the group is denoted by

$$\mathbb{G} = \{g, g^2, g^3, \cdots, g^p\}.$$

Here, $g^p = 1_{\mathbb{G}}$ is the identity group element.

We use the group $(\mathbb{G}, g, p, q)$ for the scheme constructions, where g is the generator of $\mathbb{G}$, p is the group order, and q is a large prime number satisfying $p|(q-1)$. The multiplicative group can be used for group-based cryptography because the DL problem over this group is hard, without polynomial-time solutions. However, there exist sub-exponential-time algorithms for solving the DL problem over this multiplicative group, whose time complexity is sub-exponential in the bit length of q, such as $2^8 \sqrt[3]{\log_2 q}$. To make sure that the DL problem over the multiplicative group has 2^{80} time complexity or 80-bit security level, the bit length of q must be at least 1,024 to resist sub-exponential attacks. Therefore, the length of each group element is at least 1,024 bits.

In this group description, p, q are both prime numbers but $p \ll q$. Note that in the description of security proofs, we denote by q a different meaning where q is a number as large as the query number and p is the group order satisfying $q \ll p$. There is an interesting question. Notice that $(\mathbb{F}_q, +)$ from the prime field under the modular addition operation is also a cyclic group. This modular additive group has group order q, which is a prime number. It provides better features than the modular multiplicative group whose group order is $q - 1$. So, it seems better to use this modular additive group than the modular multiplicative group. However, this is wrong and the reason is omitted here.

3.2.7 Group Choice 2: Elliptic Curve Groups

The second group choice is an elliptic curve group. An elliptic curve is a plain curve defined over a finite field $\mathbb{F}_{q^n}$, where all points are on the following curve:

$$Y^2 = X^3 + aX + b$$

along with a distinguished point at infinity, denoted by ∞. Here, $a, b \in \mathbb{F}_{q^n}$ and the space of points is denoted by $E(\mathbb{F}_{q^n})$. The finite field can be a prime field or a binary field or others, and each field has a different computational efficiency.

The group elements, group generator, group order, and group operation of the elliptic curve group are described as follows.

- **Group Elements.** We denote by $E(\mathbb{F}_{q^n})$ the space of an elliptic curve group, where all group elements in this group are points described with coordinates $(x, y) \in \mathbb{F}_{q^n} \times \mathbb{F}_{q^n}$. Theoretically, the bit length of each group element is

$$|x| + |y| = 2|\mathbb{F}_{q^n}| = 2n \cdot |q|.$$

  Notice that given an x-coordinate x and the curve, we can compute two y-coordinates $+y$ and $-y$. Therefore, with the curve, each group element (x, y) can be simplified: $(x, 1)$ to denote $(x, +y)$, or $(x, 0)$ to denote $(x, -y)$. Sometimes, we can even represent the group element with x only, because we can handle both group elements $(x, +y)$ and $(x, -y)$ in computations that will return one correct result. Therefore, the bit length of a group element is about $n|q|$.

- **Group Generator.** There exists a generator $h \in E(\mathbb{F}_{q^n})$, which can generate the group $E(\mathbb{F}_{q^n})$. The point at infinity serves as the identity group element.
- **Group Order.** The group order of the elliptic curve group is denoted by

$$|E(\mathbb{F}_{q^n})| = q^n + 1 - t,$$

where $|t| \le 2\sqrt{q^n}$ and t is the trace of the Frobenius of the elliptic curve over the field. Note that the group order is not a prime number for most curves.
- **Group Operation.** The group operation " $\cdot$ " in the elliptic curve group has two different types of operations, which depend on the input of two group elements u and v.

  - If $u = (x_u, y_u)$ and $v = (x_v, y_v)$ are two distinct points, we draw a line through u and v. This line will intersect the elliptic curve at a third point. We define $u \cdot v$ as the reflection of the third point in the x-axis.
  - Otherwise, if $u = v$, we draw the tangent line to the elliptic curve at u. This line will intersect the elliptic curve at a second point. We define $u \cdot u$ as the reflection of the second point in the x-axis.

The detailed group operation is dependent on the given group elements, curve, and finite field. We omit a detailed description of the group operation here.

This elliptic curve group is not always a group of prime order. However, we can extract a subgroup $\mathbb{G}$ of prime order p from it if p is a divisor of the group order. The extraction approach is the same as that in the modular multiplicative group. We define the group $(\mathbb{G}, g, p)$ as an elliptic curve group for scheme constructions, where $\mathbb{G}$ is a group, g is the generator of $\mathbb{G}$, and p is the group order.

The DL problem over the elliptic curve group is also hard as it does not have any polynomial-time solution. Furthermore, there is no sub-exponential-time algorithm for solving the DL problem in a general elliptic curve group, which means that we can choose the finite field as small as possible to reduce the size of the group representation. This short representation property is the primary motivation for constructing a cyclic group from an elliptic curve. For example, to have an elliptic curve group where the time complexity of solving the DL problem over this group is 2^{80}, the bit length of the prime q in the prime field $\mathbb{F}_q$ for the elliptic curve group implementation can be as small as 160, rather than 1,024 in the modular multiplicative group. The tradeoff is less computationally efficient of the group operation in the elliptic curve group compared to that in the modular multiplicative group.

In an elliptic curve group, the group element in the binary representation can be as small as the group order in the binary representation. That is, $|g| = |p|$. However, this does not mean that all elliptic curve groups have this nice feature. For l-bit security level, we must have at least $|p| = 2 \cdot l$. The size of each group element g depends on the choice of the finite field, and we have $|g| \ge |p|$ for all choices.

3.2.8 Computations over a Group

The following computations are the most common operations over a group $\mathbb{G}$ of prime order p.

- **Group Operation.** Given $g, h \in \mathbb{G}$, compute

$$g \cdot h.$$

- **Group Inverse.** Given $g \in \mathbb{G}$, compute

$$\frac{1}{g} = g^{-1}.$$

   Since $g^p = g \cdot g^{p-1} = 1$, we have $g^{-1} = g^{p-1}$.

- **Group Division.** Given $g, h \in \mathbb{G}$, compute

$$\frac{g}{h} = g \cdot h^{-1}.$$

- **Group Exponentiation.** Given $g \in \mathbb{G}$ and $x \in \mathbb{Z}_p$, compute

$$g^x.$$

Note that the operations mentioned above do not represent all computations for a group. We should also include all operations over the prime field, where the prime number is the group order. For example, given the group $(\mathbb{G}, g, p)$, an additional group element h, and $x, y \in \mathbb{Z}_p$, we can compute $g^{\frac{1}{x}} h^{-y}$.

3.3 Bilinear Pairings

Roughly speaking, a bilinear pairing provides a bilinear map that maps two group elements in elliptic curve groups to a third group element in a multiplicative group without losing its isomorphic property. Bilinear pairing was originally introduced to solve hard problems in elliptic curve groups by mapping a given problem instance in the elliptic curve group into a problem instance in a multiplicative group, running a sub-exponential-time algorithm to find the answer to the problem instance in the multiplicative group, and then using the answer to solve the hard problem in the elliptic curve group.

Bilinear pairing for scheme constructions is built from a pairing-friendly elliptic curve where it should be easy to find an isomorphism from the elliptic curve group to the multiplicative group. The instantiations of bilinear pairing, denoted by $\mathbb{G}_1 \times \mathbb{G}_2 \to \mathbb{G}_T$, fall into the following three types.

- **Symmetric.** $\mathbb{G}_1 = \mathbb{G}_2 = \mathbb{G}$. We denote a symmetric pairing by $\mathbb{G} \times \mathbb{G} \to \mathbb{G}_T$.

- Asymmetric 1. $\mathbb{G}_1 \neq \mathbb{G}_2$ with an efficient homomorphism $\psi : \mathbb{G}_2 \rightarrow \mathbb{G}_1$.
- Asymmetric 2. $\mathbb{G}_1 \neq \mathbb{G}_2$ with no efficient homomorphism between $\mathbb{G}_2$ and $\mathbb{G}_1$.

Bilinear pairing can be built from the prime-order groups $(\mathbb{G}_1, \mathbb{G}_2, \mathbb{G}_T)$ or the composite-order groups $(\mathbb{G}_1, \mathbb{G}_2, \mathbb{G}_T)$. In the following two subsections, we only introduce the symmetric pairing and the asymmetric pairing in prime-order groups, and focus on their group representations.

3.3.1 Symmetric Pairing

The definition of symmetric pairing is stated as follows. Let $\mathbb{PG} = (\mathbb{G}, \mathbb{G}_T, g, p, e)$ be a symmetric-pairing group. Here, $\mathbb{G}$ is an elliptic curve subgroup, $\mathbb{G}_T$ is a multiplicative subgroup, $|\mathbb{G}| = |\mathbb{G}_T| = p$, g is a generator of $\mathbb{G}$, and e is a map satisfying the following three properties.

- For all $u, v \in \mathbb{G}, a, b \in \mathbb{Z}_p$, $e(u^a, v^b) = e(u, v)^{ab}$.
- $e(g, g)$ is a generator of group $\mathbb{G}_T$.
- For all $u, v \in \mathbb{G}$, there exist efficient algorithms to compute $e(u, v)$.

This completes the definition of the symmetric pairing. Now, we introduce its size efficiency.

Let $E(\mathbb{F}_{q^n})[p]$ be the elliptic curve subgroup of $E(\mathbb{F}_{q^n})$ with order p over the basic field $\mathbb{F}_{q^n}$, and $\mathbb{F}_{q^{nk}}[p]$ be the multiplicative subgroup of the extension field $\mathbb{F}_{q^{nk}}$ with order p, where k is the embedding degree. The bilinear pairing is actually defined over

$$E(\mathbb{F}_{q^n})[p] \times E(\mathbb{F}_{q^n})[p] \rightarrow \mathbb{F}_{q^{nk}}[p].$$

A secure bilinear pairing requires the DL problem to be hard over both the elliptic curve group $\mathbb{G}$ and the multiplicative group $\mathbb{G}_T$. We should also make these groups as small as possible for efficient group operations. However, the DL problem in the multiplicative group defined over the extension field suffers from sub-exponential attacks. Therefore, the size of q^{nk} must be large enough to resist sub-exponential attacks. That is why we need an embedding degree k to extend the field. For l-bit security level, we have the following parameters.

$|p| = 2 \cdot l$,   to resist Pollard Rho attacks.

$|g| \approx |\mathbb{F}_{q^n}| \geq 2 \cdot l$,   which depends on the chosen elliptic curve.

$|e(g, g)| = k \cdot |\mathbb{F}_{q^n}|$, which should be large enough to resist sub-exponential attacks.

We study the different choices of the security parameter for 80-bit security level, namely $l = 80$.

- **Option 1.** We choose an elliptic curve where $|\mathbb{F}_{q^n}| = 2 \cdot l = 160$. Since the extension field $k \cdot |\mathbb{F}_{q^n}|$ must be at least 1,024 bits in the binary representation to resist sub-exponential attacks for 80-bit security, we should choose at least $k = 7$.

Therefore, we have $|p| = |g| = 160$ and $|e(g,g)| = 1,120$. Unfortunately, no such curve has been found for any $k \geq 7$. Therefore, this means that we cannot construct a symmetric pairing where the size of group elements in $\mathbb{G}$ is 160 bits for 80-bit security.

- **Option 2.** We choose the pairing group with embedding degree $k = 2$. For $k \cdot |\mathbb{F}_{q^n}| = 1,024$, we have $|\mathbb{F}_{q^n}| = 512$. Therefore, $|p| = 160$, $|g| = 512$ and $|e(g,g)| = 1,024$. There exists such an elliptic curve with a minimum size of $\mathbb{G}_T$ for 80-bit security, but we cannot use it to construct schemes with short representation for group elements particularly in $\mathbb{G}$.

3.3.2 Asymmetric Pairing

The definition of asymmetric pairing (Asymmetric 2) is stated as follows. Let $\mathbb{PG} = (\mathbb{G}_1, \mathbb{G}_2, \mathbb{G}_T, g_1, g_2, p, e)$ be an asymmetric-pairing group. Here, $\mathbb{G}_1, \mathbb{G}_2$ are elliptic curve subgroups, $\mathbb{G}_T$ is a multiplicative subgroup, $|\mathbb{G}_1| = |\mathbb{G}_2| = |\mathbb{G}_T| = p$, g_1 is a generator of $\mathbb{G}_1$, g_2 is a generator of $\mathbb{G}_2$, and e is a map satisfying the following three properties.

- For all $u \in \mathbb{G}_1, v \in \mathbb{G}_2, a, b \in \mathbb{Z}_p, e(u^a, v^b) = e(u,v)^{ab}$.
- $e(g_1, g_2)$ is a generator of group $\mathbb{G}_T$.
- For all $u \in \mathbb{G}_1, v \in \mathbb{G}_2$, there exist efficient algorithms to compute $e(u,v)$.

This completes the definition of the asymmetric pairing. Now, we introduce its size efficiency.

Let $E(\mathbb{F}_{q^n})[p]$ be the elliptic curve subgroup of $E(\mathbb{F}_{q^n})$ with order p over the basic field $\mathbb{F}_{q^n}$, $E(\mathbb{F}_{q^{nk}})[p]$ be one of the elliptic curve subgroups of $E(\mathbb{F}_{q^{nk}})$ with order p over the extension field $\mathbb{F}_{q^{nk}}$, and $\mathbb{F}_{q^{nk}}[p]$ be the multiplicative subgroup of extension field $\mathbb{F}_{q^{nk}}$ with order p, where k is the embedding degree. The bilinear pairing is actually defined over

$$E(\mathbb{F}_{q^n})[p] \times E(\mathbb{F}_{q^{nk}})[p] \to \mathbb{F}_{q^{nk}}[p].$$

Similarly, for l-bit security level, we have the following parameters.

$|p| = 2 \cdot l,$	to resist Pollard Rho attacks.
$|g_1| \approx |\mathbb{F}_{q^n}| \geq 2 \cdot l,$	which depends on the chosen elliptic curve.
$|g_2| \approx |\mathbb{F}_{q^{nk}}| \geq k \cdot 2l,$	which depends on the chosen elliptic curve and k.
$|e(g_1, g_2)| = k \cdot |\mathbb{F}_{q^n}|,$	which should be large enough to resist sub-exponential attacks.

We study the choice of security parameter for 80-bit security level, namely $l = 80$, towards short group representation in $\mathbb{G}_1$ such that $|\mathbb{F}_{q^n}| = 2 \cdot l = 160$. If $k \cdot |\mathbb{F}_{q^n}|$ must be at least 1,024 to resist sub-exponential attacks for 80-bit security, we should choose at least $k = 7$. However, the minimum k we have found for this pairing is 10. Therefore, we have $|p| = |g_1| = 160$ and $|g_2| = |e(g_1, g_2)| = 1,600$. Note that the group elements in $\mathbb{G}_2$ can be compressed into half or quarter size or even shorter representations if the bilinear pairing is the third type, in which there is no efficient homomorphism between $\mathbb{G}_1$ and $\mathbb{G}_2$.

3.3.3 Computations over a Pairing Group

A pairing group is composed of groups $(\mathbb{G}, \mathbb{G}_T)$ or $(\mathbb{G}_1, \mathbb{G}_2, \mathbb{G}_T)$ of prime order p and a bilinear map e. All computations over a pairing group are summarized as follows.

- All modular operations over $\mathbb{Z}_p$.
- All group operations over the groups $(\mathbb{G}, \mathbb{G}_T)$ or $(\mathbb{G}_1, \mathbb{G}_2, \mathbb{G}_T)$.
- The pairing computation $e(u, v)$ for all $u, v \in \mathbb{G}$ or $u \in \mathbb{G}_1, v \in \mathbb{G}_2$.

Note that all group-based schemes in the literature are constructed with the above computations, which are all efficiently computable. Some widely known computations more complicated than the above basic computations but still efficiently computable are introduced in Section 4.2.

3.4 Hash Functions

A hash function takes an arbitrary-length string as an input and returns a much shorter string as an output. The primary motivation for using hash functions, especially for group-based cryptography, is due to the limited space of $\mathbb{Z}_p$ or $\mathbb{G}$, such that we cannot embed all values in them. With the adoption of hash functions, we can securely embed strings of any length into group elements/exponents to improve the computational efficiency without using a large group. The tradeoff is that the security of group-based cryptography also depends on hash functions. If an adopted hash function is broken, the corresponding scheme will no longer be secure.

Hash functions can be classified into the following two main types according to the security definition.

- **One-Way Hash Function.** Given a one-way hash function H and an output string y, it is hard to find a pre-image input x satisfying $y = H(x)$.
- **Collision-Resistant Hash Function.** Given a collision-resistant hash function H, it is hard to find two different inputs x_1 and x_2 satisfying $H(x_1) = H(x_2)$.

When a hash function is claimed to be a cryptographic hash function in this book, it is a one-way hash function, or a collision-resistant hash function, or an ideal hash function that will be set as a random oracle in the security proof. Hash functions can be classified into the following three important types according to the output space, where the input can be any arbitrary strings.

- $H : \{0,1\}^* \to \{0,1\}^n$. The output space is the set containing all n-bit strings. To resist birthday attacks, n must be at least $2 \cdot l$ bits for l-bit security. We mainly use this kind of hash function to generate a symmetric key from the key space $\{0,1\}^n$ for hybrid encryption.
- $H : \{0,1\}^* \to \mathbb{Z}_p$. The output space is $\{0,1,2,\cdots,p-1\}$, where p is the group order. We use this kind of hash function to embed hashing values in group exponents, when the input values are not in the $\mathbb{Z}_p$ space.
- $H : \{0,1\}^* \to \mathbb{G}$. The output space is a cyclic group. That is, this hash function will hash the input string into a group element. This hash function exists only for some groups. The main groups we can hash are the group $\mathbb{G}$ in the symmetric bilinear pairing $\mathbb{G} \times \mathbb{G} \to \mathbb{G}_T$ and the group $\mathbb{G}_1$ in the asymmetric bilinear pairing $\mathbb{G}_1 \times \mathbb{G}_2 \to \mathbb{G}_T$.

How to construct cryptographic hash functions is outside the scope of this book. The above definitions and descriptions of hash functions are sufficient for constructing schemes and security proofs.

3.5 Further Reading

In this section, we briefly introduce group-based cryptography including algebraic structures, exponentiations, the discrete logarithm problem, elliptic curve cryptography, and bilinear pairings.

Algebraic Structures. Number theory and algebraic structures, such as groups, rings, and finite fields, are the foundations of modern cryptography. We refer the reader to [89, 96] for further reading about number theory. Basic knowledge of finite fields can be found in [79], while a detailed introduction can be found in [74]. Group theory plays an important role in public-key cryptography. The author in [90] gave an introduction to group theory. For how to apply group theory in cryptography, the reader is referred to the book [98].

Exponentiations. Group exponentiation is the basic computation of group-based cryptography. The simplest approach is the square-and-multiply algorithm [68]. There also exist many improved algorithms, such as the m-ary method, the sliding-window method, and the Montgomery method. A technique called Montgomery's ladder improves the computation process to withstand side-channel attacks. The work in [51] provided a useful survey of these algorithms. More specialized algorithms for elliptic curve groups were introduced in [57].

The security level that a group can achieve is determined by the group order and the algorithm for solving its discrete logarithm problem. The group order, in turn, determines the computational efficiency of group-based schemes. We refer the reader to the work in [73] for a detailed elaboration of the group size and the security level.

Discrete Logarithm Problem. Algorithms for solving the discrete logarithm problem can be divided into two categories: generic algorithms and particular algorithms.

The generic algorithms, such as the baby-step giant-step algorithm [95] and the Pollard Rho algorithm [87], work for all groups. The particular algorithms, such as the index calculus algorithm [3, 58], only work for some particular groups, such as the modular multiplicative group. A survey of these algorithms was given in [78] and [81] (Chapter 3.6).

The time complexity of generic algorithms is normally $O(\sqrt{p})$ for a group of order p, while the time complexity of the index calculus algorithm is sub-exponential. The most efficient algorithm, which is called the number field sieve and is a variant of the index calculus algorithm, has a complexity of $L_p[\frac{1}{3}, 1.923]$ (refer to [72] for the definition of L-notation). The record for solving a discrete logarithm in $GF(p)$ is a 768-bit prime [67]. In a group construction with a finite field of characteristic 2, the calculation of a logarithm in $\mathbb{F}_{2^{1279}}$ was announced in [66]. In a group construction with a finite field of characteristic 3, the latest result is given in [2]. A full list of the records sorted by date can be found in [52].

Elliptic Curve Cryptography. The notion of elliptic curve groups was independently suggested by Koblitz [69] and Miller [83]. In comparison with the modular multiplicative groups, there exists no sub-exponential algorithm for solving the discrete logarithm problem over the elliptic curve groups. The current record is the discrete logarithm of a 113-bit Koblitz curve [102] and a curve over $\mathbb{F}_{2^{127}}$ [16]. For a survey of recent progress, we refer the reader to the work [43].

The US National Institute of Standards and Technology (NIST) published the recommended size of an elliptic curve group (Table 2 of [9]). For a more direct comparison of the key size, we refer the reader to [17]. A collection of recommendations from well-known organizations is available at [19]. There are also many helpful textbooks such as [17, 18, 57, 99], which provide a detailed introduction to elliptic curve cryptography.

Bilinear Pairings. The use of bilinear pairing was first proposed in [80, 41] to attack cryptosystems. Later, numerous schemes become achievable with the help of pairings. We refer the reader to the survey in [39] of these constructions during the first few years after the bilinear pairing was invented.

Galbraith et al.'s paper [44] provides a background to pairing and classifies the pairing $\mathbb{G}_1 \times \mathbb{G}_2 \to \mathbb{G}_T$ into three types. There is another rarely used type of pairing, which was introduced by Shacham [92]. These four types are denoted Type I, II, III, and IV, respectively. The difference in these four types is the structures of groups $\mathbb{G}_1$ and $\mathbb{G}_2$. Meanwhile, the Weil pairing and the Tate pairing are classified with respect to the computation, and the work in [70] gives an efficiency comparison of these two pairings. Elegant explanations of pairings can be found in [76, 31, 97], where the structure of r-torsion, the Miller algorithm, and optimizations of the pairing computation were explained.

The elliptic curves that we use to construct a bilinear pairing are referred to as pairing-friendly curves. Finding pairing-friendly curves with an optimized group size needs the embedding degree, the modulo of the underlying group, and the ρ-value all to be considered. The most commonly applied method is called the complex multiplication (CM method) [5]. Summaries of pairing-friendly curve constructions were given in [40, 63].

Chapter 4
Foundations of Security Reduction

In this chapter, we introduce what is security reduction and how to program a correct security reduction. We start by presenting an overview of important concepts and techniques, and then proof structures for digital signatures and encryption. We classify each concept into several categories in order to guide the reader to a deep understanding of security reduction. We devise and select some examples to show how to correctly program a full security reduction. Some definitions adopted in this book may be defined differently elsewhere in the literature.

4.1 Introduction to Basic Concepts

4.1.1 Mathematical Primitives and Superstructures

Mathematics is the foundation of modern cryptography. With a mathematical primitive, we define mathematical hard problems and construct cryptographic schemes. Generally, the structure of a cryptographic scheme is more complicated than the structure of a mathematical hard problem (e.g., interactive vs. non-interactive). It is relatively hard to analyze the security of a cryptographic scheme compared to the hardness of a mathematical hard problem. Therefore, security reduction was introduced to analyze the security of cryptographic schemes. In a security reduction, if a scheme is constructed over a mathematical primitive, its underlying hard problem must be defined over the same mathematical primitive. For example, in group-based cryptography, a cyclic group or a pairing group is the mathematical primitive. If a scheme is proposed over a cyclic group $\mathbb{G}$, the underlying hard problem for the security reduction must also be defined over the same cyclic group $\mathbb{G}$. Figure 4.1 provides an overview of the relationship among these four concepts.

In computational complexity theory, a reduction transforms one problem into another problem, while in public-key cryptography, a security reduction reduces breaking a proposed scheme into solving a mathematical hard problem. How to

© Springer International Publishing AG, part of Springer Nature 2018

F. Guo et al., *Introduction to Security Reduction*,

https://doi.org/10.1007/978-3-319-93049-7_4

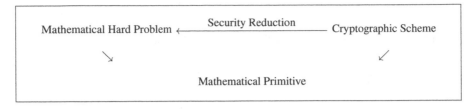

Fig. 4.1 The relationship among the four concepts

correctly program a security reduction is highly dependent on the cryptosystem, security model, proposed scheme, and hard problem. We assume that there exists a proposed scheme that needs to be proved secure and an adversary who is capable of breaking the proposed scheme. In this book, "the proposed scheme" and "the adversary" will frequently be mentioned when explaining the concepts of security reduction.

Roughly speaking, each mathematical primitive is implemented with a string as input. The bit length of the input string is a *security parameter* denoted by λ, which is an integer. In group-based cryptography, the security parameter λ refers in particular to the bit length of a group element, such as 160 bits or 1,024 bits. In this book, when we say that a cryptographic scheme (or a mathematical problem) is generated with a security parameter λ, we mean that its underlying mathematical primitive is generated with the security parameter λ.

4.1.2 Mathematical Problems and Problem Instances

A mathematical problem defined over a mathematical primitive is a mathematical object representing certain questions and answers. For each mathematical problem, there should be some descriptions of input (question) and output (answer). Mathematical problems can be classified into *computational problems* and *decisional problems*. A decisional problem can be seen as a special case of a computational problem whose output has only two answers, such as *true* and *false*.

An input string for a (mathematical) problem is referred to as a *problem instance*. A problem should have an infinite number of instances. In a security reduction, we find a correct solution (answer) to a randomly chosen instance of a problem, which indicates that this problem is efficiently solvable. Suppose a problem is generated with a security parameter λ. The level of "hardness" of solving this problem can be denoted by a function $P(\lambda)$ of λ for this problem. The functions for different problems are different, which means that their levels of hardness are not the same even though they are defined over the same mathematical primitive.

4.1.3 Cryptography, Cryptosystems, and Schemes

In this book, cryptography, cryptosystem, and scheme have the following meanings.

- Cryptography, such as public-key cryptography and group-based cryptography, is a security mechanism to provide security services for authentication, confidentiality, integrity, etc.
- A cryptosystem, such as digital signatures, public-key encryption, and identity-based encryption, is a suite of algorithms that provides a security service.
- A scheme, such as the BLS signature scheme [26], is a specific construction or implementation of the corresponding algorithms for a cryptosystem.

A cryptosystem might have many different scheme constructions. For example, many signature schemes with distinct features have been proposed in the literature. Suppose a scheme is generated with a security parameter λ. The level of "hardness" of breaking the scheme can be denoted by a function $S(\lambda)$ of λ for this scheme. The functions for different proposed schemes are different, and thus their levels of hardness are not the same even though they are constructed over the same mathematical primitive.

4.1.4 Algorithm Classification 1

In mathematics and computer science, an algorithm is a set of steps to compute an output from an input. All algorithms can be classified into *deterministic algorithms* and *probabilistic algorithms*.

A deterministic algorithm is an algorithm where, given as an input a problem instance, it will always return a correct result. A probabilistic (randomized) algorithm is an algorithm where, given as an input a problem instance, it will return a correct result by chance only, meaning that the obtained result may be either incorrect or correct with some likelihood. We denote by (t, ε) that an algorithm returns a correct result in time t with success probability ε. In comparison with deterministic algorithms, probabilistic algorithms are believed to be more efficient for solving problems. A deterministic algorithm can be seen as a specific probabilistic algorithm where the success probability is 100%. In this book, all algorithms are probabilistic algorithms unless specified otherwise.

An algorithm with (t, ε) can be applied differently in cryptography as follows.

- If this algorithm is used to measure how successfully it can return a correct result, ε is regarded as a probability as described above.
- If this algorithm is particularly used to measure how successfully it can break a scheme or solve a hard problem compared to other algorithms that cannot break the scheme or solve the hard problem, ε is regarded as an *advantage*. Advantage is a variant definition of probability, introduced in Section 4.6.2.

We have the above two different applications because it is confusing to measure whether a scheme is secure or insecure and whether a problem is hard or easy with probability. The difference between probability and advantage can be found in Section 4.6. In this book, an algorithm is mainly used for the second application and the default ε is therefore referred to as an advantage. When the algorithm is specifically proposed to break a digital signature scheme or solve a computational problem, we can also call ε probability, because the probability and the advantage are equivalent.

4.1.5 Polynomial Time and Exponential Time

Suppose a scheme is constructed (or a problem is generated) with a security parameter λ. Let $t(\lambda)$ be the time cost of an algorithm for breaking the scheme or solving the problem, where $t(\lambda)$ is a function of λ.

- We say that $t(\lambda)$ is polynomial time if there exists $n_0 > 0$ such that

$$t(\lambda) = O(\lambda^{n_0}).$$

- We say that $t(\lambda)$ is exponential time if $t(\lambda)$ can be expressed as

$$t(\lambda) = O(e^\lambda),$$

  where e is the base of the natural logarithm.

Note that intermediate time between polynomial time and exponential time is called sub-exponential time. If $t_{se}(\lambda)$ is a sub-exponential time associated with the factor λ, such as $t_{se}(\lambda) = 2^{8\sqrt[3]{\lambda}}$, we can still choose a proper λ in such a way that $t_{se}(\lambda)$ is as large as 2^{80} or even larger.

4.1.6 Negligible and Non-negligible

Suppose a scheme is constructed (or a problem is generated) with a security parameter λ. Let $\varepsilon(\lambda)$ be the advantage of an algorithm for breaking the scheme or solving the problem, where $\varepsilon(\lambda)$ is a function of λ. To explain the concepts of *negligible* and *non-negligible* clearly, we do not use the traditional definitions but borrow the definitions of polynomial time and exponential time to define these two concepts.

- We say that $\varepsilon(\lambda)$ is negligible associated with λ if $\varepsilon(\lambda)$ can be expressed as

$$\varepsilon(\lambda) = \frac{1}{\Theta(e^\lambda)}.$$

That is, the value $\varepsilon(\lambda)$ tends to zero very quickly as the input λ grows.

- We say that $\varepsilon(\lambda)$ is non-negligible associated with λ if there exists $n_0 \geq 0$ such that

$$\varepsilon(\lambda) = \frac{1}{O(\lambda^{n_0})}.$$

The minimum advantage $\varepsilon(\lambda)$ is 0, which means that there is no advantage. The maximum advantage $\varepsilon(\lambda)$ is equal to 1 in this book, which is independent of the input security parameter. The details will be introduced in Section 4.6.2.

4.1.7 Insecure and Secure

We can classify all schemes into "insecure" and "secure" as follows.

- **Insecure.** A scheme generated with a security parameter λ is insecure in a security model if there exists an adversary who can break the scheme in polynomial time with non-negligible advantage associated with λ.
- **Secure.** A scheme generated with a security parameter λ is secure in a security model if there exists no adversary who can break the scheme in polynomial time with non-negligible advantage associated with λ.

We cannot simply say that a scheme is insecure or secure, because it is associated with the input security parameter and the security model. A scheme might be insecure in one security model, but secure in another security model.

4.1.8 Easy and Hard

We can classify all mathematical problems into "easy" and "hard" as follows.

- **Easy.** A problem generated with a security parameter λ is easy if there exists an algorithm that can solve the problem in polynomial time with non-negligible advantage associated with λ.
- **Hard.** A problem generated with a security parameter λ is hard if there exists no (known) algorithm that can solve the problem in polynomial time with non-negligible advantage associated with λ.

Hard problems are those mathematical problems only believed to be hard based on the fact that all known algorithms cannot efficiently solve them. There is no mathematical proof for the hardness of a mathematical hard problem. We can only prove that solving a problem is not easier than solving another problem. Notice that some believed-to-be-hard problems might become easy in the future.

4.1.9 Algorithm Classification 2

Suppose there exists an algorithm that can break a scheme or solve a hard problem in time t with advantage ε, where the scheme or the problem is generated with a security parameter λ.

- An algorithm that can break a scheme or solve a hard problem with (t, ε) is *computationally efficient* if t is polynomial time and ε is non-negligible associated with the security parameter λ.
- An algorithm that can break a scheme or solve a hard problem with (t, ε) is *computationally inefficient* if t is polynomial time but ε is negligible associated with the security parameter λ.

In this book, a computationally efficient algorithm is treated as a *probabilistic polynomial-time* (PPT) algorithm. In the following introduction, a computationally efficient algorithm is called an efficient algorithm for short. An algorithm requiring exponential time to solve a hard problem is also computationally inefficient.

4.1.10 Algorithms in Cryptography

All algorithms in public-key cryptography can be classified into the following four types, and each type is defined for a different purpose.

- **Scheme Algorithm.** This algorithm is proposed to implement a cryptosystem. A scheme algorithm might be composed of multiple algorithms for different computation tasks. For example, a digital signature scheme usually consists of four algorithms: system parameter generation, key pair generation, signature generation, and signature verification. We require the scheme algorithm to return correct results except with negligible probability.
- **Attack Algorithm.** This algorithm is proposed to break a scheme. A scheme is secure if all attack algorithms are computationally inefficient. Suppose there exists an adversary who can break the proposed scheme in polynomial time with non-negligible advantage. This means that the adversary knows a computationally efficient attack algorithm. However, this algorithm is a black-box algorithm only known to the adversary. The steps inside the algorithm are unknown.
- **Solution Algorithm.** This algorithm is proposed to solve a hard problem. Similarly, a problem is hard if all solution algorithms for this problem are computationally inefficient. In a security reduction, if there exists a computationally efficient attack algorithm that can break a proposed scheme, we prove that there exists a computationally efficient solution algorithm that can solve a mathematical hard problem.
- **Reduction Algorithm.** This algorithm is proposed to describe how a security reduction works. A security reduction is merely a reduction algorithm. If the attack indeed exists, it shows how to use an adversary's attack on a simulated

scheme (see Section 4.3.6) to solve a mathematical hard problem. A reduction algorithm at least consists of a *simulation algorithm* (how to simulate the scheme algorithm) and a solution algorithm (how to solve an underlying hard problem).

Among the aforementioned algorithms, we only require that the advantage ε in the attack algorithm, the solution algorithm, and the reduction algorithm is non-negligible; while the probability ε in the scheme algorithm is close to 1. When we say that an adversary can break a scheme or solve a hard problem, we mean that the corresponding attack algorithm or the corresponding solution algorithm known to the adversary is computationally efficient.

4.1.11 Hard Problems in Cryptography

All mathematical hard problems can be classified into the following two types.

- **Computationally Hard Problems.** These problems, such as the discrete logarithm problem, cannot be solved in polynomial time with non-negligible advantage. This type of hard problem is used as the underlying hard problem in the security reduction.
- **Absolutely Hard Problems.** These problems cannot be solved with non-negligible advantage, even if the adversary can solve all computational hard problems in polynomial time with non-negligible advantage. Absolutely hard problems are unconditionally secure against any adversary. This type of hard problem is used in security reductions to hide secret information from the adversary.

A simple example of an absolutely hard problem is to compute x from (g, g^{x+y}), where x, y are both randomly chosen from $\mathbb{Z}_p$. More absolutely hard problems will be introduced in Section 4.7.6. We will explain why it is essential to utilize absolutely hard problems in security reductions in Section 4.5.7. When we need to assume that an adversary can solve all computational hard problems in polynomial time with non-negligible advantage, we say that the adversary is a *computationally unbounded adversary* who has unbounded computational power.

4.1.12 Security Levels

In public-key cryptography, we need to know how secure a proposed scheme is and how hard a mathematical problem is. We say that a scheme or a problem has k-bit security if an adversary must take 2^k steps/operations to break the scheme or to solve the problem. The *security level* indicates the strength of an adversary in breaking a scheme or solving a problem, which can be seen as the time cost of breaking a scheme or solving a problem. Generating a scheme with a security parameter λ does not mean that this scheme has λ-bit security. The real security level depends on the mathematical primitive and the scheme construction.

Suppose all potential attack algorithms to break a proposed scheme have been found with the following distinct time cost and advantage

$$(t_1, \varepsilon_1), \ (t_2, \varepsilon_2), \ \cdots, \ (t_l, \varepsilon_l).$$

For a simple analysis, we say that the proposed scheme has k-bit security if the minimum value within the following set

$$\left\{ \frac{t_1}{\varepsilon_1}, \ \frac{t_2}{\varepsilon_2}, \ \cdots, \ \frac{t_l}{\varepsilon_l} \right\}$$

is 2^k, where the time unit is one step/operation. This definition will be used to analyze the concrete security of a proposed scheme in this book.

The security level of a proposed scheme is not fixed. Suppose a proposed scheme has k-bit security against all existing attack algorithms. If an attack algorithm with (t^*, ε^*) satisfying $t^*/\varepsilon^* = 2^{k^*} < 2^k$ is found in the future, the proposed scheme will then have k^*-bit security instead.

4.1.13 Hard Problems and Hardness Assumptions

In this book, the concepts of hard problem and hardness assumption are treated as equivalent. However, the descriptions of these two concepts are slightly different.

- We can say that breaking a proposed scheme implies solving an underlying hard problem, denoted by A, such that the scheme is secure under the hardness assumption on A.
- We can also say that a hardness assumption is a weak assumption or a strong assumption. Weak or strong is not related to the problem but to the strength of the assumption.

A hard problem is associated with the solution while a hardness assumption is associated with the security assumption. In a security reduction, we are to solve an underlying hard problem or break an underlying hardness assumption.

4.1.14 Security Reductions and Security Proofs

In this book, security reduction and security proof are assumed to be different concepts with different components. We clarify them as follows.

- A security reduction is a part of a security proof focusing on how to reduce breaking a proposed scheme to solving an underlying hard problem. A security reduction consists of a simulation algorithm and a solution algorithm.

- A security proof consists of all components required to convince us that a proposed scheme is indeed secure. Besides a given security reduction, it should also include a correctness analysis for the proposed security reduction.

We will introduce which components should be included in the security proof of digital signatures and encryption in Sections 4.9.1, 4.10.1, and 4.11.5. Note that these two concepts may be regarded as equivalent elsewhere in the literature.

4.2 An Overview of Easy/Hard Problems

All mathematical problems can be classified into the following four types for scheme constructions and security reductions: computational easy problems, computational hard problems, decisional easy problems, and decisional hard problems. In this section, we collect some popular problems that have been widely used in the literature.

4.2.1 Computational Easy Problems

A computational problem generated with a security parameter λ is easy if there exists a polynomial-time solution algorithm that can find a correct solution to a given problem instance with overwhelming probability 1.

Let $f(x)$ and $F(x)$ be polynomials in $\mathbb{Z}_p[x]$ of degree n and $2n$, respectively. Let $a \in \mathbb{Z}_p$ be a random and unknown exponent. We have several interesting polynomial problems that are efficiently solvable.

- **Polynomial Problem 1.** Given $g, g^a, g^{a^2}, \cdots, g^{a^n} \in \mathbb{G}$, and $f(x) \in \mathbb{Z}_p[x]$, we can compute the group element

$$g^{f(a)}.$$

The polynomial $f(x)$ can be written as

$$f(x) = f_n x^n + f_{n-1} x^{n-1} + \cdots + f_1 x + f_0,$$

where $f_i \in \mathbb{Z}_p$ is the coefficient of x^i for all $i \in [0, n]$. Therefore, this element is computable by computing

$$g^{f(a)} = \prod_{i=0}^{n} (g^{a^i})^{f_i}.$$

- **Polynomial Problem 2.** Given $g, g^a, g^{a^2}, \cdots, g^{a^{n-1}} \in \mathbb{G}$, $f(x) \in \mathbb{Z}_p[x]$, and any $w \in \mathbb{Z}_p$ satisfying $f(w) = 0$, we can compute the group element

$$g^{\frac{f(a)}{a-w}}.$$

If $f(w) = 0$ for an integer $w \in \mathbb{Z}_p$, we have that $x - w$ divides $f(x)$, and

$$\frac{f(x)}{x - w}$$

is a polynomial of degree $n - 1$, where all coefficients are computable. Therefore, this element is computable because $\frac{f(x)}{x-w}$ is a polynomial of degree $n - 1$.

- **Polynomial Problem 3.** Given $g, g^a, g^{a^2}, \cdots, g^{a^{n-1}} \in \mathbb{G}$, $f(x) \in \mathbb{Z}_p[x]$, and any $w \in \mathbb{Z}_p$, we can compute the group element

$$g^{\frac{f(a)-f(w)}{a-w}}.$$

It is easy to see that $x - w$ divides $f(x) - f(w)$ and then

$$\frac{f(x) - f(w)}{x - w}$$

is a polynomial of degree $n - 1$, where all coefficients are computable. Therefore, this element is computable because $\frac{f(x)-f(w)}{x-w}$ is a polynomial of degree $n - 1$.

- **Polynomial Problem 4.** Given $g, g^a, g^{a^2}, \cdots, g^{a^{n-1}}, g^{\frac{f(a)}{a-w}} \in \mathbb{G}$, $f(x) \in \mathbb{Z}_p[x]$, and any $w \in \mathbb{Z}_p$ satisfying $f(w) \neq 0$, we can compute the group element

$$g^{\frac{1}{a-w}}.$$

Since $x - w$ divides $f(x) - f(w)$, we have

$$\frac{f(x)}{x - w} = \frac{f(x) - f(w) + f(w)}{x - w} = \frac{f(x) - f(w)}{x - w} + \frac{f(w)}{x - w},$$

which can be rewritten as

$$\frac{f(x)}{x - w} = f'_{n-1}x^{n-1} + f'_{n-2}x^{n-2} + \cdots + f'_1 x + f'_0 + \frac{d}{x - w}$$

for coefficients $f'_i \in \mathbb{Z}_p$, which are computable, and $d = f(w)$ which is a nonzero integer. Therefore, this element is computable by computing

$$g^{\frac{1}{a-w}} = \left(\frac{g^{\frac{f(a)}{a-w}}}{\prod_{i=0}^{n-1} (g^{a^i})^{f'_i}} \right)^{\frac{1}{d}}.$$

- **Polynomial Problem 5.** Given $g, g^a, g^{a^2}, \cdots, g^{a^{n-1}}, h^{as} \in \mathbb{G}$, and $e(g,h)^{f(a)s} \in \mathbb{G}_T$ where $f(0) \neq 0$, we can compute the group element

$$e(g,h)^s.$$

Let $f(x) = f_n x^n + f_{n-1}x^{n-1} + \cdots + f_1 x + f_0$. This polynomial can be rewritten as

$$f(x) = x(f_n x^{n-1} + f_{n-1} x^{n-2} + \cdots + f_1) + f_0.$$

Since $f_0 = f(0) \neq 0$, this element is computable by computing

$$e(g,h)^s = \left(\frac{e(g,h)^{f(a)s}}{e\left(h^{as}, \prod_{i=0}^{n-1}(g^{a^i})^{f_{i+1}}\right)} \right)^{\frac{1}{f_0}}.$$

- **Polynomial Problem 6.** Given $g, g^a, g^{a^2}, \cdots, g^{a^n} \in \mathbb{G}$, and $F(x) \in \mathbb{Z}_p[x]$, we can compute the group element

$$e(g,g)^{F(a)}.$$

Let $F(x) = F_{2n} x^{2n} + F_{2n-1} x^{2n-1} + \cdots + F_1 x + F_0$ be a polynomial of degree $2n$. It can be rewritten as

$$F(x) = x^n(F_{2n} x^n + F_{2n-1} x^{n-1} + \cdots + F_{n+1} x^1) + (F_n x^n + \cdots + F_1 x^1 + F_0).$$

Therefore, this element is computable by computing

$$e(g,g)^{F(a)} = e\left(g^{a^n}, \prod_{i=1}^{n}(g^{a^i})^{F_{n+i}} \right) e\left(g, \prod_{i=0}^{n}(g^{a^i})^{F_i} \right).$$

- **Polynomial Problem 7.** Given $g^{\frac{1}{a-x_1}}, g^{\frac{1}{a-x_2}}, \cdots, g^{\frac{1}{a-x_n}} \in \mathbb{G}$, and all distinct $x_i \in \mathbb{Z}_p$, we can compute the group element

$$g^{\frac{1}{(a-x_1)(a-x_2)(a-x_3)\cdots(a-x_n)}}.$$

For any $x_1, x_2, \cdots, x_n \in \mathbb{Z}_p$, a polynomial $f(x)$ can be rewritten as

$$
\begin{aligned}
f(x) = w_1 (x - x_1)(x - x_2)(x - x_3) \cdots (x - x_{n-1})(x - x_n) \\
+ w_2 (x - x_2)(x - x_3) \cdots (x - x_{n-1})(x - x_n) \\
+ w_3 (x - x_3) \cdots (x - x_{n-1})(x - x_n) \\
+ \cdots \\
+ w_n (x - x_n) \\
+ w
\end{aligned}
$$

for some $w_1, w_2, \cdots, w_n, w$ from $\mathbb{Z}_p$. The above element is computable and can be explained as follows.

We have

$$g^{\frac{1}{x-x_1} + \frac{1}{x-x_2} + \cdots + \frac{1}{x-x_i} + \frac{1}{x-x_{i+1}}} = g^{\frac{f_i(x)}{(x-x_1)(x-x_2)\cdots(x-x_i)(x-x_{i+1})}},$$

where $f_i(x)$ is a polynomial of degree i. Rewrite $f_i(x)$ as

$$
\begin{aligned}
f_i(x) = w_1 (x - x_2)(x - x_3)(x - x_4) \cdots (x - x_i)(x - x_{i+1}) \\
+ w_2 (x - x_3)(x - x_4) \cdots (x - x_i)(x - x_{i+1})
\end{aligned}
$$

$$+w_3(x-x_4)\cdots(x-x_i)(x-x_{i+1})$$
$$+\cdots$$
$$+w_i(x-x_{i+1})$$
$$+w \ .$$

If $w = 0$, we can choose a different integer $k \neq 1$ and compute

$$g^{\frac{k}{x-x_1}+\frac{1}{x-x_2}+\cdots+\frac{1}{x-x_{i+1}}} \ .$$

Otherwise, $w \neq 0$ and we have

$$g^{\frac{1}{x-x_1}+\frac{1}{x-x_2}+\cdots+\frac{1}{x-x_{i+1}}}$$
$$= g^{\frac{f_i(x)}{(x-x_1)(x-x_2)\cdots(x-x_i)(x-x_{i+1})}}$$
$$= g^{\frac{w_1}{x-x_1}+\frac{w_2}{(x-x_1)(x-x_2)}+\cdots+\frac{w_i}{(x-x_1)(x-x_2)\cdots(x-x_i)}+\frac{w}{(x-x_1)(x-x_2)\cdots(x-x_i)(x-x_{i+1})}} \ .$$

Let $\mathbb{S}_i$ be the set of group elements defined as

$$\mathbb{S}_i = \left\{ g^{\frac{1}{x-x_1}}, \ g^{\frac{1}{(x-x_1)(x-x_2)}}, \ g^{\frac{1}{(x-x_1)(x-x_2)(x-x_3)}}, \cdots, g^{\frac{1}{(x-x_1)(x-x_2)(x-x_3)\cdots(x-x_i)}} \right\},$$

which contains i group elements. Given all elements in $\mathbb{S}_i$, we can compute the new element

$$g^{\frac{1}{(x-x_1)(x-x_2)\cdots(x-x_i)(x-x_{i+1})}} = \left(\frac{g^{\frac{1}{x-x_1}+\frac{1}{x-x_2}+\cdots+\frac{1}{x-x_{i+1}}}}{g^{\frac{w_1}{x-x_1}} \cdot g^{\frac{w_2}{(x-x_1)(x-x_2)}} \cdots g^{\frac{w_i}{(x-x_1)(x-x_2)\cdots(x-x_i)}}} \right)^{\frac{1}{w}}$$

by the above approach, which is the $(i+1)$-th group element in the set $\mathbb{S}_{i+1}$. Therefore, with the given group elements, we immediately have $\mathbb{S}_1$ and then can compute $\mathbb{S}_2, \mathbb{S}_3, \cdots$ until $\mathbb{S}_n$. We solve this problem because the n-th group element in $\mathbb{S}_n$ is the solution to the problem instance.

Another type of computational easy problem can be seen as a structured problem, where the solution to a structured problem must satisfy a defined structure. For example, given $g, g^a \in \mathbb{G}$, a structured problem is to compute a pair $(r, \ g^{ar})$ for an integer $r \in \mathbb{Z}_p$. Here, the integer r can be any number chosen by the party that returns the answer. We have the following structured problems that are efficiently solvable. How to solve these problems is important, especially in the simulation of digital signatures and private keys of identity-based cryptography.

• **Structured Problem 1.** Given $g, g^a \in \mathbb{G}$, we can compute a pair

$$\left(g^r, \ g^{ar} \right)$$

for an integer $r \in \mathbb{Z}_p$, where a correct pair, denoted by (u, v), satisfies

$$e(u, g^a) = e(v, g).$$

We solve this problem by randomly choosing $r' \in \mathbb{Z}_p$ and computing

$$\left(g^{r'}, (g^a)^{r'} \right).$$

Let $r = r'$. The computed pair is the solution to the problem instance.

- **Structured Problem 2.** Given $g, g^a \in \mathbb{G}$, we can compute a pair

$$\left(g^{\frac{1}{a+r}}, g^r \right)$$

for an integer $r \in \mathbb{Z}_p$, where a correct pair, denoted by (u, v), satisfies

$$e\left(u, \ g^a \cdot v \right) = e(g, g).$$

We solve this problem by randomly choosing $r' \in \mathbb{Z}_p^*$ and computing

$$\left(g^{\frac{1}{r'}}, g^{r'-a} \right).$$

Let $r = r' - a \in \mathbb{Z}_p$. We have

$$\left(g^{\frac{1}{a+r}}, \ g^r \right) = \left(g^{\frac{1}{a+r'-a}}, \ g^{r'-a} \right) = \left(g^{\frac{1}{r'}}, g^{r'-a} \right),$$

and thus the computed pair is the solution to the problem instance.

- **Structured Problem 3.** Given $g, g^a \in \mathbb{G}$ and $w \in \mathbb{Z}_p$, we can compute a pair

$$\left(g^{\frac{r}{a+w}}, g^r \right)$$

for an integer $r \in \mathbb{Z}_p$, where a correct pair, denoted by (u, v), satisfies

$$e\left(u, \ g^a \cdot g^w \right) = e(v, g).$$

We solve this problem by randomly choosing $r' \in \mathbb{Z}_p$ and computing

$$\left(g^{r'}, \ g^{r'(a+w)} \right).$$

Let $r = r'(a+w) \in \mathbb{Z}_p$. We have

$$\left(g^{\frac{r}{a+w}}, \ g^r \right) = \left(g^{\frac{r'(a+w)}{a+w}}, \ g^{r'(a+w)} \right) = \left(g^{r'}, \ g^{r'(a+w)} \right),$$

and thus the computed pair is the solution to the problem instance.

- **Structured Problem 4.** Given $g, g^a, g^b \in \mathbb{G}$ and $w \in \mathbb{Z}_p^*$, we can compute a pair

$$\left(g^{ab} g^{(wa+1)r}, \ g^r \right)$$

for an integer $r \in \mathbb{Z}_p$, where a correct pair, denoted by (u, v), satisfies

$$e(u, \ g) = e(g^a, g^b) e(g^{wa} g, v).$$

We solve this problem by randomly choosing $r' \in \mathbb{Z}_p$ and computing

$$\left(g^{-\frac{1}{w}b + wr'a + r'}, g^{-\frac{b}{w} + r'} \right).$$

Let $r = -\frac{b}{w} + r' \in \mathbb{Z}_p$. We have

$$\left(g^{ab} g^{(wa+1)r}, \ g^r \right) = \left(g^{ab} g^{(wa+1)(-\frac{b}{w} + r')}, \ g^{-\frac{b}{w} + r'} \right)$$
$$= \left(g^{-\frac{1}{w}b + wr'a + r'}, \ g^{-\frac{b}{w} + r'} \right),$$

and thus the computed pair is the solution to the problem instance.

In the above structured problems, the integer r in the computed pair is also a random number from the point of view of the adversary if r' is secretly and randomly chosen from $\mathbb{Z}_p$. The randomness of r is extremely important for indistinguishable simulation, introduced in Section 4.7.

4.2.2 Computational Hard Problems

A computational problem generated with a security parameter λ is hard if, given as input a problem instance, the probability of finding a correct solution to this problem instance in polynomial time is a negligible function of λ, denoted by $\varepsilon(\lambda)$ (ε for short). A computational problem is definitely easy if λ is not large enough.

We give some computational hard problems in the following, where $\mathbb{G}$ is the pairing group from $e : \mathbb{G} \times \mathbb{G} \to \mathbb{G}_T$ unless it is specified otherwise.

Discrete Logarithm Problem (DL)
Instance: $g, g^a \in \mathbb{G}$, where $\mathbb{G}$ is a general cyclic group
Compute: a

Computational Diffie-Hellman Problem (CDH)
Instance: $g, g^a, g^b \in \mathbb{G}$, where $\mathbb{G}$ is a general cyclic group
Compute: g^{ab}

q-Strong Diffie-Hellman Problem (q-SDH) [21]
Instance: $g, g^a, g^{a^2}, \cdots, g^{a^q} \in \mathbb{G}$
Compute: $\left(s, g^{\frac{1}{a+s}} \right) \in \mathbb{Z}_p \times \mathbb{G}$ for any s

q-Strong Diffie-Hellman Inversion Problem (q-SDHI) [21]

Instance: $g, g^a, g^{a^2}, \cdots, g^{a^q} \in \mathbb{G}$

Compute: $g^{\frac{1}{a}}$

Bilinear Diffie-Hellman Problem (BDH) [24]

Instance: $g, g^a, g^b, g^c \in \mathbb{G}$

Compute: $e(g,g)^{abc}$

q-Bilinear Diffie-Hellman Inversion Problem (q-BDHI) [20]

Instance: $g, g^a, g^{a^2}, \cdots, g^{a^q} \in \mathbb{G}$

Compute: $e(g,g)^{\frac{1}{a}}$

q-Bilinear Diffie-Hellman Problem (q-SDH) [22]

Instance: $g, g^a, g^{a^2}, \cdots, g^{a^q}, g^{a^{q+2}}, g^{a^{q+3}}, \cdots, g^{a^{2q}}, h \in \mathbb{G}$

Compute: $e(g,h)^{a^{q+1}}$

4.2.3 Decisional Easy Problems

A decisional problem is to guess whether a target, denoted by Z, in a problem instance is true or false. If the answer to the decisional problem is true, then Z is equal to a specific element, called *true element*; otherwise, Z is different from the specific element, called *false element*. A decisional problem generated with a security parameter λ is easy if there exists a solution algorithm that can correctly guess Z in a problem instance in polynomial time with overwhelming probability 1.

We denote by "$Z = \text{True}$" that Z is a true element or Z is true for short. Similarly, we denote by "$Z = \text{False}$" that Z is a false element or Z is false for short. When the true element is clearly defined, we can alternatively write "$Z = \text{True Element}$" instead of $Z = \text{True}$. We denote by "$Z \overset{?}{=} \text{True Element}$" deciding whether Z is a true element or not. Examples can be found at the end of this subsection.

Let I be an instance of a computational problem. The decisional variant of this computational problem can be seen as setting (I, Z) as the problem instance. The aim is to decide whether Z is a correct solution to the instance I of the computational problem. Therefore, each computational problem can be modified into a decisional problem. We have the following interesting observations.

- If a computational problem is easy, its decisional variant must be easy. Otherwise, the computational problem is hard and its decisional variant can be either easy or hard depending on the problem definition.
- If the decisional variant of a computational problem is hard, the computational problem must also be hard.

We now list two decisional easy problems defined over a pairing group whose corresponding computational problems are hard.

- **Decisional Problem 1.** Given $g, g^a, g^b, Z \in \mathbb{G}$, the decisional problem is to decide whether $Z = g^{ab}$ or Z is a random element from $\mathbb{G} \backslash \{g^{ab}\}$.
  We can easily solve this problem by verifying

$$e(Z, g) \stackrel{?}{=} e(g^a, g^b),$$

because this equation holds if and only if Z is true.

- **Decisional Problem 2.** Given $g, g^a, \cdots, g^{a^n}, Z \in \mathbb{G}$, and $f(x), F(x) \in \mathbb{Z}_p[x]$, where $f(x), F(x)$ are polynomials of degree $n, 2n$, respectively, satisfying $f(x) \nmid F(x)$, the problem is to decide whether $Z = g^{F(a)/f(a)}$ or Z is a random element from $\mathbb{G} \backslash \{g^{F(a)/f(a)}\}$.
  We can easily solve this problem by verifying

$$e\left(Z, g^{f(a)}\right) \stackrel{?}{=} e(g, g)^{F(a)},$$

because this equation holds if and only if Z is true. Here, $e(g, g)^{F(a)}$ is computable as has been explained in Polynomial Problem 6.

4.2.4 Decisional Hard Problems

A decisional problem generated with a security parameter λ is hard if, given as input a problem instance whose target is Z, the advantage of returning a correct guess in polynomial time is a negligible function of λ, denoted by $\varepsilon(\lambda)$ (ε for short),

$$\varepsilon = \Pr\left[\text{Guess } Z = \text{True} | Z = \text{True}\right] - \Pr\left[\text{Guess } Z = \text{True} | Z = \text{False}\right],$$

where

- $\Pr\left[\text{Guess } Z = \text{True} | Z = \text{True}\right]$ is the probability of correctly guessing Z if Z is true.
- $\Pr\left[\text{Guess } Z = \text{True} | Z = \text{False}\right]$ is the probability of wrongly guessing Z if Z is false.

Similarly, a decisional problem is definitely easy if λ is not large enough.

We give some decisional hard problems in the following, where $\mathbb{G}$ is the pairing group from $e : \mathbb{G} \times \mathbb{G} \to \mathbb{G}_T$ unless it is specified otherwise.

	Decisional Diffie-Hellman Problem (DDH)
Instance:	$g, g^a, g^b, Z \in \mathbb{G}$, where $\mathbb{G}$ is a general cyclic group
Decide:	$Z \stackrel{?}{=} g^{ab}$

	Variant Decisional Diffie-Hellman Problem (Variant DDH) [32]
Instance:	$g, g^a, g^b, g^{ac}, Z \in \mathbb{G}$, where $\mathbb{G}$ is a general cyclic group
Decide:	$Z \stackrel{?}{=} g^{bc}$

Decisional Bilinear Diffie-Hellman Problem (DBDH) [101]

Instance: $g, g^a, g^b, g^c \in \mathbb{G}, Z \in \mathbb{G}_T$

Decide: $Z \overset{?}{=} e(g,g)^{abc}$

Decisional Linear Problem [23]

Instance: $g, g^a, g^b, g^{ac_1}, g^{bc_2}, Z \in \mathbb{G}$

Decide: $Z \overset{?}{=} g^{c_1 + c_2}$

q-DABDHE Problem [47]

Instance: $g, g^a, g^{a^2}, \cdots, g^{a^q}, h, h^{a^{q+2}} \in \mathbb{G}, Z \in \mathbb{G}_T$

Decide: $Z \overset{?}{=} e(g,h)^{a^{q+1}}$

Decisional (P, Q, f)-GDHE Problem [22]

Instance: $g^{P(x_1, x_2, \cdots, x_m)} \in \mathbb{G}, \ e(g,g)^{Q(x_1, x_2, \cdots, x_m)}, Z \in \mathbb{G}_T$

            $P = (p_1, p_2, \cdots, p_s) \in \mathbb{Z}_p[X_1, \cdots, X_m]^s$ is an s-tuple of m-variate polynomials

            $Q = (q_1, q_2, \cdots, q_s) \in \mathbb{Z}_p[X_1, \cdots, X_m]^s$ is an s-tuple of m-variate polynomials

            $f \in \mathbb{Z}_p[X_1, X_2, \cdots, X_m]$

            $f \neq \sum a_{i,j} p_i p_j + \sum b_i q_i$ holds for $\forall a_{i,j}, b_i$

Decide: $Z \overset{?}{=} e(g,g)^{f(x_1, x_2, \cdots, x_m)}$

Decisional (f, g, F)-GDDHE Problem [33]

Instance: $g, g^a, g^{a^2}, \cdots, g^{a^{n-1}}, \ g^{af(a)}, g^{b \cdot af(a)} \in \mathbb{G}$

            $h, h^a, h^{a^2}, \cdots, h^{a^{2k}}, \qquad\qquad h^{b \cdot g(a)} \in \mathbb{G}$

            $Z \in \mathbb{G}_T$

            $f(x), g(x)$ are co-prime polynomials of degree n, k, respectively

Decide: $Z \overset{?}{=} e(g,h)^{b \cdot f(a)}$

In the definition of decisional hard problems, the answer to the problem instance is either true or false. In particular, false in this book means $Z \neq g^{ab}$ in the DDH problem. There also exists a slightly different definition of false where Z is randomly chosen from $\mathbb{G}$. In this case, it is possible that $Z = g^{ab}$ holds with probability $\frac{1}{p}$ when the DDH problem is defined over a group of order p. We do not adopt this definition, in order to simplify the probability analysis. In this book, $Z = $ True in the DDH problem means $Z = g^{ab}$, while $Z = $ False means that Z is randomly chosen from $\mathbb{G} \backslash \{g^{ab}\}$. The same rule will be applied to all decisional hard problems.

4.2.5 How to Prove New Hard Problems

In public-key cryptography, it is possible that the proposed scheme looks secure without any efficient attack, but there is no hard problem that can be adopted for the security reduction. In this case, we have to create a new hard problem. A new hard problem is the same as a new proposed scheme, whose hardness is not convincing

unless there exists an analysis. Here, we introduce three popular methods for the
hardness analysis.

- The first method is by reduction. Suppose there exists an efficient solution algorithm that can solve a new hard problem, denoted by A. We construct a reduction
  algorithm that transforms a random instance of an existing hard problem, denoted by B, into an instance of the proposed problem A, such that a solution
  to the problem instance of A implies a solution to the problem instance of B.
  Since the problem B is hard, the assumption that the new hard problem A is easy
  is false. Therefore, the problem A is hard without any computationally efficient
  solution algorithm.

  For example, let the variant DDH problem be a new problem; we want to reduce
  its hardness to the DDH problem. Given a random instance (g, g^a, g^b, Z) of the
  DDH problem, we randomly choose z and generate an instance of the variant
  DDH problem as

  $$(g, g^z, g^b, g^{az}, Z).$$

  We have that Z is true in the variant DDH problem if and only if $Z = g^{ab}$, which
  is also true in the DDH problem. Therefore, the solution to the variant DDH
  problem instance is the solution to the DDH problem instance, and the variant
  DDH problem is not easier than the DDH problem. This reduction seems to be
  the same as a security reduction from breaking a proposed scheme to solving an
  underlying hard problem. However, this reduction is static and much easier than
  the security reduction. The reasons will be explained in Section 4.5.
- The second method is by membership proof. Suppose there exists a general problem that has been proved hard without any computationally efficient solution algorithm. We only need to prove that the new hard problem is a particular case of
  this general hard problem.

  For example, the decisional (P, Q, f)-GDHE problem is a general hard problem,
  and the decisional (f, g, F)-GDDHE problem is a specific problem. We only need
  to prove that the decisional (f, g, F)-GDDHE problem is a member of the decisional (P, Q, f)-GDHE problem.
- The third method is by intractability analysis in the generic group model. In
  this model, an adversary is only given a randomly chosen encoding of a group,
  instead of a specific group. Roughly speaking, the adversary cannot perform any
  group operation directly and must query all operations to an oracle, where only
  basic group operations are allowed to be queried. We analyze that the adversary
  cannot solve the hard problem under such an oracle. For example, the decisional
  (P, Q, f)-GDHE problem was analyzed in the generic group model in [22].

The methods mentioned above for hardness analysis are just used to convince us
that a new hard problem is at least as hard as an existing hard problem, or that a new
hard problem is hard under ideal conditions. The first two methods are much easier
for the beginner than the third one. Note that the third method is only suitable for
group-based hard problems.

4.2.6 Weak Assumptions and Strong Assumptions

All hardness assumptions can be classified into *weak assumptions* and *strong assumptions*, but the classification is not very precise.

- Weak assumptions over the group-based mathematical primitive are those hard problems, such as the CDH problem, whose security levels are very close to the DL problem. The security level is only associated with the input security parameter for the generation of the underlying mathematical primitive. A weak assumption is also regarded as a standard assumption.
- Strong assumptions over the group-based mathematical primitive are those hard problems, such as the q-SDH problem, whose security levels are lower than the DL problem. The security level is not only associated with the input security parameter for the generation of the underlying mathematical primitive, but also other parameters, such as the size of each problem instance.

Here, "weak" means that the time cost of breaking a hardness assumption is much greater than that for "strong." The word "weak" is better than the word "strong" in hardness assumptions, because it is harder to break a weak assumption than to break a strong assumption. A strong assumption means that the hardness assumption is relatively risky and unreliable. Weak assumption and strong assumption are two concepts used to judge whether an underlying hardness assumption for a proposed scheme is good or not.

4.3 An Overview of Security Reduction

Security reduction was invented to prove that breaking a proposed scheme implies solving a mathematical hard problem. In this section, we describe how a security reduction works and explain some important concepts in security reduction.

4.3.1 Security Models

When we propose a scheme for a cryptosystem, we usually do not analyze the security of the proposed scheme against a list of attacks, such as replay attack and collusion attack. Instead, we analyze that the proposed scheme is secure in a security model. A security model can be seen as an abstract of multiple attacks for a cryptosystem. If a proposed scheme is secure in a security model, it is secure against any attack that can be described and captured in this security model.

To model the security for a cryptosystem, a virtual party, called the *challenger*, is invented to interact with an adversary. A security model can be seen as a game (interactively) played between the challenger and the adversary. The challenger creates a scheme following the algorithm (definition) of the cryptosystem and knows secrets, such as the secret key, while the adversary aims to break this scheme. A security model mainly consists of the following definitions.

- What information the adversary can query.
- When the adversary can query information.
- How the adversary wins the game (breaks the scheme).

The security models for different cryptosystems might be entirely different, because the security services are not the same.

We give an example to show that the security model named IND-ID-CPA for IBE captures the collusion attack. The security model can be simply revisited as follows.

Setup. The challenger runs the setup algorithm of IBE, gives the master public key to the adversary, and keeps the master secret key.

Phase 1. The adversary makes private-key queries in this phase. The challenger responds to queries on any identity following the key generation algorithm of IBE.

Challenge. The adversary outputs two distinct messages m_0, m_1 from the same message space and an identity ID^* to be challenged, whose private key has not been queried in Phase 1. The challenger randomly flips a coin $c \in \{0, 1\}$ and returns the challenge ciphertext CT^* as $CT^* = E[mpk, ID^*, m_c]$, which is given to the adversary.

Phase 2. The challenger responds to private-key queries in the same way as in Phase 1 with the restriction that no private-key query is allowed on ID^*.

Guess: The adversary outputs a guess c' of c and wins the game if $c' = c$.

The collusion attack on an IBE scheme is stated as follows. If a proposed IBE scheme is insecure against the collusion attack, two users, namely ID_1, ID_2, can together use their private keys d_{ID_1}, d_{ID_2} to decrypt a ciphertext CT created for a third identity, namely ID_3. We now investigate whether or not the proposed scheme is secure in the above security model. Following the security model, the adversary can query ID_1, ID_2 for private keys and set $ID^* = ID_3$ as the challenge identity. If the proposed scheme is insecure against the collusion attack, the adversary can always correctly guess the encrypted message and so win the game. Therefore, if a proposed IBE scheme is secure in this security model, the proposed scheme is secure against the collusion attack.

A correct security model definition for a cryptosystem requires that the adversary cannot win the game in the security model. Otherwise, no matter how the scheme is constructed, the adversary can win the game and then the scheme is insecure in such a security model. To satisfy this requirement, the adversary must be prevented from making any trivial query. For example, the adversary must be prevented from querying the private key of ID^*, which would allow the adversary to simply win the game by running the decryption algorithm on the challenge ciphertext with the private key of ID^*. A security model is ideal and the best if the adversary can make any queries at any time excluding those queries that will allow trivial attacks. A proposed scheme provably secure in an ideal security model is more secure than a scheme provably secure in other security models.

4.3.2 Weak Security Models and Strong Security Models

A cryptosystem might have more than one security model for the same security service. These security models can be classified into the following two types.

- **Weak Security Model.** A security model is weak if the adversary is restricted in its set of allowed queries or has to reveal some queries in advance to the challenger. For example, in the security model of IND-sID-CPA for identity-based encryption, the adversary cannot make any decryption query and has to specify the challenge identity before seeing the master public key.
- **Strong Security Model.** A security model is strong if the adversary is not restricted in the queries it can make (except those queries allowing trivial attacks) and the adversary does not need to reveal any query in advance to the challenger. For example, in the security model of IND-ID-CCA for identity-based encryption, the adversary can make decryption queries on any ciphertext different from the challenge ciphertext, and the adversary does not need to specify the challenge identity before the challenge phase.

If a proposed scheme is secure in a strong security model, it indicates that it has strong security. The word "strong" is better than the word "weak" in the security model. Recall that these two words for hardness assumptions have the opposite senses. The reader might find that some security models are regarded as standard security models. A standard security model is the security model that has been widely accepted as a standard to define a security service for a cryptosystem. For example, existential unforgeability against chosen-message attacks is the standard security model for digital signatures. Note that a standard security model is not necessarily the strongest security model for a cryptosystem.

4.3.3 Proof by Testing

To measure whether a proposed scheme is secure or not in the corresponding security model, we can give the proposed scheme to the challenger for testing. The challenger runs the proposed scheme and calls for attacks. Any adversary can interact with the challenger and make queries to the challenger, while the challenger will respond to these queries following the security model. The proposed scheme is claimed to be secure if no adversary can win this game in polynomial time with non-negligible advantage.

Unfortunately, we cannot prove the security of the proposed scheme by testing in this way. Even though no adversary can win in this game, it does not mean that the proposed scheme is truly secure. The reason is that the adversary might hide its ability to break the proposed scheme during the call-for-attacks phase and will launch an attack to break the scheme when the proposed scheme has been adopted as a standard for applications.

4.3.4 Proof by Contradiction

A proof by contradiction is described as follows.

> A mathematical problem is believed to be *hard*.
> If a proposed scheme is *insecure*, we prove that this problem is *easy*.
> The assumption is then false, and the scheme is *secure*.

The proof by contradiction for public-key cryptography is explained as follows. Firstly, we have a mathematical problem that is believed to be hard. Then, we give a *breaking assumption* that there exists an adversary who can break the proposed scheme in polynomial time with non-negligible advantage. That is, the adversary is assumed to be able to break the proposed scheme by following the steps described in the proof by testing. Next, we show that this mathematical hard problem is easy because such an adversary exists. The contradiction indicates that the breaking assumption must be false. In other words, the scheme is secure and cannot be broken. Therefore, the proposed scheme is secure.

The contradiction occurs if and only if we can efficiently solve an underlying hard problem with the help of the adversary. If the underlying hard problem is actually easy or we cannot efficiently solve the underlying hard problem, the proof will fail to obtain a contradiction. A proof without contradiction does not mean that the proposed scheme is insecure but that the proposed scheme is not provably secure. That is, the given proof cannot convince us that the proposed scheme is provably secure.

4.3.5 What Is Security Reduction?

The process from *insecure* to *easy* in the proof by contradiction is called *security reduction*. A security reduction works if we can find a solution to a problem instance of the mathematical hard problem with the help of the adversary's attack. However, security reduction cannot directly reduce the adversary's attack on the proposed scheme to solving an underlying hard problem. This is because the proposed scheme and the problem instance are generated independently.

In the security reduction, the proposed scheme is replaced with a different but well-prepared scheme, which is associated with a problem instance. We extract a solution to the problem instance from the adversary's attack on such a different but well-prepared scheme to solve the mathematical problem. The core and difficulty of the security reduction is to generate such a different but well-prepared scheme. In the following introduction, we will introduce the following important concepts.

- The concepts of *real scheme*, *challenger*, and *real attack* associated with the proposed scheme.
- The concepts of *simulated scheme*, *simulator*, and *simulation* associated with the different but well-prepared scheme.

4.3.6 Real Scheme and Simulated Scheme

In a security reduction, both the real scheme and the simulated scheme are schemes. However, their generation and application are completely different.

- A real scheme is a scheme generated with a security parameter following the scheme algorithm described in the proposed scheme. A real scheme can be seen as a specific instantiation of the proposed scheme (algorithm). When the adversary interacts with the real scheme following the defined security model, we assume that the adversary can break this scheme. For simplicity, we can view the proposed scheme as the real scheme.
- A simulated scheme is a scheme generated with a random instance of an underlying hard problem following the reduction algorithm. In the security reduction, we want the adversary to interact with such a simulated scheme and break it with the same advantage as that of breaking the real scheme.

In a security reduction, it is not necessary to fully implement the simulated scheme. We only need to implement those algorithms involved in the responses to queries from the adversary. For example, when proving an encryption scheme in the IND-CPA security model, we do not need to implement the decryption algorithm for the simulated scheme, because the simulator is not required to respond to decryption queries from the adversary.

4.3.7 Challenger and Simulator

When the adversary interacts with a scheme, the scheme needs to respond to queries made by the adversary. To easily distinguish between the interaction with a real scheme and the interaction with a simulated scheme, two virtual parties, called the *challenger* and the *simulator*, are adopted.

- When the adversary interacts with a real scheme, we say that the adversary is interacting with the challenger, who creates a real scheme and responds to queries from the adversary. The challenger only appears in the security model and in the security description where the adversary needs to interact with a real scheme.
- When the adversary interacts with a simulated scheme, we say that the adversary is interacting with the simulator, who creates a simulated scheme and responds to queries from the adversary. The simulator only appears in the security reduction and is the party who runs the reduction algorithm.

These two parties appear in different circumstances (i.e., security model and security reduction) and perform different computations because the challenger runs the real scheme while the simulator runs the simulated scheme. We can even describe the interaction between the adversary and the scheme without mentioning the entity who runs the scheme.

4.3.8 Real Attack and Simulation

In a security reduction, to make sure that the adversary is able to break the simulated scheme with the advantage defined in the breaking assumption, we always need to prove that the simulation is indistinguishable from the real attack (on the real scheme). The concepts of real attack and simulation can be further explained as follows.

- The real attack is the interaction between the adversary and the challenger, who runs the real (proposed) scheme following the security model.
- The simulation is the interaction between the adversary and the simulator, who runs the simulated scheme following the reduction algorithm. Simulation is a part of security reduction.

If the simulation is indistinguishable from the real attack, the adversary cannot distinguish the scheme that it is interacting with is a real scheme or a simulated scheme. That is, the simulated scheme is indistinguishable from the real scheme from the point of view of the adversary. In this book, the indistinguishability between the simulation and the real attack is equivalent to that between the simulated scheme and the real scheme.

When the adversary is asked to interact with a given scheme, we stress that the given scheme can be a real scheme or a simulated scheme, or can be neither the real scheme nor the simulated scheme. In the breaking assumption, we assume that the adversary is able to break the real scheme, but we cannot directly use this assumption to deduce that the adversary will also break the simulated scheme, unless the simulated scheme is indistinguishable from the real scheme.

4.3.9 Attacks and Hard Problems

The aim of a security reduction is to reduce an adversary's attack to solving an underlying hard problem. An attack can be a computational attack or a decisional attack. A computational attack, such as forging a valid signature, requires the adversary to find a correct answer from an exponential-size answer space. A decisional attack, such as guessing the message in the challenge ciphertext in the IND-CPA security model, only requires the adversary to guess 0 or 1. Security against a decisional attack is also known as indistinguishability security. According to the types of attacks and the types of hard problems, we can classify security reductions into the following three types.

- **Computational Attacks to Computational Hard Problems.** For example, in the security model of EU-CMA for digital signatures, the adversary wins the game if it can forge a valid signature of a new message that has not been queried. The forgery is a computational attack. In the security reduction, the simulator will use the forged signature to solve a computational hard problem.

- **Decisional Attacks to Decisional Hard Problems.** For example, in the security model of IND-CPA for encryption, the adversary wins the game if it can correctly guess the message m_c in the challenge ciphertext. The guess is a decisional attack. In the security reduction, the simulator will use the adversary's guess of the encrypted message to solve a decisional hard problem.
- **Decisional Attacks to Computational Hard Problems.** This type is a special reduction because it is only available for security reductions in the random oracle model, where the simulator uses hash queries made by the adversary to solve a computational hard problem. The details of this type will be introduced in Section 4.11 for encryption schemes under computational hardness assumptions.

We rarely reduce a computational attack to solving a decisional hard problem, especially for digital signatures and encryption, although this type of reduction is not wrong.

4.3.10 Reduction Cost and Reduction Loss

Suppose there exists an adversary who can break a proposed scheme in polynomial time t with non-negligible advantage ε. Generally speaking, in the security reduction, we will construct a simulator to solve an underlying hard problem with (t', ε') defined as follows:

$$t' = t + T, \quad \varepsilon' = \frac{\varepsilon}{L}.$$

- T is referred to as the *reduction cost*, which is also known as the time cost. The size of T is mainly dependent on the number of queries from the adversary and the computation cost for a response to each query.
- L is referred to as the *reduction loss*, also called the security loss or loss factor. The size of L is dependent on the proposed security reduction. The minimum loss factor is 1, which means that there is no loss in the reduction. Many proposed schemes in the literature have loss factors that are linear in the number of queries, such as signature queries or hash queries.

In a security reduction, solving an underlying hard problem with (t', ε') is acceptable as long as T and L are polynomial, because this means that we can solve the underlying hard problem in polynomial time with non-negligible advantage. If one of them is exponentially large, the security reduction will fail as there is no contradiction.

4.3.11 Loose Reduction and Tight Reduction

In a security reduction, *loose reduction* and *tight reduction* are two concepts introduced to measure the reduction loss.

- We say that a security reduction is *loose* if L is at least linear in the number of queries, such as signature queries or hash queries, made by the adversary.
- We say that a security reduction is *tight* if L is a constant number or is small (e.g., sub-linear in the number of queries).

If L is as large as 2^k for an integer k, we say the reduction has k-bit security loss. Theoretically, for group-based cryptography, we must increase the group size with an additional k-bit security to make sure that the proposed scheme is as secure as the underlying hard problem. We rarely consider the time cost in measuring whether a security reduction is tight or not. The main reason is that the time cost of a security reduction is mainly determined by the hardness assumption and the security model, and is independent of the proposed security reduction.

4.3.12 Security Level Revisited

Suppose a proposed scheme, denoted by S, is generated with a security parameter λ. It is really hard to calculate its concrete security level because we do not know which attack is the most efficient one. However, we can calculate the lower bound security level and the upper bound security level of the proposed scheme S.

- Suppose solving a hard problem, denoted by A, can immediately be used to break the scheme S. The upper bound security level of the scheme S is the security level of the problem A. In group-based cryptography, the discrete logarithm problem is the fundamental hard problem. Solving the discrete logarithm problem implies breaking all group-based schemes. Therefore, the upper bound security level of all group-based schemes is the security level of the discrete logarithm problem defined over the group.
- Suppose breaking the scheme S can be reduced to solving an underlying hard problem, denoted by B. The lower bound security level of the scheme S is calculated from the underlying hard problem B. However, we cannot simply say that the lower bound security level of the scheme S is equal to the security level of the problem B. It still depends on the reduction cost and the reduction loss. The equality holds if and only if there is no reduction cost and no reduction loss.

We now use an example to explain the range of the security level for a proposed scheme based on the following statements.

1. A cyclic group $\mathbb{G}$ is generated for scheme constructions.
2. The discrete logarithm problem over the group $\mathbb{G}$ has 80-bit security.
3. Another problem, denoted by B, over the group $\mathbb{G}$ has only 60-bit security.
4. The proposed scheme is constructed over the group $\mathbb{G}$, and its security is reduced to the underlying hard problem B. To be precise, if there exists an adversary who can (t, ε)-break the proposed scheme, there exists a simulator who can solve the underlying hard problem B in time $2^5 \cdot t$ with advantage $\frac{\varepsilon}{2^{10}}$.

The security level of the proposed scheme is at most $\frac{t}{\varepsilon}$. Firstly, the upper bound security level of the scheme is 80 bits. Secondly, since the security level of the underlying hard problem B is 60 bits, we have

$$\frac{2^5 t}{\frac{\varepsilon}{2^{10}}} = 2^{15} \cdot \frac{t}{\varepsilon} \geq 2^{60}.$$

Thus, we obtain $\frac{t}{\varepsilon} \geq 2^{45}$, and the lower bound security level of the scheme is 45 bits. Therefore, the range of the proposed scheme's security level in bits is $[45, 80]$.

The lower bound security level of the proposed scheme is not 60 but 45 due to the reduction cost and the reduction loss. To make sure that the security level of the proposed scheme is at least 80 bits from the above deduction, we have the following two methods.

- We program a security reduction for the proposed scheme S under the discrete logarithm assumption without any reduction cost or reduction loss. That is, the quality of the security reduction from the proposed scheme to the discrete logarithm problem is perfect. However, few schemes in the literature can be tightly reduced to the discrete logarithm assumption.
- We generate the group $\mathbb{G}$ with a larger security parameter such that the underlying hard problem B has 95-bit security, and then the lower bound security level of the scheme is 80 bits. This solution works with the tradeoff that we have to increase the group length of the representation, which will decrease the computational efficiency of group operations.

The security range $[45, 80]$ does not mean that there must exist an attack algorithm that can break the scheme in 2^{45} steps. It only states that 45-bit security is the provable lower bound security level. Whether the provable lower bound security level can be increased or not is unknown and is dependent on the security reduction that we can propose.

We emphasize that in a real security reduction, it is actually very hard to calculate the lower bound security level because the reduction cost is $t + T$, and we cannot calculate the security level t/ε from $(t + T, \frac{\varepsilon}{L})$. The above argument and discussion are artificial and only given to help the reader understand the concrete security of the proposed scheme. However, it is always correct that the underlying hardness assumption should be as weak as the discrete logarithm assumption and (T, L) should be as small as possible.

4.3.13 Ideal Security Reduction

An ideal security reduction is the best security reduction that we can program for a proposed scheme. It should capture the following four features.

- **Security Model.** The security model should be the strongest security model that allows the adversary to maximally, flexibly, and adaptively make queries to the challenger and win the game with a minimum requirement.
- **Hard Problem.** The underlying hard problem adopted for the security reduction must be the hardest one among all hard problems defined over the same mathematical primitive. For example, the discrete logarithm problem is the hardest problem among all problems defined over a group.
- **Reduction Cost and Reduction Loss.** The reduction cost T and the reduction loss L are the minimized values. That is, T is linear in the number of queries made by the adversary and $L = 1$.
- **Computational Restrictions on Adversary.** There is no computational restriction on the adversary except time and advantage. For example, the adversary is allowed to access a hash function by itself. However, in the random oracle model, the adversary is not allowed to access a hash function but has to query a random oracle instead.

Unfortunately, an inherent tradeoff among these features is very common in all security reductions proposed in the literature. For example, we can construct an efficient signature scheme whose security is under a weak hardness assumption, but the security reduction must use random oracles. We can also construct a signature scheme without random oracles in the security reduction, but it is accompanied with a strong assumption or a long public key. Currently, it seems technically impossible to construct a scheme with an ideal security reduction satisfying all four features mentioned above.

4.4 An Overview of Correct Security Reduction

4.4.1 What Should Bob Do?

Suppose Bob has constructed a scheme along with its security reduction. In the given security reduction, Bob proves that if there exists an adversary who can break his scheme in polynomial time with non-negligible advantage, he can construct a simulator to solve an underlying hard problem in polynomial time with non-negligible advantage. Therefore, Bob has shown by contradiction that there exists no adversary who can break his proposed scheme, since the hard problem cannot be solved. Now, we have the following question:

> *How can Bob convince us that his security reduction is truly correct?*

The simplest way of proving the correctness of his security reduction is to demonstrate the security reduction, which outputs a solution to a hard problem.

Unfortunately, Bob cannot demonstrate this because a successful demonstration requires a successful attack and this attack indicates that the proposed scheme is insecure. Without the demonstration, another way is that Bob analyzes the correctness of his security reduction. We stress that the correctness analysis of the security reduction is the most difficult part of the security proof of public-key cryptography. In the following subsections, we introduce the basic preliminaries for understanding when a security reduction is correct.

4.4.2 Understanding Security Reduction

To program a security reduction and prove the security of a proposed scheme, we have the following important observations.

- At the beginning of the security proof, we assume that there exists an adversary who can break the proposed scheme. To be precise, when the adversary interacts with a real scheme following the corresponding security model, the adversary is able to break the real scheme.
- The adversary is assumed to be able to break any given scheme following the security model if the given scheme looks like a real scheme during the interaction. That is, the adversary can break any scheme that looks like a real scheme from the point of view of the adversary.
- In the security reduction, the adversary interacts with a given scheme that is a simulated scheme. We want the adversary to believe that the given scheme is a real scheme and break it. At the end, the adversary's attack is reduced to solving an underlying hard problem.
- We do not know whether or not the adversary will break the simulated scheme with the same advantage as that of breaking the real scheme if the adversary finds out that the given scheme is not a real scheme. We also do not know how the adversary breaks the simulated scheme when the given scheme looks like a real scheme.

The difficulties of the security reduction include how to ensure that the adversary accepts the simulated scheme as a real scheme and how to ensure that the adversary's attack can be reduced to solving an underlying hard problem.

4.4.3 Successful Simulation and Indistinguishable Simulation

In this book, *successful simulation* and *indistinguishable simulation* are two different concepts. They are explained as follows.

- **Successful Simulation.** A simulation is successful from the point of view of the simulator if the simulator does not abort in the simulation while interacting with the adversary. The simulator makes the decision to abort the simulation or not according to the reduction algorithm. We assume that the adversary cannot abort the attack before the simulation is completed. In this book, a simulation refers to a successful simulation unless specified otherwise.

- **Indistinguishable Simulation.** A successful simulation is indistinguishable from the real attack if the adversary cannot distinguish the simulated scheme from the real scheme. An unsuccessful simulation must be distinguishable from the real attack. Whether a (successful) simulation is distinguishable or indistinguishable is judged by the adversary. An indistinguishable simulation is desirable, especially when we want the adversary to break the simulated scheme with the advantage defined in the breaking assumption.

We emphasize that a correct security reduction might fail with a certain probability to generate a successful simulation. In this book, a successful simulation only means that the simulator does not abort in the simulation. That is, in a successful simulation, the simulator's responses to the adversary's queries might even be incorrect. However, to simplify the proof, the reduction algorithm should tell the simulator to abort if queries from the adversary cannot be correctly answered. For example, in the security reduction for a digital signature scheme, the simulator must abort if it cannot compute valid signatures on queried messages for the adversary. However, even with such an assumption, a successful simulation does not mean that the simulation is indistinguishable from the real attack. In Section 4.5.11, we discuss how the adversary can distinguish the simulated scheme from the real scheme.

4.4.4 Failed Attack and Successful Attack

We define a *failed attack* and a *successful attack* in order to clarify the adversary's attack on the simulated scheme.

- **Failed Attack.** An attack by the adversary fails if the attack cannot break the simulated scheme following the security model. Any output such as an error symbol $\perp$, a random string, a wrong answer, or an abort from the adversary is a failed attack.
- **Successful Attack.** An attack by the adversary is successful if the attack can break the simulated scheme following the security model. In this book, an attack refers to a successful attack unless specified otherwise.

We define these two types of attacks to simplify the description of reduction. In particular, there is no abort from the adversary at the end of the simulation. Any output that is not a successful attack is treated as a failed attack. The simulator may abort during the simulation because it cannot generate a successful simulation. An attack by the adversary is either failed or successful. If the adversary returns a failed attack, it is equivalent that the adversary returns a successful attack with probability 0. Therefore, at the end of the simulation, the adversary will launch a successful attack with a certain probability.

4.4.5 Useless Attack and Useful Attack

Suppose the adversary is given a simulated scheme. The adversary's attack on the simulated scheme can be classified into the following two types.

- **Useless Attack.** A useless attack is an attack by the adversary that cannot be reduced to solving an underlying hard problem.
- **Useful Attack.** A useful attack is an attack by the adversary that can be reduced to solving an underlying hard problem.

According to the above definitions, an attack by the adversary on the simulated scheme must be either useless or useful. We emphasize that a failed attack can be a useful attack and a successful attack can be a useless attack, depending on the cryptosystem, proposed scheme, and its security reduction.

4.4.6 Attack in Simulation

We have classified three types of simulations (i.e., successful simulation, distinguishable simulation, and indistinguishable simulation) and four types of attacks (i.e., failed attack, successful attack, useless attack, and useful attack). In Section 4.5 we will introduce and explain the following relationships that are extremely important in the security reduction.

- An attack at the end of a successful simulation can be either a failed attack or a successful attack, which is dependent on whether the successful simulation is distinguishable or not.
- An attack at the end of a distinguishable simulation can be either a failed attack or a successful attack. That is, the adversary can decide which attack it will launch. This does not contradict the breaking assumption.
- An attack at the end of an indistinguishable simulation is a successful attack with probability defined in the breaking assumption. The attack on the simulated scheme, however, can be either a useful attack or a useless attack. We emphasize that an indistinguishable simulation cannot ensure a useful attack in the security reduction.

The indistinguishability analysis of a simulation is important in all security reductions. However, it is not necessary to program an indistinguishable simulation in the entire simulation. For encryption under a decisional hardness assumption (see Section 4.10), the simulation must be distinguishable if Z is false. For encryption under a computational hardness assumption (see Section 4.11), we only require that the simulation is indistinguishable before the adversary makes a specific hash query to the random oracle.

4.4.7 Successful/Correct Security Reduction

The concepts of *successful security reduction* and *correct security reduction* are regarded as different in this book. They are explained as follows.

- **Successful Security Reduction.** We say that a security reduction is successful if the simulation is successful and the adversary's attack in the simulation is a useful attack.
- **Correct Security Reduction.** We say that a security reduction for a proposed scheme is correct if the advantage of solving an underlying hard problem using the adversary's attack is non-negligible in polynomial time if the breaking assumption holds.

A successful security reduction is desired in order to obtain a correct security reduction. That is, a security reduction is correct if the security reduction can be successful in solving an underlying hard problem in polynomial time with non-negligible advantage.

4.4.8 Components of a Security Proof

A security proof by a security reduction should have the following components in order to prove that the proposed scheme is secure.

- **Simulation.** The reduction algorithm should show how the simulator generates a simulated scheme and interacts with the adversary.
- **Solution.** The reduction algorithm should show how the simulator solves the underlying hard problem by returning a solution to a problem instance with the help of the adversary's attack on the simulated scheme.
- **Analysis.** After the simulation and solution, there should be an analysis showing that the advantage of solving the underlying hard problem is non-negligible if the breaking assumption holds.

The above three components are essential for proving that the security reduction is correct or the proposed scheme is truly secure under the underlying hardness assumption in the corresponding security model. These three components are quite different in detail depending on the cryptosystem, proposed scheme, underlying hard problem, and reduction approach.

In this book, we only show these three components for digital signatures, encryption under decisional hardness assumptions, and encryption under computational hardness assumptions.

4.5 An Overview of the Adversary

In this section, we take a close look at the adversary, who is assumed to be able to break the proposed scheme. It is important to understand which attack the adversary can launch or will launch on the simulated scheme.

4.5.1 Black-Box Adversary

The breaking assumption states that there exists an adversary who can break the proposed scheme in polynomial time with non-negligible advantage. There is no restriction on the adversary except time and advantage. The adversary in the security reduction is a black-box adversary. The most important property of a black box is that what the adversary will query and which specific attack the adversary will launch are not restricted and are unknown to the simulator.

For such a black-box adversary, we use *adaptive attack* to describe the black-box adversary's behavior. Adaptive attacks will be introduced in the next subsection. We emphasize that the adversary in the security reduction is far more than a black-box adversary. The reason will be explained soon after introducing the adaptive attack.

4.5.2 What Is an Adaptive Attack?

Let a be an integer chosen from the set $\{0, 1\}$. If a is randomly chosen, we have

$$\Pr[a = 0] = \Pr[a = 1] = \frac{1}{2}.$$

However, if a is adaptively chosen, the two probabilities $\Pr[a = 0]$ and $\Pr[a = 1]$ are unknown. An adaptive attack is a specific attack where the adversary's choices from the given space are not uniformly distributed but based on an unknown probability distribution.

An adaptive attack is composed of the following three parts in a security reduction between an adversary and a simulator. We take the security reduction for a digital signature scheme in the EU-CMA security model as an example to explain these three parts. Suppose the message space is $\{m_1, m_2, m_3, m_4, m_5\}$ with five distinct messages and the adversary will first query the signatures of two messages before forging a valid signature of a new message.

- What the adversary will query to the simulator is adaptive. We cannot claim that a particular message, for example m_3, will be queried for its signature with probability $2/5$. Instead, the adversary will query the signature of message m_i with unknown probability.

- How the adversary will query to the simulator is adaptive. The adversary might output two messages for signature queries at the same time or one at a time. For the latter, the adversary decides the message for its first signature query. Upon seeing the received signature, it will then decide the second message to be queried.
- What the adversary will output for the simulator is adaptive. If the adversary makes signature queries on the messages m_3 and m_4, we cannot claim that the forged signature will be on a random message m^* from $\{m_1, m_2, m_5\}$. Instead, the adversary will forge a signature of one of the messages from $\{m_1, m_2, m_5\}$ with unknown probabilities between $[0,1]$ satisfying

$$\Pr[m^* = m_1] + \Pr[m^* = m_2] + \Pr[m^* = m_5] = 1.$$

An adaptive attack is not just about how the adversary will query to the simulator. All choices are also made adaptively by the adversary unless restricted in the corresponding security model. For example, in a weak security model for digital signatures, the adversary must forge the signature of a message m^* designated by the simulator. In this case, m^* is not adaptively chosen by the adversary. There are some security models, such as IND-sID-CPA for IBE, where the adversary needs to output a challenge identity before seeing the master public key, but it can still adaptively choose this identity from the identity space.

4.5.3 Malicious Adversary

Suppose there are only two distinct attacks that can break the simulated scheme in a security reduction. One attack is useful and the other is useless. Consider the following question.

> *What is the probability of returning a useful attack by the adversary?*

According to the description of the black-box adversary, we know that this probability is unknown due to the adaptive attack by the adversary. However, a correct security reduction requires us to calculate the probability of returning a useful attack. To solve this problem, we amplify the black-box adversary into a malicious adversary and consider the *maximum probability* of returning a useless attack by the malicious adversary.

The malicious adversary is still a black-box adversary who will launch an adaptive attack. However, the malicious adversary will try its best to launch a useless attack unless the adversary does not know how to, as long as the useless attack does not contradict the breaking assumption. If the maximum probability of returning a useless attack is not the overwhelming probability 1, this means that the probability of returning a useful attack is non-negligible, and thus the security reduction is correct. If a security reduction works against such a malicious adversary, the security reduction definitely works against any adversary who can break the proposed scheme. The reason is that this maximum probability is the biggest likelihood that all adversaries can make the attack useless. From now on, an adversary refers to a malicious adversary unless specified otherwise.

4.5.4 The Adversary in a Toy Game

To help the reader better understand the meaning of the malicious adversary when the simulation is indistinguishable, we create the following toy game to explain the difficulty of security reduction. In this toy game,

- The simulator generates the simulated scheme with a random $b \in \{0,1\}$.
- The adversary adaptively chooses $a \in \{0,1\}$ as an attack.
- The adversary's attack is useful if and only if $a \neq b$.

In the security reduction, a can be seen as the adaptive attack launched by the adversary where both $a = 0$ and $a = 1$ can break the scheme, and b can be seen as the secret information in the simulated scheme. In the simulation, all the parameters given to the adversary may include the secret information about how to launch a useless attack. The malicious adversary intends to make this attack useless. It will try to guess b from the simulated scheme and then output an attack a in such a way that $\Pr[a = b] = 1$.

Security reduction is hard because we must program the simulation in such a way that the adversary does not know how to launch a useless attack. In the correctness analysis of the security reduction, the probability $\Pr[a \neq b]$ must be non-negligible. To achieve this, b must be random and independent of all the parameters given to the adversary, so that the adversary can only correctly guess b with probability $\frac{1}{2}$. In this case, we will have $\Pr[a \neq b] = \frac{1}{2}$ even though a is adaptively chosen by the adversary. The corresponding probability analysis will be given in Section 4.6.4.

4.5.5 Adversary's Successful Attack and Its Probability

Let $P_{\mathcal{E}}$ be the probability of returning a successful attack on the proposed scheme under the breaking assumption. In a security reduction the adversary will launch a successful attack on the simulated scheme with probability described as follows.

- If the simulated scheme is indistinguishable from the real scheme, according to the breaking assumption, the adversary will return a successful attack on the simulated scheme with probability $P_{\mathcal{E}}$.
- If the simulated scheme is distinguishable from the real scheme, the adversary will return a successful attack on the simulated scheme with malicious and adaptive probability $P^* \in [0,1]$ decided by the adversary itself. Returning a successful

attack with such malicious probability does not contradict the breaking assumption, because the simulated scheme is different from the real scheme.

The first case is very straightforward, but the second case is a little complex, because it varies and depends on the security reduction. The probability P^* is quite different in the security reductions for digital signatures and for encryption. The details can be found in Section 4.9 and Section 4.10.

4.5.6 Adversary's Computational Ability

All public-key schemes are only computationally secure. If there exists an adversary who has unbounded computational power and can solve all computational hard problems, it can definitely break any proposed scheme in polynomial time with non-negligible advantage. For example, the adversary can use its unbounded computational power to solve the DL problem, where the discrete logarithm can be applied to break all group-based schemes. Therefore, any proposed scheme is only secure against an adversary with bounded computational power.

An inherent interesting question is to explore which problems the adversary cannot solve when analyzing the security of a proposed scheme. A compact theorem template for claiming that a proposed scheme is provably secure (without mentioning its security model) can be stated as follows.

Theorem 4.5.6.1 *If the mathematical problem P is hard, the proposed scheme is secure and there exists no adversary who can break the proposed scheme in polynomial time with non-negligible advantage.*

The above theorem states that the proposed scheme is secure under the hardness assumption of problem P. It seems that the adversary's computational ability should be bounded in solving the hard problem P. That is, we only prove that the proposed scheme is secure against an adversary who cannot solve the hard problem P or other problems harder than P. This proof strategy is acceptable because we assume that the problem P is hard, and hence do not care whether the proposed scheme is secure or not against an adversary who can solve the problem P.

However, in the security reduction, the adversary's computational ability is taken to be unbounded to simplify the correctness analysis. Roughly speaking, the proposed scheme is only secure against a computationally bounded adversary, but the corresponding security reduction should even work against a computationally unbounded adversary. The reason will be given in the next subsection.

4.5.7 The Adversary's Computational Ability in a Reduction

In a security reduction, the simulation, such as a response computed by the simulator, might include some secret information (denoted by $\mathbb{I}$ in the following discussion). This piece of information tells the adversary how to generate a useless attack on the simulated scheme. For example, b in the toy game of Section 4.5.4 is the secret information, which should be unknown to the adversary. Other examples can be found at the end of this chapter. The simulator must hide this secret information. Otherwise, once the malicious adversary obtains the information $\mathbb{I}$ from the given parameters in the simulation, it will always launch a useless attack. Here, given parameters are all the information that the adversary knows from the simulated scheme, such as public key and signatures.

The simplest way to hide the information $\mathbb{I}$ is for the simulator never to reveal the information $\mathbb{I}$ to the adversary. Unfortunately, we found that all security reductions in the literature have to respond to queries where responses include the information $\mathbb{I}$. To make sure that the adversary does not know the information $\mathbb{I}$, the simulator must use some hard problems to hide it. Let P be the underlying hard problem in the security reduction. There are three different methods for the simulator to hide the information $\mathbb{I}$ in the security reduction.

- The simulator programs the security reduction in such a way that the information $\mathbb{I}$ is hidden by a set of new hard problems $P_1, P_2, \cdots, P_q$. The correctness of the security reduction requires that these new hard problems are not easier than the problem P. Otherwise, the adversary can solve them to obtain the information $\mathbb{I}$. To achieve this, we must prove that the information $\mathbb{I}$ can only be obtained by solving these hard problems, which are not easier than the underlying hard problem P. This method is challenging and impractical because we may not be able to reduce the hard problems $P_1, P_2, \cdots, P_q$ to the underlying hard problem P.
- The simulator programs the security reduction in such a way that the information $\mathbb{I}$ is hidden by the problem P. This method works because we assume that it is hard for the adversary to solve the problem P. However, how to use the problem P to hide the information $\mathbb{I}$ from the adversary is challenging. For example, P is the CDH problem. Suppose the information $\mathbb{I}$ is hidden with g^{ab} where the adversary knows (g, g^a, g^b). The simulator should not provide additional group elements, such as the group element $g^{a^2 b}$, to the adversary. Otherwise, it is no longer a CDH problem.
- The simulator programs the security reduction in such a way that the information $\mathbb{I}$ is hidden with some absolutely hard problems that cannot be solved, even if the adversary has unbounded computational power. This method is very efficient because those absolutely hard problems can be universally used and independent of the underlying hard problem P. In this case, we only need to prove that the information $\mathbb{I}$ is hidden with absolutely hard problems.

This book only introduces security reductions where the secret information is hidden with the third method. Therefore, the adversary can be a computationally unbounded adversary. This method is sufficient, but not necessary. However, it provides the most efficient method of analyzing the correctness of a security reduction. We note that the third method was adopted in most security reductions proposed in the literature.

4.5.8 The Adversary in a Reduction

A security reduction starts with the breaking assumption that there exists an adversary who can break the proposed scheme in polynomial time with non-negligible advantage. Then, we construct a simulator to generate a simulated scheme and use the adversary's attack to solve an underlying hard problem. According to the previous explanations, the adversary in the security reduction is summarized as follows.

- The adversary has unbounded computational power in solving all computational hard problems defined over the adopted mathematical primitive and breaking the simulated scheme.
- The adversary will maliciously try its best to launch a useless attack to break the simulated scheme and make the security reduction fail.

We assume that the adversary has unbounded computational power, but we cannot directly ask the adversary to solve an underlying hard problem for us. All that the adversary will do for us is to launch a successful attack on a scheme that looks like a real scheme. This is what the adversary can do and will do in a security reduction. Now, it is time to understand what the adversary knows and never knows in a security reduction.

4.5.9 What the Adversary Knows

There are three types of information that the adversary knows.

- **Scheme Algorithm.** The adversary knows the scheme algorithm of the proposed scheme. That is, the adversary knows how to precisely compute an output from an input. For example, to break a signature scheme, the adversary knows the system parameter generation algorithm, the key generation algorithm, the signing algorithm, and the verification algorithm.
- **Reduction Algorithm.** The adversary knows the reduction algorithm proposed for proving the security of the proposed scheme. Otherwise, we must prove that the adversary cannot find the reduction algorithm by itself from the scheme algorithm. For example, the adversary knows how the public key will be simulated; how the random numbers will be chosen; how queries will be answered; and how an underlying hard problem will be solved with a useful attack.
- **How to Solve All Computational Hard Problems.** The adversary has unbounded computational power and can solve all computational hard problems. For example, in group-based cryptography, suppose (g, g^a) is given to the adversary. We assume that the adversary can compute a before launching an attack. However, the adversary cannot break other cryptographic primitives, such as hash functions, when they are adopted as building blocks for constructing schemes. Otherwise, it can break the building blocks to break the simulated scheme, so that the security reduction is not successful.

We assume that the adversary knows the reduction algorithm. However, this does not mean that the adversary knows all the secret parameters chosen in the simulated scheme, although the simulated scheme is generated by the reduction algorithm. There are some secrets that the adversary never knows. Otherwise, it is impossible to obtain a successful security reduction.

4.5.10 What the Adversary Never Knows

There are three types of secrets that the adversary never knows.

- **Random Numbers.** The adversary does not know those random numbers (including group elements) chosen by the simulator when the simulator generates the simulated scheme unless they can be computed by the adversary. For example, if the simulator randomly chooses two secrets number $x, y \in \mathbb{Z}_p$, we assume that they are unknown to the adversary. However, once (g, g^{x+y}) are given to the adversary, the adversary knows $x + y$ according to the previous subsection.
- **Problem Instance.** The adversary does not know the random instance of the underlying hard problem given to the simulator. This assumption is desired to simplify the proof of indistinguishability. For example, suppose Bob proposes a scheme and a security reduction that shows that if there exists an adversary who can break the scheme, the reduction can find the solution to the instance (g, g^a) of the DL problem. In the security reduction, the adversary receives a key pair (g, g^α), which is equal to (g, g^a). Since the adversary knows that (g, g^a) is a problem instance, it will immediately find out that the given scheme is a simulated scheme and stop the attack.
- **How to Solve an Absolutely Hard Problem.** The adversary does not know how to solve an absolutely hard problem, such as computing (x, y) from the group elements (g, g^{x+y}). Another example is to compute a pair $(m^*, f(m^*))$ when given $(m_1, m_2, f(m_1), f(m_2))$ for a distinct $m^* \notin \{m_1, m_2\}$, where $f(x) \in \mathbb{Z}_p[x]$ is a random polynomial of degree 2. Some absolutely hard problems will be introduced in Section 4.7.6.

Roughly speaking, the adversary will utilize what it knows to launch a useless attack on the simulated scheme, while the simulator should utilize what the adversary never knows to force the adversary to launch a useful attack with non-negligible probability.

4.5.11 How to Distinguish the Given Scheme

In the security reduction, the adversary interacts with a given scheme that is the simulated scheme. The adversary distinguishes the simulated scheme from the real scheme by *correctness* and *randomness*, which are described as follows.

- **Correctness.** All responses to queries from the adversary in the simulated scheme must be exactly the same as in the real scheme. When the adversary makes queries to the simulated scheme, it will receive the corresponding responses accordingly. If a response is not correct, the adversary can judge the scheme to be a simulated scheme because the real scheme should respond to all queries correctly. For example, the adversary judges a signature scheme to be a simulated scheme when the received signature of message m cannot pass the verification. Another example in encryption is the decryption query. The adversary will find out that the given encryption scheme is a simulated scheme if a decryption query on a ciphertext that should be rejected by the real scheme is accepted by the given scheme.
- **Randomness.** Random numbers and random group elements in the simulated scheme should be truly random and independent. Random numbers and random group elements are used in many constructions, such as digital signatures and private keys in identity-based cryptography. If the real scheme produces random numbers/elements, they must be truly random and independent. Then, all generated random numbers/elements in the simulated scheme must also be random and independent. Otherwise, the adversary can easily determine that the given scheme is a simulated scheme. We will introduce the concept of *random and independent* in Section 4.7.

According to the descriptions of successful simulation and indistinguishable simulation in Section 4.4.3, we have the following interesting formula.

$$\text{Successful Simulation} + \text{Correctness} + \text{Randomness} = \text{Indistinguishable Simulation}.$$

An indistinguishable simulation cannot guarantee that the adversary's attack is useful. The malicious adversary can still utilize what it knows and what it receives from the simulator to find out how to launch a useless attack.

4.5.12 How to Generate a Useless Attack

The way that the adversary launches a useless attack cannot be described here in detail because it is highly dependent on the proposed scheme, the reduction algorithm, and the underlying hard problem. Here, we only give a high-level overview of what a useless attack looks like in digital signatures and encryption.

- Suppose a security reduction for a signature scheme uses a forged signature from the adversary to solve an underlying hard problem. A useless attack is a special forged signature for the simulated scheme that is valid and also computable by the simulator, so that it cannot be used to solve an underlying hard problem.
- Suppose a security reduction for an encryption scheme uses the guess of the encrypted message from the adversary to solve an underlying decisional hard problem. A useless attack is a special way of guessing the encrypted message m_c such that the message in the challenge ciphertext can always be correctly guessed

($c' = c$), no matter whether the target Z in the decisional problem instance is true or false.

The adversary can launch a useless attack because it knows the secret information in the simulation. How to hide the secret information $\mathbb{I}$ from the adversary using absolutely hard problems is an important step in a security reduction.

4.5.13 Summary of Adversary

At the end of this section, we summarize the malicious adversary in a security reduction as follows.

- When the adversary is asked to interact with a given scheme, it considers this scheme to be a simulated scheme. The adversary will use what it knows and what it can query (following the defined security model) to find whether the given scheme is indeed distinguishable from the real scheme or not.
- When the adversary finds out that the given scheme is a simulated scheme, the adversary will launch a successful attack with malicious and adaptive probability $P^* \in [0, 1]$. The detailed probability P^* is dependent on the security reduction.
- When the adversary cannot distinguish the simulation from the real attack, it will launch a successful attack with probability P_ε according to the breaking assumption.
- Without contradicting the breaking assumption, the adversary will use what it knows and what it receives to launch a useless attack on the given scheme.

In the security reduction, we prove that if there exists an adversary who can break the proposed scheme, we can construct a simulator to solve an underlying hard problem. To be more precise, a correct security reduction requires that even if the attack on the simulated scheme is launched by a malicious adversary who has unbounded computational power, the advantage of solving an underlying hard problem is still non-negligible.

4.6 An Overview of Probability and Advantage

4.6.1 Definitions of Probability

Probability is the measure of the likelihood that an event will occur. In a security proof, this event is mainly about a successful attack on a scheme or a correct solution to a problem instance. There are four important probability definitions for digital signatures, encryption, computational problems, and decisional problems, respectively.

- **Digital Signatures.** Let $\Pr[\text{Win}_{Sig}]$ be the probability that the adversary successfully forges a valid signature. Obviously, this probability satisfies

$$0 \leq \Pr[\text{Win}_{Sig}] \leq 1.$$

- **Encryption.** Let $\Pr[\text{Win}_{Enc}]$ be the probability that the adversary correctly guesses the message in the challenge ciphertext in the security model of indistinguishability. This probability satisfies

$$\frac{1}{2} \leq \Pr[\text{Win}_{Enc}] \leq 1.$$

The message in the challenge ciphertext is m_c where $c \in \{0, 1\}$, and the adversary will output 0 or 1 to guess c. Since c is randomly chosen by the challenger, no matter what the guess c' is, we have that $\Pr[\text{Win}_{Enc}] = \Pr[c' = c]$ holds with probability at least $\frac{1}{2}$.

- **Computational Problems.** Let $\Pr[\text{Win}_C]$ be the probability of computing a correct solution to an instance of a computational problem. This probability satisfies

$$0 \leq \Pr[\text{Win}_C] \leq 1.$$

- **Decisional Problems.** Let $\Pr[\text{Win}_D]$ be the probability of correctly guessing the target Z in an instance of a decisional problem. That is, if Z is a true element, the guess output is true. Otherwise, Z is a false element and the guess output is false. The probability $\Pr[\text{Win}_D]$ is dependent on the definition of the decisional problem.

  - Suppose the target Z is randomly chosen from a space having two elements where one element is true and the other is false. Then, we have

  $$\frac{1}{2} \leq \Pr[\text{Win}_D] \leq 1.$$

  - Suppose the target Z is randomly chosen from a space having n elements where only one element is true. Then, we have

  $$1 - \frac{1}{n} \leq \Pr[\text{Win}_D] \leq 1.$$

  This probability is calculated in such a way that if we cannot correctly guess the target with probability 1, we guess that Z is false. Since $n - 1$ out of n elements are false and Z is randomly chosen, we have that Z is false with probability $\frac{n-1}{n} = 1 - \frac{1}{n}$.

In the above four definitions, the adversary refers to a general adversary who intends to break a scheme or solve a problem. Note that this is not the adversary who can break the scheme or solve the problem in the breaking assumption. Otherwise, the probability cannot be, for example, $\Pr[\text{Win}_{Sig}] = 0$.

The minimum and maximum probabilities in the above four definitions are different. We cannot use a given probability to universally measure whether a proposed scheme is secure or insecure and whether a problem is hard or easy. Due to the difference, advantage is defined in such a way that we can use the same measurement to judge security/insecurity for schemes and hardness/easiness for problems.

4.6.2 Definitions of Advantage

Informally speaking, advantage is the measure of how successfully an attack algorithm can break a proposed scheme or a solution algorithm can solve a problem, compared to the idealized probability P_{ideal} in the corresponding security model. For example, $P_{ideal} = 0$ in the EU-CMA security model for digital signatures and $P_{ideal} = \frac{1}{2}$ in the indistinguishability security model.

Advantage is an adjusted probability, where the minimum advantage must be zero. Roughly speaking, we use the following method to define an advantage.

- If P_{ideal} is non-negligible, we define the advantage as

$$\text{Advantage} = \text{Probability of Successful Attack} \ - \ P_{ideal}.$$

- If P_{ideal} is negligible, we define the advantage as

$$\text{Advantage} = \text{Probability of Successful Attack}.$$

In the advantage definition, we are not interested in how large the advantage is, but only in two different results: *Negligible* and *Non-negligible*. Let ε be the advantage of breaking a proposed scheme or solving a problem. If the advantage is negligible, the proposed scheme is secure or the problem is hard. Otherwise, the proposed scheme is insecure or the problem is easy. A precise non-negligible value is not important because any non-negligible advantage indicates that the proposed scheme is insecure or the problem is easy.

There is no standard definition of maximum advantage. For example, in the definition of indistinguishability for encryption, some researchers prefer $\frac{1}{2}$ as the maximum advantage while others prefer 1. In this book, we prefer 1 as the maximum advantage for encryption to keep the consistency with digital signatures.

The definitions of advantage for digital signatures, encryption, computational problems, and decisional problems are described as follows.

- **Advantage for Digital Signatures.** The advantage of forging a valid signature in the security model of EU-CMA for digital signatures is defined as

$$\varepsilon = \Pr[\text{Win}_{Sig}].$$

We have $\varepsilon \in [0, 1]$ according to its probability definition.

- **Advantage for Encryption.** The advantage of correctly guessing the encrypted message in the security model of indistinguishability for encryption is defined as

$$
\begin{aligned}
\varepsilon &= \Pr[\text{Win}_{Enc}|c = 0] - \frac{1}{2} + \Pr[\text{Win}_{Enc}|c = 1] - \frac{1}{2} \\
&= 2\left(\Pr[\text{Win}_{Enc}|c = 0]\Pr[c = 0] + \Pr[\text{Win}_{Enc}|c = 1]\Pr[c = 1] - \frac{1}{2} \right) \\
&= 2\left(\Pr[\text{Win}_{Enc}] - \frac{1}{2} \right).
\end{aligned}
$$

  We have $\varepsilon \in [0,1]$ according to its probability definition.
- **Advantage for Computational Problems.** The advantage of finding a solution to an instance of a computational problem is defined as

$$
\varepsilon = \Pr[\text{Win}_C].
$$

  We have $\varepsilon \in [0,1]$ according to its probability.
- **Advantage for Decisional Problems.** The advantage of correctly guessing the target Z in an instance of a decisional problem is defined as

$$
\begin{aligned}
\varepsilon &= \Pr[\text{Win}_D|Z = \text{True}] - \frac{1}{2} + \Pr[\text{Win}_D|Z = \text{False}] - \frac{1}{2} \\
&= \Pr[\text{Win}_D|Z = \text{True}] - (1 - \Pr[\text{Win}_D|Z = \text{False}]) \\
&= \Pr[\text{Guess } Z = \text{True}|Z = \text{True}] - \Pr[\text{Guess } Z = \text{True}|Z = \text{False}],
\end{aligned}
$$

where the first conditional probability is the probability of correctly guessing Z if Z is true, and the second conditional probability is the probability of wrongly guessing Z if Z is false. The advantage definition for a decisional problem does not directly use the probability $\Pr[\text{Win}_D]$.

If the decisional problem is easy, then

$$
\Pr[\text{Guess } Z{=}\text{True}|Z = \text{True}] = 1, \quad \Pr[\text{Guess } Z{=}\text{True}|Z = \text{False}] = 0.
$$

That is, we have $\varepsilon = 1$. Otherwise, the decisional problem is absolutely hard, and we have

$$
\Pr[\text{Guess } Z{=}\text{True} |Z = \text{True}] = \Pr[\text{Guess } Z{=}\text{True}|Z = \text{False}] = \frac{1}{2}.
$$

That is, we have $\varepsilon = 0$, which means that the probability of correctly/wrongly guessing Z is the same. Therefore, the advantage ε is also within the range $[0,1]$.

The ranges in all the above advantage definitions are the same. If $\varepsilon = 0$, then the scheme is absolutely secure or the problem is absolutely hard. If $\varepsilon = 1$, then the scheme can be broken or the problem can be solved with success probability 1.

4.6.3 Malicious Adversary Revisited

The reason why we strengthen a black-box adversary into a malicious adversary can be explained as follows with probability and advantage.

- In a security reduction, we cannot calculate the probability of returning a useful attack by a black-box adversary unless the adversary's attack is always useful. The reason is that the adversary's attack is adaptive.
- In a security reduction, we can calculate the advantage of returning a useless attack by a malicious adversary, who tries its best to make the security reduction fail. If the advantage is 1, this means that the security reduction is incorrect.

We have to consider the advantage in the security reduction because it is hard or impossible to make the attack always useful in a security reduction. Take the security reduction for digital signatures as an example. In the EU-CMA security model, the simulator must program the security reduction in such a way that some signatures can be computed by the simulator in order to respond to signature queries. If the adversary happens to choose one of these signatures as the forged signature, the forged signature is a useless attack and thus the forged signature cannot always be a useful attack.

4.6.4 Adaptive Choice Revisited

The probability of an adaptive choice cannot be calculated. Fortunately, there are two important probability formulas associated with an adaptive choice that we can still use.

Take the toy game in Section 4.5.4 as an example, where the adversary adaptively chooses $a \in \{0,1\}$, and the simulator randomly chooses $b \in \{0,1\}$.

- The complementary event holds for all adaptive choices. That is,

$$\Pr[a = 0] + \Pr[a = 1] = 1.$$

- If b is unknown to the adversary, we have that the choice of a is independent of b, and then

$$
\begin{aligned}
\Pr[a = b] &= \Pr[a = 0 | b = 0] \Pr[b = 0] + \Pr[a = 1 | b = 1] \Pr[b = 1] \\
&= \Pr[a = 0] \Pr[b = 0] + \Pr[a = 1] \Pr[b = 1] \\
&= \frac{1}{2} \Pr[a = 0] + \frac{1}{2} \Pr[a = 1] \\
&= \frac{1}{2} \Big(\Pr[a = 0] + \Pr[a = 1] \Big) \\
&= \frac{1}{2}.
\end{aligned}
$$

The above two probability formulas are simple but they are the core of the probability analysis in all security reductions. We can only calculate the success probability associated with an adaptive attack by these two formulas.

4.6.5 Useless, Useful, Loose, and Tight Revisited

Let ε denote the advantage of breaking a proposed scheme and ε_R denote the advantage of solving an underlying hard problem by a security reduction. The concepts of useless attack, useful attack, tight reduction, and loose reduction in a security reduction can be explained as follows.

- **Useless.** The advantage ε_R is negligible. There exists an adversary who can break the proposed scheme in polynomial time with non-negligible advantage ε, but the advantage ε_R is negligible.
- **Useful.** The advantage ε_R is non-negligible. If there exists an adversary who can break the proposed scheme in polynomial time with non-negligible advantage ε, then the advantage ε_R is also non-negligible.
- **Loose.** The advantage ε_R is equal to $\frac{\varepsilon}{O(q)}$, where q denotes the number of queries made by the adversary. In practice, the size of q can be as large as $q = 2^{30}$ or $q = 2^{60}$, depending on the definition of q. For example, q can denote the number of signature queries or the number of hash queries made by the adversary. The number $q = 2^{30}$ is derived based on the fact that a key pair can be used to generate up to 2^{30} signatures, while the number $q = 2^{60}$ is derived based on the fact that the adversary can make up to 2^{60} hash queries in polynomial time.
- **Tight.** The advantage ε_R is equal to $\frac{\varepsilon}{O(1)}$, where $O(1)$ is constant and independent of the number of queries. For example, a security reduction with $O(1) = 2$ is a tight reduction. When the reduction loss is related to the security parameter λ, we still call it a tight reduction although it is only almost tight.

In the above descriptions, we do not consider the time cost and assume that the security reduction is completed in polynomial time. The above four concepts are associated with the advantage only.

4.6.6 Important Probability Formulas

Let $A_1, A_2, \cdots, A_q, B$ denote different events, and A^c be the complementary event that the event A does not occur. The following probability formulas have been used in many security reductions for calculating the advantage.

- **Equations.**

$$\Pr[B] = 1 - \Pr[B^c] \tag{6.1}$$

$$\Pr[A] = \Pr[A|B]\Pr[B] + \Pr[A|B^c]\Pr[B^c] \tag{6.2}$$

$$\Pr[A \wedge B] = \Pr[B] \cdot \Pr[A|B] \tag{6.3}$$

$$\Pr[A \wedge B] = \Pr[A] \cdot \Pr[B|A] \tag{6.4}$$

$$\Pr[A|B] = \frac{\Pr[B|A] \cdot \Pr[A]}{\Pr[B]} \tag{6.5}$$

$$\Pr[A|B] = 1 - \Pr[A^c|B] \tag{6.6}$$

$$\Pr[A_1 \wedge A_2 \wedge \cdots \wedge A_q] = 1 - \Pr[A_1^c \vee A_2^c \vee \cdots \vee A_q^c] \tag{6.7}$$

$$\Pr[A_1 \vee A_2 \vee \cdots \vee A_q] = 1 - \Pr[A_1^c \wedge A_2^c \wedge \cdots \wedge A_q^c] \tag{6.8}$$

$$\Pr[(A_1 \wedge A_2 \wedge \cdots \wedge A_q)|B] = 1 - \Pr[(A_1^c \vee A_2^c \vee \cdots \vee A_q^c)|B] \tag{6.9}$$

$$\Pr[(A_1 \vee A_2 \vee \cdots \vee A_q)|B] = 1 - \Pr[(A_1^c \wedge A_2^c \wedge \cdots \wedge A_q^c)|B] \tag{6.10}$$

- **Inequations.**

$$\Pr[A_1 \vee A_2 \vee \cdots \vee A_q] \le \sum_{i=1}^{q} \Pr[A_i] \tag{6.11}$$

$$\Pr[A_1 \wedge A_2 \wedge \cdots \wedge A_q] \ge \prod_{i=1}^{q} \Pr[A_i] \tag{6.12}$$

$$\Pr[A_1 \vee A_2 \vee \cdots \vee A_q] \le 1 - \prod_{i=1}^{q} \Pr[A_i^c] \tag{6.13}$$

$$\Pr[A_1 \wedge A_2 \wedge \cdots \wedge A_q] \ge 1 - \sum_{i=1}^{q} \Pr[A_i^c] \tag{6.14}$$

$$\Pr[A] \ge \Pr[A|B] \cdot \Pr[B] \tag{6.15}$$

- **Conditional Equations.**

$$\Pr[A|B] = \Pr[A] \quad \text{if } A \text{ and } B \text{ are independent} \tag{6.16}$$

$$\Pr[A_1 \vee A_2 \vee \cdots \vee A_q] = \sum_{i=1}^{q} \Pr[A_i] \quad \text{if all events are independent} \tag{6.17}$$

$$\Pr[A_1 \wedge A_2 \wedge \cdots \wedge A_q] = \prod_{i=1}^{q} \Pr[A_i] \quad \text{if all events are independent} \tag{6.18}$$

4.7 An Overview of Random and Independent

Random numbers (including random group elements) are very common in constructing cryptographic schemes, such as digital signature schemes and encryption schemes. Suppose each number in the set $\{A_1, A_2, \cdots, A_n\} \in \mathbb{Z}_p$ is a random number. This means that each number is chosen randomly and independently from $\mathbb{Z}_p$, and all numbers are uniformly distributed in $\mathbb{Z}_p$. In a simulated scheme, if random numbers are not randomly chosen, but generated from a function, we must prove that these simulated random numbers generated by the function are also random and independent from the point of view of the adversary. Otherwise, the simulation is distinguishable from the real attack. In this section, we explain the concept of *random and independent* and introduce how to simulate randomness, where all simulated random numbers are truly random and independent.

4.7.1 What Are Random and Independent?

Let (A, B, C) be three random integers chosen from the space $\mathbb{Z}_p$. The concept of *random and independent* can be explained as follows.

- **Random.** C is equal to any integer in $\mathbb{Z}_p$ with the same probability $\frac{1}{p}$.
- **Independent.** C cannot be computed from A and B.

The concept of random and independent is applied in the security reduction as follows. Let A, B, C be random integers chosen from $\mathbb{Z}_p$. Suppose an adversary is only given A and B. The adversary then has no advantage in guessing the integer C and can only guess the integer C correctly with probability $\frac{1}{p}$. If A, B are two integers randomly chosen from the space $\mathbb{Z}_p$ and $C = A + B \bmod p$, we still have that C is equivalent to a random number chosen from $\mathbb{Z}_p$. However, A, B, C are not independent, because C can be computed from A and B.

In a scheme construction and a security proof, when we say that $A_1, A_2, \cdots, A_q$ are all randomly chosen from an exponentially large space, such as $\mathbb{Z}_p$, we assume that they are all distinct. That is, $A_i \neq A_j$ for any $i \neq j$. This assumption will simplify the probability analysis and the proof description. We also note that for some proposed schemes in the literature, if they generate random numbers that are equal, the proposed schemes will become insecure.

4.7.2 Randomness Simulation with a General Function

In a real scheme, suppose (A, B, C) are integers randomly chosen from $\mathbb{Z}_p$. However, in the simulated scheme, (A, B, C) are generated from a function with other random integers. For example, all integers A, B, C are simulated from a function with w, x, y, z as input, where (w, x, y, z) are integers randomly chosen from $\mathbb{Z}_p$ by the simulator when running the reduction algorithm. We want to investigate whether the simulated (A, B, C) are also random and independent from the point of view of the adversary. If the simulated random integers are also random and independent, the simulated scheme is indistinguishable from the real scheme from the point of view of the random number generation.

We have the following simplified lemma for checking whether the simulated random numbers (A, B, C) are also random and independent.

Lemma 4.7.1 *Suppose a real scheme and a simulated scheme generate integers (A, B, C) with different methods described as follows.*

- *In the real scheme, let (A, B, C) be three integers randomly chosen from $\mathbb{Z}_p$.*
- *In the simulated scheme, let (A, B, C) be computed by a function with random integers (w, x, y, z) from $\mathbb{Z}_p$ as the input to the function, denoted by $(A, B, C) = F(w, x, y, z)$.*

Suppose the adversary knows the function F from the reduction algorithm but not (w, x, y, z). The simulated scheme is indistinguishable from the real scheme if for any given (A, B, C) from $\mathbb{Z}_p$, the number of solutions (w, x, y, z) satisfying $(A, B, C) = F(w, x, y, z)$ is the same. That is, any (A, B, C) from $\mathbb{Z}_p$ will be generated with the same probability in the simulated scheme.

It is not hard to verify the correctness of this lemma. We prove this lemma by arguing that any three given values (A, B, C) will appear with the same probability. Let $< w, x, y, z >$ be a vector that represents one choice of random (w, x, y, z) from $\mathbb{Z}_p$. There are p^4 different vectors in the vector space and each vector will be chosen with the same probability $1/p^4$. Suppose that for any (A, B, C), the number of $< w, x, y, z >$ generating (A, B, C) via F is n, so the probability of choosing random (w, x, y, z) satisfying $(A, B, C) = F(w, x, y, z)$ is n/p^4. Therefore, the simulated scheme is indistinguishable from the real scheme.

Consider the simulation of (A, B, C) from $\mathbb{Z}_p$ with the following functions under modular operations using random integers (w, x, y, z) from $\mathbb{Z}_p$.

$$(A, \ B, \ C) = F(x, y) = (x, \ y, \ x + y) \tag{7.19}$$
$$(A, \ B, \ C) = F(x, y, z) = (x, \ y, \ z + 3) \tag{7.20}$$
$$(A, \ B, \ C) = F(x, y, z) = (x, \ y, \ z + 4 \cdot xy) \tag{7.21}$$
$$(A, \ B, \ C) = F(w, x, y, z) = (x + w, \ y, \ z + w \cdot x) \tag{7.22}$$

We have the following observations.

- **7.19 Distinguishable.** In this function, we have

$$x = A,$$
$$y = B,$$
$$x + y = C.$$

If the given (A, B, C) satisfies $A + B = C$, the function has one solution

$$< x, y > = < A, B > .$$

Otherwise, there is no solution. Therefore, the simulated A, B, C are not random and independent. To be precise, C can be computed from $A + B$.

- **7.20 Indistinguishable.** In this function, we have

$$x = A,$$
$$y = B,$$
$$z + 3 = C.$$

For any given (A, B, C), the function has one solution

$$< x, y, z > = < A, B, C - 3 > .$$

Therefore, A, B, C are random and independent.

- **7.21 Indistinguishable.** In this function, we have

$$x = A,$$
$$y = B,$$
$$z + 4xy = C.$$

For any given (A, B, C), the function has one solution

$$< x, y, z > = < A, B, C - 4AB > .$$

Therefore, A, B, C are random and independent.

- **7.22 Indistinguishable.** In this function, we have

$$x + w = A,$$
$$y = B,$$
$$z + w \cdot x = C.$$

For any given (A, B, C), the function has p different solutions

$$< w, x, y, z > = < w, A - w, B, C - w(A - w) >,$$

where w can be any integer from $\mathbb{Z}_p$. Therefore, A, B, C are random and independent.

The full lemma can be stated as follows. This lemma will frequently be used in the correctness analysis of the schemes in this book. We stress that when $(A_1, A_2, \cdots, A_q)$ are randomly chosen from $\mathbb{Z}_p$, we have that $(g^{A_1}, g^{A_2}, \cdots, g^{A_q})$ are random and independent from $\mathbb{G}$. Therefore, in this book, the analysis of randomness and independence is associated with integers or exponents from $\mathbb{Z}_p$ only.

Lemma 4.7.2 *Suppose a real scheme and a simulated scheme generate integers $(A_1, A_2, \cdots, A_q)$ with different methods described as follows.*

- *In the real scheme, let $(A_1, A_2, \cdots, A_q)$ be integers randomly chosen from $\mathbb{Z}_p$.*
- *In the simulated scheme, let $(A_1, A_2, \cdots, A_q)$ be computed by a function with random integers $(x_1, x_2, \cdots, x_{q'})$ from $\mathbb{Z}_p$ as the input to the function, denoted by*

$$(A_1, A_2, \cdots, A_q) = F(x_1, x_2, \cdots, x_{q'}).$$

Suppose the adversary knows the function F from the reduction algorithm but not $(x_1, x_2, \cdots, x_{q'})$. *The simulated scheme is indistinguishable from the real scheme if, for any* $(A_1, A_2, \cdots, A_q)$ *from* $\mathbb{Z}_p$, *the number of solutions* $(x_1, x_2, \cdots, x_{q'})$ *satisfying* $(A_1, A_2, \cdots, A_q) = F(x_1, x_2, \cdots, x_{q'})$ *is the same. That is, every* $(A_1, A_2, \cdots, A_q)$ *from* $\mathbb{Z}_p$ *will be generated with the same probability in the simulated scheme.*

We stress that if $q' < q$, the simulated scheme is definitely distinguishable from the real scheme. For indistinguishable simulation, it is required that $q' \geq q$ must hold, but this condition is not sufficient.

4.7.3 Randomness Simulation with a Linear System

A general system of n linear equations (or linear system) over $\mathbb{Z}_p$ with n unknown secrets $(x_1, x_2, \cdots, x_n)$ can be written as

$$
\begin{aligned}
a_{11}x_1 + a_{12}x_2 + \cdots + a_{1n}x_n &= y_1 \\
a_{21}x_1 + a_{22}x_2 + \cdots + a_{2n}x_n &= y_2 \\
&\cdots \\
a_{n1}x_1 + a_{n2}x_2 + \cdots + a_{nn}x_n &= y_n
\end{aligned},
$$

where the a_{ij} are the coefficients of the system, and $y_1, y_2, \cdots, y_n$ are constant terms from $\mathbb{Z}_p$. We define $\mathbb{A}$ as the coefficient matrix,

$$
\mathbb{A} = \begin{pmatrix}
a_{11} & a_{12} & a_{13} & \cdots & a_{1n} \\
a_{21} & a_{22} & a_{23} & \cdots & a_{2n} \\
\vdots & \vdots & \vdots & \cdots & \vdots \\
a_{n1} & a_{n2} & a_{n3} & \cdots & a_{nn}
\end{pmatrix}.
$$

We have the following lemma for the simulation of random numbers by a linear system.

Lemma 4.7.3 *Suppose a real scheme and a simulated scheme generate integers* $(A_1, A_2, \cdots, A_n)$ *with different methods described as follows.*

- *In the real scheme, let* $(A_1, A_2, \cdots, A_n)$ *be n integers randomly chosen from* $\mathbb{Z}_p$.
- *In the simulated scheme, let* $(A_1, A_2, \cdots, A_n)$ *be computed by*

$$
(A_1, A_2, \cdots, A_n)^\top = \mathbb{A} \cdot X^\top = \begin{pmatrix}
a_{11} & a_{12} & a_{13} & \cdots & a_{1n} \\
a_{21} & a_{22} & a_{23} & \cdots & a_{2n} \\
\vdots & \vdots & \vdots & \cdots & \vdots \\
a_{n1} & a_{n2} & a_{n3} & \cdots & a_{nn}
\end{pmatrix} \cdot \begin{pmatrix}
x_1 \\
x_2 \\
\vdots \\
x_n
\end{pmatrix} \bmod p,
$$

where $x_1, x_2, \cdots, x_n$ *are random integers chosen from* $\mathbb{Z}_p$.

Suppose the adversary knows $\mathbb{A}$ *but not* X. *If the determinant of* $\mathbb{A}$ *is nonzero, the simulated scheme is indistinguishable from the real scheme.*

According to our knowledge of linear systems, if $|\mathbb{A}| \neq 0$ there is only one solution $< x_1, x_2, \cdots, x_n >$ for any given $(A_1, A_2, \cdots, A_n)$. According to Lemma 4.7.2, the A_i are random and independent, so the simulated scheme is indistinguishable from the real scheme. If $|\mathbb{A}| = 0$ the number of solutions can be zero or p depending on the given $(A_1, A_2, \cdots, A_n)$. The A_i are not random and independent, so the simulated scheme is distinguishable from the real scheme.

Consider the simulation of (A_1, A_2, A_3) from $\mathbb{Z}_p$ with the following functions using random integers (x_1, x_2, x_3) from $\mathbb{Z}_p$.

$$(A_1, A_2, A_3) = (x_1 + 3x_2 + 3x_3 , x_1 + x_2 + x_3 , 3x_1 + 5x_2 + 5x_3) \qquad (7.23)$$
$$(A_1, A_2, A_3) = (x_1 + 3x_2 + 3x_3 , 2x_1 + 3x_2 + 5x_3 , 9x_1 + 5x_2 + 2x_3) \ (7.24)$$

- **7.23 Distinguishable.** In this function, we have

$$x_1 + 3x_2 + 3x_3 = A_1,$$
$$x_1 + x_2 + x_3 = A_2,$$
$$3x_1 + 5x_2 + 5x_3 = A_3.$$

It is easy to verify that the determinant of the coefficient matrix satisfies

$$\begin{vmatrix} 1 & 3 & 3 \\ 1 & 1 & 1 \\ 3 & 5 & 5 \end{vmatrix} = 0.$$

Therefore, (A_1, A_2, A_3) are not random and independent. To be precise, given A_1 and A_2, we can compute A_3 by $A_3 = A_1 + 2A_2$.

- **7.24 Indistinguishable.** In this function, we have

$$x_1 + 3x_2 + 3x_3 = A_1,$$
$$2x_1 + 3x_2 + 5x_3 = A_2,$$
$$9x_1 + 5x_2 + 2x_3 = A_3.$$

It is easy to verify that the determinant of the coefficient matrix satisfies

$$\begin{vmatrix} 1 & 3 & 3 \\ 2 & 3 & 5 \\ 9 & 5 & 2 \end{vmatrix} = 53 \neq 0.$$

Therefore, (A_1, A_2, A_3) are random and independent.

Simulation by a more general linear system can be described as follows.

Lemma 4.7.4 *Suppose a real scheme and a simulated scheme generate integers* $(A_1, A_2, \cdots, A_n)$ *with different methods described as follows.*

- *In the real scheme, let $(A_1, A_2, \cdots, A_n)$ be n integers randomly chosen from $\mathbb{Z}_p$.*
- *In the simulated scheme, let $(A_1, A_2, \cdots, A_n)$ be computed by*

$$
(A_1, A_2, \cdots, A_n)^\top = \mathbb{A} \cdot X^\top =
\begin{pmatrix}
a_{11} & a_{12} & a_{13} & \cdots & a_{1q} \\
a_{21} & a_{22} & a_{23} & \cdots & a_{2q} \\
\vdots & \vdots & \vdots & \cdots & \vdots \\
a_{n1} & a_{n2} & a_{n3} & \cdots & a_{nq}
\end{pmatrix}
\cdot
\begin{pmatrix}
x_1 \\
x_2 \\
\vdots \\
x_q
\end{pmatrix}
\mod p,
$$

where $x_1, x_2, \cdots, x_q$ are random integers chosen from $\mathbb{Z}_p$.

Suppose the adversary knows $\mathbb{A}$ but not X.

- *The simulated scheme is distinguishable from the real scheme if $q < n$.*
- *The simulated scheme is indistinguishable from the real scheme if $q \geq n$ and there exists an $n \times n$ sub-matrix whose determinant is nonzero.*

4.7.4 Randomness Simulation with a Polynomial

Let $f(x) \in \mathbb{Z}_p[x]$ be a $(q-1)$-degree polynomial function defined as

$$
f(x) = a_{q-1}x^{q-1} + a_{q-2}x^{q-2} + \cdots + a_1 x + a_0,
$$

where there are q coefficients, and all coefficients a_i are randomly chosen from $\mathbb{Z}_p$. We have the following lemma for the simulation of random numbers by the polynomial function $f(x)$.

Lemma 4.7.5 *Suppose a real scheme and a simulated scheme generate integers $(A_1, A_2, \cdots, A_n)$ with different methods described as follows.*

- *In the real scheme, let $(A_1, A_2, \cdots, A_n)$ be n integers randomly chosen from $\mathbb{Z}_p$.*
- *In the simulated scheme, let $(A_1, A_2, \cdots, A_n)$ be computed by*

$$
(A_1, A_2, \cdots, A_n) = (f(m_1), f(m_2), \cdots, f(m_n)),
$$

where $m_1, m_2, \cdots, m_n$ are n distinct integers in $\mathbb{Z}_p$ and f is a $(q-1)$-degree polynomial.

Suppose the adversary knows $m_1, m_2, \cdots, m_n$ but not $f(x)$. The simulated scheme is indistinguishable from the real scheme if $q \geq n$.

We can rewrite the simulation as

$$
(A_1, A_2, \cdots, A_n)^\top = (f(m_1), f(m_2), \cdots, f(m_n))^\top
$$

$$= \begin{pmatrix} m_1^{q-1} & m_1^{q-2} & m_1^{q-3} & \cdots & m_1^0 \\ m_2^{q-1} & m_2^{q-2} & m_2^{q-3} & \cdots & m_2^0 \\ \vdots & \vdots & \vdots & \cdots & \vdots \\ m_n^{q-1} & m_n^{q-2} & m_n^{q-3} & \cdots & m_n^0 \end{pmatrix} \cdot \begin{pmatrix} a_{q-1} \\ a_{q-2} \\ \vdots \\ a_0 \end{pmatrix} \mod p.$$

The coefficient matrix is the Vandermonde matrix, whose determinant is nonzero. According to Lemma 4.7.4, the simulated scheme is indistinguishable from the real scheme.

4.7.5 Indistinguishable Simulation and Useful Attack Together

Suppose the real scheme generates random numbers $(A_1, A_2, \cdots, A_n)$ from $\mathbb{Z}_p$. In the simulated scheme, let $x_1, x_2, \cdots, x_q$ be integers randomly chosen from $\mathbb{Z}_p$ by the simulator, and $F_1, F_2, \cdots, F_n, F^*$ be functions of $(x_1, x_2, \cdots, x_q)$ defined over $\mathbb{Z}_p$ given in the reduction algorithm (thus, they are known to the adversary). In the security reduction, the following requirements might occur at the same time.

- In the simulated scheme, $(A_1, A_2, \cdots, A_n)$ is computed as

$$A_i = F_i(x_1, x_2, \cdots, x_q), \quad \text{for all } i \in [1, n].$$

  The correctness of the security reduction requires that the simulated scheme is indistinguishable from the real scheme, and thus $(A_1, A_2, \cdots, A_n)$ must be random and independent.
- The adversary outputs an attack and this attack on the simulated scheme is useless if the adversary can compute

$$A^* = F^*(x_1, x_2, \cdots, x_q).$$

  The correctness of the security reduction requires that the adversary cannot compute A^* except with negligible probability.

In the security reduction, we do not need to prove an indistinguishable simulation and a useful attack separately. Instead, we only need to prove that

$$(A_1, \cdots, A_n, A^*) = \left(F_1(x_1, x_2, \cdots, x_q), \cdots, F_n(x_1, x_2, \cdots, x_q), F^*(x_1, x_2, \cdots, x_q) \right)$$

are random and independent, so that the randomness property of $(A_1, A_2, \cdots, A_n)$ holds, and the adversary has no advantage in computing A^*, because A^* is random and independent of all given A_i. An example is given in Section 4.14.2.

4.7.6 Advantage and Probability in Absolutely Hard Problems

We give several absolutely hard problems and introduce the advantage and the probability of solving these problems by an adversary who has unbounded computational power. These examples are summarized from existing security reductions in the literature.

- Suppose (a,Z,c,x) satisfies $Z = ac + x \bmod p$, where $a,x \in \mathbb{Z}_p$ and $c \in \{0,1\}$ are randomly chosen. Given (a,Z), the adversary has no advantage in distinguishing whether Z is computed from either $a \cdot 0 + x$ or $a \cdot 1 + x$ except with probability $1/2$. The reason is that a,Z,c are random and independent.

- Suppose $(a,Z_1,Z_2,\cdots,Z_{n-1},Z_n,x_1,x_2,\cdots,x_n)$ satisfies $Z_i = a + x_i \bmod p$, where a,x_i for all $i \in [1,n]$ are randomly chosen from $\mathbb{Z}_p$. Given $(a,Z_1,Z_2,\cdots,Z_{n-1})$, the adversary has no advantage in computing $Z_n = a + x_n$ except with probability $1/p$. The reason is that $a,Z_1,Z_2,\cdots,Z_n$ are random and independent.

- Suppose $(f(x),Z_1,Z_2,\cdots,Z_n,x_1,x_2,\cdots,x_n)$ satisfies $Z_i = f(x_i)$, where $f(x) \in \mathbb{Z}_p[x]$ is an n-degree polynomial randomly chosen from $\mathbb{Z}_p$. Given $(Z_1,Z_2,\cdots,Z_n, x_1,x_2,\cdots,x_n)$, the adversary has no advantage in computing a pair $(x^*,f(x^*))$ for a new x^* different from x_i except with probability $1/p$. The reason is that $Z_1,Z_2,\cdots,Z_n,f(x^*)$ are random and independent.

- Suppose $(\mathbb{A},Z_1,Z_2,\cdots,Z_{n-1},Z_n,x_1,x_2,\cdots,x_n)$ satisfies $|\mathbb{A}| \neq 0 \bmod p$ and Z_i is computed by $Z_i = \sum_{j=1}^{n} a_{i,j}x_j \bmod p$, where $\mathbb{A}$ is an $n \times n$ matrix whose elements are from $\mathbb{Z}_p$, and x_j for all $j \in [1,n]$ are randomly chosen from $\mathbb{Z}_p$. Given $(\mathbb{A},Z_1,Z_2,\cdots,Z_{n-1})$, the adversary has no advantage in computing $Z_n = \sum_{j=1}^{n} a_{n,j}x_j$ except with probability $1/p$. The reason is that $Z_1,Z_2,\cdots,Z_n$ are random and independent.

- Suppose (g,h,Z,x,y) satisfies $Z = g^x h^y$, where $x,y \in \mathbb{Z}_p$ are randomly chosen. Given $(g,h,Z) \in \mathbb{G}$, the adversary has no advantage in computing (x,y) except with probability $1/p$. Once the adversary finds x, it can immediately compute y with Z. However, g,h,Z,x are random and independent.

- Suppose (g,h,Z,x,c) satisfies $Z = g^x h^c$, where $x \in \mathbb{Z}_p$ and $c \in \{0,1\}$ are randomly chosen. Given $(g,h,Z) \in \mathbb{G}$, the adversary has no advantage in distinguishing whether Z is computed from either $g^x h^0$ or $g^x h^1$, except with probability $1/2$. The reason is that g,h,Z,c are random and independent.

In the real security reductions, if the adversary has advantage 1 in computing the target in the above examples, it can always launch a useless attack. More absolutely hard problems can be found in the examples given in this book.

4.8 An Overview of Random Oracles

A random oracle, denoted by $\mathcal{O}$, is typically used to represent an ideal hash function H whose outputs are random and uniformly distributed in its output space. A security proof in the random oracle model [14] (namely with random oracles) for a proposed scheme means that at least one hash function in the proposed scheme is treated as a random oracle. This section introduces how to use random oracles in security reductions.

4.8.1 Security Proof with Random Oracles

Suppose a proposed scheme is constructed using a hash function H as one of the primitives. We can represent the proposed scheme using the following combination

$$Scheme + H.$$

Roughly speaking, a security proof with random oracles for this scheme is the security proof for the following combination

$$Scheme + \mathcal{O},$$

where the hash function H is set as a random oracle $\mathcal{O}$. That is, we do not analyze the security of $Scheme + H$ but $Scheme + \mathcal{O}$, and believe that $Scheme + H$ is secure if $Scheme + \mathcal{O}$ is secure. Notice that the random oracle $\mathcal{O}$ and a real hash function H are treated differently in the security reduction. The security gap between these two combinations was discussed in [85].

Proving the security of a proposed scheme in the random oracle model requires at least one hash function to be set as a random oracle. However, it does not need all hash functions to be set as random oracles. To keep consistency with the concept of indistinguishable simulation, we assume that the real scheme in the random oracle model refers to the combination $Scheme + \mathcal{O}$. Otherwise, the adversary can immediately distinguish the simulated scheme with random oracles from the real scheme with hash functions.

4.8.2 Hash Functions vs Random Oracles

The differences between hash functions and random oracles in security reductions are summarized as follows.

- **Knowledge.** Given any arbitrary string x, if H is a hash function, the adversary knows the function algorithm of H and so knows how to compute $H(x)$. However, if H is set as a random oracle, the adversary does not know $H(x)$ unless it queries x to the random oracle.
- **Input.** Hash functions and random oracles have the same input space, which is dependent on the definition of the hash function. Although the number of inputs to a hash function is exponential, the number of inputs to a random oracle is

polynomial. This is due to the fact that the random oracle only accepts queries in polynomial time, and thus the random oracle only has a polynomial number of inputs.

- **Output.** Hash functions and random oracles have the same output space, which is dependent on the definition of the hash function. Given an input, the output from a hash function is determined by the input and the hash function algorithm. However, the output from a random oracle for an input is defined by the simulator who controls the random oracle. The outputs from a hash function are not required to be uniformly distributed, but the outputs from a random oracle must be random and uniformly distributed.
- **Representation.** A hash function can be seen as a mapping from an input space to an output space, where the mapping is calculated according to the hash function algorithm. A random oracle can be viewed as a virtual hash function that is represented by a list composed of input and output only. The random oracle itself does not have any rule or algorithm to define the mapping, as long as all outputs are random and independent. See Table 4.1 for comparison.

Table 4.1 Hash function and random oracle in representation

Input	Hash Function	Output	Input	Random Oracle	Output
x_1		y_1	x_1		y_1
x_2		y_2	x_2		y_2
x_3	$H(x_i) = y_i$	y_3	x_3	Simulator	y_3
x_4		y_4	$\vdots$		$\vdots$
$\vdots$		$\vdots$	x_q		y_q

Random oracles are very helpful for the simulator in programming security reductions. The reason is that the simulator can control and select any output that looks random and helps the simulator complete the simulation or force the adversary to launch a useful attack. Security proofs in the random oracle model are, therefore, believed to be much easier than those without random oracles.

4.8.3 Hash List

In a security reduction with random oracles, hash queries and their responses from an oracle look like a list as described in Table 4.1, where only inputs and outputs are known to the adversary. The outputs can be adaptively computed by the simulator, as long as they are random and independent. How to compute these outputs should be recorded because they can be helpful for the simulator to program the security reduction. Let x be a query, y be its response, and S be the secret state used to compute y. After the simulator responds to the query on x with $y = H(x)$, the simulator should add a tuple (x, y, S) to a hash list, denoted by $\mathscr{L}$.

The hash list created by the simulator is composed of input, output, and the corresponding state S. This hash list should satisfy the following conditions.

- The hash list is empty at the beginning before any hash queries are made.
- All tuples associated with queries will be added to this hash list.
- The secret state S must be unknown to the adversary.

How to choose S in computing y is completely dependent on the proposed scheme and the security reduction. In the security reduction for some encryption schemes, we note that y can be randomly chosen without using a secret state. Examples can be found in the schemes given in this book.

4.8.4 How to Program Security Reductions with Random Oracles

For a security proof in the random oracle model, the simulator should add one more phase called H-Query (usually after the Setup phase) in the simulation to describe hash queries and responses. Note that this phase only appears in the security reduction, and it should not appear in the security model.

H-Query. The adversary makes hash queries in this phase. The simulator prepares a hash list $\mathscr{L}$ to record all queries and responses, where the hash list is empty at the beginning.

For a query x to the random oracle, if x is already in the hash list, the simulator responds to this query following the hash list. Otherwise, the simulator generates a secret state S and uses it to compute the hash output y adaptively. Then, the simulator responds to this query with $y = H(x)$ and adds the tuple (x, y, S) to the hash list.

This completes the description of the random oracle performance in the simulation. If more than one hash function is set as a random oracle, then the simulator must describe how to program each random oracle accordingly. In the random oracle model, the adversary can make queries to random oracles at any time even after the adversary wins the game. The simulator should generate all outputs in an adaptive way in order to make sure that the random oracle can help the simulator program the simulation, such as signature simulation and private-key simulation. How to adaptively respond to the hash queries from the adversary is fully dependent on the proposed scheme, the underlying hard problem, and the security reduction. Examples can be found in Section 4.12.

4.8.5 Oracle Response and Its Probability Analysis

Suppose the hash function H is set as a random oracle. We study a general case of oracle response and analyze its success probability.

H-Query. The simulator prepares a hash list $\mathscr{L}$ to record all queries and responses, where the hash list is empty at the beginning.

For a query x to the random oracle, if x is already in the hash list, the simulator responds to this query following the hash list. Otherwise, the simulator works as follows.

- The simulator chooses a random secret value z and a secret bit $c \in \{0,1\}$ (how to choose c has not yet been defined) to compute y. Here, $S = (z,c)$ is the secret state used to compute y.
- The simulator then sets $H(x) = y$ and sends y to the adversary.
- Finally, the simulator adds (x,y,z,c) to the hash list.

This completes the description of the random oracle performance in the simulation. Suppose q_H hash queries are made to the random oracle. The hash list is composed of q_H tuples as follows.

$$(x_1,y_1,z_1,c_1), \quad (x_2,y_2,z_2,c_2), \quad \cdots, \quad (x_{q_H},y_{q_H},z_{q_H},c_{q_H}).$$

Suppose the adversary does not know $(z_1,c_1),(z_2,c_2),(z_3,c_3),\cdots,(z_{q_H},c_{q_H})$. From these q_H hash queries, the adversary adaptively chooses $q+1$ out of q_H queries

$$\left(x_1', \ x_2', \ \cdots, \ x_q', \ x^*\right),$$

where $q+1 \leq q_H$. Let $c_1',c_2',\cdots,c_q',c^*$ be the corresponding secret bits for the chosen hash queries. We want to calculate the success probability, defined as

$$P = \Pr[c_1' = c_2' = \cdots = c_q' = 0 \wedge c^* = 1].$$

We stress that this probability cannot be computed once all c_i are known to the adversary. That is why we assume that the adversary does not know all c_i at the beginning.

This probability appears in many security proofs. For example, in the security proof of digital signatures in the random oracle model, the security reduction is programmed in such a way that a signature of message x is simulatable if $c = 0$ and is reducible if $c = 1$. Suppose the adversary first queries signatures on messages $x_1',x_2',\cdots,x_q'$ and then returns a forged signature of the message x^*. The probability of successful simulation and useful attack is equal to

$$\Pr[c_1' = c_2' = \cdots = c_q' = 0 \wedge c^* = 1].$$

The above success probability depends on the method of choosing c_i. Here we introduce two approaches proposed in the literature. The first approach is easy to understand, but the probability is relatively small, and the loss factor is linear in the number of all hash queries, denoted by q_H. The second approach is a bit complex, but has a larger success probability than the first one, and the loss factor is linear in the number of chosen hash queries, denoted by q.

- In the first approach, the simulator randomly chooses $i^* \in [1, q_H]$ and guesses that the adversary will output the i^*-th query as x^*. Then, for a query x_i, the simulator sets

$$\begin{cases} c_i = 1 & \text{if } i = i^* \\ c_i = 0 & \text{otherwise} \end{cases}.$$

  In this setting, P is equivalent to successfully guessing which query is chosen as x^*. Since the adversary makes q_H queries, and one of queries is chosen to be x^*, we have $P = 1/q_H$. The success probability is linear in the number of all hash queries.

- In the second approach, the simulator guesses more than one query as the potential x^* to increase the success probability. To be precise, the simulator flips a bit $b_i \in \{0, 1\}$ in such a way that $b_i = 0$ occurs with probability P_b, and $b_i = 1$ occurs with probability $1 - P_b$. Then, for a query x_i, the simulator sets

$$\begin{cases} c_i = 1 & \text{if } b_i = 1 \\ c_i = 0 & \text{otherwise} \end{cases}.$$

Since all b_i are chosen according to the probability P_b, we have

$$\begin{aligned} P &= \Pr[c_1' = c_2' = \cdots = c_q' = 0 \wedge c^* = 1] \\ &= \Pr[b_1 = b_2 = \cdots = b_q = 0 \wedge b^* = 1] \\ &= P_b^q (1 - P_b). \end{aligned}$$

The value is maximized at $P_b = 1 - 1/(1 + q)$, and then we get $P \approx 1/(eq)$ when $(1 + \frac{1}{q})^q \approx e$. This success probability is linear in the number of chosen hash queries instead of the number of all hash queries.

In the security proof, q_H is believed to be much larger than q (for example $q_H = 2^{60}$ compared to $q = 2^{30}$). Therefore, the second approach has a larger success probability than the first one. The first approach, however, is much simpler to understand than the second approach. In the security proofs for selected schemes in this book, we always adopt the first approach when one of the two approaches should be used in a security reduction. We can naturally modify the security proofs with the second approach in order to have a smaller reduction loss.

4.8.6 Summary of Using Random Oracles

We summarize the use of random oracles in security proofs, especially for digital signatures and encryption, as follows.

- A random oracle is useful in a security proof not because its outputs are random and uniformly distributed but because the adversary must query x to the random oracle in order to know the corresponding output $H(x)$, and the computations of all outputs are fully controlled by the simulator.

- When a hash function is set as a random oracle, the adversary will not receive the hash function algorithm from the simulator in the security proof. The adversary can only access the "hash function" by asking the random oracle.
- A random oracle is an ideal hash function. However, we do not need to construct such an ideal hash function in the simulation. Instead, the main task for the simulator in the security proof is to think how to respond to each input query.
- The simulator can adaptively return any element as the response to a given input query as long as all responses look random from the point of view of the adversary. This tip is very useful for security proofs in "hash-then-sign" digital signatures. To be precise, we program $H(m)$ in such a way that the corresponding signature of $H(m)$ is either simulatable or reducible.
- The hash list is empty when it is created, but the simulator can pre-define the tuple $(x, H(x), S)$ in the hash list before the adversary makes a query on x. This tip is useful when a signature generation needs to use $H(x)$, and x has not yet been queried by the adversary.
- The secret state S for x is useful for the simulator to compute signatures on x in digital signatures, or private keys on x in identity-based encryption, or to perform the decryption without knowing the corresponding secret key.
- If breaking a scheme must use a particular pair $(x, H(x))$, then the adversary must have queried x to the random oracle. This is essential in the security proof of encryption under a computational hardness assumption.
- To simplify the security proof, we assume that the simulator already knows the maximum number of queries that the adversary will make to the random oracle before the simulation. This assumption is useful in the probability calculation.

More details about how to use random oracles to program a security reduction can be found in the schemes given in this book.

4.9 Security Proofs for Digital Signatures

4.9.1 Proof Structure

Suppose there exists an adversary $\mathscr{A}$ who can break the proposed signature scheme in the corresponding security model. We construct a simulator $\mathscr{B}$ to solve a computational hard problem. Given as input an instance of this hard problem in the security proof we must show (1) how the simulator generates the simulated scheme; (2) how the simulator solves the underlying hard problem using the adversary's attack; and (3) why the security reduction is correct. A security proof is composed of the following three parts.

- **Simulation.** In this part, we show how the simulator uses the problem instance to generate a simulated scheme and interacts with the adversary following the unforgeability security model. If the simulator has to abort, the security reduction fails.

- **Solution.** In this part, we show how the simulator solves the underlying hard problem using the forged signature generated by the adversary. To be precise, the simulator should be able to extract a solution to the problem instance from the forged signature.
- **Analysis.** In this part, we need to provide the following analysis.

  1. The simulation is indistinguishable from the real attack.
  2. The probability P_S of successful simulation.
  3. The probability P_U of useful attack.
  4. The advantage ε_R of solving the underlying hard problem.
  5. The time cost of solving the underlying hard problem.

The simulation will be successful if the simulator does not abort in computing the public key and responding to all signature queries from the adversary. The simulation is indistinguishable if all computed signatures can pass the signature verification, and the simulation has the randomness property. An attack by the adversary is useful if the simulator can extract a solution to the problem instance from the forged signature.

Many security proofs only calculate the probability of successful simulation without calculating the probability of useful attack. Such an analysis is the same as ours because the probability of successful simulation in their definitions includes the usefulness of the attack. The difference is due to the different definition of successful simulation.

A security reduction for digital signatures does not have to use the forged signature to solve an underlying hard problem. With random oracles, the simulator can use hash queries instead of the forged signature to solve an underlying hard problem. However, this is a rare case. The motivation for this kind of security reduction will be explained later.

4.9.2 Advantage Calculation

Let ε be the advantage of the adversary in breaking the proposed signature scheme. The advantage of solving the underlying hard problem, denoted by ε_R, is

$$\varepsilon_R = P_S \cdot \varepsilon \cdot P_U.$$

If the simulation is successful and indistinguishable from the real attack with probability P_S, the adversary can successfully forge a valid signature with probability ε. With probability P_U, the forged signature is a useful attack and can be reduced to solving the underlying hard problem. Therefore, we obtain ε_R as the advantage of solving the underlying hard problem in the security reduction.

4.9.3 Simulatable and Reducible

In the security reduction, if the solution to the problem instance is extracted from the adversary's forged signature, we can classify all signatures in the simulated scheme into two types: *simulatable* and *reducible*.

- **Simulatable.** A signature is simulatable if it can be computed by the simulator. If the forged signature is simulatable, the forgery attack is useless. Otherwise, the simulator can compute the forged signature and perform as the adversary by itself. The security reduction will be successful without the help of the adversary. That is, the simulator can solve the underlying hard problem by itself. This security reduction is wrong.
- **Reducible.** A signature is reducible if it can be used to solve the underlying hard problem. If the forged signature is reducible, the attack is useful. Similarly, a reducible signature in the security reduction cannot be computed by the simulator. Otherwise, the simulator could solve the underlying hard problem by itself.

In a security reduction for digital signatures, each signature in the simulated scheme should be either simulatable or reducible. A successful security reduction requires that all queried signatures are simulatable, and the forged signature is reducible. Otherwise, the simulator cannot respond to signature queries from the adversary or use the forged signature to solve the underlying hard problem.

4.9.4 Simulation of Secret Key

In security proofs for digital signatures, most security proofs in the literature program the security reduction in such a way that the simulator does not know the corresponding secret key. Intuitively, if the simulator knows the secret key, then all signatures must be simulatable including the forged signature. Therefore, this reduction must be unsuccessful. However, this observation is not correct. It is possible to program a simulation where the simulator knows the secret key. An example can be found in [7]. We stress that some signatures must be still reducible even though the secret key is known to the simulator; otherwise, the security reduction must be incorrect. This is a paradox that must be addressed in this type of security reduction.

In this book, all introductions and given schemes program the security reduction in such a way that the secret key is unknown to the simulator. That is, in such a simulation, if the secret key is known to the simulator, the simulator can immediately solve the underlying hard problem.

4.9.5 Partition

In the simulation, the simulator must also hide from the adversary which signatures are simulatable and which signatures are reducible. If the adversary can always return a simulatable signature as the forged signature, the reduction has no advantage of solving the underlying hard problem. We call the approach of splitting signatures into the above two sets *partition*. The simulator must stop the adversary (who knows the reduction algorithm and can make signature queries) from finding the partition. Two different approaches are currently used to deal with the partition.

- **Intractable in Finding.** Given the simulation including queried signatures, the computationally unbounded adversary cannot find the partition with probability 1, so the forged signature returned by the adversary is still reducible with non-negligible probability P_U. To hide the partition from the computationally unbounded adversary in the security reduction, the simulator should utilize absolutely hard problems in hiding the partition in the simulation. The secret information $\mathbb{I}$, introduced in Section 4.5.7, can be treated as the partition.
- **Intractable in Distinguishing.** Given the simulation including queried signatures and two complementary partitions, the computationally unbounded adversary has no advantage in distinguishing which partition is used, so the adversary can only guess the partition correctly with probability $1/2$. Here, complementary partitions means that any signature in the simulation must be either simulatable using one partition or reducible using another partition. In this case, the adversary will return a forged signature that is reducible with probability $1/2$. The secret information $\mathbb{I}$ here is which partition is adopted in the simulation. Note that it is not necessary to construct two partitions that are complementary, as long as the adversary cannot always find which signature is simulatable in both partitions.

In comparison with the first approach, the second approach does not need to hide the partition from the adversary. We found that the partition is fixed in the reduction algorithm. To make sure that there are two different partitions in the second approach, we must propose two distinct simulation algorithms. That is, a reduction algorithm consists of at least two simulation algorithms and the corresponding solution algorithms. One such example can be found in Section 4.14.3.

4.9.6 Tight Reduction and Loose Reduction Revisited

Recalling the definitions of tight reduction and loose reduction, we have the following observations.

- If all signatures of the same message are either simulatable or reducible and a randomly chosen message is simulatable with probability P, then the reduction must be loose. Let q_s be the number of signature queries. If the adversary randomly chooses messages for signature queries, the probability of successful simulation and useful attack is $P^{q_s}(1-P) \leq \frac{1}{q_s}$. The reduction loss is linear in the number q_s, and thus the security reduction is loose.

- If the signatures of a message can be generated to be simulatable or reducible, we can achieve a tight reduction. For a signature query on a message, the simulator makes it simulatable. In this case, there is no abort in the responses to signature queries. Let $1-P$ be the probability that the forged signature is reducible. The probability of successful simulation and useful attack is $1 \cdot (1-P)$ instead of $P^{q_s}(1-P)$. If $1-P$ is constant and small, the security reduction is tight.

We found that all previous signature schemes with tight reductions use a random salt in a signature generation, where the random salt is used to switch the functionality between simulatable and reducible. Therefore, all unique signatures [77] that do not have any random salt in the signature generation seem unable to achieve tight reductions. However, with random oracles, we can program a tight reduction for a specially constructed unique signature scheme [53], where the solution to the underlying hard problem is from one of the hash queries. A simplified signature scheme is given in Section 5.8.

4.9.7 Summary of Correct Security Reduction

A correct security reduction for a digital signature scheme, where the simulator does not know the secret key, should satisfy the following conditions. We can use these conditions to check whether a security reduction is correct or not.

- The underlying hard problem is a computational hard problem.
- The simulator does not know the secret key.
- All queried signatures are simulatable without knowing the secret key.
- The simulation is indistinguishable from the real attack.
- The partition is intractable or indistinguishable.
- The forged signature is reducible.
- The advantage ε_R of solving the underlying hard problem is non-negligible.
- The time cost of the simulation is polynomial time.

A security reduction where the simulator uses hash queries to solve an underlying hard problem or knows the secret key will change the method of the security reduction. However, since these two cases are very special, we omit their introductions.

4.10 Security Proofs for Encryption Under Decisional Assumptions

4.10.1 Proof Structure

Suppose there exists an adversary $\mathscr{A}$ who can break the proposed encryption scheme in the corresponding security model. We construct a simulator $\mathscr{B}$ to solve a decisional hard problem. Given as input an instance of this hard problem (X, Z), in the security proof we must show (1) how the simulator generates the simulated scheme; (2) how the simulator solves the underlying hard problem using the adversary's attack; and (3) why the security reduction is correct. A security proof is composed of the following three parts.

- **Simulation.** In this part, we show how the simulator uses the problem instance (X, Z) to generate a simulated scheme and interacts with the adversary following the indistinguishability security model. Most importantly, the target Z in the problem instance must be embedded in the challenge ciphertext. If the simulator has to abort, it outputs a random guess of Z.
- **Solution.** In this part, we show how the simulator solves the decisional hard problem using the adversary's guess c' of c, where the message in the challenge ciphertext is m_c. The method of guessing Z is the same in all security reductions. To be precise, if $c' = c$, the simulator outputs that Z is true. Otherwise, $c' \neq c$, and it outputs that Z is false.
- **Analysis.** In this part, we need to provide the following analysis.

  1. The simulation is indistinguishable from the real attack if Z is true.
  2. The probability P_S of successful simulation.
  3. The probability P_T of breaking the challenge ciphertext if Z is true.
  4. The probability P_F of breaking the challenge ciphertext if Z is false.
  5. The advantage ε_R of solving the underlying hard problem.
  6. The time cost of solving the underlying hard problem.

The simulation will be successful if the simulator does not abort in computing the public key, responding to queries, and computing the challenge ciphertext. The simulation with a true Z is indistinguishable from the real attack if (1) all responses to queries are correct; (2) the challenge ciphertext generated with a true Z is a correct ciphertext as defined in the proposed scheme; (3) and the randomness property holds in the simulation.

In this book, breaking the ciphertext means that the adversary correctly guesses the message in the ciphertext. This proof structure is regarded as the standard structure for an encryption scheme under a decisional hardness assumption in the indistinguishability security model. The proof structure for an encryption scheme under a computational hardness assumption in the random oracle model is quite different and will be introduced in Section 4.11.5.

4.10.2 Classification of Ciphertexts

A strong security model for encryption allows the adversary to make decryption queries on any ciphertexts with the restriction that no decryption query is allowed on the challenge ciphertext. We found that all ciphertexts in the simulation can be classified into the following four types.

- **Correct Ciphertext.** A ciphertext is correct if it can be generated by the encryption algorithm. For example, taking as input $pk = (g, g_1, g_2) \in \mathbb{G}$ and message $m \in \mathbb{G}$, an encryption algorithm randomly chooses $r \in \mathbb{Z}_p$ and computes $CT = (g^r, \ g_1^r, \ g_2^r \cdot m)$. Any ciphertext that can be generated with a message m and a number r for pk is a correct ciphertext.
- **Incorrect Ciphertext.** A ciphertext is incorrect if it cannot be generated by the encryption algorithm. Continued from the above example, $(g^r, g_1^{r+1}, g_2^r \cdot m)$ is an incorrect ciphertext because it cannot be generated by the encryption algorithm with (pk, m) as the input using any random number.
- **Valid Ciphertext.** A ciphertext is valid if the decryption of the ciphertext returns a message. We stress that the message returned from the decryption can be any message as long as the output is not $\perp$.
- **Invalid Ciphertext.** A ciphertext is invalid if the decryption of the ciphertext returns an error $\perp$, without returning any message.

In the above classifications, correct ciphertext and incorrect ciphertext are associated with the ciphertext structure, while valid ciphertext and invalid ciphertext are associated with the decryption result. Note that correct ciphertext and valid ciphertext may be treated as equivalent elsewhere in the literature.

When constructing an encryption scheme, an ideal decryption algorithm should be able to accept all correct ciphertexts as valid ciphertexts, and reject all incorrect ciphertexts. In the security reduction, the simulated decryption algorithm should be able to perform the decryption identically to the proposed decryption algorithm. Otherwise, the simulated scheme may be distinguishable from the real scheme. However, it is not easy to construct such a perfect decryption in both the real scheme and the simulated scheme.

We classify ciphertexts into the above four types in order to clarify the analysis of whether the decryption simulation helps the adversary break the challenge ciphertext or not, especially when the challenge ciphertext is generated with a false Z. A ciphertext from the adversary for a decryption query can be one of the above four types, and each type should be differently responded in a correct way. This classification is desirable because in the security reduction for the proposed scheme, an incorrect ciphertext for a decryption query might be accepted such that the decryption result will help the adversary break the challenge ciphertext.

The challenge ciphertext is either a correct ciphertext or an incorrect ciphertext, which depends on Z in the ciphertext generation. For the challenge ciphertext, we further define two special types in the next subsection.

4.10.3 Classification of the Challenge Ciphertext

The target Z in the instance of the underlying decisional hard problem is either a true or a false element. The challenge ciphertext must be computed with the target Z, and it can be classified into the following two types.

- **True Challenge Ciphertext.** The challenge ciphertext created with the target Z is a true challenge ciphertext if Z is true. We have that the probability of breaking the true challenge ciphertext is

$$P_T = \Pr[c' = c | Z = \text{True}].$$

- **False Challenge Ciphertext.** The challenge ciphertext created with the target Z is a false challenge ciphertext if Z is false. We have that the probability of breaking the false challenge ciphertext is

$$P_F = \Pr[c' = c | Z = \text{False}].$$

In the simulation, if the challenge ciphertext is the true challenge ciphertext, we require that the adversary has non-negligible advantage defined in the breaking assumption in guessing the encrypted message. Otherwise, the adversary should only have negligible advantage in guessing the encrypted message in the false challenge ciphertext. To achieve this difference, the simulation of the challenge ciphertext should satisfy the conditions given in the next subsection.

4.10.4 Simulation of the Challenge Ciphertext

In a security reduction for encryption, the simulator must embed the target Z in the challenge ciphertext such that it satisfies the following conditions.

- If Z is true, the true challenge ciphertext is a correct ciphertext whose encrypted message is $m_c \in \{m_0, m_1\}$, where m_0, m_1 are two messages from the same message space provided by the adversary, and c is randomly chosen by the simulator. We should program the simulation in such a way that the simulation is indistinguishable and then the adversary can guess the encrypted message correctly with non-negligible advantage defined in the breaking assumption.
- If Z is false, the false challenge ciphertext can be either a correct ciphertext or an incorrect ciphertext. However, the challenge ciphertext cannot be an encryption of the message m_c from the point of view of the adversary. We program the simulation in such a way that the adversary cannot guess the encrypted message correctly except with negligible advantage.

If the challenge ciphertext is independent of Z, the guess of the message in the challenge ciphertext is independent of Z, and thus the guess is useless. This is why Z must be embedded in the challenge ciphertext.

4.10.5 Advantage Calculation 1

The advantage of solving the underlying hard problem is

$$
\begin{aligned}
\varepsilon_R &= \Pr\left[\text{Guess } Z = \text{True}|Z = \text{True}\right] - \Pr\left[\text{Guess } Z = \text{True}|Z = \text{False}\right] \\
&= \Pr\left[\begin{smallmatrix}\text{The simulator guesses} \\ Z \text{ is true}\end{smallmatrix}\, \Big| Z = \text{True}\right] - \Pr\left[\begin{smallmatrix}\text{The simulator guesses} \\ Z \text{ is true}\end{smallmatrix}\, \Big| Z = \text{False}\right].
\end{aligned}
$$

Let US be the event of unsuccessful simulation, and SS be the event of successful simulation. If the simulation is unsuccessful, the simulator will randomly guess Z by itself, and thus we have

$$
\Pr\left[\begin{smallmatrix}\text{The simulator guesses} \\ Z \text{ is true}\end{smallmatrix}\, \Big| US\right] = \frac{1}{2}.
$$

Otherwise, according to the proof structure, we have

$$
\Pr\left[\begin{smallmatrix}\text{The simulator guesses} \\ Z \text{ is true}\end{smallmatrix}\, \Big| SS\right] = \Pr[c' = c].
$$

By applying the law of total probability, we have

$$
\begin{aligned}
&\Pr\left[\begin{smallmatrix}\text{The simulator guesses} \\ Z \text{ is true}\end{smallmatrix}\, \Big| Z = \text{True}\right] \\
&= \Pr\left[\begin{smallmatrix}\text{The simulator guesses} \\ Z \text{ is true}\end{smallmatrix}\, \Big| Z = \text{True} \wedge SS\right]\Pr[SS] + \Pr\left[\begin{smallmatrix}\text{The simulator guesses} \\ Z \text{ is true}\end{smallmatrix}\, \Big| Z = \text{True} \wedge US\right]\Pr[US] \\
&= \Pr[c' = c|Z = \text{True}]\Pr[SS] + \frac{1}{2}\Pr[US] \\
&= P_T \cdot P_S + \frac{1}{2}(1 - P_S).
\end{aligned}
$$

$$
\begin{aligned}
&\Pr\left[\begin{smallmatrix}\text{The simulator guesses} \\ Z \text{ is true}\end{smallmatrix}\, \Big| Z = \text{False}\right] \\
&= \Pr\left[\begin{smallmatrix}\text{The simulator guesses} \\ Z \text{ is true}\end{smallmatrix}\, \Big| Z = \text{False} \wedge SS\right]\Pr[SS] + \Pr\left[\begin{smallmatrix}\text{The simulator guesses} \\ Z \text{ is true}\end{smallmatrix}\, \Big| Z = \text{False} \wedge US\right]\Pr[US] \\
&= \Pr[c' = c|Z = \text{False}]\Pr[SS] + \frac{1}{2}\Pr[US] \\
&= P_F \cdot P_S + \frac{1}{2}(1 - P_S).
\end{aligned}
$$

The above analysis yields the advantage of solving the underlying hard problem, which is

$$
\begin{aligned}
\varepsilon_R &= \Pr\left[\begin{smallmatrix}\text{The simulator guesses} \\ Z \text{ is true}\end{smallmatrix}\, \Big| Z = \text{True}\right] - \Pr\left[\begin{smallmatrix}\text{The simulator guesses} \\ Z \text{ is true}\end{smallmatrix}\, \Big| Z = \text{False}\right] \\
&= \left(P_T \cdot P_S + \frac{1}{2}(1 - P_S)\right) - \left(P_F \cdot P_S + \frac{1}{2}(1 - P_S)\right) \\
&= P_S(P_T - P_F).
\end{aligned}
$$

In the security reduction, to solve a decisional hard problem with non-negligible advantage, we should program the security reduction in such a way that P_T is as large as possible, and P_F is as small as possible. On the contrary, to make the security reduction fail, the aim of the adversary is to achieve $P_T \approx P_F$. According to the descriptions of a useful attack and a useless attack, the adversary's attack is useful if $P_T - P_F$ is non-negligible. Otherwise, it is useless.

4.10.6 Probability P_T of Breaking the True Challenge Ciphertext

We assume that there exists an adversary who can break the proposed scheme in polynomial time with non-negligible advantage ε. If the message m_c is encrypted in the real scheme, according to the definition of the advantage in the security model, we have

$$\varepsilon = 2\left(\Pr[c' = c] - \frac{1}{2}\right).$$

That is, the adversary can correctly guess the message in the challenge ciphertext of the real scheme with probability $\Pr[c' = c] = \frac{1}{2} + \frac{\varepsilon}{2}$.

If Z is true, and the simulated scheme is indistinguishable from the real scheme from the point of view of the adversary, the adversary will break the simulated scheme as it can break the real scheme and correctly guess the encrypted message with probability $\frac{1}{2} + \frac{\varepsilon}{2}$. That is, we have

$$P_T = \Pr[c' = c | Z = \text{True}] = \frac{1}{2} + \frac{\varepsilon}{2}.$$

4.10.7 Probability P_F of Breaking the False Challenge Ciphertext

If Z is false, the false challenge ciphertext should be an incorrect ciphertext or a correct ciphertext whose encrypted message is neither m_0 nor m_1. Therefore, the adversary knows that the given scheme is not a real scheme, but a simulated scheme, because the challenge ciphertext in the real scheme should be a correct ciphertext whose encrypted message is from $\{m_0, m_1\}$.

Since the adversary is malicious, even though the adversary finds out that the challenge ciphertext is false, it will not abort but try its best to guess c using what it knows in order to have $P_F \approx P_T$. Therefore, the probability P_F is

$$P_F = \Pr[c' = c | Z = \text{False}] \geq \frac{1}{2},$$

which is highly dependent on the simulation and is no smaller than $\frac{1}{2}$, where the probability $\frac{1}{2}$ is obtained by a random guess.

4.10.8 Advantage Calculation 2

According to the deduction in Section 4.10.5, the advantage of solving the underlying hard problem is

$$\varepsilon_R = \Pr\left[\text{Guess } Z = \text{True}|Z = \text{True}\right] - \Pr\left[\text{Guess } Z = \text{True}|Z = \text{False}\right]$$

$$= \Pr\left[\begin{smallmatrix}\text{The simulator guesses}\\ Z \text{ is true}\end{smallmatrix}\middle|Z = \text{True}\right] - \Pr\left[\begin{smallmatrix}\text{The simulator guesses}\\ Z \text{ is true}\end{smallmatrix}\middle|Z = \text{False}\right]$$

$$= P_S(P_T - P_F).$$

If the probability P_S is non-negligible, and the simulation with a true Z is indistinguishable, by putting the probabilities P_T and P_F together, we have

$$\varepsilon_R = P_S(P_T - P_F) = P_S\left(\frac{1}{2} + \frac{\varepsilon}{2} - P_F\right).$$

The advantage is non-negligible if and only if $P_F \approx \frac{1}{2}$. Otherwise, if $P_F = \frac{1}{2} + \frac{\varepsilon}{2}$, the advantage of solving the underlying hard problem is zero.

The aim of the simulator is to obtain a non-negligible ε_R from the security reduction against a malicious adversary. According to the above deduction, a correct security reduction requires that

- P_S is non-negligible.
- The simulated scheme is indistinguishable from the real scheme if Z is true.
- $P_F \approx \frac{1}{2}$, which means that the malicious adversary has almost no advantage in breaking the false challenge ciphertext.

The ideal probability $P_F = \frac{1}{2}$ holds if and only if the message m_c is encrypted with a one-time pad from the point of view of the adversary. The probability $P_F \approx \frac{1}{2}$ means that the false challenge ciphertext is a one-time pad from the point of view of the adversary except with negligible probability. A one-time pad is a specific encryption where the adversary has no advantage in guessing the message in the challenge ciphertext, even if it has unbounded computational power. We introduce the concept of one-time pad in the next subsection.

We found out an interesting reduction result according to the above analysis. For example, even if the simulation satisfies that $P_S = 1, \varepsilon = 1, P_F = \frac{1}{2}$ and the simulation is indistinguishable, we obtain

$$\varepsilon_R = P_S\left(\frac{1}{2} + \frac{\varepsilon}{2} - P_F\right) = \frac{1}{2} \neq 1.$$

That is, the maximum advantage of solving the decisional hard problem is not 100%, but at most 50%. The guess of Z is not always correct because the adversary, who is given the false challenge ciphertext (Z is false), might still guess c correctly with probability $\frac{1}{2}$ and output $c' = c$, so that the simulator will guess that Z is true, but actually Z is false.

4.10.9 Definition of One-Time Pad

One-time pad plays an important role in the security proof of encryption. The simplest example of a one-time pad is as follows:

$$CT = m \oplus K,$$

where $m \in \{0,1\}^n$ is a message, and $K \in \{0,1\}^n$ is a random key unknown to the adversary. For such a one-time pad, the adversary has no advantage in guessing the message in CT, except with success probability $\frac{1}{2^n}$, even if it has unbounded computational power. If CT is created for a randomly chosen message from two distinct messages $\{m_0, m_1\}$, the adversary still has no advantage and can only guess the encrypted message with success probability $\frac{1}{2}$. Therefore, a one-time pad captures perfect security in the indistinguishability security model, where the adversary has no advantage in breaking the ciphertext.

The notion of one-time pad is defined as follows.

Definition 4.10.9.1 (One-Time Pad) *Let $E(m, r, R)$ be an encryption of a given message m with a public parameter R and a secret parameter r. The ciphertext $E(m, r, R)$ is a one-time pad if, for any two distinct messages m_0, m_1 from the same message space, CT can be seen as an encryption of either the message m_0 with the secret parameter r_0 or an encryption of the message m_1 with the secret parameter r_1 under the public parameter R with the same probability:*

$$\Pr\left[CT = E(m_0, r_0, R)\right] = \Pr\left[CT = E(m_1, r_1, R)\right].$$

In the security proof of encryption, we need to prove that the false challenge ciphertext is a one-time pad from the point of view of the adversary. To be precise, given an instance (X, Z) of a decisional hard problem, we must program the security reduction in such a way that Z is embedded in the challenge ciphertext CT^*, and CT^* is a one-time pad from the point of view of the adversary if Z is false. We stress that "from the point of view of the adversary" is extremely important. We cannot simply prove that the false challenge ciphertext is a one-time pad. The reasons will be explained in Section 4.10.11.

In the security proof of group-based encryption, we are more interested in those one-time pads constructed from a cyclic group. We can use the following lemma to check whether or not a general ciphertext constructed over a cyclic group is a one-time pad from the point of view of the adversary, even if it has unbounded computational power.

Lemma 4.10.1 *Let CT be a general ciphertext defined as follows, where $m_c \in \{m_0, m_1\}$ and the adversary knows the group $(\mathbb{G}, g, p)$ and messages $m_0, m_1 \in \mathbb{G}$:*

$$CT = \left(g^{x_1}, \ g^{x_2}, \ g^{x_3}, \ \cdots, \ g^{x_n}, \ g^{x^*} \cdot m_c\right).$$

The ciphertext CT is a one-time pad if

- x^* *is a random number from* $\mathbb{Z}_p$, *and*
- x^* *is independent of* $x_1, x_2, \cdots, x_n$.

The ciphertext CT is not a one-time pad if

- x^* *is not a random number from* $\mathbb{Z}_p$ *(can be known to the adversary), or*
- x^* *is dependent on* $x_1, x_2, \cdots, x_n$ *(can be computed from* $x_1, x_2, \cdots, x_n$).

Proof. Let $C^* = g^{x^*} m_c$. From the point of view of the adversary, we have

- CT can be seen as an encryption of m_0 where $r_0 = x^* = \log_g C^* - \log_g m_0 \in \mathbb{Z}_p$.
- CT can be seen as an encryption of m_1 where $r_1 = x^* = \log_g C^* - \log_g m_1 \in \mathbb{Z}_p$.

Since x^* is random and independent of $x_1, x_2, \cdots, x_n$, we have that both $x^* = \log_g C^* - \log_g m_0$ and $x^* = \log_g C^* - \log_g m_1$ hold with the same probability $\frac{1}{p}$. Therefore, the general ciphertext is a one-time pad. Otherwise, if the adversary knows x^*, or can compute x^* from $x_1, x_2, \cdots, x_n$, the message m_c in the general ciphertext can be decrypted by the adversary, and thus it is not a one-time pad.

This completes the proof. □

To prove that CT is a one-time pad, we can also prove that $x^*, x_1, x_2, \cdots, x_n$ are random and independent. However, this is a sufficient but not necessary condition. An example is given at the end of the next subsection.

4.10.10 Examples of One-Time Pad

We give several examples to introduce what a one-time pad looks like in group-based cryptography. Suppose the adversary knows the following information.

- The cyclic group $(\mathbb{G}, g, h, p)$, where g, h are generators, and p is the group order.
- Two distinct messages m_0, m_1 from $\mathbb{G}$ and how the ciphertext is created.

In the following ciphertexts, $c \in \{0, 1\}$ and $x, y \in \mathbb{Z}_p$ are randomly chosen by the simulator. The aim of the adversary is to guess c in CT. We want to investigate whether the following constructed ciphertexts are one-time pads or not.

$$CT = \left(g^x, \ g^4 \cdot m_c \right) \tag{10.25}$$

$$CT = \left(g^x, \ g^y \cdot m_c \right) \tag{10.26}$$

$$CT = \left(g^x, \ h^x \cdot m_c \right) \tag{10.27}$$

$$CT = \left(g^x, \ g^y, \ g^{xy} \cdot m_c \right) \tag{10.28}$$

$$CT = \left(g^x, \ h^{x+y} \cdot m_c \right) \tag{10.29}$$

$$CT = \left(g^{2x+y+z}, \ g^{x+3y+z}, \ g^{4x+7y+3z} \cdot m_c \right) \tag{10.30}$$

$$CT = \left(g^{x+3y+3z}, \ g^{2x+3y+5z}, \ g^{9x+5y+2z} \cdot m_c \right) \tag{10.31}$$

$$CT = \left(g^{x+3y+3z}, \ g^{2x+6y+6z}, \ g^{9x+5y+2z} \cdot m_c \right) \tag{10.32}$$

According to Lemma 4.10.1, we have the following results.

- **10.25 No.** We have $x^* = 4$ which is not random.
- **10.26 Yes.** We have

$$(x_1, x^*) = (x, y).$$

x^* is random and independent of x_1, because (x,y) are both random numbers.

- **10.27 No.** We have

$$(x_1, x^*) = (x, x\log_g h).$$

x^* is dependent on x_1 and $\log_g h$, satisfying the equation $x^* = x_1 \log_g h$.

- **10.28 No.** We have

$$(x_1, x_2, x^*) = (x, y, xy).$$

x^* is dependent on x_1 and x_2, satisfying the equation $x^* = x_1 x_2$.

- **10.29 Yes.** We have

$$(x_1, x^*) = (x, x\log_g h + y\log_g h).$$

x^* is independent of x_1, because y is a random number that only appears in x^*.

- **10.30 No.** We have

$$(x_1, x_2, x^*) = (2x + y + z, x + 3y + z, 4x + 7y + 3z).$$

The determinant of the coefficient matrix is zero, and x^* is dependent on (x_1, x_2), satisfying $x^* = x_1 + 2x_2$.

- **10.31 Yes.** We have

$$(x_1, x_2, x^*) = (x + 3y + 3z, 2x + 3y + 5z, 9x + 5y + 2z).$$

The determinant of the coefficient matrix is nonzero. Therefore, x^* is random and independent of x_1, x_2.

- **10.32 Yes.** We have

$$(x_1, x_2, x^*) = (x + 3y + 3z, 2x + 6y + 6z, 9x + 5y + 2z).$$

The determinant of the coefficient matrix is zero where $x_2 = 2x_1$. However, x^* and x_2 are independent because there exists a 2×2 sub-matrix whose determinant is nonzero. Therefore, we have that x^* is random and independent of x_1, x_2.

The last example shows one interesting result. Even though $x_1, x_2, \cdots, x_n, x^*$ are not random and independent, it does not mean that x^* can be computed from $x_1, x_2, \cdots, x_n$, but that at least one value in $\{x_1, x_2, \cdots, x_n, x^*\}$ can be computed from others. To make sure that the last example will not occur in the analysis, we can first remove some x_i if $\{x_1, x_2, \cdots, x_n\}$ are dependent until all remaining x_i are random and independent. A detailed example can be found in Section 4.14.2.

4.10.11 Analysis of One-Time Pad

In the correctness analysis of encryption, it is not sufficient to prove that the false challenge ciphertext is a one-time pad. Instead, we must prove that breaking the false challenge ciphertext is as hard as breaking a one-time pad. That is, the false challenge ciphertext is a one-time pad from the point of view of the adversary who receives some other parameters from the simulated scheme. We have to analyze in this way because other parameters might help the adversary break the false challenge ciphertext.

Let CT^* be the challenge ciphertext defined as

$$CT^* = \left(g^{x_1},\ g^{x_2},\ g^{x_3},\ \cdots,\ g^{x_n},\ g^{x^*} \cdot m_c\right).$$

Let $g^{x_1'}, g^{x_2'}, \cdots, g^{x_n'}$ be additional information that the adversary obtained from other phases. If Z is false, we must analyze that the following ciphertext, an extension of the false challenge ciphertext, is a one-time pad:

$$\left(g^{x_1'},\ g^{x_2'},\ \cdots,\ g^{x_n'},\ g^{x_1},\ g^{x_2},\ g^{x_3},\ \cdots,\ g^{x_n},\ g^{x^*} \cdot m_c\right).$$

That is, x^* is random and independent of $x_1', x_2', \cdots, x_n', x_1, x_2, \cdots, x_n$.

The above explanation is just for an ideal result. The adversary might still have negligible advantage in breaking the false challenge ciphertext. The reason is that the adversary might obtain useful information from other phases such as the public key and responses to queries with a certain probability. For example, the following challenge ciphertext is a one-time pad if $x, y, z \in \mathbb{Z}_p$ are randomly chosen by the simulator in the simulation:

$$CT^* = \left(g^{x+3y+3z},\ g^{2x+6y+6z},\ g^{9x+5y+2z} \cdot m_c\right).$$

However, if the adversary can obtain a new group element such as g^{x+y+z} from a response to a decryption query, the challenge ciphertext is no longer a one-time pad because the adversary can compute the element $g^{9x+5y+2z}$ from the other three group elements to decrypt the message m_c.

4.10.12 Simulation of Decryption

In the security analysis, we must prove that the simulation of decryption is correct. To be precise, the simulation of decryption must satisfy the following conditions.

- If Z is true, the simulation of decryption is indistinguishable from the decryption in the real scheme. Otherwise, we cannot prove that the simulation is indistinguishable from the real attack. Here, the indistinguishability means that the simulated scheme will accept correct ciphertexts and reject incorrect ciphertexts in the same way as the real scheme. To make sure that the simulation of decryption is indistinguishable, the simplest way is for the simulator to be able to generate a valid secret key for the ciphertext decryption.

- If Z is false, the adversary cannot break the false challenge ciphertext with the help of decryption queries, i.e., the adversary cannot successfully guess the message in the challenge ciphertext with the help of decryption queries. This condition is desired when proving that the adversary has no (or negligible) advantage in breaking the false challenge ciphertext. How to stop the adversary from breaking the false challenge ciphertext using decryption queries is the most challenging task in security reduction. This is due to the fact that all ciphertexts for decryption queries can be adaptively generated by the adversary, e.g., by modifying the challenge ciphertext in the CCA security model.

The above two different conditions are desired for proving the security of encryption schemes under decisional hardness assumptions. However, when we prove encryption schemes under computational hardness assumptions in the random oracle model, the required conditions of the decryption simulation are slightly different. The reason is that there is no target Z in the given problem instance.

4.10.13 Simulation of Challenge Decryption Key

Let (pk^*, sk^*) be the key pair in a public-key encryption scheme, and (ID^*, d_{ID^*}) be the key pair in an identity-based encryption scheme that an adversary aims to challenge, where the challenge ciphertext will be created for pk^* or ID^*. For simplicity, in this section, we denote by sk^* and d_{ID^*} the challenge decryption keys.

In the security reduction for encryption, it is not necessary for the simulator to program the simulation without knowing the challenge decryption key. Currently, there are two different methods associated with the decryption key.

- In the first method, the simulator knows the challenge decryption key. The simulator can easily simulate the decryption by following the decryption algorithm because it knows the decryption key. The decryption simulation in the simulated scheme is therefore indistinguishable from the decryption in the real scheme. However, it is challenging to simulate the challenge ciphertext, so that the adversary has negligible advantage in breaking the false challenge ciphertext.
- In the second method, the simulator does not know the challenge decryption key. If Z is false, we found that it is relatively easy to generate the false challenge ciphertext satisfying the requirements. However, it is challenging to simulate the decryption correctly without knowing the decryption key. The simulator does not know the challenge decryption key in this case, but the simulator has to be able to simulate the decryption.

We cannot adaptively choose one of them to program a security reduction for a proposed scheme. Which method can be used is dependent on the proposed scheme and the underlying hard problem.

4.10.14 Probability Analysis for P_F

We have explained that if Z is false, we cannot simply analyze that the false challenge ciphertext is a one-time pad, but we must analyze that the adversary cannot break the false challenge ciphertext except with negligible advantage. To calculate the probability P_F of breaking the false challenge ciphertext, we might need to calculate the following probabilities and advantages.

- **Probability $P_F^W = \frac{1}{2}$.** The probability P_F^W of breaking the false challenge ciphertext without any decryption query is $\frac{1}{2}$. This probability is actually the probability of breaking the false challenge ciphertext in the CPA security model, where there is no decryption query. The security proof for CPA is relatively easy, because we do not need to analyze the following probability or advantages.

- **Advantage $A_F^K \overset{?}{=} 0$.** The advantage A_F^K of breaking the false challenge ciphertext with the help of the challenge decryption key is either 0 or 1. If $A_F^K = 0$, this means that the adversary cannot use the challenge decryption key to guess the message in the false challenge ciphertext, and this completes the probability analysis of P_F. Otherwise, $A_F^K = 1$, and we need to analyze the following probability or advantages.

- **Advantage $A_F^C = 0$.** The advantage A_F^C of breaking the false challenge ciphertext with the help of decryption queries on correct ciphertexts is 0. Since a correct ciphertext will always be accepted for decryption, a correct security reduction requires that decryption of correct ciphertexts must not help the adversary break the false challenge ciphertext. Otherwise, it is impossible to obtain $P_F \approx \frac{1}{2}$, and the security reduction fails.

- **Advantage $A_F^I \overset{?}{=} 0$.** The advantage A_F^I of breaking the false challenge ciphertext with the help of decryption queries on incorrect ciphertexts is either 0 or 1. If $A_F^I = 0$, decryption of incorrect ciphertexts will not help the adversary break the false challenge ciphertext, and this completes the probability analysis of P_F. Otherwise, $A_F^I = 1$, and we need to analyze the following probability.

- **Probability $P_F^A \approx 0$.** The probability P_F^A of accepting an incorrect ciphertext for decryption query is negligible, or the probability that the adversary can generate an incorrect ciphertext for decryption query to be accepted by the simulator is negligible. If $P_F^A = 0$ all incorrect ciphertexts for decryption queries will be rejected by the simulator.

We can use the following formula to define the probability P_F with the above probabilities and advantages:

$$P_F = P_F^W + A_F^K \left(A_F^C + A_F^I P_F^A \right).$$

The flowchart for analyzing the probability P_F is given in Figure 4.2. The probability analysis for CCA security is complicated because we may have to additionally analyze up to four different cases.

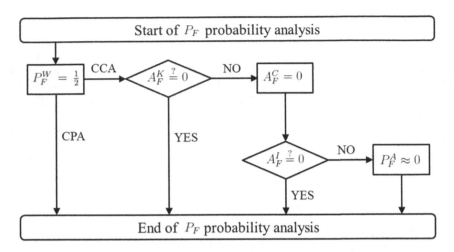

Fig. 4.2 The flowchart for analyzing probability P_F

4.10.15 Examples of Advantage Results for A_F^K and A_F^I

In the previous subsection, we introduced which probabilities and advantages we need to analyze for CCA security if Z is false. In a correct security reduction, the advantages A_F^K and A_F^I can be either 0 or 1 depending on the proposed scheme and the security reduction. We give four artificial examples to introduce $A_F^K = 0, A_F^K = 1, A_F^I = 0$, and $A_F^I = 1$ in the security reduction.

- $A_F^K = 0$. In a public-key encryption scheme, the key pair is $(pk, sk) = (h, \alpha)$ where $SP = (\mathbb{G}, g, p)$, $h = g^\alpha$, and $\alpha \in \mathbb{Z}_p$ is randomly chosen. Therefore, the challenge decryption key is α in this construction.

  Suppose the false challenge ciphertext is equal to

$$CT^* = (C_1^*, C_2^*) = \left(g^x, \ Z \cdot m_c \right),$$

  where the target (false) Z is randomly chosen from $\mathbb{G}$. This challenge ciphertext is a one-time pad from the point of view of the adversary if and only if Z is random and unknown to the adversary. Even if the challenge decryption key α can be computed by the adversary, it does not help the adversary guess the encrypted message. Therefore, we have $A_F^K = 0$.

- $A_F^K = 1$. In a public-key encryption scheme, the public key is $pk = h$, and the secret key is $sk = (\alpha, \beta, \gamma)$, where $SP = (\mathbb{G}, g_1, g_2, g_3, p)$, $h = g_1^\alpha g_2^\beta g_3^\gamma$, and $\alpha, \beta, \gamma \in \mathbb{Z}_p$ are randomly chosen. Here, g_1, g_2, g_3 are three distinct group elements. Therefore, the challenge decryption key is (α, β, γ) in this construction.

  Suppose the false challenge ciphertext is equal to

$$CT^* = (C_1^*, C_2^*, C_3^*) = \left(g_1^x,\ Z,\ Z^\alpha \cdot m_c \right),$$

where the (false) target Z is randomly chosen from $\mathbb{G}$. The message is encrypted with Z^α, and Z is given as the second element in the challenge ciphertext. Therefore, this challenge ciphertext is a one-time pad from the point of view of the adversary if and only if α is random and unknown to the adversary. It is easy to see that with the help of (α, β, γ), the adversary can easily break the false challenge ciphertext. Therefore, we have $A_F^K = 1$.

- $A_F^I = 0$. Continue the above example for $A_F^K = 1$. Even if the adversary has unbounded computational power, it still cannot compute the challenge decryption key (α, β, γ) from the public key. The false challenge ciphertext is a one-time pad from the point of view of the adversary when α is random and unknown to the adversary.

  Let $CT = (C_1, C_2, C_3)$ be an incorrect ciphertext. Suppose the decryption of this ciphertext will return to the adversary the group element $m = C_3 \cdot C_2^\gamma$ as the message. The computationally unbounded adversary can easily obtain γ from this group element because C_2, C_3 are known. However, the computed γ cannot help the adversary break the false challenge ciphertext. Therefore, we have $A_F^I = 0$. Notice that the advantage $A_F^I = 0$ holds if and only if α will not be known to the adversary from the decryption of all incorrect ciphertexts.

- $A_F^I = 1$. Continue the examples for $A_F^K = 1$ and $A_F^I = 0$. Suppose the decryption of that incorrect ciphertext will not return $m = C_3 \cdot C_2^\gamma$ but $m = C_3 \cdot C_2^{-\alpha}$ instead. Following similar analysis, the adversary can obtain α from decryption queries on incorrect ciphertexts and then break the false challenge ciphertext. Therefore, we have $A_F^I = 1$.

Whether the challenge decryption key can be computed by the adversary significantly affects the analysis. We have the following interesting observations.

- If the challenge decryption key can be computed from the public key by the computationally unbounded adversary, the decryption of either correct or incorrect ciphertexts will not help the adversary break the false challenge ciphertext. That is, $A_F^C = A_F^I = 0$. The reason is that the adversary can use the challenge decryption key to decrypt ciphertexts by itself. Therefore, in this case, we do not need to consider whether decryption queries can help the adversary break the false challenge ciphertext or not.

- If the challenge decryption key cannot be computed by the computationally unbounded adversary, the decryption of incorrect ciphertexts might help the adversary break the false challenge ciphertext. The reason is that the challenge decryption key might play an important role in the construction of a one-time pad, but the challenge decryption key might be obtained by the adversary by decryption queries on incorrect ciphertexts, so that the false challenge ciphertext is no longer a one-time pad. We stress that the decryption of incorrect ciphertexts does not always help the adversary. It depends on how the one-time pad is constructed in the security reduction.

Giving the challenge decryption key to the adversary in analysis is sufficient but not necessary, because the simulator only responds to decryption queries made by the adversary. We can even skip the analysis of whether the challenge decryption key helps the adversary. However, this is a useful assumption to simplify the analysis, especially when the challenge decryption key cannot help the adversary.

4.10.16 Advantage Calculation 3

In the advantage calculation, we have shown that

$$\varepsilon_R = \Pr\left[\text{Guess } Z = \text{True}|Z = \text{True}\right] - \Pr\left[\text{Guess } Z = \text{True}|Z = \text{False}\right]$$
$$= P_S(P_T - P_F).$$

By applying the probability of breaking the true/false challenge ciphertext, when the simulation is indistinguishable from the real attack we finally have

$$\varepsilon_R = P_S\left(\frac{1}{2} + \frac{\varepsilon}{2} - P_F^W - A_F^K\left(A_F^C + A_F^I P_F^A\right)\right).$$

- For CPA security, the advantage is equivalent to

$$\varepsilon_R = P_S\left(\frac{1}{2} + \frac{\varepsilon}{2} - P_F^W\right),$$

where we only need to analyze that P_S is non-negligible and $P_F^W = \frac{1}{2}$.
- For CCA security where $A_F^K = 0$, the advantage is equivalent to

$$\varepsilon_R = P_S\left(\frac{1}{2} + \frac{\varepsilon}{2} - P_F^W\right),$$

where we only need to analyze that P_S is non-negligible and $P_F^W = \frac{1}{2}$.
- For CCA security where $A_F^K = 1$, the advantage is equivalent to

$$\varepsilon_R = P_S\left(\frac{1}{2} + \frac{\varepsilon}{2} - P_F^W - A_F^C - A_F^I P_F^A\right),$$

where we need to analyze that P_S is non-negligible and

$$P_F^W = \frac{1}{2}, \ A_F^C = 0, \ A_F^I = 0 \text{ or } P_F^A \approx 0.$$

The property of indistinguishable simulation is desired in all cases. Note that the indistinguishability analysis is much more complicated in the CCA security model than in the CPA security model, because we also need to analyze that the decryption simulation is indistinguishable if Z is true.

4.10.17 Summary of Correct Security Reduction

A correct security reduction for an encryption scheme should satisfy the following conditions. We can use these conditions to check whether a security reduction is correct or not.

- The underlying hard problem is a decisional problem.
- The simulator uses the adversary's guess to solve the underlying hard problem.
- The simulation is indistinguishable from the real attack if Z is true.
- The probability of successful simulation is non-negligible.
- The advantage of breaking the true challenge ciphertext is ε.
- The advantage of breaking the false challenge ciphertext is negligible.
- The advantage ε_R of solving the underlying hard problem is non-negligible.
- The time cost of the simulation is polynomial time.

In a security proof with random oracles, we can prove the security of a proposed scheme under a computational hardness assumption. One main difference is how to solve the underlying hard problem. The reduction method with random oracles is given in the next section.

4.11 Security Proofs for Encryption Under Computational Assumptions

In this section, we introduce how to use random oracles to program a security reduction for an encryption scheme under a computational hardness assumption. Security reductions for encryption schemes under computational hardness assumptions and for encryption schemes under decisional hardness assumptions are quite different in the challenge ciphertext simulation, how to find a solution to the problem instance, and the correctness analysis.

4.11.1 Random and Independent Revisited

Let H be a cryptographic hash function, and x be a random input string.

- If H is a cryptographic hash function, $H(x)$ is dependent on x and the hash function algorithm. That is, $H(x)$ is computable from x and the hash function H.
- If H is set as a random oracle, $H(x)$ is random and independent of x. This is due to the fact that $H(x)$ is an element randomly chosen by the simulator.

In a security proof with random oracles, if the adversary does not query x to the random oracle, $H(x)$ is random and unknown to the adversary. This is the core of security reduction for encryption with random oracles.

4.11.2 One-Time Pad Revisited

Let $H : \{0,1\}^* \to \{0,1\}^n$ be a cryptographic hash function. We consider the following encryption of the message m_c with an arbitrary string x, where m_0, m_1 are any two distinct messages chosen from the message space $\{0,1\}^n$ and m_c is randomly chosen from $\{m_0, m_1\}$:

$$CT = \Big(x, \; H(x) \oplus m_c \Big).$$

If H is a hash function, the above ciphertext is not a one-time pad. Given x and the hash function H, the adversary can compute $H(x)$ by itself and decrypt the ciphertext to obtain the message m_c. However, if H is set as a random oracle, the adversary cannot compute $H(x)$ by itself. The adversary must query x to the random oracle to know $H(x)$. Then, we have the following two interesting results.

- **Before Querying x.** Since $H(x)$ is random and unknown to the adversary, the message is encrypted with a random and unknown encryption key. Therefore, the above ciphertext is equivalent to a one-time pad, and the adversary has no advantage in guessing the message m_c except with probability $\frac{1}{2}$.
- **After Querying x.** Once the adversary queries x to the random oracle and receives the response $H(x)$, it can immediately decrypt the message with $H(x)$. Therefore, the above ciphertext is no longer a one-time pad, and the adversary can guess the encrypted message with advantage 1.

With the above features, the simulator is able to use random oracles to program a security reduction for an encryption scheme in the indistinguishability security model to solve a computational hard problem.

4.11.3 Solution to Hard Problem Revisited

In a security reduction for an encryption scheme in the indistinguishability security model without random oracles, we use the guess of the random coin c of the adversary to solve a decisional hard problem. With the help of random oracles, we can program a security reduction to solve a computational hard problem. However, instead of using the guess of c, the simulator uses one of the hash queries.

Let $H : \{0,1\}^* \to \{0,1\}^n$ be a cryptographic hash function set as a random oracle. Let X be a given instance of a computational hard problem, and y be its solution. Suppose the challenge ciphertext in the simulation is created as

$$CT = \Big(X, \; H(y) \oplus m_c \Big).$$

The breaking assumption states that there exists an adversary who can break the above ciphertext with non-negligible advantage. That is, the adversary has non-negligible advantage in guessing m_c correctly. According to the features introduced in the previous subsection, the adversary must query y to the random oracle. Otherwise, without making the query on y to the random oracle, CT is equivalent to a one-time pad, which is contrary to the breaking assumption. Therefore, the solution to the problem instance will appear in one of the hash queries made by the adversary.

We denote by Q^* the *challenge hash query*, if the adversary has no advantage in guessing the encrypted message without making a hash query on Q^* to the random oracle. According to the breaking assumption, the adversary will make the challenge hash query on $Q^* = y$ to the random oracle with non-negligible probability. Since the number of hash queries to the random oracle is polynomial, the simulator then uses these hash queries to solve the underlying hard problem. For example, the simulator can randomly picks one of the hash queries as the solution. The success probability is $\frac{1}{q_H}$ for q_H hash queries, which is non-negligible. This is the magical part of using random oracles in proving security of encryption schemes under computational hardness assumptions in the indistinguishability security model.

4.11.4 Simulation of Challenge Ciphertext

In a security reduction for an encryption scheme in the indistinguishability security model without random oracles, we embed the target Z from the problem instance in the challenge ciphertext to obtain a true challenge ciphertext if Z is true or a false challenge ciphertext if Z is false. However, in a security reduction for an encryption scheme under a computational hardness assumption, there is no target Z in the problem instance, and thus the simulation of the challenge ciphertext must be different.

The simulation of the challenge ciphertext has one important step, which is to simulate a component associated with the challenge hash query. We give the following example to explain how to simulate the challenge ciphertext. We continue the example in the previous subsection, where the challenge ciphertext in the real scheme is set as

$$CT^* = \Big(X, H(y) \oplus m_c\Big).$$

The simulator cannot directly simulate $H(y) \oplus m_c$ in the challenge ciphertext because y is unknown to the simulator. Fortunately, this problem can be easily solved with the help of random oracles. To be precise, the simulator chooses a random string $R \in \{0,1\}^n$ to replace $H(y) \oplus m_c$. The challenge ciphertext in the simulated scheme is set as

$$CT^* = (X, R).$$

The challenge ciphertext can be seen as an encryption of the message $m_c \in \{m_0, m_1\}$ if $H(y) = R \oplus m_c$, where we have

$$CT^* = (X, R) = \Big(X, H(y) \oplus m_c\Big).$$

Unfortunately, after sending this challenge ciphertext to the adversary, the simulator may not know which hash query from the adversary is the solution y and will respond to the query on y with a random element different from $R \oplus m_c$. Therefore, the query response is wrong, and the challenge ciphertext in the simulation is distinguishable from that in the real scheme. We have the following results.

- **Before Querying** y. From the point of view of the adversary, the challenge ciphertext is an encryption of m_0 if $H(y) = R \oplus m_0$ and an encryption of m_1 if $H(y) = R \oplus m_1$. Without making a hash query on y to the random oracle, the adversary never knows $H(y)$, and thus the challenge ciphertext in the simulated scheme is indistinguishable from the challenge ciphertext in the real scheme.
  Before querying y to the random oracle, $H(y)$ is random and unknown to the adversary, so the challenge ciphertext is an encryption of m_0 or m_1 with the same probability. Therefore, the challenge ciphertext is equivalent to a one-time pad from the point of view of the adversary, and thus the adversary has no advantage in guessing the encrypted message.
- **After Querying** y. Once the adversary makes a hash query on y to the random oracle, the simulator will respond to the query with a random element $Y = H(y)$. If the simulator does not know which query is the challenge hash query $Q^* = y$, the response to the query on y is independent of R and therefore we have

$$Y \oplus m_0 = R \ \text{ or } \ Y \oplus m_1 = R$$

holds with negligible probability. Then, the simulated scheme is distinguishable from the real scheme because the encrypted message in the challenge ciphertext is neither m_0 nor m_1. However, we do not care that the simulation becomes distinguishable now, because the simulator has already received the challenge hash query from the adversary and can solve the underlying hard problem.

4.11.5 Proof Structure

We are ready to summarize the proof structure for encryption schemes under computational hardness assumptions, where at least one hash function is set as a random oracle. Suppose there exists an adversary $\mathcal{A}$ who can break the proposed encryption scheme in the corresponding security model. We construct a simulator $\mathcal{B}$ to solve a computational hard problem. Given as input an instance of this hard problem, in the security proof we must show (1) how the simulator generates the simulated scheme; (2) how the simulator solves the underlying hard problem; and (3) why the security reduction is correct. A security proof is composed of the following three parts.

- **Simulation.** In this part, we show how the simulator programs the random oracle simulation, generates the simulated scheme using the received problem instance, and interacts with the adversary following the indistinguishability security model. If the simulator aborts, the security reduction fails.
- **Solution.** In this part (at the end of the guess phase), we show how the simulator solves the computational hard problem using hash queries to the random oracle made by the adversary. To be precise, we should point out which hash query is

the challenge hash query Q^* in this simulation, how to pick the challenge hash query from all hash queries, and how to use the challenge hash query to solve the underlying hard problem.

- **Analysis.** In this part, we need to provide the following analysis.

  1. The simulation is indistinguishable from the real attack if no challenge hash query is made by the adversary.
  2. The probability P_S of successful simulation.
  3. The adversary has no advantage in breaking the challenge ciphertext if it does not make the challenge hash query to the random oracle.
  4. The probability P_C of finding the correct solution from hash queries.
  5. The advantage ε_R of solving the underlying hard problem.
  6. The time cost of solving the underlying hard problem.

The simulation will be successful if the simulator does not abort in computing the public key, responding to queries, and computing the challenge ciphertext. Before the adversary makes the challenge hash query, the simulation is indistinguishable if (1) all responses to queries are correct; (2) the challenge ciphertext is a correct ciphertext as defined in the proposed scheme from the point of view of the adversary; and (3) the randomness property holds for the simulation.

If the security reduction is correct, the solution to the problem instance can be extracted from the challenge hash query. For simplicity, we can view the challenge hash query as the solution to the problem instance. In this type of security reduction, there is no true challenge ciphertext or false challenge ciphertext.

4.11.6 Challenge Ciphertext and Challenge Hash Query

In the real scheme, the challenge ciphertext is a correct ciphertext whose encrypted message is m_c. If the adversary makes the challenge hash query to the random oracle, it can use the response to decrypt the encrypted message and then break the scheme. However, in the simulated scheme, the challenge ciphertext is a correct ciphertext if and only if there is no challenge hash query. Once the adversary makes the challenge hash query to the random oracle and the response to the challenge hash query is wrong, it will immediately find out that the challenge ciphertext is incorrect and the simulation is distinguishable.

According to the explanation in Section 4.11.4, we do not care that the simulation becomes distinguishable after the adversary has made the challenge hash query to the random oracle. In the security reduction, making the challenge hash query can be seen as a successful and useful attack by the adversary. Before the adversary launches such an attack with non-negligible probability, the simulated scheme must be indistinguishable from the real scheme, and the adversary has no advantage in breaking the challenge ciphertext. That is, the challenge ciphertext must be an encryption of either m_0 or m_1 with the same probability (i.e., one-time pad) from the point of view of the adversary.

4.11.7 Advantage Calculation

Suppose there exists an adversary who can break the proposed encryption scheme in the random oracle model with advantage ε. We have the following important lemma (originally from [24]) about calculating the advantage.

Lemma 4.11.1 *If the adversary has no advantage in breaking the challenge cipher-text without making the challenge hash query to the random oracle, the adversary will make the challenge hash query to the random oracle with probability ε.*

Proof. According to the breaking assumption, we have

$$\Pr[c' = c] = \frac{1}{2} + \frac{\varepsilon}{2}.$$

This is the success probability that the adversary can correctly guess the encrypted message in the real scheme according to the breaking assumption.

Let H^* denote the event of making the challenge hash query to the random oracle, and H^{*c} be the complementary event of H^*. According to the statement in the lemma, we have

$$\Pr[c' = c|H^*] = 1, \quad \Pr[c' = c|H^{*c}] = \frac{1}{2}.$$

Then, we obtain

$$\begin{aligned}
\Pr[c' = c] &= \Pr[c' = c|H^*]\Pr[H^*] + \Pr[c' = c|H^{*c}]\Pr[H^{*c}] \\
&= \Pr[H^*] + \frac{1}{2}\Pr[H^{*c}] \\
&= \Pr[H^*] + \frac{1}{2}(1 - \Pr[H^*]) \\
&= \frac{1}{2} + \frac{1}{2}\Pr[H^*],
\end{aligned}$$

and deduct $\Pr[H^*] = \varepsilon$. This completes the proof.   □

The advantage ε_R of solving the underlying computational hard problem is defined as

$$\varepsilon_R = P_S \cdot \varepsilon \cdot P_C.$$

If the probability that the simulation is successful and indistinguishable is P_S, and the adversary has no advantage in breaking the challenge ciphertext without making the challenge hash query, the challenge hash query will appear in the hash list with probability ε. Finally, the probability of picking the challenge hash query from the hash list is P_C. Therefore, the advantage of solving the computational hard problem is $P_S \cdot \varepsilon \cdot P_C$.

The simulator needs to pick one hash query as the challenge hash query and extracts the solution to the problem instance from it. If the simulator cannot verify which hash query is the correct one, it has to randomly pick one of the hash queries as the challenge hash query. For simplicity, if the adversary can break the challenge ciphertext with advantage 1 after making q_H hash queries, one of the hash queries must be the challenge hash query. Therefore, the probability that a randomly picked query from the hash list is the challenge hash query is $1/q_H$. There is no reduction loss in finding the solution from hash queries if the decisional variant of the computational hard problem is easy. The reason is that the simulator can test all the hash queries one by one until it finds the challenge hash query. However, if the decisional variant is also hard, it seems that this *finding loss* cannot be avoided.

4.11.8 Analysis of No Advantage

A successful reduction requires that the adversary has no advantage in breaking the challenge ciphertext if it never makes the challenge hash query to the random oracle. To satisfy this condition, the challenge ciphertext should look like a one-time pad, where $c \in \{0, 1\}$ is random and unknown, from the point of view of the adversary. That is, the generated challenge ciphertext is an encryption of either m_0 or m_1 with the same probability. We stress that an indistinguishable simulation cannot guarantee that the adversary has no advantage. The reason is that c may be non-random in the simulated challenge ciphertext.

For example, let the message space be $\{0, 1\}^{n+1}$, and $H : \{0, 1\}^* \to \{0, 1\}^n$ be a cryptographic hash function. Suppose the adversary chooses two distinct messages m_0, m_1 to be challenged, where the least significant bits (LSB) of m_0 and m_1 are 0 and 1, respectively. Suppose the challenge ciphertext in the real scheme is set as

$$\left(x, \ H(x) \oplus m_c \right),$$

and the challenge ciphertext in the simulated scheme is set as

$$CT^* = (x, \ R),$$

where R is a random string chosen from $\{0, 1\}^{n+1}$. Let $CT^* = (C_1, C_2)$. We have the following observations.

- The challenge ciphertext can be seen as an encryption of a message from $\{m_0, m_1\}$ if no challenge hash query on x is made to the random oracle. Therefore, the simulation is indistinguishable from the real attack.
- However, the message m_c in the challenge ciphertext can easily be identified from the least significant bit of C_2, because the LSB of the message is not encrypted. According to the choice of messages m_0, m_1, the bit c is equal to the LSB of C_2. Therefore, the adversary can correctly guess the encrypted message with probability 1 without making the challenge hash query to the random oracle.

The above encryption scheme is not IND-CPA secure. The adversary has non-negligible advantage in guessing the encrypted message in the challenge ciphertext, and this is why we cannot prove its security in the IND-CPA security model.

4.11.9 Requirements of Decryption Simulation

In a security reduction for an encryption scheme under a decisional hardness assumption, the decryption simulation must be indistinguishable from the real attack if Z is true, and the decryption simulation must not help the adversary break the false challenge ciphertext if Z is false. However, the requirements of the decryption simulation for this type of security reduction are slightly different. We have the following requirements before the adversary makes the challenge hash query to the random oracle.

- We require that the decryption simulation is indistinguishable from the decryption in the real scheme. Otherwise, the simulation is distinguishable from the real attack. To achieve this, in the simulated scheme, any ciphertext will be accepted or rejected identically to the real scheme.
- We require that the decryption simulation cannot help the adversary distinguish the challenge ciphertext in the simulated scheme from that in the real scheme. Otherwise, the simulation is distinguishable from the real attack. To achieve this, we can construct the scheme and program the security reduction in such a way that all incorrect ciphertexts will be rejected and only ciphertexts created by the adversary are correct. In this case, any modification of the challenge ciphertext will be judged to be an incorrect ciphertext.

The core of the decryption simulation is to find an approach that can determine whether a ciphertext for a decryption query from the adversary is correct or incorrect. If the ciphertext is correct, it must be completely generated by the adversary and the simulator must be able to simulate the decryption. Otherwise, it must be rejected. The details of the approach depend on the proposed scheme and the security reduction. We cannot give any general summary here but will provide an example in the following subsection.

4.11.10 An Example of Decryption Simulation

In this type of security reduction, the challenge decryption key is usually programmed as a key unknown to the simulator. How to simulate the decryption without knowing the challenge decryption key then becomes tricky and difficult. Fortunately, the random oracle also provides a big help in the decryption simulation. We now give a simple example to see how the decryption simulation works without having the corresponding decryption key.

Let the system parameters SP be $(\mathbb{G}, g, p, H)$, where $H : \{0,1\}^* \to \{0,1\}^n$ is a cryptographic hash function satisfying $n = |p|$ (the same bit length as p). Suppose a public-key encryption scheme generates a key pair (pk, sk), where $pk = g_1 = g^\alpha$ and $sk = \alpha$. The encryption algorithm takes as input the public key pk, a message $m \in \{0,1\}^n$, and the system parameters SP. It chooses a random number $r \in \mathbb{Z}_p$ and returns the ciphertext as

$$CT = (C_1, C_2, C_3) = \left(g^r, \; H(0||g_1^r) \oplus r, \; H(1||g_1^r) \oplus m\right).$$

The decryption algorithm first computes $C_1^\alpha = g_1^r$ and then extracts r by $H(0||C_1^\alpha) \oplus C_2$ and m by $H(1||C_1^\alpha) \oplus C_3$. Finally, it outputs the message m if and only if CT can be created with the decrypted number r and the decrypted message m.

This encryption scheme is not secure in the IND-CCA security model but only secure in the IND-CCA1 security model, where the adversary can only make decryption queries before the challenge phase. The proposed encryption scheme is secure under the CDH assumption in the random oracle model, where it is hard to compute g^{ab} from a problem instance (g, g^a, g^b).

In the security reduction, the simulator sets $\alpha = a$ with the unknown exponent a in the problem instance. We are now interested in knowing how the simulator responds to decryption queries from the adversary with the help of random oracles.

In this encryption scheme, a queried ciphertext CT is valid if CT can be created with the decrypted random number r' and the decrypted message m'. That is,

$$\left(g^{r'}, \; H(0||g_1^{r'}) \oplus r', \; H(1||g_1^{r'}) \oplus m'\right) = CT.$$

Otherwise, it is invalid, and the simulator outputs $\perp$. Consider the ciphertext $CT = (C_1, C_2, C_3)$ for a decryption query. Let $C_1 = g^r$ for some exponent $r \in \mathbb{Z}_p$. The ciphertext will be a correct ciphertext if $CT = (g^r, \; H(0||g_1^r) \oplus r, \; H(1||g_1^r) \oplus m)$ for a message m. We have the following observations.

- If the adversary does not query $0||g_1^r$ to the random oracle, $H(0||g_1^r)$ is random and unknown to the adversary, so that $C_2 = H(0||g_1^r) \oplus r$ holds with negligible probability $\frac{1}{2^n}$ for any adaptive choice of C_2.
- If the adversary does not query $1||g_1^r$ to the random oracle, $H(1||g_1^r)$ is random and unknown to the adversary, but any C_3 can still be seen as an encryption of a message, where the message is $C_3 \oplus H(1||g_1^r)$.

From the above observation, the adversary cannot generate a valid ciphertext except with negligible probability $1/2^n$ for a large n unless it queries $0||g_1^r$ to the random oracle and uses $H(0||g_1^r)$ in the ciphertext generation.

Suppose $(x_1, y_1), (x_2, y_2), \cdots, (x_q, y_q)$ are in the hash list, where x, y denote a query and a response, respectively. If CT is a valid ciphertext, one of the hash queries must be equal to $0||g_1^r$. Otherwise, the ciphertext is invalid. Therefore, the simulator can simulate the decryption without knowing the challenge decryption key as follows.

- For all $i \in [1, q]$, it starts with $i = 1$ and computes $r' = y_1 \oplus C_2$.
- It uses r' to decrypt the message m' by computing $H(1||g_1^{r'}) \oplus C_3$.
- It checks whether the ciphertext CT can be generated with (r', m'). If yes, the simulator returns m' as the decrypted message. Otherwise, the simulator sets $i = i + 1$ and repeats the above procedure.
- If all y_i cannot decrypt the ciphertext correctly, the simulator outputs $\perp$ as the decryption result on the queried ciphertext CT. That is, CT is invalid.

This completes the description of the decryption simulation. To simulate the decryption with the help of random oracles, the security reduction must satisfy two conditions. Firstly, we can use hash queries instead of the challenge decryption key to simulate the decryption. A ciphertext is valid if and only if the adversary ever made the correct hash query to the random oracle. This condition is necessary if the simulator is to simulate the decryption correctly. Secondly, there should be a mechanism for checking which hash query is the correct hash query for a decryption. Otherwise, given a ciphertext for a decryption query, the simulator might return many distinct results depending on the used hash queries.

4.11.11 Summary of Correct Security Reduction

A successful security reduction for an encryption scheme under a computational hardness assumption is slightly different from a security reduction for an encryption scheme under a decisional hardness assumption. We stress that the difference is not due to using random oracles but due to the underlying hardness assumption. An encryption scheme under a decisional hardness assumption can also be proved secure with random oracles.

Public-Key Encryption. A correct security reduction for a public-key encryption scheme under a computational hardness assumption must satisfy the following conditions.

- The underlying hard problem is a computational problem.
- The simulator does not know the secret key.
- The simulator can simulate the decryption for CCA security.
- The probability of successful simulation is non-negligible.
- Without making the challenge hash query, the adversary cannot distinguish the simulated scheme from the real scheme and has no advantage in breaking the challenge ciphertext.
- The simulator uses the challenge hash query to solve the hard problem.
- The advantage ε_R of solving the underlying hard problem is non-negligible.
- The time cost of the simulation is polynomial time.

Identity-Based Encryption. A correct security reduction for an identity-based encryption scheme under a computational hardness assumption must satisfy the following conditions.

- The underlying hard problem is a computational problem.
- The simulator does not know the master secret key.
- The simulator can simulate the private-key generation.
- The simulator can simulate the decryption for CCA security.
- The probability of successful simulation is non-negligible.
- The simulator does not know the private key of the challenge identity.

- Without making the challenge hash query, the adversary cannot distinguish the simulated scheme from the real scheme and has no advantage in breaking the challenge ciphertext.
- The simulator uses the challenge hash query to solve the hard problem.
- The advantage ε_R of solving the underlying hard problem is non-negligible.
- The time cost of the simulation is polynomial time.

We find that any provably secure encryption scheme under a decisional hardness assumption can be modified into a provably secure encryption scheme under a computational hardness assumption with random oracles. Therefore, the above summary is only suitable for some encryption schemes, especially those schemes that cannot be proved secure under decisional hardness assumptions.

4.12 Simulatable and Reducible with Random Oracles

In previous sections, we have introduced what is simulatable and what is reducible for digital signatures. These two concepts are important for digital signatures and for private keys in identity-based encryption. In this section, we summarize three different structures used in the constructions of signature schemes and other cryptographic schemes that are quite popular in group-based cryptography. These three types are introduced in the random oracle model, where random oracles are used to decide whether a signature is simulatable or reducible.

4.12.1 H-Type: Hashing to Group

The first H-type of signature structure is described as

$$\sigma_m = H(m)^a,$$

where $H : \{0,1\}^* \to \mathbb{G}$ is a cryptographic hash function. Here, $(g, g^a, g^b) \in \mathbb{G}$ is an instance of the CDH problem, and the aim is to compute g^{ab}.

Suppose H is set as a random oracle. For a query on m, the simulator responds with

$$H(m) = g^{xb+y},$$

where b is the unknown secret in the problem instance, $x \in \mathbb{Z}_p$ is adaptively chosen, and $y \in \mathbb{Z}_p$ is randomly chosen by the simulator. Because y is randomly chosen from $\mathbb{Z}_p$, $H(m)$ is random in $\mathbb{G}$.

The simulatable and reducible conditions are described as follows:

$$\sigma_m \text{ is } \begin{cases} \text{Simulatable, if } x = 0 \\ \\ \text{Reducible,} \quad \text{otherwise} \end{cases}.$$

- The H-type is simulatable if $x = 0$ because we have

$$\sigma_m = H(m)^a = (g^{0b+y})^a = g^{ya} = (g^a)^y,$$

which is computable from g^a and y without knowing a.
- The H-type is reducible if $x \neq 0$ because we have

$$\left(\frac{\sigma_m}{(g^a)^y} \right)^{\frac{1}{x}} = \left(\frac{H(m)^a}{(g^a)^y} \right)^{\frac{1}{x}} = \left(\frac{g^{(xb+y)a}}{g^{ay}} \right)^{\frac{1}{x}} = \left(g^{x \cdot ab} \right)^{\frac{1}{x}} = g^{ab},$$

which is the solution to the CDH problem instance.

The second H-type of signature structure is described as

$$\sigma_m = H(m)^{\frac{1}{a}},$$

where $H : \{0,1\}^* \rightarrow \mathbb{G}^*$ is a cryptographic hash function. Here, $(g, g^a) \in \mathbb{G}$ is an instance of the DHI problem, and the aim is to compute $g^{\frac{1}{a}}$.

Suppose H is set as a random oracle. For a query on m, the simulator responds with

$$H(m) = g^{y \cdot a + x},$$

where a is the unknown secret in the problem instance, $x \in \mathbb{Z}_p$ is adaptively chosen, and $y \in \mathbb{Z}_p^*$ is randomly chosen by the simulator. Because y is randomly chosen from $\mathbb{Z}_p^*$, $H(m)$ is random in $\mathbb{G}^*$.

The simulatable and reducible conditions are described as follows:

$$\sigma_m \text{ is } \begin{cases} \text{Simulatable, if } x = 0 \\ \\ \text{Reducible, \quad otherwise} \end{cases}.$$

- The H-type is simulatable if $x = 0$ because we have

$$\sigma_m = H(m)^{\frac{1}{a}} = (g^{ya+x})^{\frac{1}{a}} = g^y,$$

which is computable from g and y without knowing a.
- The H-type is reducible if $x \neq 0$ because we have

$$\left(\frac{\sigma_m}{g^y} \right)^{\frac{1}{x}} = \left(\frac{H(m)^{\frac{1}{a}}}{g^y} \right)^{\frac{1}{x}} = \left(\frac{g^{y+\frac{x}{a}}}{g^y} \right)^{\frac{1}{x}} = g^{\frac{1}{a}},$$

which is the solution to the DHI problem instance.

4.12.2 C-Type: Commutative

The C-type of signature structure is described as

$$\sigma_m = \left(g^{ab} H(m)^r, \, g^r \right),$$

where $H : \{0,1\}^* \rightarrow \mathbb{G}$ is a cryptographic hash function and $r \in \mathbb{Z}_p$ is a random number. Here, $(g, g^a, g^b) \in \mathbb{G}$ is an instance of the CDH problem, and the aim is to compute g^{ab}.

Suppose H is set as a random oracle. For a query on m, the simulator responds with

$$H(m) = g^{xb+y},$$

where b is the unknown secret in the problem instance, $x \in \mathbb{Z}_p$ is adaptively chosen, and $y \in \mathbb{Z}_p$ is randomly chosen by the simulator. Because y is randomly chosen from $\mathbb{Z}_p$, $H(m)$ is random in $\mathbb{G}$.

The simulatable and reducible conditions are described as follows:

$$\sigma_m \text{ is } \begin{cases} \text{Simulatable, if } x \neq 0 \\ \\ \text{Reducible,} \quad \text{otherwise} \end{cases}.$$

- The C-type is simulatable if $x \neq 0$ because we can choose a random $r' \in \mathbb{Z}_p$ and set $r = -\frac{a}{x} + r'$. Then, we have

$$\begin{aligned}
g^{ab} H(m)^r &= g^{ab} \left(g^{xb+y} \right)^{-\frac{a}{x}+r'} \\
&= g^{ab} \cdot g^{-ab+xr'b-\frac{ya}{x}+r'y} \\
&= (g^b)^{xr'} \cdot (g^a)^{-\frac{y}{x}} \cdot g^{r'y}, \\
g^r &= g^{-\frac{a}{x}+r'} \\
&= (g^a)^{-\frac{1}{x}} \cdot g^{r'},
\end{aligned}$$

which are computable from g, g^a, g^b and x, y, r'. Since r' is random in $\mathbb{Z}_p$, we have that r is also random in this simulation.
- The C-type is reducible if $x = 0$ because we have

$$\frac{g^{ab} H(m)^r}{(g^r)^y} = \frac{g^{ab}(g^{0b+y})^r}{g^{ry}} = g^{ab},$$

which is the solution to the CDH problem instance.

This type of signature structure can also be proved secure without random oracles if the hash function $H(m)$ can be replaced with a similar function. An example can be found in Section 6.4.

4.12.3 I-Type: Inverse of Group Exponent

The I-type of signature structure is described as

$$\sigma_m = h^{\frac{1}{a-H(m)}},$$

where $H : \{0,1\}^* \to \mathbb{Z}_p$ is a cryptographic hash function. Here, $(g, g^a, g^{a^2}, \cdots, g^{a^q}) \in \mathbb{G}$ is an instance of the q-SDH problem, and the aim is to compute a pair $(s, g^{\frac{1}{a+s}})$ for any $s \in \mathbb{Z}_p$.

Suppose H is set as a random oracle. For a query on m, the simulator responds with

$$H(m) = x \in \mathbb{Z}_p$$

where $x \in \mathbb{Z}_p$ is randomly chosen by the simulator, and thus $H(m)$ is random in $\mathbb{Z}_p$.

In the simulated scheme, suppose the group element h is computed by

$$h = g^{(a-x_1)(a-x_2)\cdots(a-x_q)},$$

where a is the unknown secret from the problem instance, and all x_i are randomly chosen by the simulator. The simulatable and reducible conditions are described as follows:

$$\sigma_m \text{ is } \begin{cases} \text{Simulatable, if } x \in \{x_1, x_2, \cdots, x_q\} \\ \\ \text{Reducible, \quad otherwise} \end{cases}.$$

- The I-type is simulatable if $x \in \{x_1, x_2, \cdots, x_q\}$. Without loss of generality, let $x = x_1$. We have

$$
\begin{aligned}
h^{\frac{1}{a-H(m)}} &= g^{\frac{(a-x_1)(a-x_2)\cdots(a-x_q)}{a-H(m)}} \\
&= g^{(a-x_2)(a-x_3)\cdots(a-x_q)} \\
&= \left(g^{a^{q-1}}\right)^{w'_{q-1}} \cdot \left(g^{a^{q-2}}\right)^{w'_{q-2}} \cdot (g^a)^{w'_1} \cdot g^{w'_0},
\end{aligned}
$$

where w_i is the coefficient of a^i for all i in

$$(a-x_2)(a-x_3)\cdots(a-x_q) = a^{q-1}w'_{q-1} + \cdots + a^1 w'_1 + w'_0.$$

- The I-type is reducible if $x \notin \{x_1, x_2, \cdots, x_q\}$. Let $f(a)$ be the polynomial function in $\mathbb{Z}_p[a]$ defined as

$$f(a) = (a-x_1)(a-x_2)\cdots(a-x_q).$$

Since $x \notin \{x_1, x_2, \cdots, x_q\}$, we have $z = f(x) \neq 0$ and

$$\frac{f(a) - f(x)}{a-x}$$

is a polynomial function in a of degree $q-1$, which can be rewritten as

$$\frac{f(a)-f(x)}{a-x} = a^{q-1}w_{q-1} + \cdots + a^1 w_1 + w_0.$$

Then $g^{\frac{1}{a-H(m)}}$ can be computed by

$$\left(\frac{\sigma_m}{\prod_{i=0}^{q-1}(g^{a^i})^{w_i}}\right)^{\frac{1}{z}} = \left(\frac{g^{\frac{f(a)}{a-H(m)}}}{\prod_{i=0}^{q-1}(g^{a^i})^{w_i}}\right)^{\frac{1}{z}}$$

$$= \left(\frac{g^{\frac{f(a)-z+z}{a-H(m)}}}{g^{\sum_{i=0}^{q-1}a^i w_i}}\right)^{\frac{1}{z}}$$

$$= \left(\frac{g^{\frac{f(a)-z}{a-H(m)}} \cdot g^{\frac{z}{a-H(m)}}}{g^{\sum_{i=0}^{q-1}a^i w_i}}\right)^{\frac{1}{z}}$$

$$= \left(g^{\frac{z}{a-H(m)}}\right)^{\frac{1}{z}}$$

$$= g^{\frac{1}{a-H(m)}}.$$

The pair $\left(-H(m), g^{\frac{1}{a-H(m)}}\right)$ is the solution to the q-SDH problem instance.

In this structure, it is important to have all values in $\{x_1, x_2, \cdots, x_q\}$ also random and independent of $\mathbb{Z}_p$. Otherwise, the adversary will be able to distinguish the simulation when most queries are answered with hash values from $\{x_1, x_2, \cdots, x_q\}$. For example, in a digital signature scheme, suppose the adversary makes $q+1$ hash queries to the random oracle and q signature queries to the simulator. It is required that q out of $q+1$ hash queries must be answered with values from $\{x_1, x_2, \cdots, x_q\}$ to simulate signatures. For example, if $\{H(m_1), H(m_2), \cdots, H(m_q)\} = \{1, 2, \cdots, q\}$, the simulator cannot simulate the random oracle correctly, because the set $\{H(m_1), H(m_2), \cdots, H(m_q)\}$ are not random in $\mathbb{Z}_p$.

4.13 Examples of Incorrect Security Reductions

In a security reduction, the malicious adversary can utilize what it knows (scheme algorithm, reduction algorithm, and how to solve all computational hard problems) to distinguish the given scheme or find a way to launch a useless attack on the scheme. In this section, we give three examples to explain why security reductions fail. Note that the security reductions in our given examples are incorrect but this does not mean that the proposed schemes are insecure. Actually, all the schemes in our examples can be proved secure with other security reductions.

4.13.1 Example 1: Distinguishable

SysGen: The system parameter generation algorithm takes as input a security parameter λ. It chooses a pairing group $\mathbb{PG} = (\mathbb{G}, \mathbb{G}_T, g, p, e)$, selects a cryptographic hash function $H : \{0,1\}^* \to \mathbb{Z}_p$, and returns the system parameters $SP = (\mathbb{PG}, H)$.

KeyGen: The key generation algorithm takes as input the system parameters SP. It chooses random numbers $\alpha, \beta, \gamma \in \mathbb{Z}_p$, computes $g_1 = g^\alpha, g_2 = g^\beta, g_3 = g^\gamma$, and returns a public/secret key pair (pk, sk) as follows:

$$pk = (g_1, g_2, g_3) = (g^\alpha, g^\beta, g^\gamma),$$
$$sk = (\alpha, \beta, \gamma).$$

Sign: The signing algorithm takes as input a message $m \in \mathbb{Z}_p$, the secret key sk, and the system parameters SP. It computes the signature σ_m on m as

$$\sigma_m = g^{\frac{1}{\alpha + m\beta + H(m)\gamma}}.$$

Verify: The verification algorithm takes as input a message-signature pair (m, σ_m), the public key pk, and the system parameters SP. It accepts the signature if

$$e\left(\sigma_m, g_1 g_2^m g_3^{H(m)}\right) = e(g, g).$$

Theorem 4.13.1.1 *Suppose the hash function H is a random oracle. If the 1-SDH problem is hard, the proposed scheme is provably secure in the EU-CMA security model with only two signature queries, where the adversary must select two messages m_1, m_2 for signature queries before making hash queries to the random oracle.*

Incorrect Proof. Suppose there exists an adversary $\mathscr{A}$ who can break the proposed scheme in the corresponding security model. We construct a simulator $\mathscr{B}$ to solve the 1-SDH problem. Given as input a problem instance (g, g^a) over the pairing group $\mathbb{PG}$, $\mathscr{B}$ controls the random oracle, runs $\mathscr{A}$, and works as follows.

Setup. Let $SP = \mathbb{PG}$ and H be the random oracle controlled by the simulator. The simulator randomly chooses x_1, x_2, x_3, y from $\mathbb{Z}_p$ and sets the secret key as

$$\alpha = x_1 a, \quad \beta = x_2 a + y, \quad \gamma = x_3 a,$$

where a is the unknown random number in the instance of the hard problem. The corresponding public key is

$$(g_1, g_2, g_3) = \left((g^a)^{x_1}, \ (g^a)^{x_2} g^y, \ (g^a)^{x_3}\right),$$

where all group elements are computable.

Selection. Let the message space be $\mathbb{Z}_p$. The adversary selects two messages m_1, m_2 for signature queries.

H-Query. The adversary makes hash queries in this phase. $\mathcal{B}$ prepares a hash list to record all queries and responses as follows, where the hash list is empty at the beginning.

- For a hash query on $m_i \in \{m_1, m_2\}$, the simulator computes w_i such that

$$x_1 + x_2 m_i + x_3 w_i = 0,$$

  and sets $H(m_i) = w_i$ as the response to the hash query on m_i.
- For a hash query on $m \notin \{m_1, m_2\}$, the simulator randomly chooses $w \in \mathbb{Z}_p$ and sets $H(m) = w$ as the response to the hash query on m.

The corresponding pair $(m, H(m))$ is added to the hash list.

Query. For a signature query on $m \in \{m_1, m_2\}$, the simulator computes

$$\sigma_m = g^{\frac{1}{ym}}$$

as the signature of the message m. Let $H(m) = w$. According to the random oracle, we have $x_1 + x_2 m + x_3 w = 0$ and

$$g^{\frac{1}{\alpha + m\beta + H(m)\gamma}} = g^{\frac{1}{x_1 a + (x_2 a + y)m + x_3 H(m)a}} = g^{\frac{1}{a(x_1 + x_2 m + x_3 w) + ym}} = g^{\frac{1}{ym}}.$$

Therefore, σ_m is a valid signature of the message m.

Forgery. The adversary returns a forged signature σ_{m^*} on some m^*, where

$$\sigma_{m^*} = g^{\frac{1}{\alpha + m^*\beta + H(m^*)\gamma}}.$$

Let $H(m^*) = w^*$. Since $m^* \notin \{m_1, m_2\}$, we must have $x_1 + x_2 m^* + x_3 w^* \neq 0$. Rewrite

$$\alpha + m^*\beta + H(m^*)\gamma = (x_1 + m^* x_2 + w^* x_3)a + ym^*,$$

and then

$$\left(\frac{ym^*}{x_1 + m^* x_2 + w^* x_3}, \ g^{\frac{x_1 + m^* x_2 + w^* x_3}{\alpha + m^*\beta + H(m^*)\gamma}} \right) = \left(s, g^{\frac{1}{a+s}} \right)$$

is the solution to the 1-SDH problem instance.

This completes the simulation and the solution. The analysis is omitted here. $\square$

Attack on the security reduction. The queried signature σ_m on the message m is equal to $g^{\frac{1}{ym}}$. Upon receiving the two queried signatures, the adversary finds

$$\left(\sigma_{m_1} \right)^{m_1} = \left(\sigma_{m_2} \right)^{m_2} = g^{\frac{1}{y}}.$$

The simulated scheme is distinguishable from the real scheme, because this event occurs in the real scheme with negligible probability $\frac{1}{p}$. The adversary therefore breaks the security reduction by returning an invalid signature in the forgery query phase. The proposed scheme is therefore not provably secure.

Comments on the technique. In this security reduction, a signature of m is simulatable if and only if the pair $(m, H(m))$ satisfies $x_1 + x_2 m + x_3 H(m) = 0$. Without the use of random oracles, it is hard for the simulator to simulate the two queried signatures on m_1, m_2 if $H(m_1)$ and $H(m_2)$ cannot be controlled by the simulator. This is the advantage of using random oracles in the security reduction.

4.13.2 Example 2: Useless Attack by Public Key

SysGen: The system parameter generation algorithm takes as input a security parameter λ. It chooses a pairing group $\mathbb{PG} = (\mathbb{G}, \mathbb{G}_T, g, p, e)$ and returns the system parameters $SP = \mathbb{PG}$.

KeyGen: The key generation algorithm takes as input the system parameters SP. It chooses random numbers $\alpha, \beta, \gamma \in \mathbb{Z}_p$, computes $g_1 = g^\alpha, g_2 = g^\beta, g_3 = g^\gamma$, and returns a public/secret key pair (pk, sk) as follows:

$$pk = (g_1, g_2, g_3) = (g^\alpha, g^\beta, g^\gamma),$$
$$sk = (\alpha, \beta, \gamma).$$

Sign: The signing algorithm takes as input a message $m \in \mathbb{Z}_p$, the secret key sk, and the system parameters SP. It chooses a random number $r \in \mathbb{Z}_p$ and computes the signature σ_m on m as

$$\sigma_m = (\sigma_1, \sigma_2) = \left(r, \ g^{\frac{1}{\alpha + m\beta + r\gamma}} \right).$$

Verify: The verification algorithm takes as input a message-signature pair (m, σ_m), the public key pk, and the system parameters SP. It accepts the signature if

$$e\left(\sigma_2, g_1 g_2^m g_3^{\sigma_1} \right) = e(g, g).$$

Theorem 4.13.2.1 *If the 1-SDH problem is hard, the proposed scheme is existentially unforgeable in the key-only security model, where the adversary is not allowed to query signatures.*

Incorrect Proof. Suppose there exists an adversary $\mathscr{A}$ who can break the proposed scheme in the key-only security model. We construct a simulator $\mathscr{B}$ to solve the 1-SDH problem. Given as input a problem instance (g, g^a) over the pairing group $\mathbb{PG}$, $\mathscr{B}$ runs $\mathscr{A}$ and works as follows.

Setup. Let $SP = \mathbb{PG}$. The simulator randomly chooses x, y from $\mathbb{Z}_p$ and sets the secret key as

$$\alpha = a, \quad \beta = ya + x, \quad \gamma = xa,$$

where a is the unknown random number in the instance of the hard problem. The corresponding public key is

$$(g_1, g_2, g_3) = \left(g^a, \ (g^a)^y g^x, \ (g^a)^x \right),$$

where all group elements are computable.

Forgery. The adversary returns a forged signature σ_{m^*} on some m^*, where

$$\sigma_{m^*} = \left(r^*, g^{\frac{1}{\alpha + m^* \beta + r^* \gamma}} \right).$$

If $1 + ym^* + xr^* = 0$, abort. Otherwise, we have

$$\alpha + m^* \beta + r^* \gamma = (1 + ym^* + xr^*)a + xm^*.$$

The simulator computes

$$\left(\frac{xm^*}{1 + ym^* + xr^*}, \ g^{\frac{1 + ym^* + xr^*}{\alpha + m^* \beta + r^* \gamma}} \right) = \left(s, g^{\frac{1}{a+s}} \right),$$

which is the solution to the 1-SDH problem instance.

This completes the simulation and the solution. The analysis is omitted here. $\square$

Attack on the security reduction. The adversary is able to break the security reduction and returns a useless forgery that cannot be reduced to solving the underlying hard problem, upon receiving the public key from the simulator.

The above security reduction is correct if and only if the adversary has no advantage in picking (m^*, r^*) satisfying $1 + ym^* + xr^* = 0$. Otherwise, the forged signature will be a useless attack. Unfortunately, from the reduction algorithm and the received public key, the computationally unbounded adversary knows how α, β, γ in the public key will be simulated and then knows how to compute x, y from the received public key following the functions described in the reduction algorithm. That is,

$$\alpha = a, \quad \beta = ya + x, \quad \gamma = xa.$$

To be precise, the adversary knows a by solving the DL problem in the problem instance (g, g^α), knows x by solving the DL problem in the problem instance (g^α, g^γ) and knows $ya + x$ by solving the DL problem in the problem instance (g, g^β), where

$$x = \frac{\gamma}{\alpha}, \quad y = \frac{\beta - \frac{\gamma}{\alpha}}{\alpha}.$$

Then, the adversary breaks the security reduction by returning a forged signature $\left(r^*, g^{\frac{1}{\alpha + m^* \beta + r^* \gamma}} \right)$ on the message m^* with a particular number r^* satisfying

$$1 + \frac{\beta - \frac{\gamma}{\alpha}}{\alpha} \cdot m^* + \frac{\gamma}{\alpha} \cdot r^* = 0.$$

That is, r^* is equal to

$$r^* = -\frac{1 + xm^*}{y} \bmod p.$$

The forged signature is useless for the simulator because $1 + ym^* + xr^* = 0$. The proposed scheme is therefore not provably secure.

Unbounded computational power revisited. The above attack is based on the assumption that the adversary, who has unbounded computational power, knows how to compute α, β, γ from the public key. That is, the adversary knows how to solve the DL problem, which is harder than the 1-SDH problem. This example raises an interesting question. Can this security reduction be secure against an adversary who cannot solve the 1-SDH problem? This question is not easy to answer. The answer "yes" requires us to prove that the adversary has no advantage in finding (m^*, r^*) such that $1 + ym^* + xr^* = 0$ from g^a, g^{ya+x}, and g^{xa}. Actually, the adversary does not need to solve the DL problem. An equivalent problem is, given $g^\alpha, g^\beta, g^\gamma$, to find (m^*, r^*) such that

$$g^\alpha g^{\beta m^*} g^{\gamma r^*} = g^{\frac{\gamma}{\alpha} m^*},$$

which implies $1 + ym^* + xr^* = 0$. The corresponding proof is rather complicated because we need to prove that the adversary cannot solve this problem if the 1-SDH problem is hard for the adversary. There might be other approaches for the adversary to find (m^*, r^*) such that $1 + ym^* + xr^* = 0$. We must prove that the adversary cannot find (m^*, r^*) in all cases if we want to program a correct reduction. This is why we assume that the adversary has unbounded computational power for simple analysis.

Comments on the technique. In this security reduction, a signature of m is either simulatable or reducible depending on the corresponding random number r. If $1 + ym + xr = 0$, the signature is simulatable. Otherwise, it is reducible. The partition is whether or not $1 + ym + xr = 0$ in the given signature, and it must be hard for the adversary to find it.

4.13.3 Example 3: Useless Attack by Signature

SysGen: The system parameter generation algorithm takes as input a security parameter λ. It chooses a pairing group $\mathbb{PG} = (\mathbb{G}, \mathbb{G}_T, g, p, e)$. The algorithm returns the system parameters $SP = \mathbb{PG}$.

KeyGen: The key generation algorithm takes as input the system parameters SP. It chooses random numbers $\alpha_0, \alpha_1 \in \mathbb{Z}_p$, computes $g_0 = g^{\alpha_0}, g_1 = g^{\alpha_1}$, and returns a public/secret key pair (pk, sk) as follows:

$$pk = (g_0, g_1) = (g^{\alpha_0}, g^{\alpha_1}),$$
$$sk = (\alpha_0, \alpha_1).$$

Sign: The signing algorithm takes as input a message $m \in \mathbb{Z}_p$, the secret key sk, and the system parameters SP. It chooses a random coin $c \in \{0,1\}$ and computes the signature σ_m on m as

$$\sigma_m = g^{\frac{1}{\alpha_c + m}}.$$

Verify: The verification algorithm takes as input a message-signature pair (m, σ_m), the public key pk, and the system parameters SP. It accepts the signature if

$$e(\sigma_m, g_0 g^m) = e(g, g) \quad \text{or} \quad e(\sigma_m, g_1 g^m) = e(g, g).$$

Theorem 4.13.3.1 *If the 1-SDH problem is hard, the proposed scheme is provably secure in the EU-CMA security model with only one signature query.*

Incorrect Proof. Suppose there exists an adversary $\mathcal{A}$ who can break the proposed scheme in the corresponding security model. We construct a simulator $\mathcal{B}$ to solve the 1-SDH problem. Given as input a problem instance (g, g^a) over the pairing group $\mathbb{PG}$, $\mathcal{B}$ runs $\mathcal{A}$ and works as follows.

Setup. Let $SP = \mathbb{PG}$. The simulator randomly chooses $x \in \mathbb{Z}_p, b \in \{0,1\}$ and sets the public key as

$$(g^{\alpha_0}, g^{\alpha_1}) = \begin{cases} (g^x, g^a), & \text{if } b = 0 \\ (g^a, g^x), & \text{otherwise} \end{cases},$$

where a is the unknown random number in the instance of the hard problem.

Query. For a signature query on m, the simulator computes

$$\sigma_m = g^{\frac{1}{x+m}} = g^{\frac{1}{\alpha_b + m}}.$$

σ_m is a valid signature because either $e(\sigma_m, g_0 g^m) = e(g, g)$ or $e(\sigma_m, g_1 g^m) = e(g, g)$.

Forgery. The adversary returns a forged signature σ_{m^*} on some m^*, where

$$\sigma_{m^*} = g^{\frac{1}{\alpha_{c^*} + m^*}}.$$

If $c^* = b$, abort. Otherwise, we have $\alpha_{c^*} = a$ and then

$$(m^*, \sigma^*) = \left(s, g^{\frac{1}{a+s}}\right)$$

is the solution to the 1-SDH problem instance.

This completes the simulation and the solution. The analysis is omitted here. $\quad\square$

Comments on the technique. In this security reduction, the simulator programs the simulation in such a way that any signature of a message computed with α_b is simulatable while any signature of a message computed with α_{1-b} is reducible. The partition thus is based on the value b. If the adversary does not know the value b, the forged signature with an adaptive choice α from $\{\alpha_0, \alpha_1\}$ will be reducible with probability $\Pr[c^* = 1 - b] = 1/2$. The partition b is secretly chosen by the simulator and assumed to be unknown to the adversary.

Attack on the security reduction. However, the adversary is able to break the security reduction and returns a useless forgery, upon receiving the simulated signature from the simulator. Given the reduction algorithm and the simulated signature from the simulator, the adversary knows which α was used in the signature generation by verifying the queried signature and thus knows b, and knows how to generate a forged signature that is useless. Therefore, the security reduction cannot solve the 1-SDH problem.

4.14 Examples of Correct Security Reductions

In this section, we give three examples to introduce how to program a correct security reduction. These examples are one-time signature schemes where each proposed scheme can generate one signature at most. We choose one-time signature schemes as examples because it is easy to program correct security reductions, especially the correctness analysis.

4.14.1 One-Time Signature with Random Oracles

SysGen: The system parameter generation algorithm takes as input a security parameter λ. It chooses a cyclic group $(\mathbb{G}, p, g)$, selects a cryptographic hash function $H: \{0,1\}^* \rightarrow \mathbb{Z}_p$, and returns the system parameters $SP = (\mathbb{G}, p, g, H)$.

KeyGen: The key generation algorithm takes as input the system parameters SP. It chooses random numbers $\alpha, \beta \in \mathbb{Z}_p$, computes $g_1 = g^\alpha, g_2 = g^\beta$, and returns a one-time public/secret key pair (opk, osk) as follows:

$$opk = (g_1, g_2), \quad osk = (\alpha, \beta).$$

Sign: The signing algorithm takes as input a message $m \in \{0,1\}^*$, the secret key osk, and the system parameters SP. It computes the signature σ_m on m as

$$\sigma_m = \alpha + H(m) \cdot \beta \mod p.$$

> **Verify:** The verification algorithm takes as input a message-signature pair (m, σ_m), the public key opk, and the system parameters SP. It accepts the signature if
> $$g^{\sigma_m} = g_1 g_2^{H(m)}.$$

Theorem 4.14.1.1 *Suppose the hash function H is a random oracle. If the DL problem is hard, the proposed one-time signature scheme is provably secure in the EU-CMA security model with only one signature query and reduction loss q_H, where q_H is the number of hash queries to the random oracle.*

Proof Idea. Let (g, g^a) be an instance of the DL problem that the simulator receives. To solve the DL problem with the forged signature, the simulation should satisfy the following conditions.

- Both α and β must be simulated with a. Otherwise, it is impossible to have both reducible signatures and simulatable signatures in the simulation. That is, all signatures will be either reducible or simulatable.
- The forged signature on the message m^* is reducible if $\alpha + H(m^*)\beta$ contains a. When α, β are both simulated with a, we have $\alpha + H(m^*)\beta$ for a random value $H(m^*)$ contains a except with negligible probability.
- The queried signature on the queried message m is simulatable if $\alpha + H(m)\beta$ does not contain a. When α, β are both simulated with a, to make sure that a can be removed in this queried signature, $H(m)$ must be very special and related to the setting of α, β.

Proof. Suppose there exists an adversary $\mathscr{A}$ who can break the one-time signature scheme in the EU-CMA security model with only one signature query. We construct a simulator $\mathscr{B}$ to solve the DL problem. Given as input a problem instance (g, g^a) over the cyclic group $(\mathbb{G}, p, g)$, $\mathscr{B}$ controls the random oracle, runs $\mathscr{A}$, and works as follows.

Setup. Let $SP = (\mathbb{G}, p, g)$ and H be set as a random oracle controlled by the simulator. The simulator randomly chooses $x, y \in \mathbb{Z}_p$ and sets the secret key as

$$\alpha = a, \quad \beta = -\frac{a}{x} + y.$$

The public key is

$$opk = (g_1, g_2) = \left(g^a, (g^a)^{-\frac{1}{x}} g^y \right),$$

which can be computed from the problem instance and the chosen parameters.

H-Query. The adversary makes hash queries in this phase. Before receiving queries from the adversary, $\mathscr{B}$ randomly chooses an integer $i^* \in [1, q_H]$, where q_H denotes the number of hash queries to the random oracle. Then, $\mathscr{B}$ prepares a hash list to record all queries and responses as follows, where the hash list is empty at the beginning.

For a query on m_i, if m_i is already in the hash list, $\mathcal{B}$ responds to this query following the hash list. Otherwise, let m_i be the i-th new queried message. $\mathcal{B}$ randomly chooses $w_i \in \mathbb{Z}_p$ and sets $H(m_i)$ as

$$\begin{cases} H(m_i) = x & \text{if } i = i^* \\ H(m_i) = w_i & \text{otherwise} \end{cases} .$$

Then, $\mathcal{B}$ responds to this query with $H(m_i)$ and adds $(m_i, H(m_i))$ to the hash list.

Query. The adversary makes a signature query on m. If m is not the i^*-th queried message in the hash list, abort. Otherwise, $\mathcal{B}$ computes σ_m as

$$\sigma_m = xy \bmod p.$$

Since $H(m) = H(m_{i^*}) = x$, we have

$$\sigma_m = \alpha + H(m)\beta = a + x\left(-\frac{a}{x} + y\right) = xy,$$

which is a valid signature of m.

Forgery. The adversary returns a forged signature σ_{m^*} on some m^*. Since $H(m^*) = w^* \neq H(m) = x$, we have

$$\sigma_{m^*} = a + w^*\left(-\frac{a}{x} + y\right) = a\frac{x - w^*}{x} + w^*y.$$

$\mathcal{B}$ computes

$$a = \frac{(\sigma_{m^*} - w^*y)x}{x - w^*}$$

as the solution to the DL problem instance.

This completes the simulation and the solution. The correctness is analyzed as follows.

Indistinguishable simulation. The correctness of the simulation has been explained above. The randomness of the simulation includes all random numbers in the key generation and the responses to hash queries. They are

$$a, -\frac{a}{x} + y, \ w_1, \cdots, w_{i^*-1}, x, w_{i^*+1}, \cdots, w_{q_H}.$$

According to the setting of the simulation, where a, x, y, w_i are all randomly chosen, it is easy to see that they are random and independent from the point of view of the adversary. Therefore, the simulation is indistinguishable from the real attack.

Probability of successful simulation and useful attack. If the simulator successfully guesses i^*, the queried signature on the message $m = m_{i^*}$ is simulatable, and the forged signature is reducible because the message chosen for signature query must be different from m_{i^*}. Therefore, the probability of successful simulation and useful attack is $1/q_H$.

Advantage and time cost. Suppose the adversary breaks the scheme with $(t, 1, \varepsilon)$ after making q_H hash queries. The advantage of solving the DL problem is therefore $\frac{\varepsilon}{q_H}$. Let T_s denote the time cost of the simulation. We have $T_s = O(1)$. $\mathscr{B}$ will solve the DL problem with $(t + T_s, \varepsilon/q_H)$.

This completes the proof of the theorem. □

4.14.2 One-Time Signature Without Random Oracles

SysGen: The system parameter generation algorithm takes as input a security parameter λ. It chooses a cyclic group $(\mathbb{G}, p, g)$, selects a cryptographic hash function $H : \{0, 1\}^* \to \mathbb{Z}_p$, and returns the system parameters $SP = (\mathbb{G}, p, g, H)$.

KeyGen: The key generation algorithm takes as input the system parameters SP. It chooses random numbers $\alpha, \beta, \gamma \in \mathbb{Z}_p$, computes $g_1 = g^\alpha, g_2 = g^\beta, g_3 = g^\gamma$, and returns a one-time public/secret key pair (opk, osk) as follows:

$$opk = (g_1, g_2, g_3), \quad osk = (\alpha, \beta, \gamma).$$

Sign: The signing algorithm takes as input a message $m \in \{0, 1\}^*$, the secret key sk, and the system parameters SP. It chooses a random number $r \in \mathbb{Z}_p$ and computes the signature σ_m on m as

$$\sigma_m = (\sigma_1, \sigma_2) = \left(r, \ \alpha + H(m) \cdot \beta + r \cdot \gamma \mod p \right).$$

Verify: The verification algorithm takes as input a message-signature pair (m, σ_m), the public key opk, and the system parameters SP. It accepts the signature if

$$g^{\sigma_2} = g_1 g_2^{H(m)} g_3^{\sigma_1}.$$

Theorem 4.14.2.1 *If the DL problem is hard, the above one-time signature scheme is provably secure in the EU-CMA security model with only one signature query and reduction loss about $L = 1$.*

Proof Idea. Let (g, g^a) be an instance of the DL problem. Let σ_m be the queried signature generated with a random number r, and σ_{m^*} be the forged signature generated with a random number r^*, where

$$\sigma_m = \left(r, \ \alpha + H(m)\beta + r\gamma \right),$$
$$\sigma_{m^*} = \left(r^*, \ \alpha + H(m^*)\beta + r^*\gamma \right).$$

Let $H(m^*) = u \cdot H(m)$ for a number $u \in \mathbb{Z}_p$. If the adversary knows the reduction algorithm and has unbounded computational power, we have the following interesting observations on the simulation of α, β, γ if the security reduction provides only one simulation.

- If α does not contain a, we have that $H(m)\beta + r\gamma$ is simulatable for the simulator. Let $r^* = ru$. We have

$$\sigma_{m^*} = \left(r^*, \alpha + H(m^*)\beta + r^*\gamma\right) = \left(ru, \ \alpha + u\left(H(m)\beta + r\gamma\right)\right)$$

  must be simulatable. Therefore, if the simulation of α does not contain a, the adversary can generate such a signature to launch a useless attack.
- If β does not contain a, we have that $\alpha + r\gamma$ is simulatable for the simulator. Let $r^* = r$. We have

$$\sigma_{m^*} = \left(r^*, \alpha + H(m^*)\beta + r^*\gamma\right) = \left(r, \ \alpha + H(m^*)\beta + r\gamma\right)$$

  must be simulatable. Therefore, if the simulation of β does not contain a, the adversary can generate such a signature to launch a useless attack.
- If only α, β contain a, we have that there exists only one message $H(m)$ whose signature is simulatable. However, the simulator does not know which message $H(m)$ the adversary will query. The probability of successful simulation is then negligible.

With the above analysis, all secret keys must contain a in the simulation. The simulator uses the chosen random number r to make sure that the queried signature is simulatable for any message. It also requires that the adversary cannot find the partition. Otherwise, the forged signature will be useless.

Proof. Suppose there exists an adversary $\mathscr{A}$ who can break the one-time signature scheme in the EU-CMA security model with only one signature query. We construct a simulator $\mathscr{B}$ to solve the DL problem. Given as input a problem instance (g, g^a) over the cyclic group $(\mathbb{G}, g, p)$, $\mathscr{B}$ runs $\mathscr{A}$ and works as follows.

Setup. Let $SP = (\mathbb{G}, p, g, H)$. $\mathscr{B}$ randomly chooses $x_1, x_2, y_1, y_2 \in \mathbb{Z}_p$ and sets the secret key as

$$\alpha = x_1 a + y_1, \ \beta = x_2 a + y_2, \ \gamma = a.$$

The public key is

$$opk = (g_1, g_2, g_3) = \left((g^a)^{x_1} g^{y_1}, \ (g^a)^{x_2} g^{y_2}, \ g^a\right),$$

which can be computed from the problem instance and the chosen parameters.

Query. The adversary makes a signature query on m. $\mathscr{B}$ computes σ_m as

$$\sigma_m = (\sigma_1, \sigma_2) = \left(-x_1 - H(m)x_2, \ y_1 + H(m)y_2\right).$$

Let $r = -x_1 - H(m)x_2$. We have

$$\alpha + H(m)\beta + r\gamma = (x_1 a + y_1) + H(m)(x_2 a + y_2) + ra$$
$$= a(x_1 + H(m)x_2 + r) + y_1 + H(m)y_2$$
$$= y_1 + H(m)y_2.$$

Therefore, σ_m is a valid signature of the message m.

Forgery. The adversary returns a forged signature σ_{m^*} on a message m^*. Let σ_{m^*} be

$$\sigma_{m^*} = (\sigma_1, \sigma_2) = \left(r^*, \ \alpha + H(m^*)\beta + r^*\gamma \right).$$

If $x_1 + H(m^*)x_2 + r^* = 0$, abort. Otherwise, we have

$$\alpha + H(m^*)\beta + r^*\gamma = a(x_1 + H(m^*)x_2 + r^*) + y_1 + H(m^*)y_2.$$

Finally, $\mathscr{B}$ computes

$$a = \frac{\sigma_2 - y_1 - H(m^*)y_2}{x_1 + H(m^*)x_2 + r^*}$$

as the solution to the DL problem instance.

This completes the simulation and the solution. The correctness is analyzed as follows.

Indistinguishable simulation. The correctness of the simulation has been explained above. The randomness of the simulation includes all random numbers in the key generation and the signature generation. They are

$$x_1 a + y_1, \ x_2 a + y_2, \ a, \ -x_1 - H(m)x_2.$$

The simulation is indistinguishable from the real attack because they are random and independent following the analysis below.

Probability of successful simulation and useful attack. There is no abort in the simulation. The forged signature is reducible if $r^* \neq -x_1 - H(m^*)x_2$. To prove that the adversary has no advantage in computing $-x_1 - H(m^*)x_2$, we only need to prove that $-x_1 - H(m^*)x_2$ is random and independent of the given parameters. Since σ_2 in the queried signature can be computed from the secret key and σ_1, we only need to prove that the following elements

$$(\alpha, \beta, \gamma, r, -x_1 - H(m^*)x_2)$$
$$= \left(x_1 a + y_1, \ x_2 a + y_2, \ a, \ -x_1 - H(m)x_2, \ -x_1 - H(m^*)x_2 \right)$$

are random and independent.

According to the simulation, we have

$$(\alpha, \beta, r, -x_1 - H(m^*)x_2) = \left(x_1 a + y_1, \ x_2 a + y_2, \ -x_1 - H(m)x_2, \ -x_1 - H(m^*)x_2 \right),$$

which can be rewritten as

$$\begin{pmatrix} a & 0 & 1\;0 \\ 0 & a & 0\;1 \\ -1 & -H(m) & 0\;0 \\ -1 & -H(m^*) & 0\;0 \end{pmatrix} \begin{pmatrix} x_1 \\ x_2 \\ y_1 \\ y_2 \end{pmatrix}.$$

It is not hard to find that the absolute value of the determinant of the matrix is $|H(m^*) - H(m)|$, which is nonzero. Therefore, we have that $\alpha, \beta, r, -x_1 - H(m^*)x_2$ are random and independent. Combining lemma 4.7.2 with the above result, we have that r^* is random and independent of the given parameters. Therefore, the probability of successful simulation and useful attack is $1 - \frac{1}{p} \approx 1$.

Advantage and time cost. Suppose the adversary breaks the scheme with $(t, 1, \varepsilon)$. Let T_s denote the time cost of the simulation. We have $T_s = O(1)$. $\mathcal{B}$ will solve the DL problem with $(t + T_s, \varepsilon)$.

This completes the proof of the theorem. $\qquad\qquad\qquad\qquad\qquad\qquad\qquad\square$

4.14.3 One-Time Signature with Indistinguishable Partition

The security proof in Theorem 4.14.2.1 is based on the fact that the adversary cannot find the partition $x_1 + H(m^*)x_2 + r^* = 0$ from the given parameters. In this section, we introduce a security proof composed of two different simulations whose partitions are opposite. That is, a signature generated with a random number is simulatable in one simulation and reducible in another simulation. If the adversary cannot distinguish which simulation is adopted by the simulator, any forged signature generated by the adversary will be reducible with probability $\frac{1}{2}$.

Theorem 4.14.3.1 *If the DL problem is hard, the proposed one-time signature scheme in Section 4.14.2 is provably secure in the EU-CMA security model with only one signature query and reduction loss at most $L = 2$.*

Proof. Suppose there exists an adversary $\mathcal{A}$ who can break the one-time signature scheme in the EU-CMA security model with only one signature query. We construct a simulator $\mathcal{B}$ to solve the DL problem. Given as input a problem instance (g, g^a) over the cyclic group $(\mathbb{G}, g, p)$, $\mathcal{B}$ runs $\mathcal{A}$ and works as follows.

$\mathcal{B}$ randomly chooses a secret bit $\mu \in \{0, 1\}$ and programs the simulation in two different ways.

- The reduction for $\mu = 0$ is programmed as follows.
  Setup. Let $SP = (\mathbb{G}, g, p, H)$. $\mathcal{B}$ randomly chooses $x_1, y_1, y_2 \in \mathbb{Z}_p$ and sets the secret key as $\alpha = x_1 a + y_1$, $\beta = 0a + y_2$, $\gamma = a$. The public key is

$$opk = (g_1, g_2, g_3) = \left((g^a)^{x_1} g^{y_1}, \; g^{y_2}, \; g^a \right),$$

which can be computed from the problem instance and the chosen parameters.

Query. The adversary makes a signature query on m. $\mathcal{B}$ computes σ_m as

$$\sigma_m = (\sigma_1, \sigma_2) = \left(-x_1, \ y_1 + H(m)y_2 \right).$$

Let $r = -x_1$. We have

$$\alpha + H(m)\beta + r\gamma = x_1 a + y_1 + H(m)y_2 - x_1 a = y_1 + H(m)y_2,$$

which is a valid signature of the message m.

Forgery. The adversary returns a forged signature σ_{m^*} on some m^*. Let σ_{m^*} be

$$\sigma_{m^*} = (\sigma_1, \sigma_2) = \left(r^*, \ \alpha + H(m^*)\beta + r^*\gamma \right).$$

If $r^* = -x_1$, abort. Otherwise, we have

$$\sigma_2 = \alpha + H(m^*)\beta + r^*\gamma = a(x_1 + r^*) + y_1 + H(m^*)y_2.$$

Finally, $\mathcal{B}$ computes

$$a = \frac{\sigma_2 - y_1 - H(m^*)y_2}{x_1 + r^*}$$

as the solution to the DL problem instance.

- The reduction for $\mu = 1$ is programmed as follows.
  Setup. Let $SP = (\mathbb{G}, g, p, H)$. $\mathcal{B}$ randomly chooses $x_2, y_1, y_2 \in \mathbb{Z}_p$ and sets the secret key as $\alpha = 0a + y_1$, $\beta = x_2 a + y_2$, $\gamma = a$. The public key is

$$opk = (g_1, g_2, g_3) = \left(g^{y_1}, \ (g^a)^{x_2} g^{y_2}, \ g^a \right),$$

which can be computed from the problem instance and the chosen parameters.

Query. The adversary makes a signature query on m. $\mathcal{B}$ computes σ_m as

$$\sigma_m = (\sigma_1, \sigma_2) = \left(-H(m)x_2, \ y_1 + H(m)y_2 \right).$$

Let $r = -H(m)x_2$. We have

$$\alpha + H(m)\beta + r\gamma = y_1 + H(m)(x_2 a + y_2) - H(m)x_2 a = y_1 + H(m)y_2,$$

which is a valid signature of the message m.

Forgery. The adversary returns a forged signature σ_{m^*} on some m^*. Let σ_{m^*} be

$$\sigma_{m^*} = (\sigma_1, \sigma_2) = \left(r^*, \ \alpha + H(m^*)\beta + r^*\gamma \right).$$

If $r^* = -H(m^*)x_2$, abort. Otherwise, we have

$$\sigma_2 = \alpha + H(m^*)\beta + r^*\gamma = a(H(m^*)x_2 + r^*) + y_1 + H(m^*)y_2.$$

Finally, $\mathcal{B}$ computes

$$a = \frac{\sigma_2 - y_1 - H(m^*)y_2}{H(m^*)x_2 + r^*}$$

as the solution to the DL problem instance.

This completes the simulation and the solution. The correctness is analyzed as follows.

Indistinguishable simulation. The correctness of the simulation has been explained above. The randomness of the simulation includes all random numbers in the key generation and the signature generation. They are

$$(\alpha, \beta, \gamma, r) = \begin{cases} \left(x_1 a + y_1,\ 0\ + y_2,\ a\ , -x_1 \right) & \mu = 0 \\ \left(0\ + y_1, x_2 a + y_2,\ a\ , -H(m)x_2 \right) & \mu = 1 \end{cases}.$$

According to the setting of the simulation, where x_1, x_2, y_1, y_2, a are randomly chosen, it is easy to see that they are random and independent from the point of view of the adversary no matter whether $\mu = 0$ or $\mu = 1$. Therefore, the simulation is indistinguishable from the real attack, and the adversary has no advantage in guessing μ from the simulation.

Probability of successful simulation and useful attack. There is no abort in the simulation. Let the random numbers in the queried signature and the forged signature be r and r^*, respectively. We have

- Case $\mu = 0$. The forged signature is reducible if $r^* \neq r$.
- Case $\mu = 1$. The forged signature is reducible if $\frac{r^*}{r} \neq \frac{H(m^*)}{H(m)}$.

Since the two simulations are indistinguishable, and the simulator randomly chooses one of them, the forged signature is therefore reducible with success probability $\Pr[Success]$ described as follows.

$$\begin{aligned} \Pr[Success] &= \Pr[Success|\mu = 0]\Pr[\mu = 0] + \Pr[Success|\mu = 1]\Pr[\mu = 1] \\ &= \Pr[r^* \neq r]\Pr[\mu = 0] + \Pr[r^* \neq rH(m^*)/H(m)]\Pr[\mu = 1] \\ &\geq \Pr[r^* \neq r]\Pr[\mu = 0] + \Pr[r^* = r]\Pr[\mu = 1] \\ &= \Pr[r^* \neq r]\frac{1}{2} + \Pr[r^* = r]\frac{1}{2} \\ &= \frac{1}{2}. \end{aligned}$$

Note that if the adversary returns a forged signature satisfying $r^* \notin \{r, \frac{H(m^*)r}{H(m)}\}$, the signature must be reducible for both cases. Therefore, the probability of successful simulation and useful attack is at least $\frac{1}{2}$.

Advantage and time cost. Suppose the adversary breaks the scheme with $(t, 1, \varepsilon)$. The advantage of solving the DL problem is at least $\frac{\varepsilon}{2}$. Let T_s denote the time cost of the simulation. We have $T_s = O(1)$. $\mathscr{B}$ will solve the DL problem with $\left(t + T_s, \frac{\varepsilon}{2}\right)$.

This completes the proof of the theorem.   □

4.15 Summary of Concepts

In the last section of this chapter, we revisit and classify concepts used in security proofs of public-key cryptography. It is important to fully understand these concepts and master where/how to apply them in a security proof. Note that some concepts, such as advantage and valid ciphertexts, may have different explanations elsewhere in the literature.

4.15.1 Concepts Related to Proof

Various concepts related to "proof" are interpreted differently for different purposes. So far, we have the following proof concepts.

- **Proof by Contradiction.** This concept introduces what is provable security via reduction in public-key cryptography We will revisit preliminaries and some important concepts about proof by contradiction in Section 4.15.2.
- **Security Proof.** A security proof is mainly composed of a reduction algorithm and its correctness analysis. To be precise, the correctness analysis should show that the advantage of solving an underlying hard problem using an adaptive attack by a malicious adversary is non-negligible.
- **Security Reduction.** This is a reduction run by the simulator following the reduction algorithm. A security reduction should introduce how to generate a simulated scheme and how to reduce an attack on this scheme to solving an underlying hard problem. We will revisit some important concepts about security reduction in Section 4.15.3.
- **Simulation.** This is an interaction between the adversary and the simulator who generates a simulated scheme with a problem instance. In comparison with security reduction, simulation focuses on how to program a simulation indistinguishable from the real attack. We will revisit some important concepts about simulation in Section 4.15.4.

A security proof is not a real mathematical proof showing that a proposed scheme is secure. Instead, it merely proposes a reduction algorithm and shows that if there exists an adversary who can break the proposed scheme, we can run the reduction algorithm and reduce the adversary's attack to solving an underlying hard problem. That is, a security proof is an algorithm only. Unfortunately, we cannot demonstrate this reduction algorithm to convince people that the proposed scheme is secure. What we do instead is a theoretical analysis showing that the proposed reduction algorithm indeed works. That is, we can reduce any adaptive attack by the malicious adversary who has unbounded computational power to solving an underlying hard problem with non-negligible advantage.

4.15.2 Preliminaries and Proof by Contradiction

Mathematics is the foundation of modern cryptography. We define mathematical hard problems and construct schemes over mathematical primitives. Each mathematical primitive is generated with an input security parameter λ. The computational complexity of solving a specific mathematical problem P defined over a mathematical primitive can be denoted by $P(\lambda)$, which is dependent on the problem definition and the size of λ. The complexity is also known as the security level. Suppose there are two hard problems A, B defined over the same mathematical primitive, and their security levels are $P_A(\lambda), P_B(\lambda)$, respectively. If $P_A(\lambda)$ is much higher than $P_B(\lambda)$, we say that A is a relatively weak hardness assumption while B is a relatively strong hardness assumption. Here, "weak" is better than "strong." In group-based cryptography, a cyclic group is the mathematical primitive, where the security parameter is the bit length of a group element. The security level of the discrete logarithm problem defined over a cyclic group depends on the implementation of this cyclic group and the input security parameter λ in the group implementation. For example, a modular multiplicative group generated with the security parameter $\lambda = 1,024$ has a security level roughly 2^{80}, while an elliptic curve group generated with the security parameter $\lambda = 1,024$ can have a security level up to 2^{512}.

There are two types of algorithms: deterministic algorithms and probabilistic algorithms, where a probabilistic algorithm is believed to be more efficient than a deterministic algorithm. A probabilistic algorithm is measured by a time cost t and a value $\varepsilon \in [0,1]$, which is either probability or advantage depending on the definition. If t is polynomial and ε is non-negligible, the corresponding algorithm is computationally efficient. Otherwise, if t is exponential or ε is negligible, the corresponding algorithm is computationally inefficient. All algorithms for cryptography can be classified into (1) scheme algorithms for implementing a cryptosystem, (2) attack algorithms for breaking a proposed scheme, (3) solution algorithms for solving a mathematical hard problem, and (4) reduction algorithms for specifying how to reduce an attack on the simulated scheme to solving an underlying hard problem. The probability ε for scheme algorithms must be approximately equal to 1, while the advantage ε for the other three types of algorithms can be non-negligible. A proposed scheme is secure if all attack algorithms are computationally inefficient. A mathematical problem is easy if there exists a computationally efficient solution algorithm, while a mathematical problem is believed to be hard if all known solution algorithms are computationally inefficient. We cannot mathematically prove that a problem is hard but only prove that solving this problem is not easier than solving an existing believed-to-be-hard problem by a reduction.

Proof by contradiction is adopted to prove that a proposed scheme is secure against any adversary in polynomial time with non-negligible advantage. Firstly, we have a mathematical problem that is believed to be hard. Then, we assume that there exists an adversary who can break the proposed scheme, and prove that the adversary's attack can be reduced to solving the underlying hard problem by a security reduction. Finally, we conclude that the proposed scheme is secure because the underlying hard problem becomes easy if the breaking assumption is true.

4.15.3 Security Reduction and Its Difficulty

A security model models attacks as a game played by a challenger and an adversary. It defines what/when the adversary can query and how the adversary wins the game. Every cryptosystem must have a corresponding security model. There may be many security models proposed to define the same security service for a cryptosystem. The reason is that some proposed schemes can only be proved secure in a weak security model, where the adversary's interactions with the scheme are restricted. A strong security model allows the adversary to flexibly and adaptively query more information than a weak security model. Therefore, a strong security model is better than a weak security model. To define a security model for a new cryptosystem, all queries from the adversary that will make the adversary trivially win the game must be forbidden. Otherwise, the adversary can always win the game no matter how the proposed scheme is constructed.

In the security reduction, we begin with the breaking assumption that there exists an adversary who can break the proposed scheme in polynomial time with non-negligible advantage under the corresponding security model. We construct a simulator who uses a given problem instance to generate a simulated scheme and then uses the adversary's attack on the simulated scheme to solve an underlying hard problem. A security reduction is a reduction algorithm only. It merely specifies what the simulator should do in the security reduction. In the security reduction, there always exist a reduction cost and a reduction loss when reducing the adversary's attack to solving an underlying hard problem. A security reduction is a tight reduction if the reduction loss is sub-linear in the number of queries or constant-size, i.e., independent of the number of queries made by the adversary. Otherwise, it is a loose reduction.

The adversary's attack can be classified into four categories: (1) failed attack that cannot break the scheme, (2) successful attack that can break the scheme, (3) useful attack that can be reduced to solving an underlying hard problem, and (4) useless attack that cannot be reduced to solving an underlying hard problem. The adversary may fail in launching a successful attack on the simulated scheme. The adversary's attack on the simulated scheme may be useless. A successful security reduction requires that the adversary's attack is useful, but a successful attack by the adversary cannot guarantee that the attack is useful. A correct security reduction must provide a correctness analysis showing that the advantage of solving an underlying hard problem using the adversary's attack is non-negligible.

In the breaking assumption, there is no restriction on the adversary in breaking the proposed scheme except time and advantage. The adversary is a black-box adversary, who will launch an adaptive attack including adaptive queries and an adaptive output. To be able to calculate the advantage of solving an underlying hard problem, we amplify the black-box adversary into a malicious black-box adversary who has unbounded computational power. A correct security reduction is complicated because we must give a correctness analysis showing that the advantage of solving an underlying hard problem using an adaptive attack from a computationally unbounded adversary is non-negligible. To simplify the correctness analysis of the security reduction, we assume that the adversary knows the scheme algorithm of the proposed scheme, the reduction algorithm, and how to solve all computational hard problems. On the other hand, we can program a security reduction successfully, because the adversary does not know the random number(s) chosen by the simulator, the problem instance given to the simulator, and how to solve an absolutely hard problem.

In the security reduction, the attack by the adversary and the underlying hard problem for security reductions are related. We reduce a computational attack to solving a computational hard problem. For example, in a security reduction for digital signatures, we mainly use the forged signature from the adversary to solve a computational hard problem. We reduce a decisional attack to solving a decisional hard problem. For example, in a security reduction for encryption, we mainly use the guess of the randomly chosen message m_c in the challenge ciphertext to solve a decisional hard problem. With the help of random oracles, in a security reduction for encryption, we can also reduce a decisional attack in the indistinguishability security model to solving a computational hard problem. We stress that each type of reduction is quite different in simulation, solution, and analysis.

4.15.4 Simulation and Its Requirements

The first step of the security reduction is the simulation. The simulator uses the given problem instance to generate a simulated scheme, and may abort in the simulation so that the simulation is not successful. The adversary will launch a failed attack or a successful attack in the simulation. It is not necessary to implement the full simulated scheme. Only those algorithms involved in the responses to queries are desired. The simulated scheme is indistinguishable from the real scheme when correctness and randomness hold. To be precise, all responses to queries, such as signature queries and decryption queries, must be correct. All simulated random numbers (group elements) must be truly random and independent. The indistinguishability is necessary because we only assume that the adversary can break a given scheme that looks like a real scheme from the point of view of the adversary. We cannot guarantee that the adversary will also break the given scheme with the same advantage as breaking the real scheme, if the given scheme is distinguishable from the real scheme.

In a security reduction with random oracles, the simulator controls random oracles and can embed any special integers/elements in responses to hash queries, as long as all responses are uniformly distributed. The simulator controls responses to hash queries to help program the simulation, especially for signature generation and private-key generation in identity-based encryption, without knowing the corresponding secret key. The number of hash queries to random oracles is polynomial. As long as the adversary does not query x to the random oracle, $H(x)$ is random and unknown to the adversary. A hash list is used to record all queries made by the adversary, all responses to hash queries, and all secret states for computing responses.

For digital signatures, most security reductions in the literature program the simulation in such a way that the simulator does not know the corresponding secret key, and the simulator utilizes the forged signature from the adversary to solve an underlying hard problem. All digital signatures in the simulation can be classified into simulatable signatures and reducible signatures. In the simulation, there should be a partition that specifies which signatures are simulatable and which signatures are reducible. If a security reduction is to use the forged signature to solve an underlying hard problem, all queried signatures must be simulatable, and the forged signature must be reducible. The adversary should not be able to find or distinguish the partition from the simulation. Otherwise, the adversary can always choose a simulatable signature as the forged signature so that the forgery is a useless attack.

The simulation is much more complicated for encryption than that for digital signatures. We can program the security reduction to solve either a decisional hard problem or a computational hard problem depending on the proposed scheme and the security reduction. The corresponding security reductions are very different.

- If we program the security reduction to solve a decisional hard problem, we use the adversary's guess of the message in the challenge ciphertext to solve the underlying hard problem. In the corresponding simulation, the target Z from the problem instance must be embedded in the challenge ciphertext in a way that the challenge ciphertext fulfills several conditions. To be precise, if Z is true, the simulated scheme is indistinguishable from the real scheme so that the adversary will guess the encrypted message correctly with probability $\frac{1}{2} + \frac{\varepsilon}{2}$ according to the breaking assumption. Otherwise, it should be as hard for the adversary to break the false challenge ciphertext as it is to break a one-time pad, so that the adversary has success probability only about $\frac{1}{2}$ of guessing the encrypted message. It is not easy to analyze the probability of breaking the false challenge ciphertext when the adversary can make decryption queries. To analyze the probability P_F of breaking the false challenge ciphertext, we need to analyze the probabilities and advantages of $P_F^W, A_F^K, A_F^C, A_F^I$, and P_F^A. In the simulation of encryption schemes, the challenge decryption key can be either known or unknown to the simulator, which is dependent on the proposed scheme and the security reduction.

- If we program a security reduction in the indistinguishability security model to solve a computational hard problem with the help of random oracles, the security reduction is very different from that to solve a decisional hard problem. In particular, the simulator should use one of the hash queries, namely the challenge hash query, to solve the underlying computational hard problem. There is no true/false challenge ciphertext definition in this type of simulation. Before the adversary makes the challenge hash query to the random oracle, the simulation must be indistinguishable from the real scheme, and the adversary must have no advantage in breaking the challenge ciphertext. If these conditions hold, the adversary must make the challenge hash query to the random oracle in order to fulfill the breaking assumption. In this security reduction, we usually program the simulation in such a way that the simulator does not know the challenge decryption key. For CCA security, the hash queries from the adversary must be able to help the decryption simulation. That is, all correct ciphertexts can be decrypted with the correct hash queries, and all incorrect ciphertexts will be rejected according to those hash queries made by the adversary.

In a security reduction for encryption under a decisional hardness assumption, the decryption simulation should be indistinguishable from the real attack if Z is true, and the decryption simulation should not help the adversary break the false challenge ciphertext if Z is false. In a security reduction for encryption under a computational hardness assumption, the decryption simulation should be indistinguishable from the real attack and should not help the adversary distinguish the challenge ciphertext in the simulated scheme from that in the real scheme.

4.15.5 Towards a Correct Security Reduction

A security reduction is merely a reduction algorithm specifying how to reduce the adversary's attack to solving an underlying hard problem, if such an adversary indeed exists. From a security reduction to a correct security reduction, there should be some steps analyzing that the advantage of solving the underlying hard problem with any attack by the adversary is non-negligible. In Figure 4.3, we have given all related steps. They are described as follows.

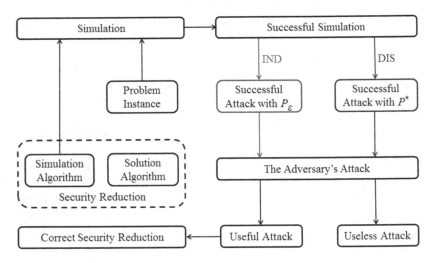

Fig. 4.3 Towards a correct security reduction

- A security reduction mainly consists of a simulation algorithm and a solution algorithm. A simulation is an interaction between the adversary and the simulated scheme that is generated using the problem instance following the simulation algorithm. The simulation is successful if the simulator does not abort during the simulation, where the simulator aborts because it cannot correctly respond to the adversary's queries.

- If the simulation is successful, the adversary will launch an attack on the simulated scheme. The attack is a successful attack with a certain probability, depending on the simulation and the reduction algorithm. To be precise, if the simulated scheme is indistinguishable (IND) from the real scheme, the adversary should launch a successful attack on the simulated scheme with probability P_ε defined in the breaking assumption. If the simulated scheme is distinguishable (DIS) from the real scheme, the adversary will launch a successful attack on the simulated scheme with malicious probability $P^* \in [0, 1]$, depending on the reduction algorithm and explained as follows.

  - For digital signatures, the adversary will launch a successful attack with probability $P^* = 0$, no matter whether the reduction is by the forged signature or hash queries.
  - For encryption under a decisional hard problem, the adversary will try to launch a successful attack with probability $P^* = P_\varepsilon$ if the simulation is distinguishable because Z is false.
  - For encryption under a computational hard problem, the adversary will try to launch a successful attack with probability $P^* = 0$ if the simulation is distinguishable before the adversary makes the challenge hash query to the random oracle.

- An attack by the adversary, no matter whether it is successful or failed, can be a useful attack depending on the cryptosystem and the reduction algorithm. Only a useful attack can be reduced to solving an underlying hard problem.

  - For digital signatures whose security reductions involve a forged signature, the adversary's attack is useful if the forged signature is reducible.
  - For encryption under a decisional hard problem, an attack is useful if the probability of correctly guessing the message in the true challenge ciphertext is $\frac{1}{2} + \frac{\varepsilon}{2}$, and the probability of correctly guessing the message in the false challenge ciphertext is at most $\frac{1}{2}$ except with negligible advantage.
  - For all cryptosystems whose security reductions involve hash queries, an attack is useful if the hash queries made by the adversary include the challenge hash query that can be used to solve an underlying hard problem.

- Finally, a security reduction is correct if the advantage of solving an underlying hard problem is non-negligible, assuming that the adversary can break the real scheme in polynomial time with non-negligible advantage.

This completes all the steps in a correctness analysis to show that a proposed security reduction is a correct security reduction.

4.15.6 Other Confusing Concepts

There are many concepts associated with the word "model" including security model, standard security model, standard model, random oracle model, and generic group model. They have totally different meanings.

- **Security Model.** A security model is defined for modeling attacks. It is a game played by the adversary and the challenger who generates a scheme for the adversary to attack. Each security model can be seen as an abstracted class of attacks, where we define how the adversary breaks the scheme. The security model should appear in the security definition for a cryptosystem.
- **Standard Security Model.** A cryptosystem can have many security models. One of these security models is selected as the standard security model. The standard security model should be widely accepted and good enough to prove the security of the proposed scheme. We emphasize that the standard security model is not the strongest security model for a cryptosystem.
- **Standard Model.** A standard model is a model of computation where the adversary is only restricted by the amount of time it takes to break a cryptosystem. Differing from the standard model, the random oracle model is a special model that has defined some further restrictions on the adversary.
- **Random Oracle Model.** The random oracle model is not a security model for a cryptosystem but an assumption where at least one hash function is set as a random oracle controlled by the simulator, and the adversary must access the random oracle to know the corresponding hash values. The random oracle model only appears in the security proof.
- **Generic Group Model.** The generic group model is an assumption proposed for analyzing whether a problem defined over cyclic groups is hard or not. In this model, the adversary cannot see the group implementation or any group element, only their encodings. Then, a problem is analyzed to be hard within this assumption. The generic group model only appears in the hardness analysis for a new hard problem.

In a security reduction, we often mention the word "indistinguishable." It is used in two different places.

- **Indistinguishable Security.** In the definition of indistinguishable security for encryption, a random message chosen by the challenger or by the simulator, either m_0 or m_1, is encrypted in the challenge ciphertext. An encryption scheme is indistinguishably secure if the adversary has negligible advantage in guessing the encrypted message in the challenge ciphertext.
- **Indistinguishable Simulation.** The adversary is given a simulated scheme, and we want the adversary to launch an attack on it with the advantage defined in the breaking assumption. This requires that the simulated scheme should be indistinguishable from the real scheme. Otherwise, the adversary could launch any attack which might be failed or successful without any restriction.

Chapter 5
Digital Signatures with Random Oracles

In this chapter, we mainly introduce the BLS scheme [26], the BB^{RO} scheme [20], and the ZSS scheme [104] under the H-Type, the C-Type, and the I-Type structures, respectively. With a random salt, we can modify the BLS scheme into the BLS^+ scheme using a random bit [65] and the $BLS^\#$ scheme using a random number [48] with tight reductions. The same approach can also be applied to the ZSS scheme, where the responses to hash queries are different due to the adoption of the q-SDH assumption. At the end, we introduce the BLS^G scheme, a simplified version of [53], based on the BLS signature scheme with a completely new and tight security reduction without the use of a random salt. The given schemes and/or proofs may be different from the original ones.

5.1 BLS Scheme

SysGen: The system parameter generation algorithm takes as input a security parameter λ. It chooses a pairing group $\mathbb{PG} = (\mathbb{G}, \mathbb{G}_T, g, p, e)$, selects a cryptographic hash function $H : \{0,1\}^* \rightarrow \mathbb{G}$, and returns the system parameters $SP = (\mathbb{PG}, H)$.

KeyGen: The key generation algorithm takes as input the system parameters SP. It randomly chooses $\alpha \in \mathbb{Z}_p$, computes $h = g^\alpha$, and returns a public/secret key pair (pk, sk) as follows:

$$pk = h, \quad sk = \alpha.$$

Sign: The signing algorithm takes as input a message $m \in \{0,1\}^*$, the secret key sk, and the system parameters SP. It returns the signature σ_m on m as

$$\sigma_m = H(m)^\alpha.$$

© Springer International Publishing AG, part of Springer Nature 2018
F. Guo et al., *Introduction to Security Reduction*,
https://doi.org/10.1007/978-3-319-93049-7_5

Verify: The verification algorithm takes as input a message-signature pair (m, σ_m), the public key pk, and the system parameters SP. It accepts the signature if

$$e(\sigma_m, g) = e\big(H(m), h\big).$$

Theorem 5.1.0.1 *Suppose the hash function H is a random oracle. If the CDH problem is hard, the BLS signature scheme is provably secure in the EU-CMA security model with reduction loss $L = q_H$, where q_H is the number of hash queries to the random oracle.*

Proof. Suppose there exists an adversary $\mathscr{A}$ who can (t, q_s, ε)-break the signature scheme in the EU-CMA security model. We construct a simulator $\mathscr{B}$ to solve the CDH problem. Given as input a problem instance (g, g^a, g^b) over the pairing group $\mathbb{PG}$, $\mathscr{B}$ controls the random oracle, runs $\mathscr{A}$, and works as follows.

Setup. Let $SP = \mathbb{PG}$ and H be the random oracle controlled by the simulator. $\mathscr{B}$ sets the public key as $h = g^a$, where the secret key α is equivalent to a. The public key is available from the problem instance.

H-Query. The adversary makes hash queries in this phase. Before receiving queries from the adversary, $\mathscr{B}$ randomly chooses an integer $i^* \in [1, q_H]$, where q_H denotes the number of hash queries to the random oracle. Then, $\mathscr{B}$ prepares a hash list to record all queries and responses as follows, where the hash list is empty at the beginning.

Let the i-th hash query be m_i. If m_i is already in the hash list, $\mathscr{B}$ responds to this query following the hash list. Otherwise, $\mathscr{B}$ randomly chooses w_i from $\mathbb{Z}_p$ and sets $H(m_i)$ as

$$H(m_i) = \begin{cases} g^{b+w_i} & \text{if } i = i^* \\ g^{w_i} & \text{otherwise} \end{cases}.$$

The simulator $\mathscr{B}$ responds to this query with $H(m_i)$ and adds $(i, m_i, w_i, H(m_i))$ to the hash list.

Query. The adversary makes signature queries in this phase. For a signature query on m_i, if m_i is the i^*-th queried message in the hash list, abort. Otherwise, we have $H(m_i) = g^{w_i}$.

$\mathscr{B}$ computes σ_{m_i} as

$$\sigma_{m_i} = (g^a)^{w_i}.$$

According to the signature definition and simulation, we have

$$\sigma_{m_i} = H(m_i)^\alpha = (g^{w_i})^a = (g^a)^{w_i}.$$

Therefore, σ_{m_i} is a valid signature of m_i.

Forgery. The adversary returns a forged signature σ_{m^*} on some m^* that has not been queried. If m^* is not the i^*-th queried message in the hash list, abort. Otherwise, we have $H(m^*) = g^{b+w_{i^*}}$.

According to the signature definition and simulation, we have

$$\sigma_{m^*} = H(m^*)^\alpha = (g^{b+w_{i^*}})^a = g^{ab+aw_{i^*}}.$$

The simulator $\mathscr{B}$ computes

$$\frac{\sigma_{m^*}}{(g^a)^{w_{i^*}}} = \frac{g^{ab+aw_{i^*}}}{(g^a)^{w_{i^*}}} = g^{ab}$$

as the solution to the CDH problem instance.

This completes the simulation and the solution. The correctness is analyzed as follows.

Indistinguishable simulation. The correctness of the simulation has been explained above. The randomness of the simulation includes all random numbers in the key generation and the responses to hash queries. They are

$$a, w_1, \cdots, w_{i^*-1}, b+w_{i^*}, w_{i^*+1}, \cdots, w_{q_H}.$$

According to the setting of the simulation, where a, b, w_i are randomly chosen, it is easy to see that they are random and independent from the point of view of the adversary. Therefore, the simulation is indistinguishable from the real attack.

Probability of successful simulation and useful attack. If the simulator successfully guesses i^*, all queried signatures are simulatable, and the forged signature is reducible because the message m_{i^*} cannot be chosen for a signature query, and it will be used for the signature forgery. Therefore, the probability of successful simulation and useful attack is $\frac{1}{q_H}$ for q_H queries.

Advantage and time cost. Suppose the adversary breaks the scheme with (t, q_s, ε) after making q_H queries to the random oracle. The advantage of solving the CDH problem is therefore $\frac{\varepsilon}{q_H}$. Let T_s denote the time cost of the simulation. We have $T_s = O(q_H + q_s)$, which is mainly dominated by the oracle response and the signature generation. Therefore, $\mathscr{B}$ will solve the CDH problem with $(t+T_s, \varepsilon/q_H)$.

This completes the proof of the theorem. $\qquad\square$

5.2 BLS$^+$ Scheme

SysGen: The system parameter generation algorithm takes as input a security parameter λ. It chooses a pairing group $\mathbb{PG} = (\mathbb{G}, \mathbb{G}_T, g, p, e)$, selects a cryptographic hash function $H : \{0,1\}^* \to \mathbb{G}$, and returns the system parameters $SP = (\mathbb{PG}, H)$.

KeyGen: The key generation algorithm takes as input the system parameters SP. It randomly chooses $\alpha \in \mathbb{Z}_p$, computes $h = g^\alpha$, and returns a public/secret key pair (pk, sk) as follows:

$$pk = h, \quad sk = \alpha.$$

Sign: The signing algorithm takes as input a message $m \in \{0,1\}^*$, the secret key sk, and the system parameters SP. It chooses a random coin $c \in \{0,1\}$ and returns the signature σ_m on m as

$$\sigma_m = (\sigma_1, \sigma_2) = \Big(c, \ H(m,c)^\alpha \Big).$$

We require that the signing algorithm always uses the same random coin c on the message m.

Verify: The verification algorithm takes as input a message-signature pair (m, σ_m), the public key pk, and the system parameters SP. Let $\sigma_m = (\sigma_1, \sigma_2)$. It accepts the signature if

$$e(\sigma_2, \ g) = e\Big(H(m, \sigma_1), \ h \Big).$$

Theorem 5.2.0.1 *Suppose the hash function H is a random oracle. If the CDH problem is hard, the BLS^+ signature scheme is provably secure in the EU-CMA security model with reduction loss $L = 2$.*

Proof. Suppose there exists an adversary $\mathscr{A}$ who can (t, q_s, ε)-break the signature scheme in the EU-CMA security model. We construct a simulator $\mathscr{B}$ to solve the CDH problem. Given as input a problem instance (g, g^a, g^b) over the pairing group $\mathbb{PG}$, $\mathscr{B}$ controls the random oracle, runs $\mathscr{A}$, and works as follows.

Setup. Let $SP = \mathbb{PG}$ and H be the random oracle controlled by the simulator. $\mathscr{B}$ sets the public key as $h = g^a$, where the secret key α is equivalent to a. The public key is available from the problem instance.

H-Query. The adversary makes hash queries in this phase. $\mathscr{B}$ prepares a hash list to record all queries and responses as follows, where the hash list is empty at the beginning.

For a query on (m_i, c_i) where $c_i \in \{0,1\}$, if m_i is already in the hash list, $\mathscr{B}$ responds to this query following the hash list. Otherwise, $\mathscr{B}$ randomly chooses $x_i \in \{0,1\}, y_i, z_i \in \mathbb{Z}_p$ and sets $H(m_i, 0), H(m_i, 1)$ as

$$\begin{cases} H(m_i, 0) = g^{b+y_i}, \ H(m_i, 1) = g^{z_i} : & x_i = 0 \\ H(m_i, 0) = g^{y_i}, \quad H(m_i, 1) = g^{b+z_i} : & x_i = 1 \end{cases}.$$

The simulator $\mathscr{B}$ responds to this query with $H(m_i, c)$ and adds $(m_i, x_i, y_i, z_i, H(m_i, 0), H(m_i, 1))$ to the hash list.

Query. The adversary makes signature queries in this phase. For a signature query on m_i, let the corresponding hashing tuple be $(m_i, x_i, y_i, z_i, H(m_i, 0), H(m_i, 1))$.

$\mathscr{B}$ computes σ_{m_i} as

$$\sigma_{m_i} = \left(c_i, H(m_i, c_i)^\alpha\right) = \begin{cases} \left(1, \ (g^a)^{z_i}\right) : & x_i = 0 \\ \\ \left(0, \ (g^a)^{y_i}\right) : & x_i = 1 \end{cases}.$$

According to the signature definition and simulation, we have

- If $x_i = 0$, then $c_i = 1$ and $H(m_i, c_i)^\alpha = H(m_i, 1)^\alpha = (g^{z_i})^a = (g^a)^{z_i}$.
- Otherwise $x_i = 1$, then $c_i = 0$ and $H(m_i, c_i)^\alpha = H(m_i, 0)^\alpha = (g^{y_i})^a = (g^a)^{y_i}$.

Therefore, σ_{m_i} is a valid signature of m_i.

Forgery. The adversary returns a forged signature σ_{m^*} on some m^* that has not been queried. Let the forged signature be $(\sigma_1^*, \sigma_2^*) = (c^*, H(m^*, c^*)^\alpha)$, and the corresponding hashing tuple be $(m^*, x^*, y^*, z^*, H(m^*, 0), H(m^*, 1))$. If $c^* \neq x^*$, abort. Otherwise, we have $c^* = x^*$ and

$$H(m^*, c^*) = \begin{cases} g^{b+y^*} : & c^* = x^* = 0 \\ \\ g^{b+z^*} : & c^* = x^* = 1 \end{cases}.$$

According to the signature definition and simulation, we have

$$\sigma_2^* = H(m^*, c^*)^\alpha = (g^{b+w^*})^a = g^{ab+aw^*} : \quad w^* = y^* \text{ or } w^* = z^*.$$

The simulator $\mathscr{B}$ computes

$$\frac{\sigma_2^*}{(g^a)^{w^*}} = \frac{g^{ab+aw^*}}{(g^a)^{w^*}} = g^{ab}$$

as the solution to the CDH problem instance.

This completes the simulation and the solution. The correctness is analyzed as follows.

Indistinguishable simulation. The correctness of the simulation has been explained above. The randomness of the simulation includes all random numbers in the key generation, the responses to hash queries, and the signature generation. They are as follows:

$$pk : a,$$
$$H(m_i, 0), H(m_i, 1) : (b + y_i, z_i) \text{ or } (y_i, b + z_i)$$
$$c_i : x_i.$$

According to the setting of the simulation, where a, b, x_i, y_i, z_i are randomly chosen, it is easy to see that they are random and independent from the point of view of the adversary. Therefore, the simulation is indistinguishable from the real attack.

Probability of successful simulation and useful attack. All queried signatures are simulatable, and the forged signature is reducible if $c^* = x^*$. According to the setting, we have

$$\begin{cases} H(m^*, 0) = g^{b+y^*}, \ H(m^*, 1) = g^{z^*} : & x^* = 0 \\ H(m^*, 0) = g^{y^*}, \quad H(m^*, 1) = g^{b+z^*} : & x^* = 1 \end{cases}.$$

The adversary has no advantage in guessing which hash query is answered with b when y^*, z^* are randomly chosen by the simulator. Therefore, x^* is random and unknown to the adversary, so that $c^* = x^*$ holds with probability $\frac{1}{2}$. Therefore, the probability of successful simulation and useful attack is $\frac{1}{2}$.

Advantage and time cost. Suppose the adversary breaks the scheme with (t, q_s, ε) after making q_H queries to the random oracle. The advantage of solving the CDH problem is therefore $\frac{\varepsilon}{2}$. Let T_s denote the time cost of the simulation. We have $T_s = O(q_H + q_s)$, which is mainly dominated by the oracle response and the signature generation. Therefore, $\mathscr{B}$ will solve the CDH problem with $(t + T_s, \varepsilon/2)$.

This completes the proof of the theorem. $\qquad\qquad\qquad\qquad\qquad\qquad\square$

5.3 BLS$^{\#}$ Scheme

SysGen: The system parameter generation algorithm takes as input a security parameter λ. It chooses a pairing group $\mathbb{PG} = (\mathbb{G}, \mathbb{G}_T, g, p, e)$, selects a cryptographic hash function $H : \{0, 1\}^* \to \mathbb{G}$, and returns the system parameters $SP = (\mathbb{PG}, H)$.

KeyGen: The key generation algorithm takes as input the system parameters SP. It randomly chooses $\alpha \in \mathbb{Z}_p$, computes $h = g^{\alpha}$, and returns a public/secret key pair (pk, sk) as follows:

$$pk = h, \ sk = \alpha.$$

Sign: The signing algorithm takes as input a message $m \in \{0, 1\}^*$, the secret key sk, and the system parameters SP. It chooses a random number $r \in \mathbb{Z}_p$ and returns the signature σ_m on m as

$$\sigma_m = (\sigma_1, \sigma_2) = \left(r, \ H(m, r)^{\alpha} \right).$$

We require that the signing algorithm always uses the same random number r for signature generation on the message m.

Verify: The verification algorithm takes as input a message-signature pair (m, σ_m), the public key pk, and the system parameters SP. Let $\sigma_m = (\sigma_1, \sigma_2)$. It accepts the signature if

$$e(\sigma_2, g) = e\Big(H(m, \sigma_1), h\Big).$$

Theorem 5.3.0.1 *Suppose the hash function H is a random oracle. If the CDH problem is hard, the BLS# signature scheme is provably secure in the EU-CMA security model with reduction loss about $L = 1$.*

Proof. Suppose there exists an adversary $\mathscr{A}$ who can (t, q_s, ε)-break the signature scheme in the EU-CMA security model. We construct a simulator $\mathscr{B}$ to solve the CDH problem. Given as input a problem instance (g, g^a, g^b) over the pairing group $\mathbb{PG}$, $\mathscr{B}$ controls the random oracle, runs $\mathscr{A}$, and works as follows.

Setup. Let $SP = \mathbb{PG}$ and H be the random oracle controlled by the simulator. $\mathscr{B}$ sets the public key as $h = g^a$, where the secret key α is equivalent to a. The public key is available from the problem instance.

H-Query. The adversary makes hash queries in this phase. $\mathscr{B}$ prepares a hash list to record all queries and responses as follows, where the hash list is empty at the beginning.

For a query on (m, r) from the adversary where $r \in \mathbb{Z}_p$, if (m, r) is already in the hash list, $\mathscr{B}$ responds to this query following the hash list. Otherwise, it randomly chooses $z \in \mathbb{Z}_p$, responds to this query with $H(m, r) = g^{b+z}$, and adds $(m, r, z, H(m, r), \mathscr{A})$ to the hash list. Here, $\mathscr{A}$ in the tuple means that the query (m, r) is generated by the adversary.

Query. The adversary makes signature queries in this phase. For a signature query on m_i, if there exists a tuple $(m_i, r_i, y_i, H(m_i, r_i), \mathscr{B})$ in the hash list, the simulator uses this tuple to generate the signature. Otherwise, $\mathscr{B}$ randomly chooses $r_i, y_i \in \mathbb{Z}_p$, sets $H(m_i, r_i) = g^{y_i}$, and adds $(m_i, r_i, y_i, H(m_i, r_i), \mathscr{B})$ to the hash list. If (m_i, r_i) was ever generated by the adversary, the simulator aborts.

$\mathscr{B}$ computes σ_{m_i} as

$$\sigma_{m_i} = \Big(r_i, H(m_i, r_i)^\alpha\Big) = \Big(r_i, (g^a)^{y_i}\Big).$$

According to the signature definition and simulation, we have

$$H(m_i, r_i)^\alpha = (g^{y_i})^a = (g^a)^{y_i}.$$

Therefore, σ_{m_i} is a valid signature of m_i.

Forgery. The adversary returns a forged signature σ_{m^*} on some m^* that has not been queried. Let the forged signature be $(\sigma_1^*, \sigma_2^*) = (r^*, H(m^*, r^*)^\alpha)$, and the corresponding hashing tuple be $(m^*, r^*, z^*, H(m^*, r^*))$. We should have

$$H(m^*, r^*) = g^{b+z^*}.$$

According to the signature definition and simulation, we have

$$\sigma_2^* = H(m^*, r^*)^\alpha = (g^{b+z^*})^a = g^{ab+az^*}.$$

The simulator $\mathscr{B}$ computes

$$\frac{\sigma_2^*}{(g^a)^{z^*}} = \frac{g^{ab+az^*}}{(g^a)^{z^*}} = g^{ab}$$

as the solution to the CDH problem instance.

This completes the simulation and the solution. The correctness is analyzed as follows.

Indistinguishable simulation. The correctness of the simulation has been explained above. The randomness of the simulation includes all random numbers in the key generation, the responses to hash queries, and the signature generation. They are as follows:

$$pk : a,$$
$$H(m, r) : z + b \text{ if } r \text{ is chosen by the adversary},$$
$$H(m_i, r_i) : y_i \text{ if } r_i \text{ is chosen by the simulator},$$
$$\text{random number} : r_i.$$

According to the setting of the simulation, where a, b, z, y_i, r_i are randomly chosen, it is easy to see that they are random and independent from the point of view of the adversary. Therefore, the simulation is indistinguishable from the real attack.

Probability of successful simulation and useful attack. The forged signature is reducible, and all queried signatures are simulatable when the random number r_i chosen in the signature query phase is different from all random numbers in the hash query phase. A randomly chosen number is different from all of the numbers in the hash query phase with probability $1 - \frac{q_H}{p}$. Therefore, the probability of successful simulation and useful attack is $(1 - \frac{q_H}{p})^{q_s} \approx 1$.

Advantage and time cost. Suppose the adversary breaks the scheme with (t, q_s, ε) after making q_H queries to the random oracle. The advantage of solving the CDH problem is therefore approximately ε. Let T_s denote the time cost of the simulation. We have $T_s = O(q_H + q_s)$, which is mainly dominated by the oracle response and the signature generation. Therefore, $\mathscr{B}$ will solve the CDH problem with $(t + T_s, \varepsilon)$.

This completes the proof of the theorem. $\qquad\qquad\qquad\qquad\qquad\qquad\qquad\square$

5.4 BB^{RO} Scheme

SysGen: The system parameter generation algorithm takes as input a security parameter λ. It chooses a pairing group $\mathbb{PG} = (\mathbb{G}, \mathbb{G}_T, g, p, e)$, selects a cryptographic hash function $H : \{0,1\}^* \rightarrow \mathbb{G}$, and returns the system parameters $SP = (\mathbb{PG}, H)$.

KeyGen: The key generation algorithm takes as input the system parameters SP. It randomly chooses $g_2 \in \mathbb{G}$, $\alpha \in \mathbb{Z}_p$, computes $g_1 = g^\alpha$, and returns a public/secret key pair (pk, sk) as follows:

$$pk = (g_1, g_2), \quad sk = \alpha.$$

Sign: The signing algorithm takes as input a message $m \in \{0,1\}^*$, the secret key sk, and the system parameters SP. It chooses a random number $r \in \mathbb{Z}_p$ and returns the signature σ_m on m as

$$\sigma_m = (\sigma_1, \sigma_2) = \left(g_2^\alpha H(m)^r, g^r\right).$$

Verify: The verification algorithm takes as input a message-signature pair (m, σ_m), the public key pk, and the system parameters SP. Let $\sigma_m = (\sigma_1, \sigma_2)$. It accepts the signature if

$$e(\sigma_1, g) = e(g_1, g_2) e\left(H(m), \sigma_2\right).$$

Theorem 5.4.0.1 *Suppose the hash function H is a random oracle. If the CDH problem is hard, the BB^{RO} signature scheme is provably secure in the EU-CMA security model with reduction loss $L = q_H$, where q_H is the number of hash queries to the random oracle.*

Proof. Suppose there exists an adversary $\mathscr{A}$ who can (t, q_s, ε)-break the signature scheme in the EU-CMA security model. We construct a simulator $\mathscr{B}$ to solve the CDH problem. Given as input a problem instance (g, g^a, g^b) over the pairing group $\mathbb{PG}$, $\mathscr{B}$ controls the random oracle, runs $\mathscr{A}$, and works as follows.

Setup. Let $SP = \mathbb{PG}$ and H be the random oracle controlled by the simulator. $\mathscr{B}$ sets the public key as

$$g_1 = g^a, \quad g_2 = g^b,$$

where the secret key α is equivalent to a. The public key is available from the problem instance.

H-Query. The adversary makes hash queries in this phase. Before any hash queries are made, $\mathscr{B}$ randomly chooses $i^* \in [1, q_H]$, where q_H denotes the number of hash queries to the random oracle. Then, $\mathscr{B}$ prepares a hash list to record all queries and responses as follows, where the hash list is empty at the beginning.

Let the i-th hash query be m_i. If m_i is already in the hash list, $\mathscr{B}$ responds to this query following the hash list. Otherwise, $\mathscr{B}$ randomly chooses w_i from $\mathbb{Z}_p$ and sets $H(m_i)$ as

$$H(m_i) = \begin{cases} g^{w_i}, & \text{if } i = i^* \\ g^{b+w_i}, & \text{otherwise} \end{cases} .$$

The simulator $\mathscr{B}$ responds to this query with $H(m_i)$ and adds $(i, m_i, w_i, H(m_i))$ to the hash list.

Query. The adversary makes signature queries in this phase. For a signature query on m_i, if m_i is the i^*-th queried message in the hash list, abort. Otherwise, we have $H(m_i) = g^{b+w_i}$.

$\mathscr{B}$ chooses a random $r_i' \in \mathbb{Z}_p$ and computes σ_{m_i} as

$$\sigma_{m_i} = \left((g^a)^{-w_i} \cdot H(m_i)^{r_i'}, \ (g^a)^{-1} g^{r_i'} \right).$$

Let $r_i = -a + r_i'$. According to the signature definition and simulation, we have

$$g_2^\alpha H(m_i)^{r_i} = g^{ab} \cdot (g^{b+w_i})^{-a+r_i'} = (g^a)^{-w_i} \cdot H(m_i)^{r_i'}$$
$$g^{r_i} = g^{-a+r_i'} = (g^a)^{-1} g^{r_i'}.$$

Therefore, σ_{m_i} is a valid signature of m_i.

Forgery. The adversary returns a forged signature σ_{m^*} on some m^* that has not been queried. If m^* is not the i^*-th queried message in the hash list, abort. Otherwise, we have $H(m^*) = g^{w_{i^*}}$.

According to the signature definition and simulation, we have

$$\sigma_{m^*} = (\sigma_1^*, \sigma_2^*) = \left(g_2^\alpha H(m^*)^r, g^r \right) = \left(g^{ab} (g^{w_{i^*}})^r, \ g^r \right).$$

The simulator $\mathscr{B}$ computes

$$\frac{\sigma_1^*}{(\sigma_2^*)^{w_{i^*}}} = \frac{g^{ab}(g^{w_{i^*}})^r}{(g^r)^{w_{i^*}}} = g^{ab}$$

as the solution to the CDH problem instance.

This completes the simulation and the solution. The correctness is analyzed as follows.

Indistinguishable simulation. The correctness of the simulation has been explained above. The randomness of the simulation includes all random numbers in the key generation, the responses to hash queries, and the signature generation. They are as follows:

$$pk : a, b,$$

$$H(m_i) : w_1, \cdots, w_{i^*-1}, b + w_{i^*}, w_{i^*+1}, \cdots, w_{q_H},$$
$$r_i : -a + r'_i.$$

According to the setting of the simulation, where a, b, w_i, r'_i are randomly chosen, it is easy to see that they are random and independent from the point of view of the adversary. Therefore, the simulation is indistinguishable from the real attack.

Probability of successful simulation and useful attack. If the simulator successfully guesses i^*, all queried signatures are simulatable, and the forged signature is reducible because the message m_{i^*} cannot be chosen for a signature query, and it will be used for the signature forgery. Therefore, the probability of successful simulation and useful attack is $\frac{1}{q_H}$ for q_H queries.

Advantage and time cost. Suppose the adversary breaks the scheme with (t, q_s, ε) after making q_H queries to the random oracle. The advantage of solving the CDH problem is therefore $\frac{\varepsilon}{q_H}$. Let T_s denote the time cost of the simulation. We have $T_s = O(q_H + q_s)$, which is mainly dominated by the oracle response and the signature generation. Therefore, $\mathscr{B}$ will solve the CDH problem with $(t + T_s, \varepsilon/q_H)$.

This completes the proof of the theorem. $\qquad\square$

5.5 ZSS Scheme

SysGen: The system parameter generation algorithm takes as input a security parameter λ. It chooses a pairing group $\mathbb{PG} = (\mathbb{G}, \mathbb{G}_T, g, p, e)$, selects a cryptographic hash function $H : \{0,1\}^* \to \mathbb{Z}_p$, and returns the system parameters $SP = (\mathbb{PG}, H)$.

KeyGen: The key generation algorithm takes as input the system parameters SP. It randomly chooses $h \in \mathbb{G}$, $\alpha \in \mathbb{Z}_p$, computes $g_1 = g^\alpha$, and returns a public/secret key pair (pk, sk) as follows:

$$pk = (g_1, h), \quad sk = \alpha.$$

Sign: The signing algorithm takes as input a message $m \in \{0,1\}^*$, the secret key sk, and the system parameters SP. It returns the signature σ_m on m as

$$\sigma_m = h^{\frac{1}{\alpha + H(m)}}.$$

Verify: The verification algorithm takes as input a message-signature pair (m, σ_m), the public key pk, and the system parameters SP. It accepts the signature if

$$e\left(\sigma_m, \, g_1 g^{H(m)}\right) = e(h, g).$$

Theorem 5.5.0.1 *Suppose the hash function H is a random oracle. If the q-SDH problem is hard, the ZSS signature scheme is provably secure in the EU-CMA security model with reduction loss $L = q_H$, where q_H is the number of hash queries to the random oracle.*

Proof. Suppose there exists an adversary $\mathscr{A}$ who can (t, q_s, ε)-break the signature scheme in the EU-CMA security model. We construct a simulator $\mathscr{B}$ to solve the q-SDH problem. Given as input a problem instance $(g, g^a, g^{a^2}, \cdots, g^{a^q})$ over the pairing group $\mathbb{PG}$, $\mathscr{B}$ controls the random oracle, runs $\mathscr{A}$, and works as follows.

Setup. Let $SP = \mathbb{PG}$ and H be the random oracle controlled by the simulator. $\mathscr{B}$ randomly chooses $w_1, w_2, \cdots, w_q$ from $\mathbb{Z}_p$ and sets the public key as

$$g_1 = g^a, \quad h = g^{(a+w_1)(a+w_2)\cdots(a+w_q)},$$

where the secret key α is equivalent to a. This requires $q = q_H$, where q_H denotes the number of hash queries to the random oracle. The public key can be computed from the problem instance and the chosen parameters.

H-Query. The adversary makes hash queries in this phase. Before any hash queries are made, $\mathscr{B}$ randomly chooses $i^* \in [1, q_H]$ and an integer $w^* \in \mathbb{Z}_p$. Then, $\mathscr{B}$ prepares a hash list to record all queries and responses as follows, where the hash list is empty at the beginning.

Let the i-th hash query be m_i. If m_i is already in the hash list, $\mathscr{B}$ responds to this query following the hash list. Otherwise, $\mathscr{B}$ sets $H(m_i)$ as

$$H(m_i) = \begin{cases} w^*, & \text{if } i = i^* \\ w_i, & \text{otherwise} \end{cases}.$$

The simulator $\mathscr{B}$ responds to this query with $H(m_i)$ and adds $(i, m_i, w_i, H(m_i))$ or $(i^*, m_{i^*}, w^*, H(m_{i^*}))$ to the hash list. Notice that $w^* \neq w_{i^*}$ in our simulation.

Query. The adversary makes signature queries in this phase. For a signature query on m_i, if m_i is the i^*-th queried message in the hash list, abort. Otherwise, we have $H(m_i) = w_i$.

$\mathscr{B}$ computes σ_{m_i} as

$$\sigma_{m_i} = g^{(a+w_1)\cdots(a+w_{i-1})(a+w_{i+1})\cdots(a+w_q)}$$

using $g, g^a, \cdots, g^{a^q}, w_1, w_2, \cdots, w_q$.

According to the signature definition and simulation, we have

$$\sigma_{m_i} = h^{\frac{1}{\alpha+H(m_i)}} = g^{\frac{(a+w_1)\cdots(a+w_i)\cdots(a+w_q)}{a+w_i}} = g^{(a+w_1)\cdots(a+w_{i-1})(a+w_{i+1})\cdots(a+w_q)}.$$

Therefore, σ_{m_i} is a valid signature of m_i.

Forgery. The adversary returns a forged signature σ_{m^*} on some m^* that has not been queried. If m^* is not the i^*-th queried message in the hash list, abort. Otherwise, we have $H(m^*) = w^*$.

According to the signature definition and simulation, we have

$$\sigma_{m^*} = h^{\frac{1}{a+H(m^*)}} = g^{\frac{(a+w_1)(a+w_2)\cdots(a+w_q)}{a+w^*}},$$

which can be rewritten as

$$g^{f(a)+\frac{d}{a+w^*}},$$

where $f(a)$ is a $(q-1)$-degree polynomial function in a, and d is a nonzero integer. The simulator $\mathscr{B}$ computes

$$\left(\frac{\sigma_{m^*}}{g^{f(a)}}\right)^{\frac{1}{d}} = \left(\frac{g^{f(a)+\frac{d}{a+w^*}}}{g^{f(a)}}\right)^{\frac{1}{d}} = g^{\frac{1}{a+w^*}}$$

and outputs $\left(w^*, g^{\frac{1}{a+w^*}}\right)$ as the solution to the q-SDH problem instance.

This completes the simulation and the solution. The correctness is analyzed as follows.

Indistinguishable simulation. The correctness of the simulation has been explained above. The randomness of the simulation includes all random numbers in the key generation and the responses to hash queries. They are as follows:

$$pk : a, \ (a+w_1)(a+w_2)\cdots(a+w_q),$$
$$H(m_i) : w_1, \cdots, w_{i^*-1}, w^*, w_{i^*+1}, \cdots, w_{q_H}.$$

According to the setting of the simulation, where $a, w_1, w_2, \cdots, w_q, w^*$ are randomly chosen, it is easy to see that they are random and independent from the point of view of the adversary. Therefore, the simulation is indistinguishable from the real attack.

Probability of successful simulation and useful attack. If the simulator successfully guesses i^*, all queried signatures are simulatable, and the forged signature is reducible because the message m_{i^*} cannot be chosen for a signature query, and it will be used for the signature forgery. Therefore, the probability of successful simulation and useful attack is $\frac{1}{q_H}$ for q_H queries.

Advantage and time cost. Suppose the adversary breaks the scheme with (t, q_s, ε) after making q_H queries to the random oracle. The advantage of solving the q-SDH problem is therefore $\frac{\varepsilon}{q_H}$. Let T_s denote the time cost of the simulation. We have $T_s = O(q_s q_H)$, which is mainly dominated by the signature generation. Therefore, $\mathscr{B}$ will solve the q-SDH problem with $(t + T_s, \frac{\varepsilon}{q_H})$.

This completes the proof of the theorem. $\square$

5.6 ZSS$^+$ Scheme

SysGen: The system parameter generation algorithm takes as input a security parameter λ. It chooses a pairing group $\mathbb{PG} = (\mathbb{G}, \mathbb{G}_T, g, p, e)$, selects a cryptographic hash function $H : \{0,1\}^* \to \mathbb{Z}_p$, and returns the system parameters $SP = (\mathbb{PG}, H)$.

KeyGen: The key generation algorithm takes as input the system parameters SP. It randomly chooses $h \in \mathbb{G}$, $\alpha \in \mathbb{Z}_p$, computes $g_1 = g^\alpha$, and returns a public/secret key pair (pk, sk) as follows:

$$pk = (g_1, h), \quad sk = \alpha.$$

Sign: The signing algorithm takes as input a message $m \in \{0,1\}^*$, the secret key sk, and the system parameters SP. It chooses a random coin $c \in \{0,1\}$ and returns the signature σ_m on m as

$$\sigma_m = (\sigma_1, \sigma_2) = \left(c, \ h^{\frac{1}{\alpha + H(m,c)}} \right).$$

We require that the signing algorithm always uses the same random coin c on the message m.

Verify: The verification algorithm takes as input a message-signature pair (m, σ_m), the public key pk, and the system parameters SP. Let $\sigma_m = (\sigma_1, \sigma_2)$. It accepts the signature if

$$e\left(\sigma_2, \ g_1 g^{H(m,\sigma_1)} \right) = e(h, g).$$

Theorem 5.6.0.1 *Suppose the hash function H is a random oracle. If the q-SDH problem is hard, the ZSS$^+$ signature scheme is provably secure in the EU-CMA security model with reduction loss $L = 2$.*

Proof. Suppose there exists an adversary $\mathscr{A}$ who can (t, q_s, ε)-break the signature scheme in the EU-CMA security model. We construct a simulator $\mathscr{B}$ to solve the q-SDH problem. Given as input a problem instance $(g, g^a, g^{a^2}, \cdots, g^{a^q})$ over the pairing group $\mathbb{PG}$, $\mathscr{B}$ controls the random oracle, runs $\mathscr{A}$, and works as follows.

Setup. Let $SP = \mathbb{PG}$ and H be the random oracle controlled by the simulator. $\mathscr{B}$ randomly chooses $y_1, y_2, \cdots, y_q, w$ from $\mathbb{Z}_p$ and sets the public key as

$$g_1 = g^a, \quad h = g^{w(a+y_1)(a+y_2)\cdots(a+y_q)},$$

where the secret key α is equivalent to a. This requires $q = q_H$, where q_H denotes the number of hash queries. The public key can be computed from the problem instance and the chosen parameters.

H-Query. The adversary makes hash queries in this phase. $\mathcal{B}$ prepares a hash list to record all queries and responses as follows, where the hash list is empty at the beginning.

For a query on (m_i, c_i) where $c_i \in \{0, 1\}$, if m_i is already in the hash list, $\mathcal{B}$ responds to this query following the hash list. Otherwise, $\mathcal{B}$ randomly chooses $x_i \in \{0, 1\}, y_i, z_i \in \mathbb{Z}_p$ and sets $H(m_i, 0), H(m_i, 1)$ as follows:

$$\begin{cases} H(m_i, 0) = y_i, & H(m_i, 1) = z_i : & x_i = 0 \\ H(m_i, 0) = z_i, & H(m_i, 1) = y_i : & x_i = 1 \end{cases}.$$

The simulator $\mathcal{B}$ responds to this query with $H(m_i, c_i)$ and adds $\big(m_i, x_i, y_i, z_i, H(m_i, 0), H(m_i, 1)\big)$ to the hash list.

Query. The adversary makes signature queries in this phase. For a signature query on m_i, let the corresponding hashing tuple be $\big(m_i, x_i, y_i, z_i, H(m_i, 0), H(m_i, 1)\big)$.

$\mathcal{B}$ computes σ_{m_i} as

$$\sigma_{m_i} = \left(x_i, \ h^{\frac{1}{\alpha + H(m_i, x_i)}} \right) = \left(x_i, \ g^{w(a+y_1)\cdots(a+y_{i-1})(a+y_{i+1})\cdots(a+y_q)} \right)$$

using $g, g^a, \cdots, g^{a^q}, y_1, y_2, \cdots, y_q$.

According to the signature definition and simulation, we have $c_i = x_i$ and $H(m_i, x_i) = y_i$ such that

$$h^{\frac{1}{\alpha + H(m_i, c_i)}} = g^{\frac{w(a+y_1)\cdots(a+y_{i-1})(a+y_i)(a+y_{i+1})\cdots(a+y_q)}{a+y_i}} = g^{w(a+y_1)\cdots(a+y_{i-1})(a+y_{i+1})\cdots(a+y_q)}.$$

Therefore, σ_{m_i} is a valid signature of m_i.

Forgery. The adversary returns a forged signature σ_{m^*} on some m^* that has not been queried. Let $\sigma_{m^*} = (\sigma_1^*, \sigma_2^*) = \left(c^*, h^{\frac{1}{\alpha + H(m^*, c^*)}} \right)$, and the corresponding hashing tuple be $(m^*, x^*, y^*, z^*, H(m^*, 0), H(m^*, 1))$. If $c^* = x^*$, abort. Otherwise, we have $c^* \neq x^*$ and then

$$H(m^*, c^*) = H(m^*, 1 - x^*) = z^*.$$

According to the signature definition and simulation, we have $z^* \notin \{y_1, y_2, \cdots, y_q\}$ and

$$\sigma_2^* = h^{\frac{1}{\alpha + H(m^*, c^*)}} = g^{\frac{w(a+y_1)(a+y_2)\cdots(a+y_q)}{a+z^*}},$$

which can be rewritten as

$$g^{f(a) + \frac{d}{a+z^*}},$$

where $f(a)$ is a $(q-1)$-degree polynomial function in a, and d is a nonzero integer.

The simulator $\mathcal{B}$ computes

$$\left(\frac{\sigma_2^*}{g^{f(a)}} \right)^{\frac{1}{d}} = \left(\frac{g^{f(a) + \frac{d}{a+z^*}}}{g^{f(a)}} \right)^{\frac{1}{d}} = g^{\frac{1}{a+z^*}}$$

and outputs $(z^*, g^{\frac{1}{a+z^*}})$ as the solution to the q-SDH problem instance.

This completes the simulation and the solution. The correctness is analyzed as follows.

Indistinguishable simulation. The correctness of the simulation has been explained above. The randomness of the simulation includes all random numbers in the key generation, the responses to hash queries, and the signature generation. They are as follows:

$$pk : a, \; w(a+y_1)(a+y_2)\cdots(a+y_q),$$
$$H(m_i,0), H(m_i,1) : (y_i,z_i) \text{ or } (z_i,y_i),$$
$$c_i : x_i.$$

According to the setting of the simulation, where a, w, y_i, z_i, x_i are randomly chosen, it is easy to see that they are random and independent from the point of view of the adversary. Therefore, the simulation is indistinguishable from the real attack.

Probability of successful simulation and useful attack. All queried signatures are simulatable, and the forged signature is reducible if $c^* \neq x^*$. According to the setting, we have

$$\begin{cases} H(m^*,0) = y^*, \;\; H(m^*,1) = z^* : \;\; x^* = 0 \\ H(m^*,0) = z^*, \;\; H(m^*,1) = y^* : \;\; x^* = 1 \end{cases}.$$

The adversary knows x^* if it finds which hash value $H(m^*,0)$ or $H(m^*,1)$ is a root of $w(a+y_1)\cdots(a+y_q)$. Since $w(a+y_1)\cdots(a+y_q), y^*, z^*$ are random and independent, the adversary has no advantage in finding x^*. Therefore, the probability of successful simulation and useful attack is $\frac{1}{2}$.

Advantage and time cost. Suppose the adversary breaks the scheme with (t, q_s, ε) after making q_H queries to the random oracle. The advantage of solving the q-SDH problem is therefore $\frac{\varepsilon}{2}$. Let T_s denote the time cost of the simulation. We have $T_s = O(q_s q_H)$, which is mainly dominated by the signature generation. Therefore, $\mathscr{B}$ will solve the q-SDH problem with $(t + T_s, \frac{\varepsilon}{2})$.

This completes the proof of the theorem.   □

5.7 ZSS$^\#$ Scheme

SysGen: The system parameter generation algorithm takes as input a security parameter λ. It chooses a pairing group $\mathbb{PG} = (\mathbb{G}, \mathbb{G}_T, g, p, e)$, selects a cryptographic hash function $H : \{0,1\}^* \rightarrow \mathbb{Z}_p$, and returns the system parameters $SP = (\mathbb{PG}, H)$.

KeyGen: The key generation algorithm takes as input the system parameters SP. It randomly chooses $h \in \mathbb{G}$, $\alpha \in \mathbb{Z}_p$, computes $g_1 = g^\alpha$, and returns a public/secret key pair (pk, sk) as follows:

$$pk = (g_1, h), \quad sk = \alpha.$$

Sign: The signing algorithm takes as input a message $m \in \{0, 1\}^*$, the secret key sk, and the system parameters SP. It chooses a random number $r \in \mathbb{Z}_p$ and returns the signature σ_m on m as

$$\sigma_m = (\sigma_1, \sigma_2) = \left(r, \ h^{\frac{1}{\alpha + H(m,r)}} \right).$$

We require that the signing algorithm always uses the same random number r on the message m.

Verify: The verification algorithm takes as input a message-signature pair (m, σ_m), the public key pk, and the system parameters SP. Let $\sigma_m = (\sigma_1, \sigma_2)$. It accepts the signature if

$$e\left(\sigma_2, \ g_1 g^{H(m,\sigma_1)} \right) = e(h, g).$$

Theorem 5.7.0.1 *Suppose the hash function H is a random oracle. If the q-SDH problem is hard, the ZSS# signature scheme is provably secure in the EU-CMA security model with reduction loss $L = 1$.*

Proof. Suppose there exists an adversary $\mathscr{A}$ who can (t, q_s, ε)-break the signature scheme in the EU-CMA security model. We construct a simulator $\mathscr{B}$ to solve the q-SDH problem. Given as input a problem instance $(g, g^a, g^{a^2}, \cdots, g^{a^q})$ over the pairing group $\mathbb{PG}$, $\mathscr{B}$ controls the random oracle, runs $\mathscr{A}$, and works as follows.

Setup. Let $SP = \mathbb{PG}$ and H be the random oracle controlled by the simulator. $\mathscr{B}$ randomly chooses $y_1, y_2, \cdots, y_q, w$ from $\mathbb{Z}_p$ and sets the public key as

$$g_1 = g^a, \quad h = g^{w(a+y_1)(a+y_2)\cdots(a+y_q)},$$

where the secret key α is equivalent to a. This requires $q = q_s$. The public key can be computed from the problem instance and the chosen parameters.

H-Query. The adversary makes hash queries in this phase. $\mathscr{B}$ prepares a hash list to record all queries and responses as follows, where the hash list is empty at the beginning.

For a query on (m, r) from the adversary, if (m, r) is already in the hash list, it responds to this query following the hash list. Otherwise, it randomly chooses $z \in \mathbb{Z}_p$ and sets $H(m, r) = z$. The simulator $\mathscr{B}$ responds to this query with $H(m, r)$ and adds

$(m, r, z, H(m, r), \mathscr{A})$ to the hash list. Here, $\mathscr{A}$ in the tuple means that the query (m, r) is generated by the adversary.

Query. The adversary makes signature queries in this phase. For a signature query on m_i, if there exists a tuple $(m_i, r_i, y_i, H(m_i, r_i), \mathscr{B})$ in the hash list, the simulator uses this tuple to generate the signature. Otherwise, $\mathscr{B}$ randomly chooses $r_i, y_i \in \mathbb{Z}_p$, sets $H(m_i, r_i) = y_i$, and adds $(m_i, r_i, y_i, H(m_i, r_i), \mathscr{B})$ to the hash list. If (m_i, r_i) was ever generated by the adversary, the simulator aborts.

$\mathscr{B}$ computes σ_{m_i} as

$$\sigma_{m_i} = \left(r_i, \ h^{\frac{1}{\alpha + H(m_i, r_i)}} \right) = \left(r_i, \ g^{w(a+y_1)\cdots(a+y_{i-1})(a+y_{i+1})\cdots(a+y_q)} \right)$$

using $g, g^a, \cdots, g^{a^q}, w, y_1, y_2, \cdots, y_q$.

According to the signature definition and simulation, we have $H(m_i, r_i) = y_i$ such that

$$h^{\frac{1}{\alpha + H(m_i, r_i)}} = g^{\frac{w(a+y_1)\cdots(a+y_{i-1})(a+y_i)(a+y_{i+1})\cdots(a+y_q)}{a+y_i}} = g^{w(a+y_1)\cdots(a+y_{i-1})(a+y_{i+1})\cdots(a+y_q)}.$$

Therefore, σ_{m_i} is a valid signature of m_i.

Forgery. The adversary returns a forged signature σ_{m^*} on some m^* that has not been queried. Let $\sigma_{m^*} = (\sigma_1^*, \sigma_2^*) = \left(r^*, h^{\frac{1}{\alpha + H(m^*, r^*)}} \right)$, and the corresponding hashing tuple be $(m^*, r^*, z^*, H(m^*, r^*))$.

According to the signature definition and simulation, we have that z^* is randomly chosen from $\mathbb{Z}_p$ and is different from $\{y_1, y_2, \cdots, y_q\}$. Then

$$\sigma_2^* = h^{\frac{1}{\alpha + H(m^*, r^*)}} = g^{\frac{w(a+y_1)(a+y_2)\cdots(a+y_q)}{a+z^*}},$$

can be rewritten as

$$g^{f(a) + \frac{d}{a+z^*}},$$

where $f(a)$ is a $(q-1)$-degree polynomial function in a, and d is a nonzero integer.

The simulator $\mathscr{B}$ computes

$$\left(\frac{\sigma_2^*}{g^{f(a)}} \right)^{\frac{1}{d}} = \left(\frac{g^{f(a) + \frac{d}{a+z^*}}}{g^{f(a)}} \right)^{\frac{1}{d}} = g^{\frac{1}{a+z^*}}$$

and outputs $\left(z^*, g^{\frac{1}{a+z^*}} \right)$ as the solution to the q-SDH problem instance.

This completes the simulation and the solution. The correctness is analyzed as follows.

Indistinguishable simulation. The correctness of the simulation has been explained above. The randomness of the simulation includes all random numbers in the key generation, the responses to hash queries, and the signature generation. They are as follows:

$$pk : a, \; w(a+y_1)(a+y_2)\cdots(a+y_q),$$
$$H(m,r) : z \text{ if } r \text{ is chosen by the adversary}$$
$$H(m_i,r_i) : y_i \text{ if } r_i \text{ is chosen by the simulator}$$
$$\text{random number} : r_i.$$

According to the setting of the simulation, where a, w, z, y_i, r_i are randomly chosen, it is easy to see that they are random and independent from the point of view of the adversary. Therefore, the simulation is indistinguishable from the real attack.

Probability of successful simulation and useful attack. The forged signature is reducible, and all queried signatures are simulatable when the random number r_i chosen in the signature query phase is different from all random numbers in the hash query phase. A randomly chosen number is not equal to the numbers in the hash query phase with probability $1 - \frac{q_H}{p}$. Therefore, the probability of successful simulation and useful attack is $(1 - \frac{q_H}{p})^{q_s} \approx 1$.

Advantage and time cost. Suppose the adversary breaks the scheme with (t, q_s, ε) after making q_H queries to the random oracle. The advantage of solving the q-SDH problem is therefore approximately ε. Let T_s denote the time cost of the simulation. We have $T_s = O(q_s^2)$, which is mainly dominated by the signature generation. Therefore, $\mathscr{B}$ will solve the q-SDH problem with $(t + T_s, \varepsilon)$.

This completes the proof of the theorem. $\qquad\qquad\qquad\qquad\qquad\qquad$ □

5.8 BLS^G Scheme

SysGen: The system parameter generation algorithm takes as input a security parameter λ. It chooses a pairing group $\mathbb{PG} = (\mathbb{G}, \mathbb{G}_T, g, p, e)$, selects a cryptographic hash function $H : \{0,1\}^* \rightarrow \mathbb{G}$, and returns the system parameters $SP = (\mathbb{PG}, H)$.

KeyGen: The key generation algorithm takes as input the system parameters SP. It randomly chooses $\alpha \in \mathbb{Z}_p$, computes $h = g^\alpha$, and returns a public/secret key pair (pk, sk) as follows:

$$pk = h, \; sk = \alpha.$$

Sign: The signing algorithm takes as input a message $m \in \{0,1\}^*$, the secret key sk, and the system parameters SP. It returns the signature σ_m on m as

$$\sigma_m = (\sigma_1, \sigma_2, \sigma_3) = \left(H(m)^\alpha, H\left(m||\sigma_m^1\right)^\alpha, H\left(m||\sigma_m^2\right)^\alpha \right),$$

---

where $\sigma_m^i = (\sigma_1, \sigma_2, \cdots, \sigma_i)$. We call σ_i a block signature in this signature scheme. The final signature σ_m is equivalent to σ_m^3.

Verify: The verification algorithm takes as input a message-signature pair (m, σ_m), the public key pk, and the system parameters SP. It accepts the signature if and only if

$$e(\sigma_1, g) = e\big(H(m), h\big), \text{ and}$$
$$e(\sigma_2, g) = e\big(H\big(m\|\sigma_m^1\big), h\big), \text{ and}$$
$$e(\sigma_3, g) = e\big(H\big(m\|\sigma_m^2\big), h\big).$$

Theorem 5.8.0.1 *Suppose the hash function H is a random oracle. If the CDH problem is hard, the BLS^G signature scheme is provably secure in the EU-CMA security model with reduction loss $2\sqrt{q_H}$, where q_H is the number of hash queries to the random oracle.*

Proof. Suppose there exists an adversary $\mathscr{A}$ who can (t, q_s, ε)-break the signature scheme in the EU-CMA security model. We construct a simulator $\mathscr{B}$ to solve the CDH problem. Given as input a problem instance (g, g^a, g^b) over the pairing group $\mathbb{PG}$, $\mathscr{B}$ controls the random oracle, runs $\mathscr{A}$, and works as follows.

Setup. Let $SP = \mathbb{PG}$ and H be the random oracle controlled by the simulator. $\mathscr{B}$ sets the public key as $h = g^a$, where the secret key α is equivalent to a. The public key is available from the problem instance.

H-Query. The adversary makes hash queries in this phase. Before receiving queries from the adversary, $\mathscr{B}$ randomly chooses an integer $c^* \in \{0, 1\}$ and then chooses another random value k^* from the range $[1, q_H^{1-\frac{c^*}{2}}]$, where q_H denotes the number of hash queries to the random oracle. To be precise, the range is $[1, q_H]$ if $c^* = 0$, and the range is $[1, q_H^{\frac{1}{2}}]$ if $c^* = 1$. Then, $\mathscr{B}$ prepares a hash list to record all queries and responses as follows, where the hash list is empty at the beginning.

For each tuple, the format is defined and described as follows:

$$(x, I_x, T_x, O_x, U_x, z_x),$$

x refers to the query input.
I_x refers to the identity, either the adversary $\mathscr{A}$ or the simulator $\mathscr{B}$.
T_x refers to the type of the hash query.
O_x refers to the order index of the query within the same type.
U_x refers to the response to x, i.e., $U_x = H(x)$.
z_x refers to the secret for computing U_x.

Let the hash query be x or the adversary query $H(x)$. If x is already in this hash list, $\mathscr{B}$ responds to this query following the hash list. Otherwise, the simulator responds to this query as follows:

Response of object I_x. The object I_x is to identify who is the first to generate and submit x to the random oracle. The query is meaningful in that both the adversary and the simulator can make to the random oracle, although the random oracle is controlled by the simulator. If the first query on x is first generated and submitted by the adversary, we say that this query is made first by the adversary and set $I_x = \mathscr{A}$. Otherwise, we set $I_x = \mathscr{B}$.

Take a new message m as an example. Suppose the adversary first queries $H(m)$, $H(m||\sigma_m^1)$ to the random oracle and then queries the signature of m to the simulator. Notice that the signature generation on the message m requires the simulator to know all the following values

$$H(m), \ H(m||\sigma_m^1), \ H(m||\sigma_m^2).$$

The hash list does not record how to respond to hash query $H(m||\sigma_m^2)$. Therefore, the simulator must query $H(m||\sigma_m^2)$ to the random oracle first before generating its signature. Notice that the adversary might query $H(m||\sigma_m^2)$ again for signature verification after receiving the signature, but this hash query is first generated and made by the simulator. Therefore, we define

- For $x \in \{m, \ m||\sigma_m^1\}$, the corresponding I_x for x is $I_x = \mathscr{A}$.

- For $x = m||\sigma_m^2$, the corresponding I_x for x is $I_x = \mathscr{B}$.

Response of object T_x. We assume "$||$" is a concatenation notation that will never appear within messages. The simulator can also run the verification algorithm to verify whether each block signature is correct or not. Therefore, it is easy to distinguish the input structure of all hash queries. We define four types of hash queries to the random oracle.

Type i. $x = m||\sigma_m^i$. Here, σ_m^i denotes the first i block signatures of m, and i refers to any integer $i \in \{0, 1, 2\}$. We assume $m||\sigma_m^0 = m$ for easy analysis.

Type D. x is a query different from the previous three types. For example, $x = m||R_m$ but $R_m \neq \sigma_m^i$ for any $i \in \{0, 1, 2\}$, or $x = m||\sigma_m^{i'}$ for any $i' \geq 3$.

The object T_x is set as follows. If $I_x = \mathscr{B}$, then $T_x = \perp$. Otherwise, suppose $I_x = \mathscr{A}$. Then, the simulator can run the verification algorithm to know which type x belongs to and set

$$T_x = \begin{cases} i & \text{if } x \text{ belongs to } \textbf{Type i} \text{ for any } i \in \{0, 1, 2\} \\ \perp & \text{otherwise } x \text{ belongs to } \textbf{Type D} \end{cases}.$$

We emphasize that T_x and O_x are used to mark "valid" queries generated by the adversary only. We define **Type D** because that the adversary can generate any arbitrary string as a query to the random oracle. The last type of queries will never be used in the signature generation or the signature forgery.

Response of object O_x. The object O_x is set as follows.

- If $T_x = \perp$, then $O_x = \perp$.

- Otherwise, suppose $T_x = c$. Then, $O_x = k$ if x is the k-th new query added to the hash list in those queries where $T_x = c$.

To calculate the integer k for the new query x, the simulator must count how many queries have been added to the hash list, where only those queries with the same T_x will be counted. We emphasize that the setting of O_x needs to know the value T_x first.

For the objects I_x, T_x, and O_x, there are only three cases in all tuples in the hash list. They are

$$(I_x, T_x, O_x) = (\mathscr{A}, c, k), \ (I_x, T_x, O_x) = (\mathscr{A}, \perp, \perp), \ (I_x, T_x, O_x) = (\mathscr{B}, \perp, \perp),$$

where $c \in \{0, 1, 2\}$ and $k \in [1, q_H]$.

Response of objects (U_x, z_x). Let (I_x, T_x, O_x) be the response to the query x according to the above description. The simulator randomly chooses $z_x \in \mathbb{Z}_p$ and sets the response U_x to x according to the chosen (c^*, k^*) as follows:

$$U_x = H(x) = \begin{cases} g^{b+z_x} & \text{if } (T_x, O_x) = (c^*, k^*) \\ g^{z_x} & \text{otherwise} \end{cases}.$$

We denote by z_x the secret for the response to x. In the following, if the query x needs to be written as $x = m||\sigma_m^i$, the corresponding secret will be rewritten as z_m^i.

Finally, the simulator adds the defined tuple $(x, I_x, T_x, O_x, U_x, z_x)$ for the new query x to the hash list. This completes the description of the hash query and its response.

For the tuple $(x, I_x, T_x, O_x, U_x, z_x)$, we have that $H(x)^\alpha = U_x^a = (g^a)^{z_x}$ is computable by the simulator for any query x as long as $(T_x, O_x) \neq (c^*, k^*)$. If $(T_x, O_x) = (c^*, k^*)$, we have

$$H(x)^\alpha = U_x^a = (g^{b+z_x})^a = g^{ab+az_x}.$$

For the tuple $(x, I_x, T_x, O_x, U_x, z_x)$, we denote by $m_{i,j}$ the message in the query input x if $(T_x, O_x) = (i, j)$. We define

$$\mathscr{M}_i = \{m_{i,1}, m_{i,2}, \cdots, m_{i,q_i}\}$$

to be the message set with q_i messages, where $\mathscr{M}_i$ contains all messages in those tuples belonging to **Type i** ($T_x = i$). According to the setting of the oracle responses, for those hash queries belonging to **Type i** for all $i \in \{0, 1, 2\}$, there are three message sets $\mathscr{M}_0, \mathscr{M}_1, \mathscr{M}_2$ at most to capture all messages in these queries. All queried messages mentioned above are described in Table 5.1, where the query associated with the message $m_{i,j}$ is made before another query associated with the message $m_{i,j'}$ if $j < j'$.

Without knowing the signature σ_m of m before making hash queries associated with m, the adversary must make hash queries $H(m), H(m||\sigma_m^1), H(m||\sigma_m^2)$ in sequence because σ_m^i in the query $m||\sigma_m^i$ contains

$$H(m)^\alpha, H(m||\sigma_m^1)^\alpha, \cdots, H(m||\sigma_m^{i-1})^\alpha.$$

Table 5.1 Messages queried by the adversary where $T_x \neq \perp$

$$\mathcal{M}_0 = \{ m_{0,1}, m_{0,2}, m_{0,3}, \cdots, \cdots, \cdots, m_{0,q_0} \}$$
$$\mathcal{M}_1 = \{ m_{1,1}, m_{1,2}, m_{1,3}, \cdots, \cdots, \cdots, m_{1,q_1} \}$$
$$\mathcal{M}_2 = \{ m_{2,1}, m_{2,2}, m_{2,3}, \cdots, \cdots, m_{2,q_2} \}$$

For a message m, the adversary can query all three hash queries $H(m)$, $H(m||\sigma_m^1)$, $H(m||\sigma_m^2)$ or fewer, such as $H(m)$, $H(m||\sigma_m^1)$, for this message before its signature query. Therefore, the following inequality and subset relationships hold:

$$q_2 \leq q_1 \leq q_0, \quad \mathcal{M}_2 \subseteq \mathcal{M}_1 \subseteq \mathcal{M}_0.$$

Suppose the adversary can finally forge a valid signature of a message m^*. The adversary must at least make the hash query $H(m^*||\sigma_{m^*}^2)$ in order to compute $H(m^*||\sigma_{m^*}^2)^\alpha$, which guarantees $q_2 \geq 1$. Since the number of hash queries is at most q_H, we have $q_0 < q_H$. We stress that the number q_1 is adaptively decided by the adversary. However, it must be

$$q_1 < \sqrt{q_H} \text{ or } q_1 \geq \sqrt{q_H}.$$

Query: The adversary makes signature queries in this phase. For a signature query on the message m that is adaptively chosen by the adversary, the simulator computes the signature σ_m as follows.

If m is never queried to the random oracle, the simulator works as follows from $i = 1$ to $i = 3$, where i is increased by one each time.

- Add a query on $m||\sigma_m^{i-1}$ and its response to the hash list ($m||\sigma_m^0 = m$). According to the setting of the random oracle simulation, the corresponding tuple is

$$\left(m||\sigma_m^{i-1}, \mathcal{B}, \perp, \perp, g^{z_m^{i-1}}, z_m^{i-1} \right).$$

- Compute the block signature σ_i as

$$\sigma_i = H \left(m||\sigma_m^{i-1} \right)^\alpha = (g^a)^{z_m^{i-1}}.$$

In the above signature generation, σ_i for all $i \in \{1,2,3\}$ is computable by the simulator, and the signature of σ_m is equal to $\sigma_m^3 = (\sigma_1, \sigma_2, \sigma_3)$. Therefore, the signature of m is computable by the simulator.

Suppose the message m was ever queried to the random oracle by the adversary, where the following queries associated with the message m were made by the adversary

$$m||\sigma_m^0, \cdots, m||\sigma_m^{r_m} : r_m \in \{0,1,2\}.$$

Here, the integer r_m is adaptively decided by the adversary. Let $(x, I_x, T_x, O_x, U_x, z_x)$ be the tuple for $x = m||\sigma_m^{r_m}$. That is, $T_x = r_m$.

- If $(T_x, O_x) = (c^*, k^*)$, the simulator aborts because

$$H(m||\sigma_m^{rm}) = g^{b+z_x}, \quad \sigma_{rm+1} = H(m||\sigma_m^{rm})^\alpha = U_x^a = (g^{b+z_x})^a = g^{ab+az_x},$$

which cannot be computed by the simulator, and thus the simulator fails to simulate the signature for the adversary, in particular the block signature σ_{rm+1}.

- Otherwise, $(T_x, O_x) \neq (c^*, k^*)$. Then, σ_{rm+1} is computable by the simulator because

$$H(m||\sigma_m^{rm}) = g^{z_x}, \quad \sigma_{rm+1} = H(m||\sigma_m^{rm})^\alpha = (g^a)^{z_x}.$$

Similarly to the case that m is never queried to the random oracle, the simulator can generate and make hash queries

$$H(m||\sigma_m^{rm+1}), \cdots, H(m||\sigma_m^2)$$

to the random oracle. Finally, it computes the signature σ_m for the adversary.

Therefore, σ_m is a valid signature of the message m. This completes the description of the signature generation.

Forgery: The adversary returns a forged signature σ_{m^*} on some m^* that has not been queried. Since the adversary cannot make a signature query on some m^*, we have that the following queries to the random oracle were made by the adversary:

$$m^*||\sigma_{m^*}^0, \; m^*||\sigma_{m^*}^1, \; m^*||\sigma_{m^*}^2.$$

The solution to the problem instance does not have to be associated with the forged message m^*. The simulator solves the hard problem as follows.

- The simulator searches the hash list to find the first tuple $(x, I_x, T_x, O_x, U_x, z_x)$ satisfying

$$(T_x, O_x) = (c^*, k^*).$$

If this tuple does not exist, abort. Otherwise, let the message m_{c^*, k^*} in this tuple be denoted by $\hat{m}$ for short. That is, $m_{c^*, k^*} = \hat{m}$ and we have $\hat{m} \in \mathcal{M}_{c^*}$. Note that $\hat{m}$ may be different from m^*. This tuple is therefore equivalent to

$$(x, I_x, T_x, O_x, U_x, z_x) = \left(\hat{m}||\sigma_{\hat{m}}^{c^*}, \; \mathscr{A}, \; c^*, \; k^*, \; g^{bz_{\hat{m}}^{c^*}}, \; z_{\hat{m}}^{c^*} \right).$$

That is $H(\hat{m}||\sigma_{\hat{m}}^{c^*}) = g^{b+z_{\hat{m}}^{c^*}}$ contains the instance g^b.

- The simulator searches the hash list to find the second tuple $(x', I_{x'}, T_{x'}, O_{x'}, U_{x'}, z_{x'})$, where x' is the query about the message $\hat{m}$ and $T_{x'} = c^* + 1$. If this tuple does not exist, abort. Otherwise, we have $\hat{m} \in \mathcal{M}_{c^*+1}$ and

$$x' = \hat{m}||\sigma_{\hat{m}}^{c^*+1},$$

where $\sigma_{\hat{m}}^{c^*+1}$ contains $\sigma_{c^*+1} = H(m||\sigma_m^{c^*})^\alpha$.
- The simulator computes and outputs

$$\frac{H(\hat{m}||\sigma_{\hat{m}}^{c^*})^\alpha}{(g^a)^{z_{\hat{m}}^{c^*}}} = \frac{g^{ab+az_{\hat{m}}^{c^*}}}{(g^a)^{z_{\hat{m}}^{c^*}}} = g^{ab}$$

as the solution to the CDH problem instance.

This completes the simulation and the solution. The correctness is analyzed as follows.

Indistinguishable simulation. The correctness of the simulation has been explained above. The randomness of the simulation includes all random numbers in the key generation and the responses to hash queries. They are $a, z_x, b + z_{x'}$. According to the setting of the simulation, where a, b, z_i are randomly chosen, it is easy to see that they are random and independent from the point of view of the adversary. Therefore, the simulation is indistinguishable from the real attack. In particular, the adversary does not know which hash query is answered with b. That is, c^* is random and unknown to the adversary.

Probability of successful simulation and useful attack. According to the assumption, the adversary will break the signature scheme with advantage ε. The adversary will make the hash query $H(m^*||\sigma_{m^*}^2)$ with probability at least ε, such that $m^* \in \mathcal{M}_2$ and thus $q_2 \geq 1$. The number of hash query is q_H. Since $q_0 + q_1 + q_2 = q_H$, we have $q_0 < q_H$.

The reduction is successful if the simulator does not abort in either the query phase or the forgery phase. According to the setting of the simulation, the reduction is successful if $\hat{m} \in \mathcal{M}_{c^*}$ and $\hat{m} \in \mathcal{M}_{c^*+1}$.

- If $c^* = 0$, we have $\hat{m} \in \mathcal{M}_0$ and $\hat{m} \in \mathcal{M}_1$. In this case, $k^* \in [1, q_H]$ and $|\mathcal{M}_0| = q_0 < q_H$. We have that any message in $\mathcal{M}_0$ will be chosen as $\hat{m}$ with probability $\frac{1}{q_H}$ according to the simulation. Since $\mathcal{M}_1 \subseteq \mathcal{M}_0$, the success probability is

$$\frac{q_1}{q_H}.$$

- If $c^* = 1$, we have $\hat{m} \in \mathcal{M}_1$ and $\hat{m} \in \mathcal{M}_2$. In this case, $k^* \in [1, \sqrt{q_H}]$ and $|\mathcal{M}_1| = q_1$. If $q_1 < \sqrt{q_H}$, we have that any message in $\mathcal{M}_1$ will be chosen as $\hat{m}$ with probability $\frac{1}{\sqrt{q_H}}$ according to the simulation. Since $\mathcal{M}_2 \subseteq \mathcal{M}_1$, the success probability is

$$\frac{q_2}{\sqrt{q_H}}.$$

Let $\Pr[suc]$ be the probability of successful simulation and useful attack when $q_2 \geq 1$. We calculate the following probability of success:

$$\Pr[suc] = \Pr[suc|c^* = 0]\Pr[c^* = 0] + \Pr[suc|c^* = 1]\Pr[c^* = 1]$$
$$= \Pr[\hat{m} \in \mathcal{M}_0 \cap \mathcal{M}_1|c^* = 0]\Pr[c^* = 0] + \Pr[\hat{m} \in \mathcal{M}_1 \cap \mathcal{M}_2|c^* = 1]\Pr[c^* = 1]$$
$$= \frac{1}{2}\Pr[\hat{m} \in \mathcal{M}_0 \cap \mathcal{M}_1|c^* = 0] + \frac{1}{2}\Pr[\hat{m} \in \mathcal{M}_1 \cap \mathcal{M}_2|c^* = 1]$$

$$\geq \frac{1}{2} \Pr[\hat{m} \in \mathcal{M}_0 \cap \mathcal{M}_1 | c^* = 0, q_1 \geq \sqrt{q_H}] \Pr[q_1 \geq \sqrt{q_H}]$$

$$+ \frac{1}{2} \Pr[\hat{m} \in \mathcal{M}_1 \cap \mathcal{M}_2 | c^* = 1, q_1 < \sqrt{q_H}] \Pr[q_1 < \sqrt{q_H}]$$

$$= \frac{1}{2\sqrt{q_H}} \Pr[q_1 \geq \sqrt{q_H}] + \frac{1}{2\sqrt{q_H}} \Pr[q_1 < \sqrt{q_H}]$$

$$= \frac{1}{2\sqrt{q_H}}.$$

Therefore, the success probability is at least $\frac{1}{2\sqrt{q_H}}$ for q_H queries.

Advantage and time cost. Suppose the adversary breaks the scheme with (t, q_s, ε) after making q_H queries to the random oracle. The advantage of solving the CDH problem is therefore $\varepsilon/(2\sqrt{q_H})$. Let T_s denote the time cost of the simulation. We have $T_s = O(q_H + q_s)$, which is mainly dominated by the oracle response and the signature generation. Therefore, $\mathcal{B}$ will solve the CDH problem with $(t + T_s, \varepsilon/(2\sqrt{q_H}))$.

This completes the proof of the theorem. $\qquad\qquad\qquad\qquad\qquad\qquad\quad \Box$

Chapter 6
Digital Signatures Without Random Oracles

In this chapter, we mainly introduce signature schemes under the q-SDH hardness assumption and the CDH assumption. We start by introducing the Boneh-Boyen short signature scheme [21] and then its variant, namely the Gentry scheme, which is modified from his IBE scheme [47]. Most stateless signature schemes without random oracles must produce signatures at least 320 bits in length for 80-bit security. Then, we introduce the GMS scheme [54], which achieves a less than 320-bit length of signature in the stateful setting. The other two signature schemes are the Waters scheme modified from his IBE scheme [101] and the Hohenberger-Waters scheme [61]. The Waters scheme requires a long public key, and the Hohenberger-Waters scheme addressed this problem in the stateful setting. The given schemes and/or proofs may be different from the original ones.

6.1 Boneh-Boyen Scheme

SysGen: The system parameter generation algorithm takes as input a security parameter λ. It chooses a pairing group $\mathbb{PG} = (\mathbb{G}, \mathbb{G}_T, g, p, e)$ and returns the system parameters $SP = \mathbb{PG}$.

KeyGen: The key generation algorithm takes as input the system parameters SP. It randomly chooses $h \in \mathbb{G}$, $\alpha, \beta \in \mathbb{Z}_p$, computes $g_1 = g^\alpha, g_2 = g^\beta$, and returns a public/secret key pair (pk, sk) as follows:

$$pk = (g_1, g_2, h), \quad sk = (\alpha, \beta).$$

Sign: The signing algorithm takes as input a message $m \in \mathbb{Z}_p$, the secret key sk, and the system parameters SP. It randomly chooses $r \in \mathbb{Z}_p$ and returns the signature σ_m on m as

© Springer International Publishing AG, part of Springer Nature 2018   173
F. Guo et al., *Introduction to Security Reduction*,
https://doi.org/10.1007/978-3-319-93049-7_6

$$\sigma_m = (\sigma_1, \sigma_2) = \left(r, \ h^{\frac{1}{\alpha + m\beta + r}} \right).$$

We require that the signing algorithm always uses the same random number r for signature generation on the message m.

Verify: The verification algorithm takes as input a message-signature pair (m, σ_m), the public key pk, and the system parameters SP. Let $\sigma_m = (\sigma_1, \sigma_2)$. It accepts the signature if

$$e\left(\sigma_2, \ g_1 g_2^m g^{\sigma_1} \right) = e(g, h).$$

Theorem 6.1.0.1 *If the q-SDH problem is hard, the Boneh-Boyen signature scheme is provably secure in the EU-CMA security model with reduction loss $L = 2$.*

Proof. Suppose there exists an adversary $\mathscr{A}$ who can (t, q_s, ε)-break the signature scheme in the EU-CMA security model. We construct a simulator $\mathscr{B}$ to solve the q-SDH problem. Given as input a problem instance $\left(g, g^a, g^{a^2}, \cdots, g^{a^q} \right)$ over the pairing group $\mathbb{PG}$, $\mathscr{B}$ runs $\mathscr{A}$ and works as follows.

$\quad$ $\mathscr{B}$ chooses a secret bit $\mu \in \{0, 1\}$ and programs the reduction in two different ways.

- The reduction for $\mu = 0$ is programmed as follows.

  Setup. Let $SP = \mathbb{PG}$. $\mathscr{B}$ randomly chooses $y, w_0, w_1, w_2, \cdots, w_q$ from $\mathbb{Z}_p$ and sets the public key as

  $$g_1 = g^a, \quad g_2 = g^y, \quad h = g^{w_0(a+w_1)(a+w_2)\cdots(a+w_q)},$$

  where $\alpha = a, \beta = y$ and we require $q = q_s$. The public key can be computed from the problem instance and the chosen parameters.

  Query. The adversary makes signature queries in this phase. For the i-th signature query on m_i, $\mathscr{B}$ computes the signature σ_{m_i} as

  $$\sigma_{m_i} = (\sigma_1, \sigma_2) = \left(w_i - ym_i, \ g^{w_0(a+w_1)\cdots(a+w_{i-1})(a+w_{i+1})\cdots(a+w_q)} \right)$$

  using $g, g^a, \cdots, g^{a^q}, y, w_0, w_1, \cdots, w_q$.
  Let $r_i = w_i - ym_i$. According to the signature definition and simulation, we have

  $$h^{\frac{1}{\alpha + m_i\beta + r_i}} = g^{\frac{w_0(a+w_1)(a+w_2)\cdots(a+w_q)}{a+m_iy+w_i-ym_i}} = g^{w_0(a+w_1)\cdots(a+w_{i-1})(a+w_{i+1})\cdots(a+w_q)}.$$

  Therefore, σ_{m_i} is a valid signature of m_i.

  Forgery. The adversary returns a forged signature σ_{m^*} on some m^* that has not been queried. Let $\sigma_{m^*} = (\sigma_1^*, \sigma_2^*) = \left(r^*, h^{\frac{1}{\alpha + m^*\beta + r^*}} \right)$. According to the signature definition and simulation, if $m^*\beta + r^* = m_i\beta + r_i$ for some queried signature of m_i, abort. Otherwise, let $c = m^*\beta + r^*$. We have $c \neq w_i = m_i\beta + r_i$ for all $i \in [1, q_s]$, and then

$$\sigma_2^* = h^{\frac{1}{a+m^*\beta+r^*}} = g^{\frac{w_0(a+w_1)(a+w_2)\cdots(a+w_q)}{a+c}},$$

which can be rewritten as

$$g^{f(a)+\frac{d}{a+c}},$$

where $f(a)$ is a $(q-1)$-degree polynomial function, and d is a nonzero integer. The simulator $\mathcal{B}$ computes

$$\left(\frac{\sigma_2^*}{g^{f(a)}}\right)^{\frac{1}{d}} = \left(\frac{g^{f(a)+\frac{d}{a+c}}}{g^{f(a)}}\right)^{\frac{1}{d}} = g^{\frac{1}{a+c}}$$

and outputs $\left(c, g^{\frac{1}{a+c}}\right)$ as the solution to the q-SDH problem instance.

- The reduction for $\mu = 1$ is programmed as follows.

Setup. Let $SP = \mathbb{PG}$. $\mathcal{B}$ randomly chooses $x, w_0, w_1, w_2, \cdots, w_q$ from $\mathbb{Z}_p$ and sets the public key as

$$g_1 = g^x, \quad g_2 = g^a, \quad h = g^{w_0(a+w_1)(a+w_2)\cdots(a+w_q)},$$

where $\alpha = x, \beta = a$ and we require $q = q_s$. The public key can be computed from the problem instance and the chosen parameters.

Query. The adversary makes signature queries in this phase. For the i-th signature query on $m_i \neq 0$, $\mathcal{B}$ computes the signature σ_{m_i} as

$$\sigma_{m_i} = (\sigma_1, \sigma_2) = \left(w_i m_i - x, \; g^{\frac{w_0}{m_i}(a+w_1)\cdots(a+w_{i-1})(a+w_{i+1})\cdots(a+w_q)}\right)$$

using $g, g^a, \cdots, g^{a^q}, x, w_0, w_1, \cdots, w_q$.
Let $r_i = w_i m_i - x$. According to the signature definition and simulation, we have

$$h^{\frac{1}{a+m_i\beta+r_i}} = g^{\frac{w_0(a+w_1)(a+w_2)\cdots(a+w_q)}{x+m_i a+w_i m_i - x}} = g^{\frac{w_0}{m_i}(a+w_1)\cdots(a+w_{i-1})(a+w_{i+1})\cdots(a+w_q)}.$$

Therefore, σ_{m_i} is a valid signature of m_i. Note that if $m_i = 0$, $\mathcal{B}$ can randomly choose $r_i \in \mathbb{Z}_p$ to generate the signature, because $\alpha + m_i\beta + r_i = x + r_i$, which is computable by the simulator.

Forgery. The adversary returns a forged signature σ_{m^*} on some m^* that has not been queried. Let $\sigma_{m^*} = (\sigma_1^*, \sigma_2^*) = \left(r^*, h^{\frac{1}{a+m^*\beta+r^*}}\right)$. According to the signature definition and simulation, if $m^*\beta + r^* \neq m_i\beta + r_i$ for all $i \in [1, q_s]$, abort. Otherwise, we have

$$m^*\beta + r^* = m_i\beta + r_i$$

for some i. That is, $m^*a + r^* = m_i a + r_i$.

The simulator $\mathscr{B}$ computes

$$a = \frac{r_i - r^*}{m^* - m_i}$$

and solves the q-SDH problem immediately using a.

This completes the simulation and the solution. The correctness is analyzed as follows.

Indistinguishable simulation. The correctness of the simulation has been explained above. The randomness of the simulation includes all random numbers in the key generation and the signature generation. Let $h = g^\gamma$. They are $\alpha, \beta, \gamma, r_1, r_2, \cdots, r_{q_s}$ equivalent to

$$\begin{cases} \left(a, \, y, \, w_0(a + w_1) \cdots (a + w_q), \, w_1 - ym_1, w_2 - ym_2, \cdots, w_{q_s} - ym_{q_s} \right) : & \mu = 0 \\ \left(x, \, a, \, w_0(a + w_1) \cdots (a + w_q), \, w_1 m_1 - x, w_2 m_2 - x, \cdots, w_{q_s} m_{q_s} - x \right) : & \mu = 1 \end{cases}.$$

According to the setting of the simulation, where a, x, y, w_0, w_i are randomly chosen, it is easy to see that they are random and independent from the point of view of the adversary no matter whether $\mu = 0$ or $\mu = 1$. Therefore, the simulation is indistinguishable from the real attack, and the adversary has no advantage in guessing μ from the simulation.

Probability of successful simulation and useful attack. There is no abort in the simulation. Let the random numbers in the queried signature and the forged signature be r_i and r^*, respectively. We have

- Case $\mu = 0$. The forged signature is reducible if $m^*\beta + r^* \neq m_i\beta + r_i$ for all i.
- Case $\mu = 1$. The forged signature is reducible if $m^*\beta + r^* = m_i\beta + r_i$ for some i.

Since the two simulations are indistinguishable and the simulator randomly chooses one simulation, the forged signature is therefore reducible with success probability $\Pr[Success]$ described as follows:

$$\begin{aligned} &\Pr[Success] \\ &= \Pr[Success|\mu = 0]\Pr[\mu = 0] + \Pr[Success|\mu = 1]\Pr[\mu = 1] \\ &= \Pr[m^*\beta + r^* \neq m_i\beta + r_i]\Pr[\mu = 0] + \Pr[m^*\beta + r^* = m_i\beta + r_i]\Pr[\mu = 1] \\ &= \frac{1}{2}\left(\Pr[m^*\beta + r^* \neq m_i\beta + r_i] + \Pr[m^*\beta + r^* = m_i\beta + r_i] \right) \\ &= \frac{1}{2}. \end{aligned}$$

Therefore, the probability of successful simulation and useful attack is $\frac{1}{2}$.

Advantage and time cost. Suppose the adversary breaks the scheme with (t, q_s, ε). The advantage of solving the q-SDH problem is $\frac{\varepsilon}{2}$. Let T_s denote the time cost of the simulation. We have $T_s = O(q_s^2)$, which is mainly dominated by the signature generation. Therefore, $\mathscr{B}$ will solve the q-SDH problem with $(t + T_s, \varepsilon/2)$.

This completes the proof of the theorem. □

6.2 Gentry Scheme

SysGen: The system parameter generation algorithm takes as input a security parameter λ. It chooses a pairing group $\mathbb{PG} = (\mathbb{G}, \mathbb{G}_T, g, p, e)$ and returns the system parameters $SP = \mathbb{PG}$.

KeyGen: The key generation algorithm takes as input the system parameters SP. It randomly chooses $\alpha, \beta \in \mathbb{Z}_p$, computes $g_1 = g^\alpha, g_2 = g^\beta$, and returns a public/secret key pair (pk, sk) as follows:

$$pk = (g_1, g_2), \quad sk = (\alpha, \beta).$$

Sign: The signing algorithm takes as input a message $m \in \mathbb{Z}_p$, the secret key sk, and the system parameters SP. It randomly chooses $r \in \mathbb{Z}_p$ and computes the signature σ_m on m as

$$\sigma_m = (\sigma_1, \sigma_2) = \left(r, \ g^{\frac{\beta - r}{\alpha - m}} \right).$$

We require that the signing algorithm always uses the same random number r for signature generation on the message m.

Verify: The verification algorithm takes as input a message-signature pair (m, σ_m), the public key pk, and the system parameters SP. Let $\sigma_m = (\sigma_1, \sigma_2)$. It accepts the signature if

$$e\left(\sigma_2, \ g_1 g^{-m} \right) = e\left(g_2 g^{-\sigma_1}, g \right).$$

Theorem 6.2.0.1 *If the q-SDH problem is hard, the Gentry signature scheme is provably secure in the EU-CMA security model with reduction loss about $L = 1$.*

Proof. Suppose there exists an adversary $\mathscr{A}$ who can (t, q_s, ε)-break the signature scheme in the EU-CMA security model. We construct a simulator $\mathscr{B}$ to solve the q-SDH problem. Given as input a problem instance $(g, g^a, g^{a^2}, \cdots, g^{a^q})$ over the pairing group $\mathbb{PG}$, $\mathscr{B}$ runs $\mathscr{A}$ and works as follows.

Setup. Let $SP = \mathbb{PG}$. $\mathscr{B}$ randomly chooses $w_0, w_1, w_2, \cdots, w_q$ from $\mathbb{Z}_p$ and sets the public key as

$$g_1 = g^a, \quad g_2 = g^{w_q a^q + w_{q-1} a^{q-1} + \cdots + w_1 a + w_0},$$

where $\alpha = a, \beta = f(a) = w_q a^q + w_{q-1} a^{q-1} + \cdots + w_1 a + w_0$ and we require $q = q_s + 1$. Here, $f(a) \in \mathbb{Z}_p[a]$ is a q-degree polynomial function in a. The public key can be computed from the problem instance and the chosen parameters.

Query. The adversary makes signature queries in this phase. For the i-th signature query on m_i, $\mathcal{B}$ computes the signature σ_{m_i} as

$$\sigma_{m_i} = (\sigma_1, \sigma_2) = \left(f(m_i), \; g^{f_{m_i}(a)} \right),$$

where $f_{m_i}(x)$ is a $(q-1)$-degree polynomial defined as

$$f_{m_i}(x) = \frac{f(x) - f(m_i)}{x - m_i}.$$

We have that σ_{m_i} is computable using $g, g^a, \cdots, g^{a^q}, f_{m_i}(x), f(x)$. Let $r_i = f(m_i)$. According to the signature definition and simulation, we have

$$g^{\frac{\beta - r_i}{\alpha - m_i}} = g^{\frac{f(a) - f(m_i)}{a - m_i}} = g^{f_{m_i}(a)}.$$

Therefore, σ_{m_i} is a valid signature of m_i.

Forgery. The adversary returns a forged signature σ_{m^*} on some m^* that has not been queried. Let $\sigma_{m^*} = (\sigma_1^*, \sigma_2^*) = \left(r^*, g^{\frac{\beta - r^*}{\alpha - m^*}} \right)$. According to the signature definition and simulation, if $f(m^*) = r^*$, abort. Otherwise, we have $r^* \neq f(m^*)$ and then

$$\sigma_2^* = g^{\frac{\beta - r^*}{\alpha - m^*}} = g^{\frac{f(a) - r^*}{a - m^*}},$$

which can be rewritten as

$$g^{f^*(a) + \frac{d}{a - m^*}},$$

where $f^*(a)$ is a $(q-1)$-degree polynomial function in a, and d is a nonzero integer. The simulator $\mathcal{B}$ computes

$$\left(\frac{\sigma_2^*}{g^{f^*(a)}} \right)^{\frac{1}{d}} = \left(\frac{g^{f(a) + \frac{d}{a - m^*}}}{g^{f^*(a)}} \right)^{\frac{1}{d}} = g^{\frac{1}{a - m^*}}$$

and outputs $\left(-m^*, g^{\frac{1}{a - m^*}} \right)$ as the solution to the q-SDH problem instance.

This completes the simulation and the solution. The correctness is analyzed as follows.

Indistinguishable simulation. The correctness of the simulation has been explained above. The randomness of the simulation includes all random numbers in the key generation and the signature generation. They are

$$a, \; f(a), \; f(m_1), \; f(m_2), \; \cdots, f(m_{q_s}).$$

The simulation is indistinguishable from the real attack because the random numbers are random and independent following the analysis below.

Probability of successful simulation and useful attack. There is no abort in the simulation. The forged signature is reducible if $r^* \neq f(m^*)$. To prove that the adversary has no advantage in computing $f(m^*)$, we only need to prove that the following integers are random and independent:

$$(\alpha, \beta, r_1, \cdots, r_{q_s}, f(m^*)) = \Big(a,\; f(a),\; f(m_1),\; f(m_2),\; \cdots, f(m_{q_s}), f(m^*)\Big).$$

This can be rewritten as

$$f(a) = w_q a^q + \cdots + w_1 a + w_0,$$
$$f(m_1) = w_q m_1{}^q + \cdots + w_1 m_1 + w_0,$$
$$f(m_2) = w_q m_2{}^q + \cdots + w_1 m_2 + w_0,$$
$$\cdots$$
$$f(m_{q_s}) = w_q m_{q_s}{}^q + \cdots + w_1 m_{q_s} + w_0,$$
$$f(m^*) = w_q m^{*q} + \cdots + w_1 m^* + w_0.$$

Since $w_0, w_1, \cdots, w_q$ are all random and independent, the randomness property holds because the determinant of the coefficient matrix is nonzero:

$$\begin{vmatrix} a^q & a^{q-2} & \cdots & a & 1 \\ m_1^a & m_1^{q-1} & \cdots & m_1 & 1 \\ m_2^a & m_2^{q-1} & \cdots & m_2 & 1 \\ \cdots \\ m_{q_s}^a & m_{q_s}^{q-1} & \cdots & m_{q_s} & 1 \\ m^{*a} & m^{*q-1} & \cdots & m^* & 1 \end{vmatrix} = \prod_{1 \leq i < j \leq q+1} (x_i - x_j) : \quad x_i, x_j \in \{a, m_1, \cdots, m_{q_s}, m^*\}.$$

Therefore, any adaptive choice of r^* satisfying $r^* = f(m^*)$ holds with probability $1/p$. Therefore, the probability of successful simulation and useful attack is $1 - \frac{1}{p} \approx 1$ for any adaptive choice r^* from the adversary.

Advantage and time cost. Suppose the adversary breaks the scheme with (t, q_s, ε). Let T_s denote the time cost of the simulation. We have $T_s = O(q_s^2)$, which is mainly dominated by the signature generation. Therefore, $\mathscr{B}$ will solve the q-SDH problem with $(t + T_s, \varepsilon)$.

This completes the proof of the theorem. $\qquad\qquad\qquad\qquad\qquad\qquad\qquad\square$

6.3 GMS Scheme

SysGen: The system parameter generation algorithm takes as input a security parameter λ. It chooses a pairing group $\mathbb{PG} = (\mathbb{G}, \mathbb{G}_T, g, p, e)$ and returns the system parameters $SP = \mathbb{PG}$.

KeyGen: The key generation algorithm takes as input the system parameters SP. It randomly chooses $u_{0,1}, u_{1,1}, u_{0,2}, u_{1,2}, \cdots, u_{0,n}, u_{1,n} \in \mathbb{G}$, $\alpha \in \mathbb{Z}_p$, computes $g_1 = g^\alpha$, selects the upper bound on the number of signatures, denoted by N, and returns a public/secret key pair (pk, sk) as follows:

$$pk = (g_1, u_{0,1}, u_{1,1}, u_{0,2}, u_{1,2}, \cdots, u_{0,n}, u_{1,n}, N), \quad sk = (\alpha, c),$$

where c is a counter initialized with $c = 0$.

Sign: The signing algorithm takes as input a message $m \in \{0,1\}^n$, the secret key sk, and the system parameters SP. It increases its counter by one, $c := c+1$. If $c > N$, abort. Otherwise, it chooses a random bit $b \in \{0,1\}$ and returns the signature σ_m on m as

$$\sigma_m = (\sigma_1, \sigma_2, \sigma_3) = \left(\left(\prod_{i=1}^n u_{m_{[i]}, i} \right)^{\frac{1}{\alpha + c|b}}, \ c, \ b \right).$$

We require that the algorithm always uses the same bit b for the same message. Here, "|" denotes bitwise concatenation.

Verify: The verification algorithm takes as input a message-signature pair (m, σ_m), the public key pk, and the system parameters SP. Let $\sigma_m = (\sigma_1, \sigma_2, \sigma_3)$. It accepts the signature if $\sigma_2 \leq N$, $\sigma_3 \in \{0,1\}$ and

$$e\left(\sigma_1, \ g_1 g^{\sigma_2 | \sigma_3} \right) = e\left(\prod_{i=1}^n u_{m_{[i]}, i}, \ g \right).$$

Theorem 6.3.0.1 *If the q-SDH problem is hard, the GMS signature scheme is provably secure in the EU-CMA security model with reduction loss at most $L = 2n$.*

Proof. Suppose there exists an adversary $\mathscr{A}$ who can (t, q_s, ε)-break the signature scheme in the EU-CMA security model. We construct a simulator $\mathscr{B}$ to solve the q-SDH problem. Given as input a problem instance $(g, g^a, g^{a^2}, \cdots, g^{a^q})$ over the pairing group $\mathbb{PG}$, $\mathscr{B}$ runs $\mathscr{A}$ and works as follows.

$\mathscr{B}$ chooses a secret bit $\mu \in \{0,1\}$ and programs the reduction in two different ways. If $\mu = 0$, the simulator guesses that the adversary will forge a signature with a tuple (c^*, b^*) that was used by the simulator in the signature generation. If $\mu = 1$, the simulator guesses that the adversary will forge a signature with a tuple (c^*, b^*) that was never used by the simulator in the signature generation.

- The reduction for $\mu = 0$ is programmed as follows.

  Setup. Let $SP = \mathbb{PG}$. $\mathcal{B}$ randomly chooses

  $$w_{0,1}, w_{1,1}, w_{0,2}, w_{1,2}, \cdots, w_{0,n}, w_{1,n} \in \mathbb{Z}_p,$$
  $$d_{0,1}, d_{0,2}, d_{0,3}, \cdots, d_{0,q_s} \in \{0,1\},$$
  $$k_1, k_2, \cdots, k_{q_s} \in [1,n],$$

and sets $d_{1,c} = 1 - d_{0,c}$ for all $c \in [1,q_s]$. Let $F(x)$ be the polynomial of degree $2q_s$ defined as

$$F(x) = \prod_{c=1}^{q_s}(x+c|0)(x+c|1) = \prod_{c=1}^{q_s}(x+c|d_{0,c})(x+c|d_{1,c}).$$

For simplicity, we set polynomials

$$F_{0,i}(x) = F(x), \quad F_{1,i}(x) = F(x), \quad i \in [1,n].$$

For all $c \in [1,q_s]$, the polynomials $F_{0,k_c}(x), F_{1,k_c}(x)$ will be replaced by

$$F_{0,k_c}(x) := \frac{F(x)}{x+c|d_{1,c}}, \quad F_{1,k_c}(x) := \frac{F(x)}{x+c|d_{0,c}}.$$

After all replacements, for all $c \in [1,q_s]$, we have that

- $F_{0,i}(x), F_{1,i}(x)$ for any $i \in [1,n] \setminus \{k_c\}$ include the roots $c|d_{0,c}$ and $c|d_{1,c}$.
- $F_{0,k_c}(x)$ does not include the root $c|d_{1,c}$ but only $c|d_{0,c}$.
- $F_{1,k_c}(x)$ does not include the root $c|d_{0,c}$ but only $c|d_{1,c}$.

The simulator sets the public key as

$$g_1 = g^a, \quad u_{0,i} = g^{w_{0,i} \cdot F_{0,i}(a)}, \quad u_{1,i} = g^{w_{1,i} \cdot F_{1,i}(a)}, \quad i \in [1,n],$$

where $\alpha = a$ and we require $q = 2q_s$. The public key can be computed from the problem instance and the chosen parameters.

Query. The adversary makes signature queries in this phase. For a signature query on m, let the updated counter for this signature generation be c, and $m[i]$ be the i-th bit of message m. Then, we have that the polynomials $F_{m[i],i}(x)$ for all $i \in [1,n]$ including $F_{m[k_c],k_c}(x)$ contain the root $c|d_{m[k_c],c}$. $\mathcal{B}$ sets $b = d_{m[k_c],c}$. Let $F_m(x)$ be

$$F_m(x) = \frac{\sum_{i=1}^n w_{m[i],i} \cdot F_{m[i],i}(x)}{x+c|b}.$$

We have that $F_m(x)$ is a polynomial of degree at most $(q-1)$.
$\mathcal{B}$ computes the signature σ_m as

$$\sigma_m = (\sigma_1, \sigma_2, \sigma_3) = \left(g^{F_m(x)}, \quad c, \quad b\right),$$

using $g, g^a, \cdots, g^{a^q}, F_m(x)$.

According to the signature definition and simulation, we have

$$\left(\prod_{i=1}^{n} u_{m_{[i]},i}\right)^{\frac{1}{a+c|b}} = \left(g^{\sum_{i=1}^{n} w_{m[i],i} \cdot F_{m[i],i}(a)}\right)^{\frac{1}{a+c|b}} = g^{F_m(a)}.$$

Therefore, σ_m is a valid signature of m.

Forgery. The adversary returns a forged signature σ_{m^*} on some m^* that has not been queried. Let σ_{m^*} be

$$\sigma_{m^*} = (\sigma_1^*, \sigma_2^*, \sigma_3^*) = \left(\left(\prod_{i=1}^{n} u_{m^*[i],i}\right)^{\frac{1}{a+c^*|b^*}}, c^*, b^*\right).$$

The simulator continues the simulation if

- The tuple (c^*, b^*) was ever used by the simulator in the signature generation for a message, denoted by m.
- $m[k_{c^*}] \neq m^*[k_{c^*}]$, where $m[k_{c^*}]$ and $m^*[k_{c^*}]$ are the k_{c^*}-th bit of messages m and m^*, respectively.

According to the signature definition and simulation, we have that only one of the polynomials $F_{0,k_{c^*}}(x), F_{1,k_{c^*}}(x)$ contains the root $c^*|b^*$, and this polynomial is $F_{m[k_{c^*}],k_{c^*}}(x)$. That is, the polynomial $F_{m^*[k_{c^*}],k_{c^*}}(x)$ does not contain the root $c^*|b^*$. Therefore,

$$F_{m^*}(x) = \frac{\sum_{i=1}^{n} w_{m^*[i],i} \cdot F_{m^*[i],i}(x)}{x + c^*|b^*},$$

can be rewritten as

$$f(x) + \frac{z}{x + c^*|b^*},$$

where $f(x)$ is a $(q-1)$-degree polynomial function in x, and z is a nonzero integer.

The simulator $\mathscr{B}$ computes

$$\left(\frac{\sigma_1^*}{g^{f(a)}}\right)^{\frac{1}{z}} = \left(\frac{g^{f(a) + \frac{z}{a + c^*|b^*}}}{g^{f(a)}}\right)^{\frac{1}{z}} = g^{\frac{1}{a + c^*|b^*}}$$

and outputs $\left(c^*|b^*, g^{\frac{1}{a+c^*|b^*}}\right)$ as the solution to the q-SDH problem instance.

- The reduction for $\mu = 1$ is programmed as follows.

Setup. Let $SP = \mathbb{PG}$. $\mathscr{B}$ randomly chooses

$$w_{0,1}, w_{1,1}, w_{0,2}, w_{1,2}, \cdots, w_{0,n}, w_{1,n} \in \mathbb{Z}_p,$$

$$b_1, b_2, b_3, \cdots, b_{q_s} \in \{0, 1\}.$$

Let $F(x)$ be the polynomial of degree q_s defined as

$$F(x) = \prod_{c=1}^{q_s} (x + c|b_c).$$

The simulator sets the public key as

$$g_1 = g^a, \quad u_{0,i} = g^{w_{0,i} \cdot F(a)}, \quad u_{1,i} = g^{w_{1,i} \cdot F(a)}, \quad i \in [1,n],$$

where $\alpha = a$ and we require $q = q_s$. The public key can be computed from the problem instance and the chosen parameters.

Query. The adversary makes signature queries in this phase. For a signature query on m, let the updated counter for this signature generation be c. $\mathcal{B}$ sets $b = b_c$. Let $F_m(x)$ be

$$F_m(x) = \frac{\sum_{i=1}^{n} w_{m[i],i} \cdot F_{m[i],i}(x)}{x + c|b}.$$

We have that $F_m(x)$ is a polynomial of degree at most $q - 1$.
$\mathcal{B}$ computes the signature σ_m as

$$\sigma_m = (\sigma_1, \sigma_2, \sigma_3) = \left(g^{F_m(x)}, \ c, \ b \right),$$

using $g, g^a, \cdots, g^{a^q}, F_m(x)$.
According to the signature definition and simulation, we have

$$\left(\prod_{i=1}^{n} u_{m[i],i} \right)^{\frac{1}{\alpha+c|b}} = \left(g^{\sum_{i=1}^{n} w_{m[i],i} \cdot F_{m[i],i}(a)} \right)^{\frac{1}{a+c|b}} = g^{F_m(a)}.$$

Therefore, σ_m is a valid signature of m.

Forgery. The adversary returns a forged signature $\sigma_{m^*} = (\sigma_1^*, \sigma_2^*, \sigma_3^*)$ on some m^* that has not been queried. Let σ_{m^*} be

$$\sigma_{m^*} = (\sigma_1^*, \sigma_2^*, \sigma_3^*) = \left(\left(\prod_{i=1}^{n} u_{m^*[i],i} \right)^{\frac{1}{\alpha+c^*|b^*}}, c^*, b^* \right).$$

The simulator continues the simulation if the tuple (c^*, b^*) was never used by the simulator in the signature generation for any message, so that the polynomial $F(x)$ does not contain the root $c^*|b^*$. Therefore,

$$F_{m^*}(x) = \frac{\sum_{i=1}^{n} w_{m^*[i],i} \cdot F(x)}{x + c^*|b^*},$$

can be rewritten as

$$f(x) + \frac{z}{x + c^*|b^*},$$

where $f(x)$ is a $(q-1)$-degree polynomial function in x, and z is a nonzero integer.

The simulator $\mathscr{B}$ computes

$$\left(\frac{\sigma_1^*}{g^{f(a)}}\right)^{\frac{1}{z}} = \left(\frac{g^{f(a)+\frac{z}{a+c^*|b^*}}}{g^{f(a)}}\right)^{\frac{1}{z}} = g^{\frac{1}{a+c^*|b^*}}$$

and outputs $\left(c^*|b^*, g^{\frac{1}{a+c^*|b^*}}\right)$ as the solution to the q-SDH problem instance.

This completes the simulation and the solution. The correctness is analyzed as follows.

Indistinguishable simulation. The correctness of the simulation has been explained above. The randomness of the simulation includes all random numbers in the key generation and the signature generation. They are

$$\begin{cases} a, & w_{0,i} \cdot F_{0,i}(a), & w_{1,i} \cdot F_{1,i}(a), & d_{m[k_c],c}: & \mu = 0 \\ a, & w_{0,i} \cdot F(a), & w_{1,i} \cdot F(a), & b_c: & \mu = 1 \end{cases}.$$

According to the setting of the simulation, where $a, w_{0,i}, w_{1,i}, d_{m[k_c],c}, b_c$ are randomly chosen, it is easy to see that they are random and independent from the point of view of the adversary no matter whether $\mu = 0$ or $\mu = 1$. Therefore, the simulation is indistinguishable from the real attack, and the adversary has no advantage in guessing μ from the simulation.

Probability of successful simulation and useful attack. There is no abort in the simulation. Let the random bit in the forged signature of m^* be b^*. We have

- Case $\mu = 0$. The forged signature is reducible if $m^*[k_{c^*}] \neq m[k_{c^*}]$ using the tuple (c^*, b^*), where $m[k_{c^*}]$ is the k_{c^*}-bit of the message m queried by the adversary. Since m and m^* differ on at least one bit and k_{c^*} is randomly chosen by the simulator, we have that the success probability of $m^*[k_{c^*}] \neq m[k_{c^*}]$ is at least $\frac{1}{n}$.
- Case $\mu = 1$. The forged signature is always reducible with success probability 1, because the tuple (c^*, b^*) was never used by the simulator in the signature generation.

Let $\mu^* \in \{0,1\}$ be the type of attack launched by the adversary, where $\mu^* = 0$ means that $c^*|b^*$ in the forged signature was used by the simulator in the signature generation, and $\mu^* = 1$ means that $c^*|b^*$ in the forged signature was never used by the simulator in the signature generation. Since the two simulations are indistinguishable and the simulator randomly chooses one simulation, the forged signature is reducible with success probability $\Pr[Success]$ described as follows:

$$\begin{aligned} \Pr[Success] &= \Pr[Success|\mu = 0]\Pr[\mu = 0] + \Pr[Success|\mu = 1]\Pr[\mu = 1] \\ &= \Pr[\mu^* = 0 \wedge m^*[k_{c^*}] \neq m[k_{c^*}]]\Pr[\mu = 0] + \Pr[\mu^* = 1]\Pr[\mu = 1] \\ &= \Pr[\mu^* = 0]\Pr[m^*[k_{c^*}] \neq m[k_{c^*}]]\Pr[\mu = 0] + \Pr[\mu^* = 1]\Pr[\mu = 1] \end{aligned}$$

$$= \Pr[\mu^* = 0]\frac{1}{2n} + \Pr[\mu^* = 1]\frac{1}{2}$$

$$\geq \Pr[\mu^* = 0]\frac{1}{2n} + \Pr[\mu^* = 1]\frac{1}{2n}$$

$$= \frac{1}{2n}\Big(\Pr[\mu^* = 0] + \Pr[\mu^* = 1]\Big)$$

$$= \frac{1}{2n}.$$

Therefore, the probability of successful simulation and useful attack is at least $\frac{1}{2n}$.

Advantage and time cost. Suppose the adversary breaks the scheme with (t, q_s, ε). The advantage of solving the q-SDH problem is therefore $\frac{\varepsilon}{2n}$. Let T_s denote the time cost of the simulation. We have $T_s = O(q_s^2)$, which is mainly dominated by the signature generation. Therefore, $\mathscr{B}$ will solve the q-SDH problem with $\big(t + T_s, \frac{\varepsilon}{2n}\big)$.

This completes the proof of the theorem. $\square$

6.4 Waters Scheme

SysGen: The system parameter generation algorithm takes as input a security parameter λ. It chooses a pairing group $\mathbb{PG} = (\mathbb{G}, \mathbb{G}_T, g, p, e)$ and returns the system parameters $SP = \mathbb{PG}$.

KeyGen: The key generation algorithm takes as input the system parameters SP. It randomly chooses $g_2, u_0, u_1, u_2, \cdots, u_n \in \mathbb{G}$, $\alpha \in \mathbb{Z}_p$, computes $g_1 = g^\alpha$, and returns a public/secret key pair (pk, sk) as follows:

$$pk = (g_1, g_2, u_0, u_1, u_2, \cdots, u_n), \quad sk = \alpha.$$

Sign: The signing algorithm takes as input a message $m \in \{0, 1\}^n$, the secret key sk, and the system parameters SP. Let $m[i]$ be the i-th bit of message m. It chooses a random number $r \in \mathbb{Z}_p$ and returns the signature σ_m on m as

$$\sigma_m = (\sigma_1, \sigma_2) = \left(g_2^\alpha \left(u_0 \prod_{i=1}^n u_i^{m[i]} \right)^r, g^r \right).$$

Verify: The verification algorithm takes as input a message-signature pair (m, σ_m), the public key pk, and the system parameters SP. Let $\sigma_m = (\sigma_1, \sigma_2)$. It accepts the signature if

$$e(\sigma_1, g) = e(g_1, g_2)e\left(u_0 \prod_{i=1}^n u_i^{m[i]}, \sigma_2 \right).$$

Theorem 6.4.0.1 *If the CDH problem is hard, the Waters signature scheme is provably secure in the EU-CMA security model with reduction loss $L = 4(n+1)q_s$, where q_s is the number of signature queries.*

Proof. Suppose there exists an adversary $\mathscr{A}$ who can (t, q_s, ε)-break the signature scheme in the EU-CMA security model. We construct a simulator $\mathscr{B}$ to solve the CDH problem. Given as input a problem instance (g, g^a, g^b) over the pairing group $\mathbb{PG}$, $\mathscr{B}$ runs $\mathscr{A}$ and works as follows.

Setup. Let $SP = \mathbb{PG}$. $\mathscr{B}$ sets $q = 2q_s$ and randomly chooses integers $k, x_0, x_1, \cdots, x_n,$ $y_0, y_1, \cdots, y_n$ satisfying

$$
\begin{aligned}
k &\in [0, n], \\
x_0, x_1, \cdots, x_n &\in [0, q-1], \\
y_0, y_1, \cdots, y_n &\in \mathbb{Z}_p.
\end{aligned}
$$

It sets the public key as

$$
g_1 = g^a, \quad g_2 = g^b, \quad u_0 = g^{-kqa+x_0 a+y_0}, u_i = g^{x_i a + y_i},
$$

where $\alpha = a$. The public key can be computed from the problem instance and the chosen parameters.

We define $F(m), J(m), K(m)$ as

$$
F(m) = -kq + x_0 + \sum_{i=1}^{n} m[i] \cdot x_i,
$$

$$
J(m) = y_0 + \sum_{i=1}^{n} m[i] \cdot y_i,
$$

$$
K(m) = \begin{cases} 0 & \text{if } x_0 + \sum_{i=1}^{n} m[i] \cdot x_i = 0 \mod q \\ 1 & \text{otherwise} \end{cases}.
$$

Then, we have

$$
u_0 \prod_{i=1}^{n} u_i^{m[i]} = g^{F(m)a + J(m)}.
$$

Query. The adversary makes signature queries in this phase. For a signature query on m, if $K(m) = 0$, the simulator aborts. Otherwise, $\mathscr{B}$ randomly chooses $r' \in \mathbb{Z}_p$ and computes the signature σ_m as

$$
\sigma_m = (\sigma_1, \sigma_2) = \left(g_2^{-\frac{J(m)}{F(m)}} \left(u_0 \prod_{i=1}^{n} u_i^{m[i]} \right)^{r'}, \ g_2^{-\frac{1}{F(m)}} g^{r'} \right).
$$

We have that σ_m is computable using $g, g_1, F(m), J(m), r', m$ and the public key.
    Let $r = -\frac{1}{F(m)} b + r'$. We have

$$g_2^\alpha \left(u_0 \prod_{i=1}^n u_i^{m[i]} \right)^r = g^{ab} \left(g^{F(m)a+J(m)} \right)^{-\frac{1}{F(m)}b+r'}$$

$$= g^{ab} \cdot g^{-ab+r'F(m)a-\frac{J(m)}{F(m)}b+J(m)r'}$$

$$= g^{-\frac{J(m)}{F(m)}b} g^{r'(F(m)a+J(m))}$$

$$= g_2^{-\frac{J(m)}{F(m)}} \left(u_0 \prod_{i=1}^n u_i^{m[i]} \right)^{r'},$$

$$g^r = g^{-\frac{1}{F(m)}b+r'}$$

$$= g_2^{-\frac{1}{F(m)}} g^{r'}.$$

Therefore, σ_m is a valid signature of m.

Forgery. The adversary returns a forged signature σ_{m^*} on some m^* that has not been queried. Let the signature be

$$\sigma_{m^*} = (\sigma_1^*, \sigma_2^*) = \left(g_2^\alpha \left(u_0 \prod_{i=1}^n u_i^{m^*[i]} \right)^r, g^r \right).$$

According to the signature definition and simulation, if $F(m^*) \neq 0$, abort. Otherwise, we have $F(m^*) = 0$ and then

$$\sigma_1^* = g_2^\alpha \left(u_0 \prod_{i=1}^n u_i^{m^*[i]} \right)^r = g^{ab} \left(g^{F(m^*)a+J(m^*)} \right)^r = g^{ab} (g^r)^{J(m^*)}.$$

The simulator $\mathscr{B}$ computes

$$\frac{\sigma_1^*}{(\sigma_2^*)^{J(m^*)}} = \frac{g^{ab} (g^r)^{J(m^*)}}{g^{rJ(m^*)}} = g^{ab}$$

as the solution to the CDH problem instance.

This completes the simulation and the solution. The correctness is analyzed as follows.

Indistinguishable simulation. The correctness of the simulation has been explained above. The randomness of the simulation includes all random numbers in the key generation and the signature generation. They are

$$a, \; b, \; x_0 b + y_0, \; x_1 b + y_1, \; x_2 b + y_2, \cdots, x_n b + y_n, \quad -\frac{b}{F(m_i)} + r_i'.$$

According to the setting of the simulation, where a, b, y_i, r_i' are randomly chosen, it is easy to see that the simulation is indistinguishable from the real attack.

Probability of successful simulation and useful attack. A successful simulation and a useful attack require that

$$K(m_1) = 1, \ K(m_2) = 1, \ \cdots, \ K(m_{q_s}) = 1, \ F(m^*) = 0.$$

We have

$$0 \le x_0 + \sum_{i=1}^{n} m[i] x_i \le (n+1)(q-1),$$

where the range $[0, (n+1)(q-1)]$ contains integers $0q, 1q, 2q, \cdots, nq \ (n < q)$.
Let $X = x_0 + \sum_{i=1}^{n} m[i] x_i$. Since all x_i and k are randomly chosen, we have

$$\Pr[F(m^*) = 0] = \Pr\left[X = 0 \bmod q\right] \cdot \Pr\left[X = kq \middle| X = 0 \bmod q\right] = \frac{1}{(n+1)q}.$$

Since the pair (m_i, m^*) for any i differ on at least one bit, $K(m_i)$ and $F(m^*)$ differ on the coefficient of at least one x_j, and then

$$\Pr[K(m_i) = 0 | F(m^*) = 0] = \frac{1}{q}.$$

Based on the above results, we obtain

$$
\begin{aligned}
&\Pr[K(m_1) = 1 \wedge \cdots \wedge K(m_{q_s}) = 1 \wedge F(m^*) = 0] \\
&= \Pr[K(m_1) = 1 \wedge \cdots \wedge K(m_{q_s}) = 1 | F(m^*) = 0] \cdot \Pr[F(m^*) = 0] \\
&= (1 - \Pr[K(m_1) = 0 \vee \cdots \vee K(m_{q_s}) = 0 | F(m^*) = 0]) \cdot \Pr[F(m^*) = 0] \\
&\ge \left(1 - \sum_{i=1}^{q_s} \Pr[K(m_i) = 0 | F(m^*) = 0]\right) \cdot \Pr[F(m^*) = 0] \\
&= \frac{1}{(n+1)q} \cdot \left(1 - \frac{q_s}{q}\right) \\
&= \frac{1}{4(n+1)q_s},
\end{aligned}
$$

which is the probability of successful simulation and useful attack.

Advantage and time cost. Suppose the adversary breaks the scheme with (t, q_s, ε). The advantage of solving the CDH problem is therefore $\frac{\varepsilon}{4(n+1)q_s}$. Let T_s denote the time cost of the simulation. We have $T_s = O(q_s)$, which is mainly dominated by the signature generation. Therefore, $\mathscr{B}$ will solve the CDH problem with $\left(t + T_s, \frac{\varepsilon}{4(n+1)q_s}\right)$.

This completes the proof of the theorem. □

6.5 Hohenberger-Waters Scheme

SysGen: The system parameter generation algorithm takes as input a security parameter λ. It chooses a pairing group $\mathbb{PG} = (\mathbb{G}, \mathbb{G}_T, g, p, e)$ and returns the system parameters $SP = \mathbb{PG}$.

KeyGen: The key generation algorithm takes as input the system parameters SP. It randomly chooses $u_1, u_2, u_3, v_1, v_2 \in \mathbb{G}$, $\alpha \in \mathbb{Z}_p$, computes $g_1 = g^\alpha$, selects the upper bound on the number of signatures, denoted by N, and returns a public/secret key pair (pk, sk) as follows:

$$pk = (g_1, u_1, u_2, u_3, v_1, v_2, N), \quad sk = (\alpha, c),$$

where c is a counter initialized with $c = 0$.

Sign: The signing algorithm takes as input a message $m \in \mathbb{Z}_p$, the secret key sk, and the system parameters SP. It chooses random numbers $r, s \in \mathbb{Z}_p$ and increases the counter by one, $c := c + 1$. If $c > N$, abort. Otherwise, the algorithm returns the signature σ_m on m as

$$\sigma_m = (\sigma_1, \sigma_2, \sigma_3, \sigma_4) = \left(\left(u_1^m u_2^r u_3 \right)^\alpha \left(v_1^c v_2 \right)^s, \ g^s, \ r, \ c \right).$$

Verify: The verification algorithm takes as input a message-signature pair (m, σ_m), the public key pk, and the system parameters SP. Let $\sigma_m = (\sigma_1, \sigma_2, \sigma_3, \sigma_4)$. It accepts the signature if $\sigma_4 \leq N$ and

$$e(\sigma_1, \ g) = e\left(u_1^m u_2^{\sigma_3} u_3, \ g_1 \right) e\left(v_1^{\sigma_4} v_2, \sigma_2 \right).$$

Theorem 6.5.0.1 *If the CDH problem is hard, the Hohenberger-Waters signature scheme is provably secure in the EU-CMA security model with reduction loss $L = N$.*

Proof. Suppose there exists an adversary $\mathscr{A}$ who can (t, q_s, ε)-break the signature scheme in the EU-CMA security model. We construct a simulator $\mathscr{B}$ to solve the CDH problem. Given as input a problem instance (g, g^a, g^b) over the pairing group $\mathbb{PG}$, $\mathscr{B}$ runs $\mathscr{A}$ and works as follows.

Setup. Let $SP = \mathbb{PG}$. $\mathscr{B}$ randomly chooses $x_1, y_1, y_2, x_3, y_3, z_1, z_2 \in \mathbb{Z}_p$, $x_2 \in \mathbb{Z}_p^*$, and $c_0 \in [1, N]$. It sets the public key as

$$g_1 = g^a,$$
$$u_1 = g^{bx_1+y_1}, \quad u_2 = g^{bx_2+y_2}, \quad u_3 = g^{bx_3+y_3},$$
$$v_1 = g^{-b+z_1}, \quad v_2 = g^{c_0 b + z_2},$$

where $\alpha = a$ and a, b are unknown secrets from the problem instance. The public key can be computed from the problem instance and the chosen parameters.

Query. The adversary makes signature queries in this phase. For a signature query on m, let the updated counter for this signature generation be c. The simulation of this signature falls into the following two cases.

- $c \neq c_0$. $\mathcal{B}$ randomly chooses $r, s' \in \mathbb{Z}_p$ such that $mx_1 + rx_2 + x_3 \neq 0$. We have

$$u_1^m u_2^r u_3 = g^{b(mx_1 + rx_2 + x_3) + (my_1 + ry_2 + y_3)}, \quad v_1^c v_2 = g^{b(c_0 - c) + z_1 c + z_2}.$$

It computes the signature σ_m as

$$
\sigma_m = (\sigma_1, \sigma_2, \sigma_3, \sigma_4)
$$
$$
= \left(g_1^{my_1 + ry_2 + y_3 - \frac{z_1 + z_2}{c_0 - c} \cdot (mx_1 + rx_2 + x_3)} \cdot (v_1^c v_2)^{s'}, \ g_1^{-\frac{mx_1 + rx_2 + x_3}{c_0 - c}} \cdot g^{s'}, \ r, \ c \right).
$$

Let $s = -\frac{mx_1 + rx_2 + x_3}{c_0 - c} a + s'$. We have

$$
(u_1^m u_2^r u_3)^\alpha (v_1^c v_2)^s
$$
$$
= g^{ab(mx_1 + rx_2 + x_3) + a(my_1 + ry_2 + y_3)} \cdot \left(g^{b(c_0 - c) + z_1 c + z_2} \right)^{-\frac{mx_1 + rx_2 + x_3}{c_0 - c} a + s'}
$$
$$
= g^{ab(mx_1 + rx_2 + x_3) + a(my_1 + ry_2 + y_3)} \cdot g^{-ab(mx_1 + rx_2 + x_3)} \cdot g^{-a \frac{z_1 c + z_2}{c_0 - c} \cdot (mx_1 + rx_2 + x_3)} \cdot (v_1^c v_2)^{s'}
$$
$$
= g_1^{my_1 + ry_2 + y_3 - \frac{z_1 c + z_2}{c_0 - c} \cdot (mx_1 + rx_2 + x_3)} \cdot (v_1^c v_2)^{s'},
$$
$$
g^s = g_1^{-\frac{mx_1 + rx_2 + x_3}{c_0 - c}} \cdot g^{s'}.
$$

Therefore, σ_m is a valid signature of m.

- $c = c_0$. $\mathcal{B}$ randomly chooses $s \in \mathbb{Z}_p$ and computes r satisfying $mx_1 + rx_2 + x_3 = 0$. That is, s is randomly chosen and

$$
r = -\frac{mx_1 + x_3}{x_2}.
$$

It computes the signature σ_m as

$$
\sigma_m = (\sigma_1, \sigma_2, \sigma_3, \sigma_4) = \left(g_1^{my_1 + ry_2 + y_3} \cdot (v_1^c v_2)^s, \ g^s, \ r, \ c \right).
$$

We have

$$
(u_1^m u_2^r u_3)^\alpha (v_1^c v_2)^s = g^{ab(mx_1 + rx_2 + x_3) + a(my_1 + ry_2 + y_3)} \cdot (v_1^c v_2)^s
$$
$$
= g^{a(my_1 + ry_2 + y_3)} (v_1^c v_2)^s
$$
$$
= g_1^{my_1 + ry_2 + y_3} \cdot (v_1^c v_2)^s.
$$

Therefore, σ_m is a valid signature of m.

Forgery. The adversary returns a forged signature σ_{m^*} on some m^* that has not been queried. Let the signature be

$$\sigma_{m^*} = (\sigma_1^*, \sigma_2^*, \sigma_3^*, \sigma_4^*) = \left((u_1^{m^*} u_2^{r^*} u_3)^\alpha (v_1^{c^*} v_2)^s, \; g^s, \; r^*, c^* \right).$$

According to the signature definition and simulation, the simulation is successful if

$$c^* = c_0 \quad \text{and} \quad m^* x_1 + r^* x_2 + x_3 \neq 0.$$

If it is successful, we have

$$
\begin{aligned}
\sigma_1^* &= \left(u_1^{m^*} u_2^{r^*} u_3 \right)^\alpha \left(v_1^{c^*} v_2 \right)^s \\
&= g^{ab(m^* x_1 + r^* x_2 + x_3) + a(m^* y_1 + r^* y_2 + y_3)} \cdot \left(g^{z_1 c^* + z_2} \right)^s \\
&= g^{ab(m^* x_1 + r^* x_2 + x_3) + a(m^* y_1 + r^* y_2 + y_3)} \cdot \left(\sigma_2^* \right)^{z_1 c^* + z_2}.
\end{aligned}
$$

The simulator $\mathscr{B}$ computes

$$
\left(\frac{\sigma_1^*}{g_1^{m^* y_1 + r^* y_2 + y_3} \left(\sigma_2^* \right)^{z_1 c^* + z_2}} \right)^{\frac{1}{m^* x_1 + r^* x_2 + x_3}} = g^{ab}
$$

as the solution to the CDH problem instance.

This completes the simulation and the solution. The correctness is analyzed as follows.

Indistinguishable simulation. The correctness of the simulation has been explained above. The randomness of the simulation includes all random numbers in the key generation and the signature generation. They are

$$
\begin{aligned}
pk &: a, \; bx_1 + y_1, \; bx_2 + y_2, \; bx_3 + y_3, \; -b + z_1, \; c_0 b + z_2, \\
(r,s) \text{ when } c \neq c_0 &: r_c, \quad -\frac{m_c x_1 + r_c x_2 + x_3}{c_0 - c} a + s_c' \quad (r = r_c, \; s = s_c), \\
(r,s) \text{ when } c = c_0 &: -\frac{m_{c_0} x_1 + x_3}{x_2}, \; s_{c_0} \quad \left(r = -\frac{m_{c_0} x_1 + x_3}{x_2}, \; s = s_{c_0} \right).
\end{aligned}
$$

Since s_c', r_c, s_{c_0} are randomly chosen, we only need to consider the randomness of

$$
a, \; bx_1 + y_1, \; bx_2 + y_2, \; bx_3 + y_3, \; -b + z_1, \; c_0 b + z_2, \; -\frac{m_{c_0} x_1 + x_3}{x_2}.
$$

According to the setting of the simulation, where $a, b, x_1, x_3, y_1, y_2, y_3, z_1, z_2$ are randomly chosen, it is easy to see that the simulation is indistinguishable from the real attack. In particular, the adversary has no advantage in guessing c_0 from the given parameters.

Probability of successful simulation and useful attack. There is no abort in the simulation. The forged signature is reducible if

$$c^* = c_0, \quad m^* x_1 + r^* x_2 + x_3 \neq 0.$$

Since c_0 is random and unknown to the adversary according to the above analysis, we have that $c^* = c_0$ holds with probability $\frac{1}{N}$ for any adaptive choice c^*. To prove that the adversary has no advantage in computing r^* satisfying $m^* x_1 + r^* x_2 + x_3 = 0$, we only need to prove that

$$-\frac{m^* x_1 + x_3}{x_2}$$

is random and independent from the point of view of the adversary. It is easy to see that the following integers associated with x_1, x_2, x_3 are random and independent:

$$b x_1 + y_1, \ b x_2 + y_2, \ b x_3 + y_3, \ -\frac{m_{c_0} x_1 + x_3}{x_2}, \ -\frac{m^* x_1 + x_3}{x_2}.$$

Any adaptive choice r^* satisfies $m^* x_1 + r^* x_2 + x_3 = 0$ with probability $1/p$. Therefore, the probability of successful simulation and useful attack is $\frac{1}{N}(1 - 1/p) \approx 1/N$.

Advantage and time cost. Suppose the adversary breaks the scheme with (t, q_s, ε). The advantage of solving the CDH problem is therefore $\frac{\varepsilon}{N}$. Let T_s denote the time cost of the simulation. We have $T_s = O(q_s)$, which is mainly dominated by the signature generation. Therefore, $\mathscr{B}$ will solve the CDH problem with $(t + T_s, \frac{\varepsilon}{N})$.

This completes the proof of the theorem. $\square$

Chapter 7
Public-Key Encryption with Random Oracles

In this chapter, we mainly use a variant of ElGamal encryption to introduce how to prove the security of encryption schemes under computational hardness assumptions. The basic scheme is called the hashed ElGamal scheme [1]. The twin ElGamal scheme and the iterated ElGamal scheme are from [29] and [55], respectively, and introduce two totally different approaches for addressing the reduction loss of finding a correct solution from hash queries. The ElGamal encryption scheme with CCA security is introduced using the Fujisaki-Okamoto transformation [42]. The given schemes and/or proofs may be different from the original ones.

7.1 Hashed ElGamal Scheme

SysGen: The system parameter generation algorithm takes as input a security parameter λ. It chooses a cyclic group $(\mathbb{G}, p, g)$, selects a cryptographic hash function $H : \{0,1\}^* \rightarrow \{0,1\}^n$, and returns the system parameters $SP = (\mathbb{G}, p, g, H)$.

KeyGen: The key generation algorithm takes as input the system parameters SP. It randomly chooses $\alpha \in \mathbb{Z}_p$, computes $g_1 = g^\alpha$, and returns a public/secret key pair (pk, sk) as follows:

$$pk = g_1, \quad sk = \alpha.$$

Encrypt: The encryption algorithm takes as input a message $m \in \{0,1\}^n$, the public key pk, and the system parameters SP. It chooses a random number $r \in \mathbb{Z}_p$ and returns the ciphertext CT as

$$CT = (C_1, C_2) = \left(g^r, \ H(g_1^r) \oplus m\right).$$

© Springer International Publishing AG, part of Springer Nature 2018
F. Guo et al., *Introduction to Security Reduction*,
https://doi.org/10.1007/978-3-319-93049-7_7

Decrypt: The decryption algorithm takes as input a ciphertext CT, the secret key sk, and the system parameters SP. Let $CT = (C_1, C_2)$. It decrypts the message by computing

$$C_2 \oplus H(C_1^\alpha) = H(g_1^r) \oplus m \oplus H(g^{\alpha r}) = m.$$

Theorem 7.1.0.1 *Suppose the hash function H is a random oracle. If the CDH problem is hard, the Hashed ElGamal encryption scheme is provably secure in the IND-CPA security model with reduction loss $L = q_H$, where q_H is the number of hash queries to the random oracle.*

Proof. Suppose there exists an adversary $\mathscr{A}$ who can (t, ε)-break the encryption scheme in the IND-CPA security model. We construct a simulator $\mathscr{B}$ to solve the CDH problem. Given as input a problem instance (g, g^a, g^b) over the cyclic group $(\mathbb{G}, g, p)$, $\mathscr{B}$ controls the random oracle, runs $\mathscr{A}$, and works as follows.

Setup. Let $SP = (\mathbb{G}, g, p)$ and H be the random oracle controlled by the simulator. $\mathscr{B}$ sets the public key as $g_1 = g^a$ where $\alpha = a$. The public key is available from the problem instance.

H-Query. The adversary makes hash queries in this phase. $\mathscr{B}$ prepares a hash list to record all queries and responses as follows, where the hash list is empty at the beginning.

Let the i-th hash query be x_i. If x_i is already in the hash list, $\mathscr{B}$ responds to this query following the hash list. Otherwise, $\mathscr{B}$ randomly chooses $y_i \in \{0, 1\}^n$ and sets $H(x_i) = y_i$. The simulator $\mathscr{B}$ responds to this query with $H(x_i)$ and adds (x_i, y_i) to the hash list.

Challenge. $\mathscr{A}$ outputs two distinct messages $m_0, m_1 \in \{0, 1\}^n$ to be challenged. The simulator randomly chooses $R \in \{0, 1\}^n$ and sets the challenge ciphertext CT^* as

$$CT^* = (g^b, \ R),$$

where g^b is from the problem instance. The challenge ciphertext can be seen as an encryption of the message $m_c \in \{m_0, m_1\}$ using the random number b if $H(g_1^b) = R \oplus m_c$:

$$CT^* = (g^b, \ R) = \left(g^b, H(g_1^b) \oplus m_c \right).$$

The challenge ciphertext is therefore a correct ciphertext from the point of view of the adversary, if there is no hash query on g_1^b to the random oracle.

Guess. $\mathscr{A}$ outputs a guess or $\bot$. The challenge hash query is defined as

$$Q^* = g_1^b = (g^b)^\alpha = g^{ab}.$$

The simulator randomly selects one value x from the hash list $(x_1, y_1), (x_2, y_2), \cdots,$ (x_{q_H}, y_{q_H}) as the challenge hash query. The simulator can immediately use this hash query to solve the CDH problem.

This completes the simulation and the solution. The correctness is analyzed as follows.

Indistinguishable simulation. The correctness of the simulation has been explained above. The randomness of the simulation includes all random numbers in the key generation, the responses to hash queries, and the challenge ciphertext generation. They are

$$a, y_1, y_2, \cdots, y_{q_H}, b.$$

According to the setting of the simulation, where a, b, y_i are randomly chosen, it is easy to see that the randomness property holds, and thus the simulation is indistinguishable from the real attack.

Probability of successful simulation. There is no abort in the simulation, and thus the probability of successful simulation is 1.

Advantage of breaking the challenge ciphertext. If $H(g^{ab}) = R \oplus m_0$, the challenge ciphertext is an encryption of m_0. If $H(g^{ab}) = R \oplus m_1$, the challenge ciphertext is an encryption of m_1. If the query g^{ab} is not made, $H(g^{ab})$ is random and unknown to the adversary, so that it has no advantage in breaking the challenge ciphertext.

Probability of finding solution. Since the adversary has advantage ε in guessing the chosen message according to the breaking assumption, the adversary will query g^{ab} to the random oracle with probability ε according to Lemma 4.11.1. The adversary makes q_H hash queries in total. Therefore, a random choice of x is equal to g^{ab} with probability $\frac{\varepsilon}{q_H}$.

Advantage and time cost. Let T_s denote the time cost of the simulation. We have $T_s = O(1)$. Therefore, the simulator $\mathscr{B}$ will solve the CDH problem with $\left(t + T_s, \frac{\varepsilon}{q_H}\right)$.

This completes the proof of the theorem. $\qquad\qquad\qquad\qquad\qquad\square$

7.2 Twin Hashed ElGamal Scheme

SysGen: The system parameter generation algorithm takes as input a security parameter λ. It chooses a cyclic group $(\mathbb{G}, p, g)$, selects a cryptographic hash function $H : \{0, 1\}^* \rightarrow \{0, 1\}^n$, and returns the system parameters $SP = (\mathbb{G}, p, g, H)$.

KeyGen: The key generation algorithm takes as input the system parameters SP. It randomly chooses $\alpha, \beta \in \mathbb{Z}_p$, computes $g_1 = g^\alpha, g_2 = g^\beta$, and returns a

---

public/secret key pair (pk, sk) as follows:

$$pk = (g_1, g_2), \quad sk = (\alpha, \beta).$$

Encrypt: The encryption algorithm takes as input a message $m \in \{0, 1\}^n$, the public key pk, and the system parameters SP. It chooses a random number $r \in \mathbb{Z}_p$ and returns the ciphertext CT as

$$CT = (C_1, C_2) = \left(g^r, \ H(g_1^r \| g_2^r) \oplus m \right).$$

Decrypt: The decryption algorithm takes as input a ciphertext CT, the secret key sk, and the system parameters SP. Let $CT = (C_1, C_2)$. It decrypts the message by computing

$$C_2 \oplus H\left(C_1^\alpha \| C_1^\beta \right) = H(g_1^r \| g_2^r) \oplus m \oplus H\left(g^{\alpha r} \| g^{\beta r} \right) = m.$$

Theorem 7.2.0.1 *Suppose the hash function H is a random oracle. If the CDH problem is hard, the Twin Hashed ElGamal encryption scheme is provably secure in the IND-CPA security model with reduction loss $L = 1$.*

Proof. Suppose there exists an adversary $\mathscr{A}$ who can (t, ε)-break the encryption scheme in the IND-CPA security model. We construct a simulator $\mathscr{B}$ to solve the CDH problem. Given as input a problem instance (g, g^a, g^b) over the cyclic group $(\mathbb{G}, g, p)$, $\mathscr{B}$ controls the random oracle, runs $\mathscr{A}$, and works as follows.

Setup. Let $SP = (\mathbb{G}, g, p)$ and H be the random oracle controlled by the simulator. $\mathscr{B}$ randomly chooses $z_1, z_2 \in \mathbb{Z}_p$ and sets the public key as

$$(g_1, g_2) = \left(g^a, g^{z_1}(g^a)^{z_2} \right),$$

where $\alpha = a$ and $\beta = z_1 + z_2 a$. The public key can be computed from the problem instance and the chosen parameters.

H-Query. The adversary makes hash queries in this phase. $\mathscr{B}$ prepares a hash list to record all queries and responses as follows, where the hash list is empty at the beginning.

Let the i-th hash query be x_i. If x_i is already in the hash list, $\mathscr{B}$ responds to this query following the hash list. Otherwise, $\mathscr{B}$ randomly chooses $y_i \in \{0, 1\}^n$ and sets $H(x_i) = y_i$. The simulator $\mathscr{B}$ responds to this query with $H(x_i)$ and adds (x_i, y_i) to the hash list.

Challenge. $\mathscr{A}$ outputs two distinct messages $m_0, m_1 \in \{0, 1\}^n$ to be challenged. The simulator randomly chooses $R \in \{0, 1\}^n$ and sets the challenge ciphertext CT^* as

$$CT^* = (g^b, \ R),$$

where g^b is from the problem instance. The challenge ciphertext can be seen as an encryption of the message $m_c \in \{m_0, m_1\}$ using the random number b if $H(g_1^b \| g_2^b) = R \oplus m_c$:

$$CT^* = (g^b, \ R) = \left(g^b, H(g_1^b \| g_2^b) \oplus m_c \right).$$

The challenge ciphertext is therefore a correct ciphertext from the point of view of the adversary, if there is no hash query on $g_1^b \| g_2^b$ to the random oracle.

Guess. $\mathscr{A}$ outputs a guess or $\perp$. In the above simulation, the challenge hash query is defined as

$$Q^* = g_1^b \| g_2^b = g^{ab} \| g^{z_1 b + z_2 ab}.$$

Suppose $(x_1, y_1), (x_2, y_2), \cdots, (x_{q_H}, y_{q_H})$ are in the hash list, where each query x_i can be denoted by $x_i = u_i \| v_i$. If x_i does not satisfy this structure, we can delete it.
   The simulator finds the query $x^* = u^* \| v^*$ from the hash list satisfying

$$(g^b)^{z_1} \cdot (u^*)^{z_2} = v^*$$

as the challenge hash query and returns $u^* = g^{ab}$ as the solution to the CDH problem instance. In this security reduction, the second group element is only used for helping the simulator find the challenge hash query from the hash list.

   This completes the simulation and the solution. The correctness is analyzed as follows.

Indistinguishable simulation. The correctness of the simulation has been explained above. The randomness of the simulation includes all random numbers in the key generation, the responses to hash queries, and the challenge ciphertext generation. They are

$$a, \ z_1 + z_2 a, \ y_1, \ y_2, \ \cdots, \ y_{q_H}, \ b.$$

According to the setting of the simulation, where a, b, z_1, z_2, y_i are randomly chosen, it is easy to see that the randomness property holds, and thus the simulation is indistinguishable from the real attack.

Probability of successful simulation. There is no abort in the simulation, and thus the probability of successful simulation is 1.

Advantage of breaking the challenge ciphertext. If $H(g_1^b \| g_2^b) = R \oplus m_0$, the challenge ciphertext is an encryption of m_0. If $H(g_1^b \| g_2^b) = R \oplus m_1$, the challenge ciphertext is an encryption of m_1. If the query $g_1^b \| g_2^b$ is not made, we have that $H(g_1^b \| g_2^b)$ is random and unknown to the adversary, so that it has no advantage in breaking the challenge ciphertext.

Probability of finding solution. Since the adversary has advantage ε in guessing the chosen message according to the breaking assumption, the adversary will query g^{ab} to the random oracle with probability ε according to Lemma 4.11.1. The adversary makes q_H hash queries in total. We claim that the adversary has no advantage in generating a query $x = u \| v$ satisfying

$$u \neq g^{ab} \text{ and } g^{bz_1} u^{z_2} = v.$$

Let $u = g^{a'b}$ and $v = g^{wb}$ where $a' \neq a$. If the adversary can compute such a query, the adversary must be able to find w satisfying

$$z_1 + z_2 a' = w.$$

According to our simulation, $a, z_1 + z_2 a, z_1 + z_2 a'$ are random and independent for any $a' \neq a$, so that w is random in $\mathbb{Z}_p$ from the point of view of the adversary. Therefore, the adversary has probability at most q_H/p in generating an incorrect query that passes the verification, which is negligible. In other words, only the challenge hash query can pass the verification, and thus the simulator can find the correct solution from hash queries with probability 1.

Advantage and time cost. Let T_s denote the time cost of the simulation. We have $T_s = O(q_H)$, which is mainly dominated by finding the solution. Therefore, the simulator $\mathcal{B}$ will solve the CDH problem with $(t + T_s, \varepsilon)$.

This completes the proof of the theorem. $\square$

7.3 Iterated Hashed ElGamal Scheme

SysGen: The system parameter generation algorithm takes as input a security parameter λ. It chooses a cyclic group $(\mathbb{G}, p, g)$, selects a cryptographic hash function $H : \{0,1\}^* \to \{0,1\}^n$, and returns the system parameters $SP = (\mathbb{G}, p, g, H)$.

KeyGen: The key generation algorithm takes as input the system parameters SP. It randomly chooses $\alpha_1, \alpha_2 \in \mathbb{Z}_p$, computes $g_1 = g^{\alpha_1}, g_2 = g^{\alpha_2}$, and returns a public/secret key pair (pk, sk) as follows:

$$pk = (g_1, g_2), \quad sk = (\alpha_1, \alpha_2).$$

Encrypt: The encryption algorithm takes as input a message $m \in \{0,1\}^n$, the public key pk, and the system parameters SP. It picks a random $r \in \mathbb{Z}_p$ and returns the ciphertext CT as

$$CT = (C_1, C_2) = \left(g^r, H(A_2) \oplus m \right),$$

where $A_1 = H(0)\|g_1^r\|1$, $A_2 = H(A_1)\|g_2^r\|2$. Here, $H(0)$ denotes an arbitrary but fixed string for all ciphertext generations.

Decrypt: The decryption algorithm takes as input a ciphertext CT, the secret key sk, and the system parameters SP. Let $CT = (C_1, C_2)$. It computes

$$B_1 = H(0)||C_1^{\alpha_1}||1, \quad B_2 = H(B_1)||C_2^{\alpha_2}||2,$$

and decrypts the message by computing $C_2 \oplus H(B_2) = m$.

Theorem 7.3.0.1 *Suppose the hash function H is a random oracle. If the CDH problem is hard, the Iterated Hashed ElGamal encryption scheme is provably secure in the IND-CPA security model with reduction loss $L = 2\sqrt{q_H}$, where q_H is the number of hash queries to the random oracle.*

Proof. Suppose there exists an adversary $\mathscr{A}$ who can (t,ε)-break the encryption scheme in the IND-CPA security model. We construct a simulator $\mathscr{B}$ to solve the CDH problem. Given as input a problem instance (g, g^a, g^b) over the cyclic group $(\mathbb{G}, g, p)$, $\mathscr{B}$ controls the random oracle, runs $\mathscr{A}$, and works as follows.

Setup. Let $SP = (\mathbb{G}, g, p)$ and H be the random oracle controlled by the simulator. $\mathscr{B}$ randomly picks $i^* \in \{1, 2\}$ and sets the secret key in such a way that $\alpha_{i^*} = a$ from the problem instance and another value, denoted by $z \in \mathbb{Z}_p$, is randomly chosen by the simulator. The public key $pk = (g_1, g_2) = (g^{\alpha_1}, g^{\alpha_2})$ can therefore be computed from the problem instance and the chosen parameters.

H-Query. The adversary makes hash queries in this phase. $\mathscr{B}$ prepares a hash list to record all queries and responses as follows, where the hash list is empty at the beginning.

Let the i-th hash query be x_i. If x_i is already in the hash list, $\mathscr{B}$ responds to this query following the hash list. Otherwise, $\mathscr{B}$ randomly chooses $y_i \in \{0,1\}^n$ and sets $H(x_i) = y_i$. The simulator $\mathscr{B}$ responds to this query with $H(x_i)$ and adds (x_i, y_i) to the hash list.

Challenge. $\mathscr{A}$ outputs two distinct messages $m_0, m_1 \in \{0,1\}^n$ to be challenged. The simulator randomly chooses $R \in \{0,1\}^n$ and sets the challenge ciphertext CT^* as

$$CT^* = (g^b, \ R),$$

where g^b is from the problem instance. The challenge ciphertext can be seen as an encryption of the message $m_c \in \{m_0, m_1\}$ using the random number b if $H(Q_2^*) = R \oplus m_c$, where $Q_1^* = H(0)||g_1^b||1, Q_2^* = H(Q_1^*)||g_2^b||2$:

$$CT^* = (g^b, \ R) = \left(g^b, H(Q_2^*) \oplus m_c\right).$$

The challenge ciphertext is therefore a correct ciphertext from the point of view of the adversary, if there is no hash query on Q_2^* to the random oracle.

Guess. $\mathscr{A}$ outputs a guess or $\perp$. In the above simulation, there are two challenge hash queries defined as

$$Q_1^* = H(0)||g_1^b||1 = H(0)||g^{\alpha_1 b}||1,$$
$$Q_2^* = H(Q_1^*)||g_2^b||2 = H(Q_1^*)||g^{\alpha_2 b}||2.$$

The solution to the CDH problem instance is $g^{\alpha_{i^*} b} = g^{ab}$ within the challenge hash query $Q_{i^*}^*$. Suppose $(x_1, y_1), (x_2, y_2), \cdots, (x_{q_H}, y_{q_H})$ are in the hash list, where each query x_i can be denoted by $x_i = u_i \| v_i \| w_i$. Here, $u_i \in \{H(0), y_1, y_2, \cdots, y_{q_H}\}$, $v_i \in \mathbb{G}$, and $w_i \in \{1, 2\}$. If x_i does not satisfy this structure, we can delete it.

Table 7.1 All hash queries with valid structure in the hash list

$(u_1 \| v_1 \| 1, y_1)$		$(u_2 \| v_2 \| 1, y_2)$	$\cdots$	$(u_k \| v_k \| 1, y_k)$	
$\mathbb{Y}_1 = \begin{cases} (y_1 \| v_{11} \| 2, y_{11}) \\ (y_1 \| v_{12} \| 2, y_{12}) \\ \vdots \\ (y_1 \| v_{1n_1} \| 2, y_{1n_1}) \end{cases}$	$\mathbb{Y}_2 = \begin{cases} (y_2 \| v_{21} \| 2, y_{21}) \\ (y_2 \| v_{22} \| 2, y_{22}) \\ \vdots \\ (y_2 \| v_{2n_2} \| 2, y_{2n_2}) \end{cases}$		$\cdots$	$\mathbb{Y}_k = \begin{cases} (y_k \| v_{k1} \| 2, y_{k1}) \\ (y_k \| v_{k2} \| 2, y_{k2}) \\ \vdots \\ (y_k \| v_{kn_k} \| 2, y_{kn_k}) \end{cases}$	

All hash queries are of one of the forms shown in Table 7.1. Suppose all hash queries in the first row are in the query set $\mathbb{Y}_0$. In the first column of the second row, all hash queries in the query set, denoted by $\mathbb{Y}_1$, use y_1. All other rows and columns have a similar structure and definition. If the challenge hash queries exist in the hash list, all hash queries in the set $\mathbb{Y}_0$ must have only one query whose v is equal to $g^{\alpha_1 b}$ because all distinct hash queries in the set $\mathbb{Y}_0$ have the same $u = H(0)$ and $w = 1$. Similarly, all hash queries in the set $\mathbb{Y}_i$ must have at most one query whose v is equal to $g^{\alpha_2 b}$. We stress that $v_{ij} = v_{i'j'}$ may hold, where v_{ij} is from $\mathbb{Y}_i$, and $v_{i'j'}$ is from $\mathbb{Y}_{i'}$.

In the above simulation, if $i^* = 1$, this means that $\alpha_1 = a$ and $\alpha_2 = z$, where z is randomly chosen by the simulator. Therefore, $g^{\alpha_2 b} = (g^b)^z$ can be computed by the simulator, and the simulator can check whether v in the hash query $u \| v \| w$ from $\mathbb{Y}_i$ is equal to g^{bz} or not. Next, we describe how to pick the challenge hash query.

- If $i^* = 1$, the simulator checks each hash query in $\mathbb{Y}_0$ as follows. For the query $u_i \| v_i \| 1$ whose response is y_i, the simulator checks whether there exists $j \in [1, n_i]$ such that $v_{in_j} = g^{bz}$ (a query from $\mathbb{Y}_i$). If yes, this query is kept in $\mathbb{Y}_0$. Otherwise, this query is removed from $\mathbb{Y}_0$. Suppose $\mathbb{Y}_0^*$ is the final set after removing all hash queries as described above. The simulator randomly picks one query from $\mathbb{Y}_0^*$ as the challenge hash query $Q_1^* = u^* \| v^* \| 1$ and extracts v^* as the solution to the CDH problem instance.
- If $i^* = 2$, the simulator randomly picks one query from the sets $\mathbb{Y}_1 \cup \mathbb{Y}_2 \cup \cdots \cup \mathbb{Y}_k$ as the challenge hash query $Q_2^* = u^* \| v^* \| 2$ and extracts v^* as the solution to the CDH problem instance.

This completes the simulation and the solution. The correctness is analyzed as follows.

Indistinguishable simulation. The correctness of the simulation has been explained above. The randomness of the simulation includes all random numbers in the key generation, the responses to hash queries, and the challenge ciphertext generation. They are

$$a, z, y_1, y_2, \cdots, y_{q_H}, b.$$

According to the setting of the simulation, where a, b, z, y_i are randomly chosen, it is easy to see that the randomness property holds, and thus the simulation is indistinguishable from the real attack. In particular, the adversary has no advantage in guessing the randomly chosen $i^* \in \{1, 2\}$.

Probability of successful simulation. There is no abort in the simulation, and thus the probability of successful simulation is 1.

Advantage of breaking the challenge ciphertext. According to the simulation, we have

- The challenge ciphertext is an encryption of the message m_0 if

$$Q_1^* = H(0)||g^{\alpha_1 b}||1, \; Q_2^* = H(Q_1^*)||g^{\alpha_2 b}||2, \; H(Q_2^*) = R \oplus m_0.$$

- The challenge ciphertext is an encryption of the message m_1 if

$$Q_1^* = H(0)||g^{\alpha_1 b}||1, \; Q_2^* = H(Q_1^*)||g^{\alpha_2 b}||2, \; H(Q_2^*) = R \oplus m_1.$$

Without making the challenge query Q_2^* to the random oracle, which requires the adversary to query Q_1^* first, $H(Q_2^*)$ is random and unknown to the adversary, so that it has no advantage in breaking the challenge ciphertext.

Probability of finding solution. Since the adversary has advantage ε in guessing the chosen message according to the breaking assumption, the adversary will query Q_1^* and Q_2^* to the random oracle with probability ε according to Lemma 4.11.1. The adversary makes q_H hash queries in total. Therefore, we have

$$n_1 + n_2 + \cdots + n_k + k \leq q_H.$$

Let suc be the probability of successfully picking the challenge hash query. We have the following probability of success:

$$\Pr[suc] = \Pr[suc|i^* = 1] \Pr[i^* = 1] + \Pr[suc|i^* = 2] \Pr[i^* = 2]$$
$$= \frac{1}{2} \cdot \Pr[suc|i^* = 1] + \frac{1}{2} \cdot \Pr[suc|i^* = 2].$$

To prove $\Pr[suc] \geq \frac{1}{2\sqrt{q_H}}$, we only need to prove

$$\Pr[suc|i^* = d] \geq \frac{1}{\sqrt{q_H}}, \quad \text{for } \mathbf{some} \; d \in \{1, 2\}.$$

On the other hand, if the adversary can adaptively make hash queries against the above probability, this means that

$$\Pr[suc|i^* = 1] < \frac{1}{\sqrt{q_H}} \; (1), \quad \text{and} \quad \Pr[suc|i^* = 2] < \frac{1}{\sqrt{q_H}} \; (2).$$

The above two probabilities must hold because the adversary does not know the value i^*.

- If $i^* = 1$, the adversary must make hash queries in such a way that $k \geq 1 + \sqrt{q_H}$. Suppose $\{(x_1, y_1), (x_2, y_2), \cdots, (x_k, y_k)\}$ are all the hash queries and responses from the set $\mathbb{Y}_0$. It is also the case that the query set $\mathbb{Y}_i$ for all $i \in [1, k]$ must have one hash query whose v is equal to $g^{\alpha_2 b}$. Otherwise, (x_i, y_i) will be removed from $\mathbb{Y}_0$ because of how the simulator picks the challenge hash query. If some queries are removed, and the remaining number is less than $\sqrt{q_H}$, we have $\Pr[suc|i^* = 1] \geq \frac{1}{\sqrt{q_H}}$.
- Suppose the probability (1) holds. If $i^* = 2$, there are k hash queries in the set $\mathbb{Y}_1 \cup \mathbb{Y}_2 \cup \cdots \cup \mathbb{Y}_k$ whose v is equal to $g^{\alpha_2 b}$. Let $N = |\mathbb{Y}_1 \cup \mathbb{Y}_2 \cup \cdots \cup \mathbb{Y}_k|$. In this case, to make sure that the probability (2) holds, the total number of hash queries must satisfy $N \geq k\sqrt{q_H} + 1$. Otherwise, $N < k\sqrt{q_H} + 1$, and we have

$$\frac{k}{N} \geq \frac{k}{k\sqrt{q_H}} = \frac{1}{\sqrt{q_H}},$$

which contradicts the probability (2) requirement.

If the probabilities (1) and (2) hold, we have $k \geq 1 + \sqrt{q_H}$ and then

$$N \geq k\sqrt{q_H} + 1 > \sqrt{q_H} \cdot \sqrt{q_H} = q_H,$$

which contradicts the assumption of q_H hash queries at most. Therefore, we have

$$\Pr[suc|i^* = 1] \geq \frac{1}{\sqrt{q_H}}, \quad \text{or} \quad \Pr[suc|i^* = 2] \geq \frac{1}{\sqrt{q_H}}$$

and then obtain $\Pr[suc] \geq \frac{1}{2\sqrt{q_H}}$. Therefore, the simulator can find the correct solution from hash queries with probability at least $\frac{\varepsilon}{2\sqrt{q_H}}$.

Advantage and time cost. Let T_s denote the time cost of the simulation. We have $T_s = O(\sqrt{q_H})$. Therefore, the simulator $\mathcal{B}$ will solve the CDH problem with $\left(t + T_s, \frac{\varepsilon}{2\sqrt{q_H}}\right)$.

This completes the proof of the theorem. $\square$

7.4 Fujisaki-Okamoto Hashed ElGamal Scheme

SysGen: The system parameter generation algorithm takes as input a security parameter λ. It chooses a cyclic group $(\mathbb{G}, p, g)$, selects three cryptographic hash functions $H_1 : \{0,1\}^* \to \mathbb{Z}_p, H_2, H_3 : \{0,1\}^* \to \{0,1\}^n$, and returns the system parameters $SP = (\mathbb{G}, p, g, H_1, H_2, H_3)$.

KeyGen: The key generation algorithm takes as input the system parameters SP. It randomly chooses $\alpha \in \mathbb{Z}_p$, computes $g_1 = g^\alpha$, and returns a public/secret key pair (pk, sk) as follows:

$$pk = g_1, \quad sk = \alpha.$$

Encrypt: The encryption algorithm takes as input a message $m \in \{0,1\}^n$, the public key pk, and the system parameters SP. It works as follows:

- Choose a random string $\sigma \in \{0,1\}^n$.
- Compute $C_3 = H_3(\sigma) \oplus m$ and $r = H_1(\sigma \| m \| C_3)$.
- Compute $C_1 = g^r$ and $C_2 = H_2(g_1^r) \oplus \sigma$.

The ciphertext CT is defined as

$$CT = (C_1, C_2, C_3) = \left(g^r, \; H_2(g_1^r) \oplus \sigma, \; H_3(\sigma) \oplus m \right).$$

Decrypt: The decryption algorithm takes as input a ciphertext CT, the secret key sk, and the system parameters SP. Let $CT = (C_1, C_2, C_3)$. The decryption works as follows:

- Decrypt σ by computing $C_2 \oplus H_2(C_1^\alpha) = H_2(g_1^r) \oplus \sigma \oplus H_2(g^{ar}) = \sigma$.
- Decrypt the message by computing $C_3 \oplus H_3(\sigma) = H_3(\sigma) \oplus m \oplus H_3(\sigma) = m$.
- Return the message m if $C_1 = g^{H_1(\sigma \| m \| C_3)}$.

Theorem 7.4.0.1 *Suppose the hash functions H_1, H_2, H_3 are random oracles. If the CDH problem is hard, the Fujisaki-Okamoto Hashed ElGamal encryption scheme is provably secure in the IND-CCA security model with reduction loss $L = q_{H_2}$, where q_{H_2} is the number of hash queries to the random oracle H_2.*

Proof. Suppose there exists an adversary $\mathscr{A}$ who can (t, q_d, ε)-break the encryption scheme in the IND-CCA security model. We construct a simulator $\mathscr{B}$ to solve the CDH problem. Given as input a problem instance (g, g^a, g^b) over the cyclic group $(\mathbb{G}, g, p)$, $\mathscr{B}$ controls the random oracles, runs $\mathscr{A}$, and works as follows.

Setup. Let $SP = (\mathbb{G}, g, p)$ and H_1, H_2, H_3 be random oracles controlled by the simulator. $\mathscr{B}$ sets the public key as $g_1 = g^a$ where $\alpha = a$. The public key is available from the problem instance.

H-Query. The adversary makes hash queries in this phase. $\mathscr{B}$ prepares three hash lists to record all queries and responses as follows, where the hash lists are empty at the beginning.

- Let the i-th hash query to H_1 be x_i. If x_i is already in the hash list, $\mathscr{B}$ responds to this query following the hash list. Otherwise, $\mathscr{B}$ randomly chooses $X_i \in \mathbb{Z}_p$, sets $H_1(x_i) = X_i$ and adds (x_i, X_i) to the hash list.
- Let the i-th hash query to H_2 be y_i. If y_i is already in the hash list, $\mathscr{B}$ responds to this query following the hash list. Otherwise, $\mathscr{B}$ randomly chooses $Y_i \in \{0,1\}^n$, sets $H_2(y_i) = Y_i$ and adds (y_i, Y_i) to the hash list.
- Let the i-th hash query to H_3 be z_i. If z_i is already in the hash list, $\mathscr{B}$ responds to this query following the hash list. Otherwise, $\mathscr{B}$ randomly chooses $Z_i \in \{0,1\}^n$, sets $H_3(z_i) = Z_i$ and adds (z_i, Z_i) to the hash list.

Let the number of hash queries to random oracles H_1, H_2, H_3 be $q_{H_1}, q_{H_2}, q_{H_3}$, respectively.

Phase 1. The adversary makes decryption queries in this phase. For a decryption query on $CT = (C_1, C_2, C_3)$, the simulator searches the hash lists to see whether there exist three pairs $(x, X), (y, Y), (z, Z)$ such that

$$x = z||m||C_3,$$
$$y = g_1^X = g_1^{H_1(x)},$$
$$C_1 = g^X = g^{H_1(x)},$$
$$C_2 = Y \oplus z = H_2(y) \oplus z,$$
$$C_3 = Z \oplus m = H_3(z) \oplus m.$$

We have the following cases.

- **Case 1.** All three queries exist. The simulator returns m as the decryption result.
- **Case 2.** There exists only one query $(x, H_1(x)) = (x, X)$ to the random oracle H_1 satisfying $C_1 = g^{H_1(x)}$. Let $x = z||m||C_3$. With such a query, the simulator knows z and can compute y. Then, the simulator adds queries $(y, H_2(y)), (z, H_2(z))$ to the random oracle. Based on these three queries, the simulator can easily decide whether the queried ciphertext is valid or not. If valid, return the message; otherwise, return $\perp$.
- **Case 3.** No query exists satisfying the ciphertext structure. Then, the simulator returns $\perp$.

Challenge. $\mathscr{A}$ outputs two distinct messages $m_0, m_1 \in \{0,1\}^n$ to be challenged. The simulator randomly chooses $R_1, R_2 \in \{0,1\}^n$ and sets the challenge ciphertext CT^* as

$$CT^* = (g^b, \ R_1, \ R_2),$$

where g^b is from the problem instance. The challenge ciphertext can be seen as an encryption of the message $m_c \in \{m_0, m_1\}$ using the random number σ^* if

- $H_3(\sigma^*) \oplus m_c = R_2,$
- $H_1(\sigma^*||m_c||R_2) = b,$
- $H_2(g_1^b) \oplus \sigma^* = RZ_1.$

That is, we have

$$CT^* = (g^b, \ R_1, \ R_2) = \left(g^b, \ H_2(g_1^b) \oplus \sigma^*, \ H_3(\sigma^*) \oplus m_c \right).$$

The challenge ciphertext is therefore a correct ciphertext from the point of view of the adversary if it does not query g_1^b, σ^*, $\sigma^* \| m_c \| C_3$ to random oracles H_2, H_3, H_1, respectively.

Phase 2. The simulator responds to decryption queries in the same way as in Phase 1 with the restriction that no decryption query is allowed on CT^*.

Guess. $\mathscr{A}$ outputs a guess or $\bot$. The challenge hash query is defined as

$$Q^* = g_1^b = (g^b)^\alpha = g^{ab},$$

which is a query to the random oracle H_2. The simulator randomly selects one value y from the hash list $(y_1, Y_1), (y_2, Y_2), \cdots, (y_{q_{H_2}}, Y_{q_{H_2}})$ as the challenge hash query. The simulator can immediately use this hash query to solve the CDH problem.

This completes the simulation and the solution. The correctness is analyzed as follows.

Indistinguishable simulation. The decryption simulation is correct except with negligible probability according to the following analysis.

- For case 1, the simulator can correctly respond to a decryption query on $CT = (C_1, C_2, C_3)$ following the description in Phase 1.
- For case 2, with $(x, H_1(x))$ where $x = (z \| m \| C_3)$ satisfying $C_1 = g^{H_1(x)}$, the simulator can compute $y = g_1^{H_1(x)}$ and extract z. Since the adversary did not query y, z to the random oracles, we have that $H_2(y) \oplus C_2$ and $H_3(z) \oplus C_3$ must be random in $\{0, 1\}^n$, so that they are equal to z and m provided by the adversary in x with negligible probability.
- For case 3 without $(x, H_1(x))$ satisfying $C_1 = g^{H_1(x)}$, we have the following two sub-cases.

  - $C_1 = g^b$. The ciphertext CT for every decryption query must be different from the challenge ciphertext $CT^* = (C_1^*, C_2^*, C_3^*)$. For such a decryption query, the simulator cannot compute g_1^b to simulate the decryption. However, the hash query $H_1(\sigma^* \| m_c \| Z_2) = b$ will determine C_2^*, C_3^*. That is, all ciphertexts where $C_1 = g^b$ are invalid except the challenge ciphertext. Therefore, the simulator can perform the decryption correctly by returning $\bot$ to the adversary.
  - $C_1 \neq g^b$. The simulator performs an incorrect decryption simulation for CT if and only if there exist three hash queries and responses $(x, X), (y, Y), (z, Z)$ **after** this decryption simulation, where these three queries satisfy

$$x = (z \| m \| C_3),$$
$$y = g_1^{H_1(x)},$$
$$C_1 = g^{H_1(x)},$$

$$C_2 = H_2(y) \oplus z,$$
$$C_3 = H_3(z) \oplus m.$$

The simulation fails because the decryption returns $\perp$ before these hash queries, but the decryption should return m after these hash queries. Since $H_1(x) = X$ is randomly chosen, $C_1 = g^{H_1(x)}$ holds with negligible probability.

Therefore, the simulator performs the decryption simulation correctly except with negligible probability. In particular, the decryption response will not generate any new hash query and its response for the adversary.

The correctness of the simulation including the public key, decryption, and the challenge ciphertext has been explained above. The randomness of the simulation includes all random numbers in the key generation, the responses to hash queries, and the challenge ciphertext generation. They are

$$a, \; X_i, Y_i, Z_i, \; b.$$

According to the setting of the simulation, where a, b, X_i, Y_i, Z_i are randomly chosen, it is easy to see that the randomness property holds, and thus the simulation is indistinguishable from the real attack.

Probability of successful simulation. There is no abort in the simulation, and thus the probability of successful simulation is 1.

Advantage of breaking the challenge ciphertext. According to the simulation, we have

- The challenge ciphertext is an encryption of the message m_0 if

$$H_2(g_1^b) = R_1 \oplus \sigma^*, \;\; H_3(\sigma^*) = R_2 \oplus m_0, \;\; H_1(\sigma^*||m_0||R_2) = b.$$

- The challenge ciphertext is an encryption of the message m_1 if

$$H_2(g_1^b) = R_1 \oplus \sigma^*, \;\; H_3(\sigma^*) = R_2 \oplus m_1, \;\; H_1(\sigma^*||m_1||R_2) = b.$$

Without making the challenge query $Q^* = g_1^b$ to the random oracle, the adversary can break the challenge ciphertext if and only if there exist queries to H_3, H_1 satisfying the equations. Note that the upper bound of the success probability is the sum of the probability that a query to H_3 is answered with $R_2 \oplus m_c$ and the probability that a query to H_1 is answered with b. The success probability is at most $(2q_{H_3} + q_{H_1})/p$, which is negligible. Furthermore, any decryption response will not help the adversary obtain additional hash queries or their responses. Therefore, the adversary has no advantage in breaking the challenge ciphertext except with negligible probability.

Probability of finding solution. According to the definition and simulation, if the adversary does not query $g_1^b = g^{ab}$ to the random oracle H_2, the adversary has no advantage in guessing the encrypted message except with negligible probability. Since the adversary has advantage ε in guessing the chosen message according to the breaking assumption, the adversary will query g^{ab} to the random oracle with probability ε according to Lemma 4.11.1. Therefore, a random choice of y from the hash list for H_2 will be equal to g^{ab} with probability $\frac{\varepsilon}{q_{H_2}}$.

Advantage and time cost. Let T_s denote the time cost of the simulation. We have $T_s = O(q_{H_1})$, which is mainly dominated by the decryption. Therefore, the simulator $\mathcal{B}$ will solve the CDH problem with $(t + T_s, \frac{\varepsilon}{q_{H_2}})$.

This completes the proof of the theorem.   □

Chapter 8
Public-Key Encryption Without Random Oracles

In this chapter, we introduce the ElGamal encryption scheme and the Cramer-Shoup encryption scheme [32]. The first scheme is widely known, and we give it here to help the reader understand how to analyze the correctness of a security reduction. The second scheme is the first practical encryption scheme without random oracles with CCA security. The given schemes and/or proofs may be different from the original ones.

8.1 ElGamal Scheme

SysGen: The system parameter generation algorithm takes as input a security parameter λ. It chooses a cyclic group $(\mathbb{G}, p, g)$ and returns the system parameters $SP = (\mathbb{G}, p, g)$.

KeyGen: The key generation algorithm takes as input the system parameters SP. It randomly chooses $\alpha \in \mathbb{Z}_p$, computes $g_1 = g^\alpha$, and returns a public/secret key pair (pk, sk) as follows:

$$pk = g_1, \quad sk = \alpha.$$

Encrypt: The encryption algorithm takes as input a message $m \in \mathbb{G}$, the public key pk, and the system parameters SP. It chooses a random number $r \in \mathbb{Z}_p$ and returns the ciphertext CT as

$$CT = (C_1, C_2) = \left(g^r, \ g_1^r \cdot m \right).$$

Decrypt: The decryption algorithm takes as input a ciphertext CT, the secret key sk, and the system parameters SP. Let $CT = (C_1, C_2)$. It decrypts the message by computing

© Springer International Publishing AG, part of Springer Nature 2018
F. Guo et al., *Introduction to Security Reduction*,
https://doi.org/10.1007/978-3-319-93049-7_8

$$C_2 \cdot C_1^{-\alpha} = g_1^r m \cdot (g^r)^{-\alpha} = m.$$

Theorem 8.1.0.1 *If the DDH problem is hard, the ElGamal encryption scheme is provably secure in the IND-CPA security model with reduction loss $L = 2$.*

Proof. Suppose there exists an adversary $\mathscr{A}$ who can (t, ε)-break the encryption scheme in the IND-CPA security model. We construct a simulator $\mathscr{B}$ to solve the DDH problem. Given as input a problem instance (g, g^a, g^b, Z) over the cyclic group $(\mathbb{G}, g, p)$, $\mathscr{B}$ runs $\mathscr{A}$ and works as follows.

Setup. Let $SP = (\mathbb{G}, g, p)$. $\mathscr{B}$ sets the public key as $g_1 = g^a$ where $\alpha = a$. The public key is available from the problem instance.

Challenge. $\mathscr{A}$ outputs two distinct messages $m_0, m_1 \in \mathbb{G}$ to be challenged. The simulator randomly chooses $c \in \{0, 1\}$ and sets the challenge ciphertext CT^* as

$$CT^* = \left(g^b, \; Z \cdot m_c \right),$$

where g^b and Z are from the problem instance. Let $r = b$. If $Z = g^{ab}$, we have

$$CT^* = \left(g^b, \; Z \cdot m_c \right) = \left(g^r, \; g_1^r \cdot m_c \right).$$

Therefore, CT^* is a correct challenge ciphertext whose encrypted message is m_c.

Guess. $\mathscr{A}$ outputs a guess c' of c. The simulator outputs true if $c' = c$. Otherwise, false.

This completes the simulation and the solution. The correctness is analyzed as follows.

Indistinguishable simulation. The correctness of the simulation has been explained above. The randomness of the simulation includes all random numbers in the key generation and the challenge ciphertext generation. They are a in the secret key and b in the challenge ciphertext. According to the setting of the simulation, where a, b are randomly chosen, it is easy to see that the randomness property holds, and thus the simulation is indistinguishable from the real attack.

Probability of successful simulation. There is no abort in the simulation, and thus the probability of successful simulation is 1.

Probability of breaking the challenge ciphertext.

If Z is true, the simulation is indistinguishable from the real attack, and thus the adversary has probability $\frac{1}{2} + \frac{\varepsilon}{2}$ of guessing the encrypted message correctly.

If Z is false, it is easy to see that the challenge ciphertext is a one-time pad because the message is encrypted using Z, which is random and cannot be calculated from the other parameters given to the adversary. Therefore, the adversary only has probability $1/2$ of guessing the encrypted message correctly.

Advantage and time cost. The advantage of solving the DDH problem is

$$P_S(P_T - P_F) = \left(\frac{1}{2} + \frac{\varepsilon}{2}\right) - \frac{1}{2} = \frac{\varepsilon}{2}.$$

Let T_s denote the time cost of the simulation. We have $T_s = O(1)$. Therefore, the simulator $\mathcal{B}$ will solve the DDH problem with $(t + T_s, \varepsilon/2)$.

This completes the proof of the theorem. □

8.2 Cramer-Shoup Scheme

SysGen: The system parameter generation algorithm takes as input a security parameter λ. It chooses a cyclic group $(\mathbb{G}, p, g)$, selects a cryptographic hash function $H : \{0,1\}^* \to \mathbb{Z}_p$, and returns the system parameters $SP = (\mathbb{G}, p, g, H)$.

KeyGen: The key generation algorithm takes as input the system parameters SP. It randomly chooses $g_1, g_2 \in \mathbb{G}$, $\alpha_1, \alpha_2, \beta_1, \beta_2, \gamma_1, \gamma_2 \in \mathbb{Z}_p$, computes $u = g_1^{\alpha_1} g_2^{\alpha_2}, v = g_1^{\beta_1} g_2^{\beta_2}, h = g_1^{\gamma_1} g_2^{\gamma_2}$, and returns a public/secret key pair (pk, sk) as follows:

$$pk = (g_1, g_2, u, v, h), \quad sk = (\alpha_1, \alpha_2, \beta_1, \beta_2, \gamma_1, \gamma_2).$$

Encrypt: The encryption algorithm takes as input a message $m \in \mathbb{G}$, the public key pk, and the system parameters SP. It chooses a random number $r \in \mathbb{Z}_p$ and returns the ciphertext CT as

$$CT = (C_1, C_2, C_3, C_4) = \left(g_1^r, \ g_2^r, \ h^r m, \ u^r v^{wr}\right),$$

where $w = H(C_1, C_2, C_3)$.

Decrypt: The decryption algorithm takes as input a ciphertext CT, the secret key sk, and the system parameters SP. Let $CT = (C_1, C_2, C_3, C_4)$. It works as follows:

- Compute $w = H(C_1, C_2, C_3)$.
- Verify that $C_4 = C_1^{\alpha_1 + w\beta_1} \cdot C_2^{\alpha_2 + w\beta_2}$.
- Return the message m by computing $m = C_3 \cdot C_1^{-\gamma_1} C_2^{-\gamma_2}$.

Theorem 8.2.0.1 *If the Variant DDH problem is hard, the Cramer-Shoup encryption scheme is provably secure in the IND-CCA security model with reduction loss about $L = 2$.*

Proof. Suppose there exists an adversary $\mathcal{A}$ who can (t, q_d, ε)-break the encryption scheme in the IND-CCA security model. We construct a simulator $\mathcal{B}$ to solve the

Variant DDH problem. Given as input a problem instance $X = (g_1, g_2, g_1^{a_1}, g_2^{a_2})$ over the cyclic group $(\mathbb{G}, g, p)$, $\mathscr{B}$ runs $\mathscr{A}$ and works as follows.

Setup. Let $SP = (\mathbb{G}, g, p, H)$, where $H : \{0,1\}^* \to \mathbb{Z}_p$ is a cryptographic hash function. $\mathscr{B}$ randomly chooses $\alpha_1, \alpha_2, \beta_1, \beta_2, \gamma_1, \gamma_2 \in \mathbb{Z}_p$ and sets the public key as

$$pk = (g_1, g_2, u, v, h) = \left(g_1, \ g_2, \ g_1^{\alpha_1} g_2^{\alpha_2}, \ g_1^{\beta_1} g_2^{\beta_2}, \ g_1^{\gamma_1} g_2^{\gamma_2} \right).$$

The public key can be computed from the problem instance and the chosen parameters.

Phase 1. The adversary makes decryption queries in this phase. For a decryption query on CT, since the simulator knows the secret key, it runs the decryption algorithm and returns the decryption result to the adversary.

Challenge. $\mathscr{A}$ outputs two distinct messages $m_0, m_1 \in \mathbb{G}$ to be challenged. The simulator randomly chooses $c \in \{0,1\}$ and sets the challenge ciphertext CT^* as

$$CT^* = (C_1^*, C_2^*, C_3^*, C_4^*) = \left(g_1^{a_1}, \ g_2^{a_2}, \ g_1^{a_1 \gamma_1} g_2^{a_2 \gamma_2} \cdot m_c, \ (g_1^{a_1})^{\alpha_1 + w^* \beta_1} (g_2^{a_2})^{\alpha_2 + w^* \beta_2} \right),$$

where $w^* = H(C_1^*, C_2^*, C_3^*)$ and $g_1^{a_1}, g_2^{a_2}$ are from the problem instance. Let $r = a_1$. If $a_1 = a_2$, we have

$$CT^* = \left(g_1^{a_1}, \ g_2^{a_2}, \ g_1^{a_1 \gamma_1} g_2^{a_2 \gamma_2} \cdot m_c, \ (g_1^{a_1})^{\alpha_1 + w^* \beta_1} (g_2^{a_2})^{\alpha_2 + w^* \beta_2} \right)$$
$$= \left(g_1^r, \ g_2^r, \ h^r m, \ u^r v^{w^* r} \right).$$

Therefore, CT^* is a correct challenge ciphertext whose encrypted message is m_c.

Phase 2. The simulator responds to decryption queries in the same way as in Phase 1 with the restriction that no decryption query is allowed on CT^*.

Guess. $\mathscr{A}$ outputs a guess c' of c. The simulator outputs true if $c' = c$. Otherwise, false.

This completes the simulation and the solution. The correctness is analyzed as follows.

Indistinguishable simulation. According to the setting of the simulation, the simulator knows the secret key, and thus can perform a decryption simulation indistinguishable from the real attack.

The correctness of the simulation including the public key, decryption, and the challenge ciphertext has been explained above. The randomness of the simulation includes all random numbers in the key generation and the challenge ciphertext generation. They are

$$\alpha_1, \alpha_2, \beta_1, \beta_2, \gamma_1, \gamma_2, a_1 = a_2.$$

According to the setting of the simulation, where $\alpha_1, \alpha_2, \beta_1, \beta_2, \gamma_1, \gamma_2, a_1$ are randomly chosen, it is easy to see that the randomness property holds, and thus the simulation is indistinguishable from the real attack.

Probability of successful simulation. There is no abort in the simulation, and thus the probability of successful simulation is 1.

Probability of breaking the challenge ciphertext.

If Z is true, the simulation is indistinguishable from the real attack, and thus the adversary has probability $\frac{1}{2} + \frac{\varepsilon}{2}$ of guessing the encrypted message correctly.

If Z is false, in the following we show that the adversary has success probability at most $\frac{1}{2} + \frac{q_d}{p - q_d}$ of guessing the encrypted message.

Let $g_2 = g_1^z$ for some integer $z \in \mathbb{Z}_p$. The adversary knows

$$z, \quad \alpha_1 + z\alpha_2, \quad \beta_1 + z\beta_2, \quad \gamma_1 + z\gamma_2$$

from the public key and

$$a_1, \quad a_2, \quad a_1(\alpha_1 + w^*\beta_1) + za_2(\alpha_2 + w^*\beta_2), \quad a_1\gamma_1 + a_2z\gamma_2 + \log_{g_1} m_c$$

from the challenge ciphertext. If γ_1, γ_2 are unknown to the adversary, and there is no decryption query, we have that $\gamma_1 + z\gamma_2$ and $a_1\gamma_1 + a_2z\gamma_2$ are random and independent because the determinant of the following coefficient matrix is nonzero:

$$\begin{vmatrix} 1 & z \\ a_1 & a_2z \end{vmatrix} = z(a_2 - a_1) \neq 0.$$

In this case, the challenge ciphertext can be seen as a one-time pad encryption of the message m_c from the point of view of the adversary, so that the adversary has no advantage in guessing the bit c. Next, we show that the decryption queries do not help the adversary break the challenge ciphertext except with negligible probability.

If a decryption query on $CT = \left(g_1^{r_1}, g_2^{r_2}, C_3, C_4\right)$ passes the verification, the decryption will return $C_3 \cdot g_1^{-r_1\gamma_1} g_2^{-r_2\gamma_2}$ to the adversary, and the adversary will know

$$r_1\gamma_1 + r_2z\gamma_2.$$

If $r_1 = r_2$ (the ciphertext is treated as a correct ciphertext), what the adversary knows is equivalent to $\gamma_1 + z\gamma_2$, and thus the adversary gets no additional information to break the one-time pad property. Otherwise, with $\gamma_1 + z\gamma_2$ and $r_1\gamma_1 + r_2z\gamma_2$, the adversary can compute γ_1, γ_2 to break the one-time pad property. Therefore, in the remainder of this proof, we prove that any incorrect ciphertext $CT = \left(g_1^{r_1}, g_2^{r_2}, C_3, C_4\right)$ different from the challenge ciphertext will be rejected except with negligible probability.

- If $(g_1^{r_1}, g_2^{r_2}, C_3) = (C_1^*, C_2^*, C_3^*)$ and $C_4 \neq C_4^*$, such an incorrect ciphertext will be rejected because only the ciphertext with $C_4 = C_4^*$ can pass the verification.
- If $(g_1^{r_1}, g_2^{r_2}, C_3) \neq (C_1^*, C_2^*, C_3^*)$, we have $H(g_1^{r_1}, g_2^{r_2}, C_3) = w \neq w^*$ because the hash function is secure. This ciphertext can pass the verification if

$$C_4 = g_1^{r_1(\alpha_1 + w\beta_1)} \cdot g_2^{r_2(\alpha_2 + w\beta_2)} = g_1^{r_1(\alpha_1 + w\beta_1) + r_2z(\alpha_2 + w\beta_2)}.$$

That is, it can pass the verification if the adversary can compute the number $r_1(\alpha_1 + w\beta_1) + r_2 z(\alpha_2 + w\beta_2)$.

According to the simulation, all the parameters associated with $\alpha_1, \alpha_2, \beta_1, \beta_2$ including the target $r_1(\alpha_1 + w\beta_1) + r_2 z(\alpha_2 + w\beta_2)$ are

$$\alpha_1 + z\alpha_2$$
$$\beta_1 + z\beta_2$$
$$a_1(\alpha_1 + w^*\beta_1) + za_2(\alpha_2 + w^*\beta_2)$$
$$r_1(\alpha_1 + w\beta_1) + r_2 z(\alpha_2 + w\beta_2).$$

The matrix of the corresponding coefficients for $(\alpha_1, \alpha_2, \beta_1, \beta_2)$ is

$$\begin{pmatrix} 1 & z & 0 & 0 \\ 0 & 0 & 1 & z \\ a_1 & za_2 & a_1 w^* & za_2 w^* \\ r_1 & zr_2 & r_1 w & zr_2 w \end{pmatrix},$$

where the absolute value of its determinant is $z(r_2 - r_1)(a_2 - a_1)(w^* - w) \neq 0$. Therefore, $r_1(\alpha_1 + w\beta_1) + r_2 z(\alpha_2 + w\beta_2)$ is random and independent of the other given parameters, so that the adversary has no advantage except with probability $\frac{1}{p}$ of generating C_4 to pass the verification.

When the adversary generates an incorrect ciphertext for a decryption query, the adaptive choice of C_4 the first time has success probability $\frac{1}{p}$, and the adaptive choice of C_4 the second time has success probability $\frac{1}{p-1}$. Therefore, the probability of successfully generating an incorrect ciphertext that can pass the verification is at most $\frac{q_d}{p-q_d}$ for q_d decryption queries. The adversary also has probability $\frac{1}{2}$ of guessing c correctly from the encryption. Therefore, the adversary has success probability at most $\frac{1}{2} + \frac{q_d}{p-q_d}$ of guessing the encrypted message.

Advantage and time cost. The advantage of solving the DDH problem is

$$P_S(P_T - P_F) = \left(\frac{1}{2} + \frac{\varepsilon}{2}\right) - \left(\frac{1}{2} + \frac{q_d}{p-q_d}\right) = \frac{\varepsilon}{2} - \frac{q_d}{p-q_d} \approx \frac{\varepsilon}{2}.$$

Let T_s denote the time cost of the simulation. We have $T_s = O(q_d)$, which is mainly dominated by the decryption. Therefore, the simulator $\mathscr{B}$ will solve the Variant DDH problem with $(t + T_s, \varepsilon/2)$.

This completes the proof of the theorem.   □

Chapter 9
Identity-Based Encryption with Random Oracles

In this chapter, we introduce the Boneh-Franklin IBE scheme [24] under the H-Type, the Boneh-Boyen^{RO} IBE scheme [20] and the Park-Lee IBE scheme [86] under the C-Type, and the Sakai-Kasahara IBE scheme [91, 30] under the I-Type. The given schemes and/or proofs may be different from the original ones.

9.1 Boneh-Franklin Scheme

Setup: The setup algorithm takes as input a security parameter λ. It selects a pairing group $\mathbb{PG} = (\mathbb{G}, \mathbb{G}_T, g, p, e)$, selects two cryptographic hash functions $H_1 : \{0,1\}^* \to \mathbb{G}, H_2 : \{0,1\}^* \to \{0,1\}^n$, randomly chooses $\alpha \in \mathbb{Z}_p$, computes $g_1 = g^\alpha$, and returns a master public/secret key pair (mpk, msk) as follows:

$$mpk = (\mathbb{PG}, g_1, H_1, H_2), \quad msk = \alpha.$$

KeyGen: The key generation algorithm takes as input an identity $ID \in \{0,1\}^*$ and the master key pair (mpk, msk). It returns the private key d_{ID} of ID as

$$d_{ID} = H_1(ID)^\alpha.$$

Encrypt: The encryption algorithm takes as input a message $m \in \{0,1\}^n$, an identity ID, and the master public key mpk. It chooses a random number $r \in \mathbb{Z}_p$ and returns the ciphertext CT as

$$CT = (C_1, C_2) = \left(g^r,\ H_2\Big(e(H_1(ID), g_1)^r \Big) \oplus m \right).$$

Decrypt: The decryption algorithm takes as input a ciphertext CT for ID, the private key d_{ID}, and the master public key mpk. Let $CT = (C_1, C_2)$. It decrypts

© Springer International Publishing AG, part of Springer Nature 2018
F. Guo et al., *Introduction to Security Reduction*,
https://doi.org/10.1007/978-3-319-93049-7_9

the message by computing

$$m = H_2\left(e(C_1, d_{ID})\right) \oplus C_2.$$

Theorem 9.1.0.1 *Suppose the hash functions H_1, H_2 are random oracles. If the BDH problem is hard, the Boneh-Franklin identity-based encryption scheme is provably secure in the IND-ID-CPA security model with reduction loss $L = q_{H_1} q_{H_2}$, where q_{H_1}, q_{H_2} are the number of hash queries to the random oracles H_1, H_2, respectively.*

Proof. Suppose there exists an adversary $\mathscr{A}$ who can (t, q_k, ε)-break the encryption scheme in the IND-ID-CPA security model. We construct a simulator $\mathscr{B}$ to solve the BDH problem. Given as input a problem instance (g, g^a, g^b, g^c) over the pairing group $\mathbb{PG}$, $\mathscr{B}$ controls the random oracles, runs $\mathscr{A}$, and works as follows.

Setup. $\mathscr{B}$ sets $g_1 = g^a$ where $\alpha = a$. The master public key except two hash functions is therefore available from the problem instance, where the two hash functions are set as random oracles controlled by the simulator.

H-Query. The adversary makes hash queries in this phase. Before any hash queries are made, $\mathscr{B}$ randomly chooses $i^* \in [1, q_{H_1}]$, where q_{H_1} denotes the number of hash queries to the random oracle H_1. Then, $\mathscr{B}$ prepares two hash lists to record all queries and responses as follows, where the hash lists are empty at the beginning.

- Let the i-th hash query to H_1 be ID_i. If ID_i is already in the hash list, $\mathscr{B}$ responds to this query following the hash list. Otherwise, $\mathscr{B}$ randomly chooses $x_i \in \mathbb{Z}_p$ and sets $H_1(ID_i)$ as

$$H_1(ID_i) = \begin{cases} g^{x_i} & \text{if } i \neq i^* \\ g^b & \text{otherwise} \end{cases}.$$

  The simulator responds to this query with $H_1(ID_i)$ and adds $(i, ID_i, x_i, H_1(ID_i))$ to the hash list.
- Let the i-th hash query to H_2 be y_i. If y_i is already in the hash list, $\mathscr{B}$ responds to this query following the hash list. Otherwise, $\mathscr{B}$ randomly chooses $Y_i \in \{0,1\}^n$, responds to this query with $H_2(y_i) = Y_i$, and adds $(y_i, H_2(y_i))$ to the hash list.

Phase 1. The adversary makes private-key queries in this phase. For a private-key query on ID_i, let $(i, ID_i, x_i, H_1(ID_i))$ be the corresponding tuple. If $i = i^*$, abort. Otherwise, according to the simulation, we have $H_1(ID_i) = g^{x_i}$. The simulator computes $d_{ID_i} = (g^a)^{x_i}$, which is equal to $H_1(ID_i)^{\alpha}$. Therefore, d_{ID_i} is a valid private key for ID_i.

Challenge. $\mathscr{A}$ outputs two distinct messages $m_0, m_1 \in \{0,1\}^n$ and one identity ID^* to be challenged. Let the corresponding tuple of a hash query on ID^* to H_1 be $(i, ID^*, x, H_1(ID^*))$. If $i \neq i^*$, abort. Otherwise, we have $i = i^*$ and $H_1(ID^*) = g^b$.

The simulator randomly chooses $R \in \{0,1\}^n$ and sets the challenge ciphertext CT^* as

$$CT^* = (g^c, \; R),$$

where g^c is from the problem instance. The challenge ciphertext can be seen as an encryption of the message $m_{coin} \in \{m_0, m_1\}$ using the random number c, if $H_2(e(g,g)^{abc}) = R \oplus m_{coin}$:

$$CT^* = (g^c, \; R) = \left(g^c, \; H_2\left(e(H_1(ID^*), g_1)^c\right) \oplus m_{coin}\right).$$

The challenge ciphertext is therefore a correct ciphertext from the point of view of the adversary if there is no hash query on $e(g,g)^{abc}$ to the random oracle H_2.

Phase 2. The simulator responds to private-key queries in the same way as in Phase 1 with the restriction that no private-key query is allowed on ID^*.

Guess. $\mathscr{A}$ outputs a guess or $\perp$. The challenge hash query is defined as

$$Q^* = e(H_1(ID^*), g_1)^c = e(g,g)^{abc},$$

which is a query to the random oracle H_2. The simulator randomly selects one value y from the hash list $(y_1, Y_1), (y_2, Y_2), \cdots, (y_{q_{H_2}}, Y_{q_{H_2}})$ as the challenge hash query. The simulator can immediately use this hash query to solve the BDH problem.

This completes the simulation and the solution. The correctness is analyzed as follows.

Indistinguishable simulation. The correctness of the simulation has been explained above. The randomness of the simulation includes all random numbers in the master-key generation, the responses to hash queries, the private-key generation, and the challenge ciphertext generation. They are

$$a, x_1, \cdots, x_{i^*-1}, b, x_{i^*+1}, \cdots, x_{q_{H_1}}, Y_1, Y_2, \cdots, Y_{q_{H_2}}, c.$$

According to the setting of the simulation, where all of them are randomly chosen, the randomness property holds, and thus the simulation is indistinguishable from the real attack.

Probability of successful simulation. If the identity ID^* to be challenged is the i^*-th identity queried to the random oracle, the adversary cannot query its private key so that the simulation will be successful in the query phase and the challenge phase. The success probability is therefore $1/q_{H_1}$ for q_{H_1} queries to H_1.

Advantage of breaking the challenge ciphertext. According to the simulation, we have

- The challenge ciphertext is an encryption of the message m_0 if

$$H_2\left(e(g,g)^{abc}\right) = R \oplus m_0.$$

- The challenge ciphertext is an encryption of the message m_1 if

$$H_2\left(e(g,g)^{abc}\right) = R \oplus m_1.$$

Without making the challenge query $Q^* = e(g,g)^{abc}$ to the random oracle, the adversary has no advantage in breaking the challenge ciphertext.

Probability of finding solution. According to the definition and simulation, if the adversary does not query $Q^* = e(g,g)^{abc}$ to the random oracle H_2, the adversary has no advantage in guessing the encrypted message. Since the adversary has advantage ε in guessing the chosen message according to the breaking assumption, the adversary will query $e(g,g)^{abc}$ to the random oracle with probability ε according to Lemma 4.11.1. Therefore, a random choice of y from the hash list for H_2 will be equal to $e(g,g)^{abc}$ with probability $\frac{\varepsilon}{q_{H_2}}$.

Advantage and time cost. Let T_s denote the time cost of the simulation. We have $T_s = O(q_{H_1} + q_k)$, which is mainly dominated by the oracle response and the key generation. Therefore, the simulator $\mathscr{B}$ will solve the BDH problem with $\left(t + T_s, \frac{\varepsilon}{q_{H_1} q_{H_2}}\right)$.

This completes the proof of the theorem. □

9.2 Boneh-Boyen^{RO} Scheme

Setup: The setup algorithm takes as input a security parameter λ. It selects a pairing group $\mathbb{PG} = (\mathbb{G}, \mathbb{G}_T, g, p, e)$, selects a cryptographic hash function $H : \{0,1\}^* \to \mathbb{G}$, randomly chooses $g_2 \in \mathbb{G}$, $\alpha \in \mathbb{Z}_p$, computes $g_1 = g^\alpha$, and returns a master public/secret key pair (mpk, msk) as follows:

$$mpk = (\mathbb{PG}, g_1, g_2, H), \quad msk = \alpha.$$

KeyGen: The key generation algorithm takes as input an identity $ID \in \{0,1\}^*$ and the master key pair (mpk, msk). It randomly chooses $r \in \mathbb{Z}_p$ and returns the private key d_{ID} of ID as

$$d_{ID} = (d_1, d_2) = \left(g_2^\alpha H(ID)^r, g^r\right).$$

Encrypt: The encryption algorithm takes as input a message $m \in \mathbb{G}_T$, an identity ID, and the master public key mpk. It chooses a random number $s \in \mathbb{Z}_p$ and returns the ciphertext CT as

$$CT = (C_1, C_2, C_3) = \left(H(ID)^s, g^s, e(g_1, g_2)^s \cdot m\right).$$

Decrypt: The decryption algorithm takes as input a ciphertext CT for ID, the private key $d_{ID} = (d_1, d_2)$, and the master public key mpk. Let $CT = (C_1, C_2, C_3)$. It decrypts the message by computing

$$C_3 \cdot \frac{e(d_2, C_1)}{e(d_1, C_2)} = e(g_1, g_2)^s m \cdot \frac{e(g^r, H(ID)^s)}{e\left(g_2^\alpha H(ID)^r, g^s\right)} = e(g_1, g_2)^s m \cdot \frac{1}{e(g_1, g_2)^s} = m.$$

Theorem 9.2.0.1 *Suppose the hash function H is a random oracle. If the DBDH problem is hard, the Boneh-Boyen^{RO} identity-based encryption scheme is provably secure in the IND-ID-CPA security model with reduction loss $L = 2q_H$, where q_H is the number of hash queries to the random oracle.*

Proof. Suppose there exists an adversary $\mathscr{A}$ who can (t, q_k, ε)-break the encryption scheme in the IND-ID-CPA security model. We construct a simulator $\mathscr{B}$ to solve the DBDH problem. Given as input a problem instance (g, g^a, g^b, g^c, Z) over the pairing group $\mathbb{PG}$, $\mathscr{B}$ controls the random oracle, runs $\mathscr{A}$, and works as follows.

Setup. $\mathscr{B}$ sets $g_1 = g^a, g_2 = g^b$ where $\alpha = a$. The master public key except the hash function is therefore available from the problem instance, where the hash function is set as a random oracle controlled by the simulator.

H-Query. The adversary makes hash queries in this phase. Before any hash queries are made, $\mathscr{B}$ randomly chooses $i^* \in [1, q_H]$, where q_H denotes the number of hash queries to the random oracle. Then, $\mathscr{B}$ prepares a hash list to record all queries and responses as follows, where the hash list is empty at the beginning.

Let the i-th hash query to H be ID_i. If ID_i is already in the hash list, $\mathscr{B}$ responds to this query following the hash list. Otherwise, $\mathscr{B}$ randomly chooses $x_i \in \mathbb{Z}_p$ and sets $H(ID_i)$ as

$$H(ID_i) = \begin{cases} g^{b+x_i} & \text{if } i \neq i^* \\ g^{x_i} & \text{otherwise} \end{cases}.$$

The simulator $\mathscr{B}$ responds to this query with $H(ID_i)$ and adds the tuple $(i, ID_i, x_i, H(ID_i))$ to the hash list.

Phase 1. The adversary makes private-key queries in this phase. For a private-key query on ID_i, let $(i, ID_i, x_i, H(ID_i))$ be the corresponding tuple. If $i = i^*$, abort. Otherwise, according to the simulation, we have $H(ID_i) = g^{b+x_i}$.

The simulator randomly chooses $r_i' \in \mathbb{Z}_p$ and computes d_{ID_i} as

$$d_{ID_i} = \left((g^a)^{-x_i} \cdot H(ID)^{r_i}, \ (g^a)^{-1} g^{r_i'}\right).$$

Let $r_i = -a + r_i'$. We have

$$g_2^\alpha H(ID)^{r_i} = g^{ab} \cdot (g^{b+x_i})^{-a+r_i'} = (g^a)^{-x_i} \cdot H(ID)^{r_i},$$
$$g^{r_i} = (g^a)^{-1} g^{r_i'}.$$

Therefore, d_{ID_i} is a valid private key for ID_i.

Challenge. $\mathscr{A}$ outputs two distinct messages $m_0, m_1 \in \mathbb{G}_T$ and one identity ID^* to be challenged. Let the corresponding tuple of a hash query on ID^* to H be $(i, ID^*, x^*, H(ID^*))$. If $i \neq i^*$, abort. Otherwise, we have $i = i^*$ and $H(ID^*) = g^{x^*}$.

The simulator randomly chooses $coin \in \{0, 1\}$ and sets the challenge ciphertext CT^* as

$$CT^* = (g^{cx^*},\ g^c,\ Z \cdot m_{coin}).$$

Let $r = c$. If $Z = e(g, g)^{abc}$, we have

$$CT^* = (g^{cx^*},\ g^c,\ Z \cdot m_{coin}) = \left(H(ID^*)^c,\ g^c,\ e(g_1, g_2)^c \cdot m_{coin} \right).$$

Therefore, CT^* is a correct challenge ciphertext for ID^* whose encrypted message is m_{coin}.

Phase 2. The simulator responds to private-key queries in the same way as in Phase 1 with the restriction that no private-key query is allowed on ID^*.

Guess. $\mathscr{A}$ outputs a guess $coin'$ of $coin$. The simulator outputs true if $coin' = coin$. Otherwise, false.

This completes the simulation and the solution. The correctness is analyzed as follows.

Indistinguishable simulation. The correctness of the simulation has been explained above. The randomness of the simulation includes all random numbers in the master-key generation, the responses to hash queries, the private-key generation, and the challenge ciphertext generation. They are

$$a, b, x_1, \cdots, x_{i^*-1}, b + x_{i^*}, x_{i^*+1}, \cdots, x_{q_H}, -a + r'_i,\ c.$$

According to the setting of the simulation, where a, b, c, x_i, r'_i are randomly chosen, it is easy to see that the randomness property holds, and thus the simulation is indistinguishable from the real attack.

Probability of successful simulation. If the identity ID^* to be challenged is the i^*-th identity queried to the random oracle, the adversary cannot query its private key so that the simulation will be successful in the query phase and the challenge phase. The success probability is therefore $1/q_H$ for q_H queries to H.

Probability of breaking the challenge ciphertext.

If Z is true, the simulation is indistinguishable from the real attack, and thus the adversary has probability $\frac{1}{2} + \frac{\varepsilon}{2}$ of guessing the encrypted message correctly.

If Z is false, it is easy to see that the challenge ciphertext is a one-time pad because the message is encrypted using Z, which is random and cannot be calculated from the other parameters given to the adversary. Therefore, the adversary only has probability $1/2$ of guessing the encrypted message correctly.

Advantage and time cost. The advantage of solving the DBDH problem is

$$P_S(P_T - P_F) = \frac{1}{q_H} \left(\frac{1}{2} + \frac{\varepsilon}{2} - \frac{1}{2} \right) = \frac{\varepsilon}{2q_H}.$$

Let T_s denote the time cost of the simulation. We have $T_s = O(q_H + q_k)$, which is mainly dominated by the oracle response and the key generation. Therefore, the simulator $\mathscr{B}$ will solve the DBDH problem with $\left(t + T_s, \frac{\varepsilon}{2q_H} \right)$.

This completes the proof of the theorem. $\qquad\qquad\qquad\qquad\qquad\qquad$ $\square$

9.3 Park-Lee Scheme

Setup: The setup algorithm takes as input a security parameter λ. It selects a pairing group $\mathbb{PG} = (\mathbb{G}, \mathbb{G}_T, g, p, e)$, selects a cryptographic hash function $H : \{0,1\}^* \to \mathbb{G}$, randomly chooses $g_2 \in \mathbb{G}$, $\alpha \in \mathbb{Z}_p$, computes $g_1 = g^\alpha$, and returns a master public/secret key pair (mpk, msk) as follows:

$$mpk = (\mathbb{PG}, g_1, g_2, H), \quad msk = \alpha.$$

KeyGen: The key generation algorithm takes as input an identity $ID \in \{0,1\}^*$ and the master key pair (mpk, msk). It randomly chooses $r, t_k \in \mathbb{Z}_p$ and returns the private key d_{ID} of ID as

$$d_{ID} = (d_1, d_2, d_3, d_4) = \left(g_2^{\alpha + r}, \ g^r, \ \left(H(ID)g_2^{t_k} \right)^r, \ t_k \right).$$

Encrypt: The encryption algorithm takes as input a message $m \in \mathbb{G}_T$, an identity ID, and the master public key mpk. It randomly chooses $s, t_c \in \mathbb{Z}_p$ and returns the ciphertext CT as

$$CT = (C_1, C_2, C_3, C_4) = \left(\left(H(ID)g_2^{t_c} \right)^s, \ g^s, \ t_c, \ e(g_1, g_2)^s \cdot m \right).$$

Decrypt: The decryption algorithm takes as input a ciphertext CT for ID, the private key $d_{ID} = (d_1, d_2)$, and the master public key mpk. Let $CT = (C_1, C_2, C_3, C_4)$. If $C_3 = d_4$, output $\perp$. Otherwise, it decrypts the message by computing

$$C_4 \cdot \left(\frac{e(d_2, C_1)}{e(d_3, C_2)} \right)^{\frac{1}{C_3 - d_4}} \cdot \frac{1}{e(d_1, C_2)}$$

$$= e(g_1, g_2)^s m \cdot \left(\frac{e(H(ID), g)^{rs} e(g_2, g)^{rst_c}}{e(H(ID), g)^{rs} e(g_2, g)^{rst_k}} \right)^{\frac{1}{t_c - t_k}} \cdot \frac{1}{e(g_1, g_2)^s \cdot e(g_2, g)^{rs}}$$

$$= e(g_1, g_2)^s m \cdot e(g_2, g)^{rs} \cdot \frac{1}{e(g_1, g_2)^s \cdot e(g_2, g)^{rs}} = m.$$

Theorem 9.3.0.1 *Suppose the hash function H is a random oracle. If the DBDH problem is hard, the Park-Lee identity-based encryption scheme is provably secure in the IND-ID-CPA security model with reduction loss $L = 2$.*

Proof. Suppose there exists an adversary $\mathscr{A}$ who can (t, q_k, ε)-break the encryption scheme in the IND-ID-CPA security model. We construct a simulator $\mathscr{B}$ to solve the DBDH problem. Given as input a problem instance (g, g^a, g^b, g^c, Z) over the pairing group $\mathbb{PG}$, $\mathscr{B}$ controls the random oracle, runs $\mathscr{A}$, and works as follows.

Setup. $\mathscr{B}$ sets $g_1 = g^a, g_2 = g^b$ where $\alpha = a$. The master public key except the hash function is therefore available from the problem instance, where the hash function is set as a random oracle controlled by the simulator.

H-Query. The adversary makes hash queries in this phase. $\mathscr{B}$ prepares a hash list to record all queries and responses as follows, where the hash list is empty at the beginning.

For a query on ID, $\mathscr{B}$ randomly chooses $x_{ID}, y_{ID} \in \mathbb{Z}_p$ and sets $H(ID)$ as

$$H(ID) = g^{y_{ID}} g_2^{-x_{ID}}.$$

The simulator $\mathscr{B}$ responds to this query with $H(ID)$ and adds $(ID, x_{ID}, y_{ID}, H(ID))$ to the hash list.

Phase 1. The adversary makes private-key queries in this phase. For a private-key query on ID, let $(ID, x_{ID}, y_{ID}, H(ID))$ be the corresponding tuple in the hash list. The simulator randomly chooses $r' \in \mathbb{Z}_p$ and computes d_{ID} as

$$d_{ID} = \left((g^b)^{r'}, \ g^{r'}(g^a)^{-1}, \ g^{r' y_{ID}}(g^a)^{-y_{ID}}, \ x_{ID} \right).$$

Let $r = r' - a$ and $t_k = x_{ID}$. We have

$$g_2^{\alpha+r} = g^{b(a+r'-a)} = (g^b)^{r'},$$
$$g^r = g^{r'-a} = g^{r'}(g^a)^{-1},$$
$$\left(H(ID)g_2^{t_k}\right)^r = (g^{y_{ID}} g_2^{-x_{ID}} g_2^{x_{ID}})^{r'-a} = g^{r' y_{ID}}(g^a)^{-y_{ID}},$$
$$t_k = x_{ID}.$$

Therefore, d_{ID} is a valid private key for ID.

Challenge. $\mathscr{A}$ outputs two distinct messages $m_0, m_1 \in \mathbb{G}_T$ and one identity ID^* to be challenged. Let the corresponding tuple of a hash query on ID^* to H be $(ID^*, x_{ID^*}, y_{ID^*}, H(ID^*))$.

The simulator randomly chooses $coin \in \{0, 1\}$ and sets the challenge ciphertext CT^* as

$$CT^* = \left(g^{c y_{ID^*}}, \ g^c, \ x_{ID^*}, \ Z \cdot m_{coin} \right).$$

Let $s = c$ and $t_c = x_{ID^*}$. If $Z = e(g, g)^{abc}$, we have

$$CT^* = (g^{c y_{ID^*}}, \ g^c, \ x_{ID^*}, \ Z \cdot m_{coin}) = \left((H(ID^*)g_2^{t_c})^s, \ g^s, \ t_c, \ e(g_1, g_2)^s \cdot m_{coin} \right).$$

Therefore, CT^* is a correct challenge ciphertext for ID^* whose encrypted message is m_{coin}.

Phase 2. The simulator responds to private-key queries in the same way as in Phase 1 with the restriction that no private-key query is allowed on ID^*.

Guess. $\mathscr{A}$ outputs a guess $coin'$ of $coin$. The simulator outputs true if $coin' = coin$. Otherwise, false.

This completes the simulation and the solution. The correctness is analyzed as follows.

Indistinguishable simulation. The correctness of the simulation has been explained above. The randomness of the simulation includes all random numbers in the master-key generation, the responses to hash queries, the private-key generation, and the challenge ciphertext generation. They are

$$mpk : a,b,$$
$$H(ID) : y_{ID} - x_{ID}b,$$
$$(r,t_k) : r' - a, \ x_{ID},$$
$$CT^* : c, \ x_{ID^*}.$$

According to the setting of the simulation, where a,b,c,x_{ID},y_{ID},r' are randomly chosen, it is easy to see that the randomness property holds, and thus the simulation is indistinguishable from the real attack.

Probability of successful simulation. There is no abort in the simulation, and thus the probability of successful simulation is 1.

Probability of breaking the challenge ciphertext.

If Z is true, the simulation is indistinguishable from the real attack, and thus the adversary has probability $\frac{1}{2} + \frac{\varepsilon}{2}$ of guessing the encrypted message correctly.

If Z is false, it is easy to see that the challenge ciphertext is a one-time pad because the message is encrypted using Z, which is random and cannot be calculated from the other parameters given to the adversary. Therefore, the adversary only has probability $1/2$ of guessing the encrypted message correctly.

Advantage and time cost. The advantage of solving the DBDH problem is

$$P_S(P_T - P_F) = \frac{1}{2} + \frac{\varepsilon}{2} - \frac{1}{2} = \frac{\varepsilon}{2}.$$

Let T_s denote the time cost of the simulation. We have $T_s = O(q_H + q_k)$, which is mainly dominated by the oracle response and the key generation. Therefore, the simulator $\mathscr{B}$ will solve the DBDH problem with $\left(t + T_s, \frac{\varepsilon}{2}\right)$.

This completes the proof of the theorem. $\qquad\qquad\square$

9.4 Sakai-Kasahara Scheme

Setup: The setup algorithm takes as input a security parameter λ. It selects a pairing group $\mathbb{PG} = (\mathbb{G}, \mathbb{G}_T, g, p, e)$, selects two cryptographic hash functions $H_1 : \{0,1\}^* \to \mathbb{Z}_p, H_2 : \{0,1\}^* \to \{0,1\}^n$, randomly chooses $h \in \mathbb{G}$, $\alpha \in \mathbb{Z}_p$, computes $g_1 = g^\alpha$, and returns a master public/secret key pair (mpk, msk) as follows:

$$mpk = (\mathbb{PG}, g_1, h, H_1, H_2), \quad msk = \alpha.$$

KeyGen: The key generation algorithm takes as input an identity $ID \in \{0,1\}^*$ and the master key pair (mpk, msk). It returns the private key d_{ID} of ID as

$$d_{ID} = h^{\frac{1}{\alpha + H_1(ID)}}.$$

Encrypt: The encryption algorithm takes as input a message $m \in \{0,1\}^n$, an identity ID, and the master public key mpk. It chooses a random number $r \in \mathbb{Z}_p$ and returns the ciphertext CT as

$$CT = (C_1, C_2) = \left(\left(g_1 g^{H_1(ID)} \right)^r, \ H_2(e(g,h)^r) \oplus m \right).$$

Decrypt: The decryption algorithm takes as input a ciphertext CT for ID, the private key d_{ID}, and the master public key mpk. Let $CT = (C_1, C_2)$. It decrypts the message by computing

$$C_2 \oplus H_2 \left(e(C_1, d_{ID}) \right) = m.$$

Theorem 9.4.0.1 *Suppose the hash functions H_1, H_2 are random oracles. If the q-BDHI problem is hard, the Sakai-Kasahara identity-based encryption scheme is provably secure in the IND-ID-CPA security model with reduction loss $L = q_{H_1} q_{H_2}$, where q_{H_1}, q_{H_2} are the number of hash queries to the random oracles H_1, H_2, respectively.*

Proof. Suppose there exists an adversary $\mathscr{A}$ who can (t, q_k, ε)-break the encryption scheme in the IND-ID-CPA security model. We construct a simulator $\mathscr{B}$ to solve the q-BDHI problem. Given as input a problem instance $(g, g^a, g^{a^2}, \cdots, g^{a^q})$ over the pairing group $\mathbb{PG}$, $\mathscr{B}$ controls the random oracles, runs $\mathscr{A}$, and works as follows.

Setup. $\mathscr{B}$ randomly chooses $w^*, w_1, w_2, \cdots, w_q \in \mathbb{Z}_p$. Let $f(x)$ be the polynomial in $\mathbb{Z}_p[x]$ defined as

$$f(x) = \prod_{i=1}^q (x - w^* + w_i).$$

We have that $f(x)$ does not contain the root zero.

The simulator $\mathscr{B}$ sets

$$g_1 = g^{a-w^*}, \quad h = g^{f(a)},$$

where $\alpha = a - w^*$. We require $q = q_{H_1}$, where q_{H_1} is the number of hash queries to H_1. The master public key except two hash functions can be computed from the problem instance and the chosen parameters, where the two hash functions are set as random oracles controlled by the simulator.

H-Query. The adversary makes hash queries in this phase. Before any hash queries are made, $\mathscr{B}$ randomly chooses $i^* \in [1, q_{H_1}]$. Then, $\mathscr{B}$ prepares two hash lists to record all queries and responses as follows, where the hash lists are empty at the beginning.

- Let the i-th hash query to H_1 be ID_i. If ID_i is already in the hash list, $\mathscr{B}$ responds to this query following the hash list. Otherwise, $\mathscr{B}$ sets $H_1(ID_i)$ as

$$H_1(ID_i) = \begin{cases} w_i & \text{if } i \neq i^* \\ w^* & \text{otherwise} \end{cases},$$

where w_i, w^* are random numbers chosen in the setup phase. In the simulation, w_{i^*} is not used in the responses to hash queries. The simulator $\mathscr{B}$ responds to this query with $H_1(ID_i)$ and adds the tuple $(i, ID_i, w_i, H_1(ID_i))$ or the tuple $(i^*, ID_{i^*}, w^*, H_1(ID_{i^*}))$ to the hash list.
- Let the i-th hash query to H_2 be y_i. If y_i is already in the hash list, $\mathscr{B}$ responds to this query following the hash list. Otherwise, $\mathscr{B}$ randomly chooses $Y_i \in \{0,1\}^n$, responds to this query with $H_2(y_i) = Y_i$, and adds $(y_i, H_2(y_i))$ to the hash list.

Phase 1. The adversary makes private-key queries in this phase. For a private-key query on ID, let $(i, ID_i, w_i, H(ID_i))$ be the corresponding tuple. If $i = i^*$, abort. Otherwise, according to the simulation, $H(ID_i) = w_i$. Let $f_{ID_i}(x)$ be defined as

$$f_{ID_i}(x) = \frac{f(x)}{x - w^* + w_i}.$$

We have that $f_{ID_i}(x)$ is a polynomial in x according to the definition of $f(x)$.

The simulator computes $d_{ID_i} = g^{f_{ID_i}(a)}$ from $g, g^a, \cdots, g^{a^q}, f_{ID_i}(x)$. Since

$$g^{f_{ID_i}(a)} = g^{\frac{f(a)}{a - w^* + w_i}} = h^{\frac{1}{\alpha + H_1(ID_i)}},$$

we have that d_{ID_i} is a valid private key for ID_i.

Challenge. $\mathscr{A}$ outputs two distinct messages $m_0, m_1 \in \{0,1\}^n$ and one identity ID^* to be challenged. Let the corresponding tuple of a hash query on ID^* to H_1 be $(i, ID^*, w^*, H_1(ID^*))$. If $i \neq i^*$, abort. Otherwise, we have $i = i^*$ and $H_1(ID^*) = w^*$.

The simulator randomly chooses $r' \in \mathbb{Z}_p$, $R \in \{0,1\}^n$ and sets the challenge ciphertext CT^* as

$$CT^* = (g^{r'}, R).$$

The challenge ciphertext can be seen as an encryption of the message $m_c \in \{m_0, m_1\}$ using the random number $r^* = \frac{r'}{a}$ if $H_2(e(g, h)^{r^*}) = R \oplus m_c$:

$$CT^* = (g^{r'}, \ R) = \left(\left(g_1 g^{H_1(ID^*)} \right)^{r^*}, \ H_2\left(e(g, h)^{r^*} \right) \oplus m_c \right).$$

The challenge ciphertext is therefore a correct ciphertext from the point of view of the adversary, if there is no hash query on $e(g, h)^{r^*}$ to the random oracle.

Phase 2. The simulator responds to private-key queries in the same way as in Phase 1 with the restriction that no private-key query is allowed on ID^*.

Guess. $\mathscr{A}$ outputs a guess or $\bot$. The challenge hash query is defined as

$$Q^* = e(g, h)^{r^*} = e(g, g)^{r' \frac{f(a)}{a}},$$

which is a query to the random oracle H_2. The simulator randomly selects one value y from the hash list $(y_1, Y_1), (y_2, Y_2), \cdots, (y_{q_{H_2}}, Y_{q_{H_2}})$ as the challenge hash query. We define

$$\frac{r' f(x)}{x} = F(x) + \frac{d}{x},$$

where $F(x)$ is a $(q-1)$-degree polynomial, and d is a nonzero integer according to the fact that $x \nmid f(x)$. The simulator can use this hash query to compute

$$\left(\frac{Q^*}{e(g, g)^{F(a)}} \right)^{\frac{1}{d}} = \left(\frac{e(g, g)^{\frac{r' f(a)}{a}}}{e(g, g)^{F(a)}} \right)^{\frac{1}{d}} = \left(e(g, g)^{\frac{d}{a}} \right)^{\frac{1}{d}} = e(g, g)^{\frac{1}{a}}.$$

as the solution to the q-BDHI problem instance.

This completes the simulation and the solution. The correctness is analyzed as follows.

Indistinguishable simulation. The correctness of the simulation has been explained above. The randomness of the simulation includes all random numbers in the master-key generation, the responses to hash queries, and the challenge ciphertext generation. They are

$$mpk : a - w^*, \ f(a) = \prod_{i=1}^{q} (x - w^* + w_i),$$

$$H(ID) : w_1, \cdots, w_{i^*-1}, w^*, w_{i^*+1}, \cdots, w_q,$$

$$CT^* : \frac{r'}{a}.$$

According to the setting of the simulation, where $a, w_1, \cdots, w_q, w^*, r'$ are randomly chosen, it is easy to see that the randomness property holds, and thus the simulation is indistinguishable from the real attack.

Probability of successful simulation. If the identity ID^* to be challenged is the i^*-th identity queried to the random oracle, the adversary cannot query its private key so that the simulation will be successful in the query phase and the challenge phase. The success probability is therefore $1/q_{H_1}$ for q_{H_1} queries to H_1.

Advantage of breaking the challenge ciphertext. According to the simulation, we have

- The challenge ciphertext is an encryption of the message m_0 if

$$H_2\left(e(g,h)^{r^*}\right) = R \oplus m_0.$$

- The challenge ciphertext is an encryption of the message m_1 if

$$H_2\left(e(g,h)^{r^*}\right) = R \oplus m_1.$$

Without making the challenge query $Q^* = e(g,h)^{r^*}$ to the random oracle, the adversary has no advantage in breaking the challenge ciphertext.

Probability of finding solution. According to the definition and simulation, if the adversary does not query $Q^* = e(g,h)^{r^*}$ to the random oracle H_2, the adversary has no advantage in guessing the encrypted message. Since the adversary has advantage ε in guessing the chosen message according to the breaking assumption, the adversary will query $e(g,h)^{r^*}$ to the random oracle with probability ε according to Lemma 4.11.1. Therefore, a random choice of y from the hash list for H_2 will be equal to $e(g,h)^{r^*}$ with probability $\frac{\varepsilon}{q_{H_2}}$.

Advantage and time cost. Let T_s denote the time cost of the simulation. We have $T_s = O(q_k q_{H_1})$, which is mainly dominated by the key generation. Therefore, the simulator $\mathscr{B}$ will solve the q-BDHI problem with $\left(t + T_s, \frac{\varepsilon}{q_{H_1} q_{H_2}}\right)$.

This completes the proof of the theorem. □

Chapter 10
Identity-Based Encryption Without Random Oracles

In this chapter, we start by introducing the Boneh-Boyen IBE scheme [20], which is selectively secure under the DBDH assumption. Then, we introduce a variant version of Boneh-Boyen IBE for CCA security without the use of one-time signatures [28] but with a chameleon hash function [94]. Then, we introduce the Waters IBE scheme [101] and the Gentry IBE scheme [47], which are both fully secure under the C-Type and the I-Type, respectively. The given schemes and/or proofs may be different from the original ones.

10.1 Boneh-Boyen Scheme

Setup: The setup algorithm takes as input a security parameter λ. It selects a pairing group $\mathbb{PG} = (\mathbb{G}, \mathbb{G}_T, g, p, e)$, randomly chooses $g_2, h, u, v \in \mathbb{G}$, $\alpha \in \mathbb{Z}_p$, computes $g_1 = g^\alpha$, selects a cryptographic hash function $H : \{0,1\}^* \to \mathbb{Z}_p$, selects a strongly unforgeable one-time signature scheme $\mathscr{S}$, and returns a master public/secret key pair (mpk, msk) as follows:

$$mpk = (\mathbb{PG}, g_1, g_2, h, u, v, H, \mathscr{S}), \quad msk = \alpha.$$

KeyGen: The key generation algorithm takes as input an identity $ID \in \mathbb{Z}_p$ and the master key pair (mpk, msk). It chooses a random number $r \in \mathbb{Z}_p$. It returns the private key d_{ID} of ID as

$$d_{ID} = (d_1, d_2) = \left(g_2^\alpha (h u^{ID})^r, \ g^r \right).$$

Encrypt: The encryption algorithm takes as input a message $m \in \mathbb{G}_T$, an identity ID, and the master public key mpk. The encryption works as follows:

© Springer International Publishing AG, part of Springer Nature 2018
F. Guo et al., *Introduction to Security Reduction*,
https://doi.org/10.1007/978-3-319-93049-7_10

- Run the key generation algorithm of $\mathscr{S}$ to generate a key pair (opk, osk).
- Choose a random number $s \in \mathbb{Z}_p$ and compute

$$(C_1, C_2, C_3, C_4) = \left((hu^{ID})^s, \ (hv^{H(opk)})^s, \ g^s, \ e(g_1, g_2)^s \cdot m \right).$$

- Run the signing algorithm of $\mathscr{S}$ to sign (C_1, C_2, C_3, C_4) using the secret key osk. Let the corresponding signature be σ.

The final ciphertext on m is

$$\begin{aligned}
CT &= (C_1, C_2, C_3, C_4, C_5, C_6) \\
&= \left((hu^{ID})^s, \ (hv^{H(opk)})^s, \ g^s, \ e(g_1, g_2)^s \cdot m, \ \sigma, \ opk \right).
\end{aligned}$$

Decrypt: The decryption algorithm takes as input a ciphertext $CT = (C_1, C_2, C_3, C_4, C_5, C_6)$ for ID, the private key d_{ID}, and the master public key mpk. It works as follows:

- Verify that C_5 is a signature of (C_1, C_2, C_3, C_4) using the public key C_6.
- Choose a random number $t \in \mathbb{Z}_p$ and compute $d_{ID|opk}$ as

$$d_{ID|opk} = (d_1', d_2', d_3') = \left(g_2^{\alpha} (hu^{ID})^r (hv^{H(opk)})^t, \ g^r, \ g^t \right).$$

- Decrypt the message by computing

$$\begin{aligned}
\frac{e(C_1, d_2') e(C_2, d_3')}{e(C_3, d_1')} \cdot C_4 &= \frac{e\left((hu^{ID})^s, g^r \right) e\left((hv^{H(opk)})^s, g^t \right)}{e\left(g^s, g_2^{\alpha} (hu^{ID})^r (hv^{H(opk)})^t \right)} \cdot C_4 \\
&= e(g_1, g_2)^{-s} \cdot e(g_1, g_2)^s m \\
&= m.
\end{aligned}$$

Theorem 10.1.0.1 *If the DBDH problem is hard and the adopted one-time signature scheme is strongly unforgeable, the Boneh-Boyen identity-based encryption scheme is provably secure in the IND-sID-CCA security model with reduction loss* $L = 2$.

Proof. Suppose there exists an adversary $\mathscr{A}$ who can $(t, q_k, q_d, \varepsilon)$-break the encryption scheme in the IND-sID-CCA security model. We construct a simulator $\mathscr{B}$ to solve the DBDH problem. Given as input a problem instance (g, g^a, g^b, g^c, Z) over the pairing group $\mathbb{PG}$, $\mathscr{B}$ runs $\mathscr{A}$ and works as follows.

Init: The adversary outputs an identity $ID^* \in \mathbb{Z}_p$ to be challenged.

Setup. Let H be a cryptographic hash function, and $\mathscr{S}$ be a secure one-time signature scheme. $\mathscr{B}$ simulates other parameters in the master public key as follows.

- Run $\mathscr{S}$ to generate a key pair (opk^*, osk^*).
- Randomly choose $x_1, x_2, x_3 \in \mathbb{Z}_p$.
- Set the master public key as

$$g_1 = g^a, \quad g_2 = g^b, \quad h = g^{-b+x_1}, \quad u = g^{\frac{b}{ID^*}+x_2}, \quad v = g^{\frac{b}{H(opk^*)}+x_3},$$

where $\alpha = a$ and a, b are from the problem instance.

The master public key can therefore be computed from the problem instance and the chosen parameters.

According to the above simulation, we have

$$hu^{ID} = g^{b\left(\frac{ID}{ID^*}-1\right)+(x_1+ID\cdot x_2)},$$

$$hv^{H(opk)} = g^{b\left(\frac{H(opk)}{H(opk^*)}-1\right)+(x_1+H(opk)\cdot x_3)}.$$

Phase 1. The adversary makes private-key queries and decryption queries in this phase.

For a private-key query on $ID \neq ID^*$, let $hu^{ID} = g^{w_1 b + w_2}$. The simulator randomly chooses $r' \in \mathbb{Z}_p$ and computes d_{ID} as

$$d_{ID} = \left((g^a)^{-\frac{w_2}{w_1}} (hu^{ID})^{r'}, \ (g^a)^{-\frac{1}{w_1}} g^{r'} \right).$$

Let $r = -\frac{a}{w_1} + r'$. We have

$$g_2^\alpha (hu^{ID})^r = g^{ab} \cdot (g^{w_1 b + w_2})^{-\frac{a}{w_1}+r'} = (g^a)^{-\frac{w_2}{w_1}} (hu^{ID})^{r'},$$

$$g^r = (g^a)^{-\frac{1}{w_1}} g^{r'}.$$

Therefore, d_{ID} is a valid private key for ID.

For a decryption query on (ID, CT), let $CT = (C_1, C_2, C_3, C_4, C_5, C_6)$. If the ciphertext passes the verification, $C_6 = opk$ must not be equal to opk^* according to the definition and simulation. We also have $H(opk) \neq H(opk^*)$. Let $hv^{H(opk)} = g^{w_3 b + w_4}$. The simulator randomly chooses $r, t' \in \mathbb{Z}_p$ and computes $d_{ID|opk} = (d_1', d_2', d_3')$ as

$$d_{ID|opk} = \left((hu^{ID})^r (g^a)^{-\frac{w_4}{w_3}} (hv^{H(opk)})^{t'}, \ g^r, \ (g^a)^{-\frac{1}{w_3}} g^{t'} \right).$$

Let $t = -\frac{a}{w_3} + t'$. We have

$$g_2^\alpha (hu^{ID})^r (hv^{H(opk)})^t = g^{ab} \cdot (hu^{ID})^r \cdot (g^{w_3 b + w_4})^{-\frac{a}{w_3}+t'}$$

$$= (hu^{ID})^r \cdot (g^a)^{-\frac{w_4}{w_3}} (hv^{H(opk)})^{t'},$$

$$g^t = (g^a)^{-\frac{1}{w_3}} g^{t'}.$$

Therefore, $d_{ID|opk}$ is valid for $ID|opk$. The simulator uses this private key to decrypt the ciphertext CT.

Challenge. $\mathscr{A}$ outputs two distinct messages $m_0, m_1 \in \mathbb{G}_T$ to be challenged. The simulator randomly chooses $coin \in \{0,1\}$ and sets the challenge ciphertext CT^* as

$$
\begin{aligned}
CT^* &= (C_1^*, C_2^*, C_3^*, C_4^*, C_5^*, C_6^*) \\
&= \left(g^{c(x_1 + ID^* \cdot x_2)},\ g^{c(x_1 + H(opk^*) \cdot x_3)},\ g^c,\ Z \cdot m_{coin},\ \sigma^*,\ opk^* \right),
\end{aligned}
$$

where σ^* is a signature of $(C_1^*, C_2^*, C_3^*, C_4^*)$ using osk^*. Let $s = c$. If $Z = e(g,g)^{abc}$, we have

$$
\left(hu^{ID^*} \right)^s = g^{bc\left(\frac{ID^*}{ID^*} - 1 \right) + c(x_1 + ID^* \cdot x_2)} = (g^c)^{x_1 + ID^* \cdot x_2},
$$

$$
\left(hv^{H(opk^*)} \right)^s = g^{bc\left(\frac{H(opk^*)}{H(opk^*)} - 1 \right) + c(x_1 + H(opk^*) \cdot x_3)} = (g^c)^{x_1 + H(opk^*) \cdot x_3},
$$

$$
g^s = g^c,
$$

$$
e(g_1, g_2)^s \cdot m_{coin} = Z \cdot m_{coin}.
$$

Therefore, CT^* is a correct challenge ciphertext for ID^* whose encrypted message is m_{coin}.

Phase 2. The simulator responds to private-key queries and decryption queries in the same way as in Phase 1 with the restriction that no private-key query is allowed on ID^* and no decryption query is allowed on (ID^*, CT^*).

Guess. $\mathscr{A}$ outputs a guess $coin'$ of $coin$. The simulator outputs true if $coin' = coin$. Otherwise, false.

This completes the simulation and the solution. The correctness is analyzed as follows.

Indistinguishable simulation. According to the assumption of a strongly unforgeable one-time signature scheme, the adversary cannot make a decryption query on a ciphertext whose opk is equal to opk^*. If $opk \neq opk^*$, the simulator can always generate the corresponding private key to decrypt the ciphertext. Therefore, the simulator performs a perfect decryption simulation.

The correctness of the simulation has been explained above. The randomness of the simulation includes all random numbers in the master-key generation, the private-key generation, and the challenge ciphertext generation. They are

$$
mpk : a,\ b,\ -b + x_1,\ \frac{b}{ID^*} + x_2,\ \frac{b}{H(opk^*)} + x_3,
$$

$$
sk_{ID} : -\frac{a}{w_1} + r',
$$

$$
CT^* : c.
$$

According to the setting of the simulation, where $a, b, x_1, x_2, x_3, r', c$ are randomly chosen, it is easy to see that the randomness property holds, and thus the simulation is indistinguishable from the real attack.

Probability of successful simulation. There is no abort in the simulation, and thus the probability of successful simulation is 1.

Probability of breaking the challenge ciphertext.

If Z is true, the simulation is indistinguishable from the real attack, and thus the adversary has probability $\frac{1}{2} + \frac{\varepsilon}{2}$ of guessing the encrypted message correctly.

If Z is false, and there is no decryption query, it is easy to see that the challenge ciphertext is a one-time pad because the message is encrypted using Z, which is random and unknown to the adversary. In the simulation, Z is independent of the challenge decryption key. Therefore, the decryption queries cannot help the adversary find Z to break the challenge ciphertext. The adversary only has probability $1/2$ of guessing the encrypted message correctly.

Advantage and time cost. The advantage of solving the DBDH problem is

$$P_S(P_T - P_F) = \frac{1}{2} + \frac{\varepsilon}{2} - \frac{1}{2} = \frac{\varepsilon}{2}.$$

Let T_s denote the time cost of the simulation. We have $T_s = O(q_k + q_d)$, which is mainly dominated by the key generation and the decryption. Therefore, the simulator $\mathscr{B}$ will solve the DBDH problem with $(t + T_s, \frac{\varepsilon}{2})$.

This completes the proof of the theorem. $\qquad\square$

10.2 Boneh-Boyen$^+$ Scheme

Setup: The setup algorithm takes as input a security parameter λ. It selects a pairing group $\mathbb{PG} = (\mathbb{G}, \mathbb{G}_T, g, p, e)$, randomly chooses $g_2, h, u, v, w \in \mathbb{G}$, $\alpha \in \mathbb{Z}_p$, computes $g_1 = g^\alpha$, selects a cryptographic hash function $H : \{0,1\}^* \to \mathbb{Z}_p$, and returns a master public/secret key pair (mpk, msk) as follows:

$$mpk = (\mathbb{PG}, g_1, g_2, h, u, v, w, H), \quad msk = \alpha.$$

KeyGen: The key generation algorithm takes as input an identity $ID \in \mathbb{Z}_p$ and the master key pair (mpk, msk). It chooses a random number $r \in \mathbb{Z}_p$ and returns the private key d_{ID} of ID as

$$d_{ID} = (d_1, d_2) = \left(g_2^\alpha (hu^{ID})^r, \ g^r \right).$$

Encrypt: The encryption algorithm takes as input a message $m \in \mathbb{G}_T$, an identity ID, and the master public key mpk. It chooses random numbers $s, z \in \mathbb{Z}_p$ and returns the ciphertext as

$$CT = \left(C_1, C_2, C_3, C_4, C_5\right) = \left((hu^{ID})^s, \; (hv^{H(C)}w^z)^s, \; g^s, \; e(g_1, g_2)^s \cdot m, \; z\right),$$

where $C = (C_1, C_3, C_4)$.

Decrypt: The decryption algorithm takes as input a ciphertext $CT = (C_1, C_2, C_3, C_4, C_5)$ for ID, the private key d_{ID}, and the master public key mpk. Let $C = (C_1, C_3, C_4)$. It works as follows.

- Verify that

$$e(C_1, g) = e\left(hu^{ID}, C_3\right) \quad \text{and} \quad e(C_2, g) = e\left(hv^{H(C)}w^{C_5}, C_3\right).$$

- Choose a random number $t \in \mathbb{Z}_p$ and compute $d_{ID|CT}$ as

$$d_{ID|CT} = (d_1', d_2', d_3') = \left(g_2^{\alpha}(hu^{ID})^r (hv^{H(C)}w^{C_5})^t, \; g^r, \; g^t\right).$$

- Decrypt the message by computing

$$\frac{e(C_1, d_2')e(C_2, d_3')}{e(C_3, d_1')} \cdot C_4 = \frac{e\left((hu^{ID})^s, g^r\right) e\left((hv^{H(C)}w^{C_5})^s, g^t\right)}{e\left(g^s, g_2^{\alpha}(hu^{ID})^r (hv^{H(C)}w^{C_5})^t\right)} \cdot C_4$$

$$= e(g_1, g_2)^{-s} \cdot e(g_1, g_2)^s m$$

$$= m.$$

Theorem 10.2.0.1 *If the DBDH problem is hard, the Boneh-Boyen$^+$ identity-based encryption scheme is provably secure in the IND-sID-CCA security model with reduction loss $L = 2$.*

Proof. Suppose there exists an adversary $\mathscr{A}$ who can $(t, q_k, q_d, \varepsilon)$-break the encryption scheme in the IND-sID-CCA security model. We construct a simulator $\mathscr{B}$ to solve the DBDH problem. Given as input a problem instance (g, g^a, g^b, g^c, Z) over the pairing group $\mathbb{PG}$, $\mathscr{B}$ runs $\mathscr{A}$ and works as follows.

Init: The adversary outputs an identity $ID^* \in \mathbb{Z}_p$ to be challenged.

Setup. Let H be a cryptographic hash function. The simulator $\mathscr{B}$ randomly chooses $x_1, x_2, x_3, x_4, y_1, y_2 \in \mathbb{Z}_p$ and sets the master public key as

$$g_1 = g^a, \; g_2 = g^b, \; h = g^{-b+x_1}, \; u = g^{\frac{b}{ID^*}+x_2}, \; v = g^{y_1 b + x_3}, \; w = g^{y_2 b + x_4},$$

where $\alpha = a$ and a, b are from the problem instance. The master public key can therefore be computed from the problem instance and the chosen parameters.

According to the above simulation, we have

$$hu^{ID} = g^{b\left(\frac{ID}{ID^*}-1\right)+(x_1+ID \cdot x_2)},$$
$$hv^{H(C)}w^z = g^{b(y_1H(C)+y_2z-1)+(x_1+H(C)x_3+zx_4)}.$$

Phase 1. The adversary makes private-key queries and decryption queries in this phase.

For a private-key query on $ID \neq ID^*$, let $hu^{ID} = g^{w_1b+w_2}$. The simulator randomly chooses $r' \in \mathbb{Z}_p$ and computes d_{ID} as

$$d_{ID} = \left((g^a)^{-\frac{w_2}{w_1}}(hu^{ID})^{r'}, \ (g^a)^{-\frac{1}{w_1}}g^{r'}\right).$$

Let $r = -\frac{a}{w_1} + r'$. We have

$$g_2^\alpha(hu^{ID})^r = g^{ab} \cdot (g^{w_1b+w_2})^{-\frac{a}{w_1}+r'} = (g^a)^{-\frac{w_2}{w_1}}(hu^{ID})^{r'},$$
$$g^r = (g^a)^{-\frac{1}{w_1}}g^{r'}.$$

Therefore, d_{ID} is a valid private key for ID.

For a decryption query on (ID, CT), let $CT = (C_1, C_2, C_3, C_4, C_5)$ and $C = (C_1, C_3, C_4)$. If $ID \neq ID^*$, the simulator can generate the corresponding private key to perform decryption. For $ID = ID^*$, the simulator continues the following decryption if it passes the verification. If $y_1H(C) + y_2C_5 - 1 = 0$, abort the simulation. Otherwise, let $hv^{H(C)}w^{C_5} = g^{w_3b+w_4}$. We have $w_3 \neq 0$. The simulator randomly chooses $r, t \in \mathbb{Z}_p$ and computes $d_{ID|CT} = (d_1', d_2', d_3')$ as

$$d_{ID|CT} = \left((hu^{ID})^r(g^a)^{-\frac{w_4}{w_3}}(hv^{H(C)}w^{C_5})^{t'}, \ g^r, \ (g^a)^{-\frac{1}{w_3}}g^{t'}\right).$$

Let $t = -\frac{a}{w_3} + t'$. We have

$$g_2^\alpha(hu^{ID})^r(hv^{H(C)}w^{C_5})^t = g^{ab} \cdot (hu^{ID})^r \cdot (g^{w_3b+w_4})^{-\frac{a}{w_3}+t'}$$
$$= (hu^{ID})^r \cdot (g^a)^{-\frac{w_4}{w_3}}(hv^{H(C)}w^{C_5})^{t'},$$
$$g^t = (g^a)^{-\frac{1}{w_3}}g^{t'}.$$

Therefore, $d_{ID|CT}$ is valid for $ID|CT$. The simulator uses this private key to decrypt the ciphertext CT.

Challenge. $\mathscr{A}$ outputs two distinct messages $m_0, m_1 \in \mathbb{G}_T$ to be challenged. The simulator randomly chooses $coin \in \{0, 1\}$ and sets the challenge ciphertext CT^* as

$$CT^* = (C_1^*, C_2^*, C_3^*, C_4^*, C_5^*)$$

$$= \left(g^{c(x_1+ID^* \cdot x_2)}, \ g^{c(x_1+H(C^*) \cdot x_3 + z^* x_4)}, \ g^c, \ Z \cdot m_{coin}, \ z^* \right),$$

where $C^* = (C_1^*, C_3^*, C_4^*)$, and z^* is the value satisfying $y_1 H(C^*) + y_2 z^* - 1 = 0$. Let $s = c$. If $Z = e(g,g)^{abc}$, we have

$$\left(hu^{ID^*} \right)^s = g^{bc\left(\frac{ID^*}{ID^*} - 1 \right) + c(x_1 + ID^* \cdot x_2)} = (g^c)^{x_1 + ID^* \cdot x_2},$$

$$\left(hv^{H(C^*)} w^{C_5^*} \right)^s = g^{bc(y_1 H(C^*) + y_2 z^* - 1) + c(x_1 + H(C^*) x_3 + z^* x_4)} = (g^c)^{x_1 + H(C^*) \cdot x_3 + z^* x_4},$$

$$g^s = g^c,$$

$$e(g_1, g_2)^s \cdot m_{coin} = Z \cdot m_{coin}.$$

Therefore, CT^* is a correct challenge ciphertext for ID^* whose encrypted message is m_{coin}.

Phase 2. The simulator responds to private-key queries and decryption queries in the same way as in Phase 1 with the restriction that no private-key query is allowed on ID^* and no decryption query is allowed on (ID^*, CT^*).

Guess. $\mathscr{A}$ outputs a guess $coin'$ of $coin$. The simulator outputs true if $coin' = coin$. Otherwise, false.

This completes the simulation and the solution. The correctness is analyzed as follows.

Indistinguishable simulation. According to the setting of the simulation, given a ciphertext $CT = (C_1, C_2, C_3, C_4, C_5)$ for a decryption query, the simulator can perform a perfect decryption simulation if $ID \neq ID^*$. If $ID = ID^*$, we have the following cases.

- $y_1 H(C) + y_2 C_5 - 1 = 0$. In this case, the simulator has to abort because it cannot compute the corresponding private key $d_{ID^*|CT}$ for decryption.
- $y_1 H(C) + y_2 C_5 - 1 \neq 0$. In this case, the simulator can compute the private key $d_{ID^*|CT}$ for decryption.

If the adversary has no advantage in computing $C_5 = \frac{1 - y_1 H(C)}{y_2}$, the simulator will perform the decryption simulation successfully except with negligible probability. From the given parameters, the adversary knows the following information:

$$a, \ b, \ -b + x_1, \ \frac{b}{ID^*} + x_2, \ y_1 b + x_3, \ y_2 b + x_4, \ -\frac{a}{w_1} + r', \ c, \ \frac{1 - y_1 H(C^*)}{y_2}.$$

It is not hard to see that the above integers and $\frac{1 - y_1 H(C)}{y_2}$ are random and independent because $x_1, x_2, x_3, x_4, y_1, y_2$ are randomly chosen.

The correctness of the simulation has been explained above. The randomness of the simulation includes all random numbers in the master-key generation, the private-key generation, and the challenge ciphertext generation. They are

$$a, \ b, \ -b+x_1, \ \frac{b}{ID^*}+x_2, \ y_1b+x_3, \ y_2b+x_4, \ -\frac{a}{w_1}+r', \ c, \ \frac{1-y_1H(C^*)}{y_2}.$$

They are random and independent according to the above analysis of the decryption simulation. Therefore, the simulation is indistinguishable from the real attack.

Probability of successful simulation. There is no abort in the simulation except $C_5 = \frac{1-y_1H(C)}{y_2}$ in a decryption query, and thus the probability of successful simulation is $1 - \frac{q_d}{p-q_d} \approx 1$, where the i-th adaptive choice of C_5 is equal to the random number $\frac{1-y_1H(C)}{y_2}$ with probability $1/(p-i+1)$.

Probability of breaking the challenge ciphertext.

If Z is true, the simulation is indistinguishable from the real attack, and thus the adversary has probability $\frac{1}{2}+\frac{\varepsilon}{2}$ of guessing the encrypted message correctly.

If Z is false, and there is no decryption query, it is easy to see that the challenge ciphertext is a one-time pad because the message is encrypted using Z, which is random and unknown to the adversary. In the simulation, Z is independent of the challenge decryption key. Therefore, the decryption queries cannot help the adversary find Z to break the challenge ciphertext. The adversary only has probability $1/2$ of guessing the encrypted message correctly.

Advantage and time cost. The advantage of solving the DBDH problem is

$$P_S(P_T - P_F) = \frac{1}{2}+\frac{\varepsilon}{2}-\frac{1}{2} = \frac{\varepsilon}{2}.$$

Let T_s denote the time cost of the simulation. We have $T_s = O(q_k + q_d)$, which is mainly dominated by the key generation and the decryption. Therefore, the simulator $\mathcal{B}$ will solve the DBDH problem with $(t+T_s, \frac{\varepsilon}{2})$.

This completes the proof of the theorem. $\qquad\qquad\square$

10.3 Waters Scheme

> **Setup:** The setup algorithm takes as input a security parameter λ. It selects a pairing group $\mathbb{PG} = (\mathbb{G}, \mathbb{G}_T, g, p, e)$, randomly chooses $g_2, u_0, u_1, u_2, \cdots, u_n \in \mathbb{G}$, $\alpha \in \mathbb{Z}_p$, computes $g_1 = g^{\alpha}$, and returns a master public/secret key pair (mpk, msk) as follows:
>
> $$mpk = (\mathbb{PG}, g_1, g_2, u_0, u_1, \cdots, u_n), \quad msk = \alpha.$$
>
> **KeyGen:** The key generation algorithm takes as input an identity $ID \in \{0,1\}^n$ and the master key pair (mpk, msk). Let $ID[i]$ be the i-th bit of ID. It chooses a random number $r \in \mathbb{Z}_p$. It returns the private key d_{ID} of ID as

$$d_{ID} = (d_1, d_2) = \left(g_2^{\alpha} \left(u_0 \prod_{i=1}^{n} u_i^{ID[i]} \right)^r, g^r \right).$$

Encrypt: The encryption algorithm takes as input a message $m \in \mathbb{G}_T$, an identity ID, and the master public key mpk. It chooses a random number $s \in \mathbb{Z}_p$ and returns the ciphertext CT as

$$CT = \left(\left(u_0 \prod_{i=1}^{n} u_i^{ID[i]} \right)^s, g^s, e(g_1, g_2)^s \cdot m \right).$$

Decrypt: The decryption algorithm takes as input a ciphertext CT for ID, the private key d_{ID}, and the master public key mpk. Let $CT = (C_1, C_2, C_3)$. It decrypts the message by computing

$$\frac{e(C_1, d_2)}{e(C_2, d_1)} \cdot C_3 = \frac{e\left((u_0 \prod_{i=1}^{n} u_i^{ID[i]})^s, g^r \right)}{e\left(g^s, g_2^{\alpha} (u_0 \prod_{i=1}^{n} u_i^{ID[i]})^r \right)} \cdot C_3 = e(g_1, g_2)^{-s} \cdot e(g_1, g_2)^s m = m.$$

Theorem 10.3.0.1 *If the DBDH problem is hard, the Waters identity-based encryption scheme is provably secure in the IND-ID-CPA security model with reduction loss $L = 8(n+1)q_k$, where q_k is the number of private-key queries.*

Proof. Suppose there exists an adversary $\mathcal{A}$ who can (t, q_k, ε)-break the encryption scheme in the IND-ID-CPA security model. We construct a simulator $\mathcal{B}$ to solve the DBDH problem. Given as input a problem instance (g, g^a, g^b, g^c, Z) over the pairing group $\mathbb{PG}$, $\mathcal{B}$ runs $\mathcal{A}$ and works as follows.

Setup. $\mathcal{B}$ sets $q = 2q_k$ and randomly chooses $k, x_0, x_1, \cdots, x_n, y_0, y_1, \cdots, y_n$ satisfying

$$k \in [0, n],$$
$$x_0, x_1, \cdots, x_n \in [0, q-1],$$
$$y_0, y_1, \cdots, y_n \in \mathbb{Z}_p.$$

It sets the master public key as

$$g_1 = g^a, \quad g_2 = g^b, \quad u_0 = g^{-kqa + x_0 a + y_0}, \quad u_i = g^{x_i a + y_i},$$

where $\alpha = a$. The master public key can therefore be computed from the problem instance and the chosen parameters.

We define $F(ID), J(ID), K(ID)$ as

$$F(ID) = -kq + x_0 + \sum_{i=1}^{n} ID[i] \cdot x_i,$$

$$J(ID) = y_0 + \sum_{i=1}^{n} ID[i] \cdot y_i,$$

$$K(ID) = \begin{cases} 0 & \text{if } x_0 + \sum_{i=1}^{n} ID[i] \cdot x_i = 0 \mod q \\ 1 & \text{otherwise} \end{cases}.$$

Then, we have

$$u_0 \prod_{i=1}^{n} u_i^{ID[i]} = g^{F(ID)a + J(ID)}.$$

Phase 1. The adversary makes private-key queries in this phase. For a private-key query on ID, if $K(ID) = 0$, the simulator aborts. Otherwise, $\mathscr{B}$ randomly chooses $r' \in \mathbb{Z}_p$ and computes the private key d_{ID} as

$$d_{ID} = (d_1, d_2) = \left(g_2^{-\frac{J(ID)}{F(ID)}} \left(u_0 \prod_{i=1}^{n} u_i^{ID[i]} \right)^{r'}, \; g_2^{-\frac{1}{F(ID)}} g^{r'} \right).$$

We have that d_{ID} is computable using $g, g_1, F(ID), J(ID), r', ID$ and the master public key.

Let $r = -\frac{b}{F(ID)} + r'$. We have

$$g_2^{\alpha} \left(u_0 \prod_{i=1}^{n} u_i^{ID[i]} \right)^{r} = g^{ab} \left(g^{F(ID)a + J(ID)} \right)^{-\frac{b}{F(ID)} + r'}$$

$$= g^{ab} \left(g^{F(ID)a + J(ID)} \right)^{-\frac{b}{F(ID)} + r'}$$

$$= g^{ab} \cdot g^{-ab + r'F(ID)a - \frac{J(ID)}{F(ID)}b + J(ID)r'}$$

$$= g^{-\frac{J(ID)}{F(ID)}b} g^{r'(F(ID)a + J(ID))}$$

$$= g_2^{-\frac{J(ID)}{F(ID)}} \left(u_0 \prod_{i=1}^{n} u_i^{ID[i]} \right)^{r'},$$

$$g^{r} = g^{-\frac{b}{F(ID)} + r'}$$

$$= g_2^{-\frac{1}{F(ID)}} g^{r'}.$$

Therefore, d_{ID} is a valid private key for ID.

Challenge. $\mathscr{A}$ outputs two distinct messages $m_0, m_1 \in \mathbb{G}_T$ and one identity $ID^* \in \{0,1\}^n$ to be challenged. According to the encryption and the simulation, if $F(ID^*) \neq 0$, abort. Otherwise, we have $F(ID^*) = 0$ and

$$u_0 \prod_{i=1}^{n} u_i^{ID^*[i]} = g^{F(ID^*)a + J(ID^*)} = g^{J(ID^*)}.$$

The simulator randomly chooses $coin \in \{0,1\}$ and sets the challenge ciphertext CT^* as

$$CT^* = (C_1^*, C_2^*, C_3^*) = \left((g^c)^{J(ID^*)}, \ g^c, \ Z \cdot m_{coin} \right),$$

where c, Z are from the problem instance. Let $s = c$. If $Z = e(g,g)^{abc}$, we have

$$\left(u_0 \prod_{i=1}^{n} u_i^{ID^*[i]} \right)^s = \left(g^{J(ID^*)} \right)^c = (g^c)^{J(ID^*)},$$

$$g^s = g^c,$$

$$e(g_1, g_2)^s \cdot m_{coin} = Z \cdot m_{coin}.$$

Therefore, CT^* is a correct challenge ciphertext for ID^* whose encrypted message is m_{coin}.

Phase 2. The simulator responds to private-key queries in the same way as in Phase 1 with the restriction that no private-key query is allowed on ID^*.

Guess. $\mathscr{A}$ outputs a guess $coin'$ of $coin$. The simulator outputs true if $coin' = coin$. Otherwise, false.

This completes the simulation and the solution. The correctness is analyzed as follows.

Indistinguishable simulation. The correctness of the simulation has been explained above. The randomness of the simulation includes all random numbers in the master-key generation, the private-key generation, and the challenge ciphertext generation. They are

$$mpk : a, \ b, \ -kqa + x_0a + y_0, \ x_1a + y_1, x_2a + y_2, \cdots, x_na + y_n,$$

$$d_{ID} : -\frac{b}{F(ID)} + r',$$

$$CT^* : c.$$

It is easy to see that the randomness property holds because $a, b, y_0, y_1, \cdots, y_n, r', c$ are randomly chosen. Therefore, the simulation is indistinguishable from the real attack.

Probability of successful simulation. The simulation is successful if no abort occurs in the query phase or the challenge phase. That is,

$$K(ID_1) = 1, \ K(ID_2) = 1, \ \cdots, \ K(ID_{q_k}) = 1, \ F(ID^*) = 0.$$

We have

$$0 \le x_0 + \sum_{i=1}^{n} ID[i]x_i \le (n+1)(q-1),$$

where the range $[0, (n+1)(q-1)]$ contains integers $0q, 1q, 2q, \cdots, nq \ (n < q)$.

Let $X = x_0 + \sum_{i=1}^{n} ID[i]x_i$. Since all x_i and k are randomly chosen, we have

$$\Pr[F(ID^*) = 0] = \Pr\left[X = 0 \bmod q\right] \cdot \Pr\left[X = kq \middle| X = 0 \bmod q\right] = \frac{1}{(n+1)q}.$$

Since the pair (ID_i, ID^*) for any i differ on at least one bit, $K(ID_i)$ and $F(ID^*)$ differ on the coefficient of at least one x_j so that

$$\Pr[K(ID_i) = 0 | F(ID^*) = 0] = \frac{1}{q}.$$

Based on the above results, we have

$$
\begin{aligned}
&\Pr[K(ID_1) = 1 \wedge \cdots \wedge K(ID_{q_k}) = 1 \wedge F(ID^*) = 0] \\
&= \Pr[K(ID_1) = 1 \wedge \cdots \wedge K(ID_{q_k}) = 1 | F(ID^*) = 0] \cdot \Pr[F(ID^*) = 0] \\
&= \left(1 - \Pr[K(ID_1) = 0 \vee \cdots \vee K(ID_{q_k}) = 0 | F(ID^*) = 0]\right) \cdot \Pr[F(ID^*) = 0] \\
&\geq \left(1 - \sum_{i=1}^{q_k} \Pr[K(ID_i) = 0 | F(ID^*) = 0]\right) \cdot \Pr[F(ID^*) = 0] \\
&= \frac{1}{(n+1)q} \cdot \left(1 - \frac{q_k}{q}\right) \\
&= \frac{1}{4(n+1)q_k}.
\end{aligned}
$$

Probability of breaking the challenge ciphertext.

If Z is true, the simulation is indistinguishable from the real attack, and thus the adversary has probability $\frac{1}{2} + \frac{\varepsilon}{2}$ of guessing the encrypted message correctly.

If Z is false, it is easy to see that the challenge ciphertext is a one-time pad because the message is encrypted using Z, which is random and unknown to the adversary. Therefore, the adversary only has probability $1/2$ of guessing the encrypted message correctly.

Advantage and time cost. The advantage of solving the DBDH problem is

$$P_S(P_T - P_F) = \frac{1}{4(n+1)q_k}\left(\frac{1}{2} + \frac{\varepsilon}{2} - \frac{1}{2}\right) = \frac{\varepsilon}{8(n+1)q_k}.$$

Let T_s denote the time cost of the simulation. We have $T_s = O(q_k)$, which is mainly dominated by the key generation. Therefore, the simulator $\mathscr{B}$ will solve the DBDH problem with $\left(t + T_s, \frac{\varepsilon}{8(n+1)q_k}\right)$.

This completes the proof of the theorem.   □

10.4 Gentry Scheme

Setup: The setup algorithm takes as input a security parameter λ. It selects a pairing group $\mathbb{PG} = (\mathbb{G}, \mathbb{G}_T, g, p, e)$, selects a cryptographic hash function $H : \{0,1\}^* \rightarrow \mathbb{Z}_p$, randomly chooses $\alpha, \beta_1, \beta_2, \beta_3 \in \mathbb{Z}_p$, computes $g_1 = g^\alpha, h_1 = g^{\beta_1}, h_2 = g^{\beta_2}, h_3 = g^{\beta_3}$, and returns a master public/secret key pair (mpk, msk) as follows:

$$mpk = (\mathbb{PG}, g_1, h_1, h_2, h_3, H), \quad msk = (\alpha, \beta_1, \beta_2, \beta_3).$$

KeyGen: The key generation algorithm takes as input an identity $ID \in \mathbb{Z}_p$ and the master key pair (mpk, msk). It chooses random numbers $r_1, r_2, r_3 \in \mathbb{Z}_p$ and returns the private key d_{ID} of ID as

$$d_{ID} = (d_1, d_2, d_3, d_4, d_5, d_6) = \left(r_1, \; g^{\frac{\beta_1 - r_1}{\alpha - ID}}, \; r_2, \; g^{\frac{\beta_2 - r_2}{\alpha - ID}}, \; r_3, \; g^{\frac{\beta_3 - r_3}{\alpha - ID}} \right).$$

We require the same random numbers r_1, r_2, r_3 for the same identity ID.

Encrypt: The encryption algorithm takes as input a message $m \in \mathbb{G}_T$, an identity ID, and the master public key mpk. It chooses a random number $s \in \mathbb{Z}_p$ and returns the ciphertext CT as

$$CT = (C_1, C_2, C_3, C_4) = \left((g_1 g^{-ID})^s, \; e(g,g)^s, \; e(h_3,g)^s \cdot m, \; e(h_1,g)^s e(h_2,g)^{sw} \right),$$

where $w = H(C_1, C_2, C_3)$.

Decrypt: The decryption algorithm takes as input a ciphertext CT for ID, the private key d_{ID}, and the master public key mpk. Let $CT = (C_1, C_2, C_3, C_4)$. It works as follows:

- Compute $w = H(C_1, C_2, C_3)$.
- Verify that

$$e(C_1, d_2 d_4^w) \cdot C_2^{d_1 + d_3 w} = e\left(g^{(\alpha - ID)s}, g^{\frac{\beta_1 - r_1 + w(\beta_2 - r_2)}{\alpha - ID}} \right) \cdot e(g,g)^{s(r_1 + r_2 w)} = C_4.$$

- Decrypt the message by computing

$$\frac{C_3}{e(C_1, d_6) \cdot C_2^{d_5}} = \frac{e(h_3,g)^s \cdot m}{e\left(g^{(\alpha - ID)s}, g^{\frac{\beta_3 - r_3}{\alpha - ID}} \right) \cdot e(g,g)^{sr_3}} = m.$$

Theorem 10.4.0.1 *If the q-DABDHE problem is hard, the Gentry identity-based encryption scheme is provably secure in the IND-ID-CCA security model with reduction loss $L = 2$.*

Proof. Suppose there exists an adversary $\mathscr{A}$ who can $(t, q_k, q_d, \varepsilon)$-break the encryption scheme in the IND-ID-CCA security model. We construct a simulator $\mathscr{B}$ to solve the q-DABDHE problem. Given as input a problem instance $(g_0, g_0^{a^{q+2}}, g, g^a, g^{a^2}, \cdots, g^{a^q}, Z)$ over the pairing group $\mathbb{PG}$, $\mathscr{B}$ runs $\mathscr{A}$ and works as follows.

Setup. $\mathscr{B}$ randomly chooses three q-degree polynomials $F_1(x), F_2(x), F_3(x)$ in $\mathbb{Z}_p[x]$. It sets the master public key as

$$g_1 = g^a, \quad h_1 = g^{F_1(a)}, \quad h_2 = g^{F_2(a)}, \quad h_3 = g^{F_3(a)},$$

where $\alpha = a, \beta = F_1(a), \beta_2 = F_2(\alpha), \beta_3 = F_3(\alpha)$, and we require $q = q_k + 1$. The master public key can therefore be computed from the problem instance and the chosen parameters.

In the following simulation, we assume that the queried ID for a private-key query, a decryption query, and challenge is not equal to $\alpha = a$, which can be verified by $g^{ID} = g_1$. Otherwise, we can use a to solve the hard problem immediately.

Phase 1. The adversary makes private-key queries and decryption queries in this phase.

For a private-key query on ID, let $f_{ID,i}(x)$ for all $i \in \{1,2,3\}$ be defined as

$$f_{ID,i}(x) = \frac{F_i(x) - F_i(ID)}{x - ID}.$$

We have that $f_{ID,i}(x)$ for all $i \in \{1,2,3\}$ are polynomials.

The simulator computes the private key d_{ID} as

$$d_{ID} = \left(F_1(ID), \ g^{f_{ID,1}(a)}, \ F_2(ID), \ g^{f_{ID,2}(a)}, \ F_3(ID), \ g^{f_{ID,3}(a)} \right),$$

which is computable from $g, g^a, g^{a^2}, \cdots, g^{a^q}, f_{ID,1}(x), f_{ID,2}(x), f_{ID,3}(x)$. Let $r_1 = F_1(ID), r_2 = F_2(ID), r_3 = F_3(ID)$. We have

$$r_i = F_i(ID), \quad i \in \{1,2,3\},$$
$$g^{\frac{\beta_i - r_i}{\alpha - ID}} = g^{\frac{F_i(\alpha) - F_i(ID)}{\alpha - ID}} = g^{f_{ID,i}(a)}, \quad i \in \{1,2,3\}.$$

Therefore, d_{ID} is a valid private key for ID.

For a decryption query on (ID, CT), the simulator runs the private-key simulation as above to compute d_{ID} and runs the decryption algorithm on CT using d_{ID}.

Challenge. $\mathscr{A}$ outputs two distinct messages $m_0, m_1 \in \mathbb{G}_T$ and one identity $ID^* \in \{0,1\}^n$ to be challenged. Let $d_{ID^*} = (d_1^*, d_2^*, d_3^*, d_4^*, d_5^*, d_6^*)$ be the private key for ID^*, which is also computable. The simulator randomly chooses $c \in \{0,1\}$ and sets the challenge ciphertext $CT^* = (C_1^*, C_2^*, C_3^*, C_4^*)$ as

$$C_1^* = g_0^{a^{q+2}-(ID^*)^{q+2}},$$

$$C_2^* = Z \cdot e\left(g_0, \prod_{i=0}^{q} g^{f_i a_i}\right),$$

$$C_3^* = e(C_1^*, \ d_6^*) \cdot (C_2^*)^{d_5^*} \cdot m_c,$$

$$C_4^* = e\left(C_1^*, \ d_2^*(d_4^*)^{w^*}\right) \cdot (C_2^*)^{d_1^* + d_3^* w^*},$$

where $w^* = H(C_1^*, C_2^*, C_3^*)$ and f_i is the coefficient of x^i in the polynomial

$$\frac{x^{q+2} - (ID^*)^{q+2}}{x - ID^*}.$$

Let $s = \left(\log_g g_0\right) \cdot \frac{a^{q+2} - (ID^*)^{q+2}}{a - ID^*}$. If $Z = e(g_0, g)^{a^{q+1}}$, we have

$$\left(g_1 g^{-ID^*}\right)^s = \left(g^{\alpha - ID^*}\right)^{\left(\log_g g_0\right) \cdot \frac{a^{q+2} - (ID^*)^{q+2}}{a - ID^*}} = g_0^{a^{q+2} - (ID^*)^{q+2}},$$

$$e(g, g)^s = e(g, g)^{\left(\log_g g_0\right) \cdot \frac{a^{q+2} - (ID^*)^{q+2}}{a - ID^*}}$$

$$= e(g_0, g)^{a^{q+1}} \prod_{i=0}^{q} e(g_0, g)^{f_i a^i}$$

$$= Z \cdot e\left(g_0, \prod_{i=0}^{q} g^{f_i a^i}\right),$$

$$e(h_3, g)^s \cdot m_c = e\left(g^{(\alpha - ID^*)s}, g^{\frac{\beta_3 - d_5^*}{\alpha - ID^*}}\right) \cdot \left(e(g, g)^s\right)^{d_5^*} \cdot m_c$$

$$= e(C_1^*, \ d_6^*) \cdot (C_2^*)^{d_5^*} \cdot m_c,$$

$$e(h_1, g)^s e(h_2, g)^{s w^*} = e\left(g^{(\alpha - ID^*)s}, g^{\frac{\beta_1 - d_1^* + w^*(\beta_2 - d_3^*)}{\alpha - ID^*}}\right) \cdot \left(e(g, g)^s\right)^{(d_1^* + d_3^* w^*)}$$

$$= e\left(C_1^*, \ d_2^*(d_4^*)^{w^*}\right) \cdot (C_2^*)^{d_1^* + d_3^* w^*}.$$

Therefore, CT^* is a correct challenge ciphertext for ID^* whose encrypted message is m_c.

Phase 2. The simulator responds to private-key queries and decryption queries in the same way as in Phase 1 with the restriction that no private-key query is allowed on ID^* and no decryption query is allowed on (ID^*, CT^*).

Guess. $\mathscr{A}$ outputs a guess c' of c. The simulator outputs true if $c' = c$. Otherwise, false.

This completes the simulation and the solution. The correctness is analyzed as follows.

Indistinguishable simulation. According to the setting of the simulation, the simulator can compute any private key, and thus it performs the decryption simulation correctly.

The correctness of the simulation has been explained above. The randomness of the simulation includes all random numbers in the master-key generation, the private-key generation, and the challenge ciphertext generation. They are

$$mpk : a, F_1(a), F_2(a), F_3(a),$$
$$r_1, r_2, r_3 : F_1(ID), F_2(ID), F_3(ID),$$
$$s : (\log_g g_0) \cdot \frac{a^{q+2} - (ID^*)^{q+2}}{a - ID^*}.$$

It is easy to see that the randomness property holds because $a, F_1(x), F_2(x), F_3(x), \log_g g_0$ are randomly chosen with the help of the following discussion, where $F_1(x), F_2(x), F_3(x)$ are $(q_k + 1)$-degree polynomials. Therefore, the simulation is indistinguishable from the real attack.

To prove that the randomness property holds, we only need to prove that $F_i(ID^*)$ and $F_i(a), F_i(ID_j)$ for all $i \in \{1, 2, 3\}$ and $j \in [1, q_k]$ are random and independent.

Without loss of generality, let $F_i(x) = F(x)$ be the polynomial defined as

$$F(x) = x_q x^q + x_{q-1} x^{q-1} + \cdots + x_1 x + x_0.$$

Since the polynomial is randomly chosen, all x_i are random and independent. We also have

$$F(a) = x_q(a)^q + x_{q-1}(a)^{q-1} + \cdots + x_1(a) + x_0,$$
$$F(ID^*) = x_q(ID^*)^q + x_{q-1}(ID^*)^{q-1} + \cdots + x_1(ID^*) + x_0,$$
$$F(ID_1) = x_q(ID_1)^q + x_{q-1}(ID_1)^{q-1} + \cdots + x_1(ID_1) + x_0,$$
$$F(ID_2) = x_q(ID_2)^q + x_{q-1}(ID_2)^{q-1} + \cdots + x_1(ID_2) + x_0,$$
$$\cdots$$
$$F(ID_{q_k}) = x_q(ID_{q_k})^q + x_{q-1}(ID_{q_k})^{q-1} + \cdots + x_1(ID_{q_k}) + x_0,$$

which can be rewritten as

$$\left(F(a), F(ID^*), F(ID_1), \cdots, F(ID_{q_k}) \right)$$

$$= (x_q, x_{q-1}, \cdots, x_1, x_0) \cdot \begin{pmatrix} a^q & a^{q-1} & \cdots & a & 1 \\ (ID^*)^q & (ID^*)^{q-1} & \cdots & ID^* & 1 \\ (ID_1)^q & (ID_1)^{q-1} & \cdots & ID_1 & 1 \\ (ID_2)^q & (ID_2)^{q-1} & \cdots & ID_2 & 1 \\ \cdots & \cdots & \cdots & \cdots & \cdots \\ (ID_{q_k})^q & (ID_{q_k})^{q-1} & \cdots & ID_{q_k} & 1 \end{pmatrix}^{\perp}.$$

The matrix is a $(q_k + 2) \times (q_k + 2)$ matrix, and the determinant of this matrix is

$$\prod_{y_i,y_j \in \{a,ID^*,ID_1,ID_2,\cdots,ID_{q_k}\}, i \neq j} (y_i - y_j) \neq 0.$$

Therefore, $F_i(ID^*)$ and $F_i(a), F_i(ID_j)$ for all $i \in \{1,2,3\}$ and $j \in [1,q_k]$ are random and independent.

Probability of successful simulation. There is no abort in the simulation, and thus the probability of successful simulation is 1.

Probability of breaking the challenge ciphertext.

If Z is true, the simulation is indistinguishable from the real attack, and thus the adversary has probability $\frac{1}{2} + \frac{\varepsilon}{2}$ of guessing the encrypted message correctly.

If Z is false, we show that the adversary only has success probability $1/2 + \frac{q_d}{p-q_d}$ of guessing the encrypted message as follows.

Since Z is random, without loss of generality, let $Z = e(g_0, g)^{a^{q+1}} \cdot e(g,g)^z$ for some random and nonzero integer z. C_1^*, C_2^*, C_3^* in the challenge ciphertext can be rewritten as

$$C_1^* = g^{s(\alpha - ID^*)}, \ C_2^* = e(g,g)^{s+z}, \ C_3^* = e(g,g)^{zd_5^*} \cdot e(h_3,g)^s \cdot m_c.$$

Furthermore, only C_3^* contains the random number d_5^*. Therefore, if the adversary cannot learn d_5^* from the query, the challenge ciphertext is a one-time pad from the point of view of the adversary.

According to the randomness property, the adversary can only learn d_5^* from a decryption query on (ID^*, CT). For a decryption query on (ID^*, CT), let $CT = (C_1, C_2, C_3, C_4)$ where $C_1 = (g_1 g^{ID^*})^{s'}$, $C_2 = e(g,g)^{s''}$, and $w = H(C_1, C_2, C_3)$. If $s' = s''$ (treated as a correct ciphertext) and the ciphertext is accepted, the simulator will return

$$\frac{C_3}{e(C_1, d_6^*) \cdot C_2^{d_5^*}} = \frac{C_3}{e(h_3,g)^{s'}},$$

where the adversary learns nothing about d_5^* from the decryption result. Otherwise, $s' \neq s''$ (treated as an incorrect ciphertext), and in the following we prove that such an incorrect ciphertext will be rejected except with negligible probability.

- Suppose $(C_1, C_2, C_3) = (C_1^*, C_2^*, C_3^*)$ such that $H(C_1, C_2, C_3) = w = w^*$. For such an incorrect ciphertext to pass the verification requires $C_4 = C_4^*$. However, this ciphertext cannot be queried because it is the challenge ciphertext.
- Suppose $(C_1, C_2, C_3) \neq (C_1^*, C_2^*, C_3^*)$. Since the hash function is secure, we have $H(C_1, C_2, C_3) = w \neq w^*$. For such an incorrect ciphertext to pass the verification requires the adversary to be able to compute C_4 satisfying

$$\begin{aligned}
C_4 &= e(C_1, d_2^*(d_4^*)^w) \cdot C_2^{d_1^* + d_3^* w} \\
&= e\left(g^{(\alpha - ID^*)s'}, g^{\frac{\beta_1 - d_1^* + w(\beta_2 - d_3^*)}{\alpha - ID^*}}\right) \cdot \left(e(g,g)^{s''}\right)^{(d_1^* + d_3^* w)} \\
&= e(g,g)^{s'(\beta_1 + w\beta_2)} \cdot e(g,g)^{(d_1^* + d_3^* w)(s'' - s')},
\end{aligned}$$

which requires the computationally unbounded adversary to know $d_1^* + d_3^* w$.
On the other hand, according to the simulation of the challenge ciphertext, the adversary will know

$$s(\beta_1 + w^* \beta_2) + (d_1^* + d_3^* w^*) z$$

from C_4^*, which is equivalent to $d_1^* + d_3^* w^*$ from the point of view of the computationally unbounded adversary. Furthermore, similarly to d_5^*, we have that d_1^* and d_3^* are random and independent of the master public key and the private keys. Therefore, we only need to prove that $d_1^* + d_3^* w$ cannot be computed from $d_1^* + d_3^* w^*$. It is easy to see that $d_1^* + d_3^* w$ and $d_1^* + d_3^* w^*$ are random and independent.

Therefore, the adversary has no advantage in generating the correct C_4 to pass the verification. Suppose the adversary generates an incorrect ciphertext for a decryption query by randomly choosing C_4. The adaptive choice of C_4 the first time has success probability $\frac{1}{p}$, and the adaptive choice of C_4 the second time has success probability $\frac{1}{p-1}$. Therefore, the probability of successfully generating an incorrect ciphertext that can pass the verification is at most $\frac{q_d}{p-q_d}$ for q_d decryption queries. The adversary also has probability $\frac{1}{2}$ of guessing c correctly from the encryption. Therefore, the adversary has success probability at most $\frac{1}{2} + \frac{q_d}{p-q_d}$ of guessing the encrypted message.

Advantage and time cost. The advantage of solving the q-DABDHE problem is

$$P_S(P_T - P_F) = \left(\frac{1}{2} + \frac{\varepsilon}{2} \right) - \left(\frac{1}{2} + \frac{q_d}{p - q_d} \right) \approx \frac{\varepsilon}{2}.$$

Let T_s denote the time cost of the simulation. We have $T_s = O(q_k^2 + q_d)$, which is mainly dominated by the key generation and the decryption. Therefore, the simulator $\mathcal{B}$ will solve the q-DABDHE problem with $\left(t + T_s, \frac{\varepsilon}{2} \right)$.

This completes the proof of the theorem. $\qquad\qquad\qquad\qquad\qquad\square$

References

1. Abdalla, M., Bellare, M., Rogaway, P.: The oracle Diffie-Hellman assumptions and an analysis of DHIES. In: D. Naccache (ed.) CT-RSA 2001, LNCS, vol. 2020, pp. 143–158. Springer (2001)
2. Adj, G., Canales-Martínez, I., Cruz-Cortés, N., Menezes, A., Oliveira, T., Rivera-Zamarripa, L., Rodríguez-Henríquez, F.: Computing discrete logarithms in cryptographically-interesting characteristic-three finite fields. IACR Cryptology ePrint Archive **2016**, 914 (2016)
3. Adleman, L.M.: A subexponential algorithm for the discrete logarithm problem with applications to cryptography. In: FOCS 1979, pp. 55–60. IEEE Computer Society (1979)
4. An, J.H., Dodis, Y., Rabin, T.: On the security of joint signature and encryption. In: L.R. Knudsen (ed.) EUROCRYPT 2002, LNCS, vol. 2332, pp. 83–107. Springer (2002)
5. Atkin, A.O.L., Morain, F.: Elliptic curves and primality proving. Mathematics of computation **61**(203), 29–68 (1993)
6. Attrapadung, N., Cui, Y., Galindo, D., Hanaoka, G., Hasuo, I., Imai, H., Matsuura, K., Yang, P., Zhang, R.: Relations among notions of security for identity based encryption schemes. In: J.R. Correa, A. Hevia, M.A. Kiwi (eds.) LATIN 2006, LNCS, vol. 3887, pp. 130–141. Springer (2006)
7. Bader, C., Hofheinz, D., Jager, T., Kiltz, E., Li, Y.: Tightly-secure authenticated key exchange. In: Y. Dodis, J.B. Nielsen (eds.) TCC 2015, LNCS, vol. 9014, pp. 629–658. Springer (2015)
8. Bader, C., Jager, T., Li, Y., Schäge, S.: On the impossibility of tight cryptographic reductions. In: M. Fischlin, J. Coron (eds.) EUROCRYPT 2016, LNCS, vol. 9666, pp. 273–304. Springer (2016)
9. Barker, E., Barker, W., Burr, W., Polk, W., Smid, M.: Recommendation for key management part 1: General (revision 3). NIST special publication **800**(57), 1–147 (2012)
10. Bellare, M., Boldyreva, A., Micali, S.: Public-key encryption in a multi-user setting: Security proofs and improvements. In: B. Preneel (ed.) EUROCRYPT 2000, LNCS, vol. 1807, pp. 259–274. Springer (2000)
11. Bellare, M., Desai, A., Pointcheval, D., Rogaway, P.: Relations among notions of security for public-key encryption schemes. In: H. Krawczyk (ed.) CRYPTO 1998, LNCS, vol. 1462, pp. 26–45. Springer (1998)
12. Bellare, M., Miner, S.K.: A forward-secure digital signature scheme. In: M.J. Wiener (ed.) CRYPTO 1999, LNCS, vol. 1666, pp. 431–448. Springer (1999)
13. Bellare, M., Namprempre, C.: Authenticated encryption: Relations among notions and analysis of the generic composition paradigm. In: T. Okamoto (ed.) ASIACRYPT 2000, LNCS, vol. 1976, pp. 531–545. Springer (2000)
14. Bellare, M., Rogaway, P.: Random oracles are practical: A paradigm for designing efficient protocols. In: D.E. Denning, R. Pyle, R. Ganesan, R.S. Sandhu, V. Ashby (eds.) CCS 1993, pp. 62–73. ACM (1993)

© Springer International Publishing AG, part of Springer Nature 2018

F. Guo et al., *Introduction to Security Reduction*,

https://doi.org/10.1007/978-3-319-93049-7

15. Bellare, M., Rogaway, P.: Optimal asymmetric encryption. In: A.D. Santis (ed.) EURO-CRYPT 1994, LNCS, vol. 950, pp. 92–111. Springer (1994)
16. Bernstein, D.J., Engels, S., Lange, T., Niederhagen, R., Paar, C., Schwabe, P., Zimmermann, R.: Faster elliptic-curve discrete logarithms on FPGAs. Tech. rep., Cryptology ePrint Archive, Report 2016/382 (2016)
17. Blake, I., Seroussi, G., Smart, N.: Elliptic Curves in Cryptography, London Mathematical Society Lecture Note Series, vol. 265. Cambridge University Press (1999)
18. Blake, I., Seroussi, G., Smart, N.: Advances in Elliptic Curve Cryptography, London Mathematical Society Lecture Note Series, vol. 317. Cambridge University Press (2005)
19. BlueKrypt: Cryptographic Key Length Recommendation. Available at: https://www.keylength.com
20. Boneh, D., Boyen, X.: Efficient selective-ID secure identity-based encryption without random oracles. In: C. Cachin, J. Camenisch (eds.) EUROCRYPT 2004, LNCS, vol. 3027, pp. 223–238. Springer (2004)
21. Boneh, D., Boyen, X.: Short signatures without random oracles. In: C. Cachin, J. Camenisch (eds.) EUROCRYPT 2004, LNCS, vol. 3027, pp. 56–73. Springer (2004)
22. Boneh, D., Boyen, X., Goh, E.: Hierarchical identity based encryption with constant size ciphertext. In: R. Cramer (ed.) EUROCRYPT 2005, LNCS, vol. 3494, pp. 440–456. Springer (2005)
23. Boneh, D., Boyen, X., Shacham, H.: Short group signatures. In: M.K. Franklin (ed.) CRYPTO 2004, LNCS, vol. 3152, pp. 41–55. Springer (2004)
24. Boneh, D., Franklin, M.K.: Identity-based encryption from the Weil pairing. In: J. Kilian (ed.) CRYPTO 2001, LNCS, vol. 2139, pp. 213–229. Springer (2001)
25. Boneh, D., Franklin, M.K.: Identity-based encryption from the Weil pairing. SIAM J. Comput. 32(3), 586–615 (2003)
26. Boneh, D., Lynn, B., Shacham, H.: Short signatures from the Weil pairing. In: C. Boyd (ed.) ASIACRYPT 2001, LNCS, vol. 2248, pp. 514–532. Springer (2001)
27. Canetti, R., Halevi, S., Katz, J.: A forward-secure public-key encryption scheme. In: E. Biham (ed.) EUROCRYPT 2003, LNCS, vol. 2656, pp. 255–271. Springer (2003)
28. Canetti, R., Halevi, S., Katz, J.: Chosen-ciphertext security from identity-based encryption. In: C. Cachin, J. Camenisch (eds.) EUROCRYPT 2004, LNCS, vol. 3027, pp. 207–222. Springer (2004)
29. Cash, D., Kiltz, E., Shoup, V.: The twin Diffie-Hellman problem and applications. In: N.P. Smart (ed.) EUROCRYPT 2008, LNCS, vol. 4965, pp. 127–145. Springer (2008)
30. Chen, L., Cheng, Z.: Security proof of Sakai-Kasahara's identity-based encryption scheme. In: N.P. Smart (ed.) IMA 2005, LNCS, vol. 3796, pp. 442–459. Springer (2005)
31. Costello, C.: Pairings for beginners. Available at: http://www.craigcostello.com.au/pairings/PairingsForBeginners.pdf
32. Cramer, R., Shoup, V.: A practical public key cryptosystem provably secure against adaptive chosen ciphertext attack. In: H. Krawczyk (ed.) CRYPTO 1998, LNCS, vol. 1462, pp. 13–25. Springer (1998)
33. Delerablée, C.: Identity-based broadcast encryption with constant size ciphertexts and private keys. In: K. Kurosawa (ed.) ASIACRYPT 2007, LNCS, vol. 4833, pp. 200–215. Springer (2007)
34. Diffie, W., Hellman, M.E.: New directions in cryptography. IEEE Trans. Information Theory 22(6), 644–654 (1976)
35. Dodis, Y., Franklin, M.K., Katz, J., Miyaji, A., Yung, M.: Intrusion-resilient public-key encryption. In: M. Joye (ed.) CT-RSA 2003, LNCS, vol. 2612, pp. 19–32. Springer (2003)
36. Dodis, Y., Katz, J., Xu, S., Yung, M.: Key-insulated public key cryptosystems. In: L.R. Knudsen (ed.) EUROCRYPT 2002, LNCS, vol. 2332, pp. 65–82. Springer (2002)
37. Dolev, D., Dwork, C., Naor, M.: Non-malleable cryptography (extended abstract). In: ACM STOC, pp. 542–552 (1991)
38. Dolev, D., Dwork, C., Naor, M.: Non-malleable Cryptography. Weizmann Science Press of Israel (1998)

39. Dutta, R., Barua, R., Sarkar, P.: Pairing-based cryptographic protocols: A survey. IACR Cryptology ePrint Archiv **2004**, 64 (2004)
40. Freeman, D., Scott, M., Teske, E.: A taxonomy of pairing-friendly elliptic curves. J. Cryptology **23**(2), 224–280 (2010)
41. Frey, G., Rück, H.G.: A remark concerning m-divisibility and the discrete logarithm in the divisor class group of curves. Mathematics of computation **62**(206), 865–874 (1994)
42. Fujisaki, E., Okamoto, T.: Secure integration of asymmetric and symmetric encryption schemes. In: M.J. Wiener (ed.) CRYPTO 1999, LNCS, vol. 1666, pp. 537–554. Springer (1999)
43. Galbraith, S.D., Gaudry, P.: Recent progress on the elliptic curve discrete logarithm problem. Des. Codes Cryptography **78**(1), 51–72 (2016)
44. Galbraith, S.D., Paterson, K.G., Smart, N.P.: Pairings for cryptographers. Discrete Applied Mathematics **156**(16), 3113–3121 (2008)
45. Gay, R., Hofheinz, D., Kiltz, E., Wee, H.: Tightly CCA-secure encryption without pairings. In: M. Fischlin, J. Coron (eds.) EUROCRYPT 2016, LNCS, vol. 9665, pp. 1–27. Springer (2016)
46. Gay, R., Hofheinz, D., Kohl, L.: Kurosawa-Desmedt meets tight security. In: J. Katz, H. Shacham (eds.) CRYPTO 2017, LNCS, vol. 10403, pp. 133–160. Springer (2017)
47. Gentry, C.: Practical identity-based encryption without random oracles. In: S. Vaudenay (ed.) EUROCRYPT 2006, LNCS, vol. 4004, pp. 445–464. Springer (2006)
48. Goh, E., Jarecki, S.: A signature scheme as secure as the Diffie-Hellman problem. In: E. Biham (ed.) EUROCRYPT 2003, LNCS, vol. 2656, pp. 401–415. Springer (2003)
49. Goldwasser, S., Micali, S.: Probabilistic encryption. J. Comput. Syst. Sci. **28**(2), 270–299 (1984)
50. Goldwasser, S., Micali, S., Rivest, R.L.: A digital signature scheme secure against adaptive chosen-message attacks. SIAM J. Comput. **17**(2), 281–308 (1988)
51. Gordon, D.M.: A survey of fast exponentiation methods. J. Algorithms **27**(1), 129–146 (1998)
52. Grémy, L.: Computations of discrete logarithms sorted by date. Available at: http://perso.ens-lyon.fr/laurent.gremy/dldb
53. Guo, F., Chen, R., Susilo, W., Lai, J., Yang, G., Mu, Y.: Optimal security reductions for unique signatures: Bypassing impossibilities with a counterexample. In: J. Katz, H. Shacham (eds.) CRYPTO 2017, LNCS, vol. 10402, pp. 517–547. Springer (2017)
54. Guo, F., Mu, Y., Susilo, W.: Short signatures with a tighter security reduction without random oracles. Comput. J. **54**(4), 513–524 (2011)
55. Guo, F., Susilo, W., Mu, Y., Chen, R., Lai, J., Yang, G.: Iterated random oracle: A universal approach for finding loss in security reduction. In: J.H. Cheon, T. Takagi (eds.) ASIACRYPT 2016, LNCS, vol. 10032, pp. 745–776 (2016)
56. Hanaoka, Y., Hanaoka, G., Shikata, J., Imai, H.: Identity-based hierarchical strongly key-insulated encryption and its application. In: B.K. Roy (ed.) ASIACRYPT 2005, LNCS, vol. 3788, pp. 495–514. Springer (2005)
57. Hankerson, D., Menezes, A.J., Vanstone, S.: Guide to Elliptic Curve Cryptography. Springer Professional Computing. Springer (2004)
58. Hellman, M.E., Reyneri, J.M.: Fast computation of discrete logarithms in GF(q). In: D. Chaum, R.L. Rivest, A.T. Sherman (eds.) CRYPTO 1982, pp. 3–13. Plenum Press, New York (1982)
59. Herzberg, A., Jakobsson, M., Jarecki, S., Krawczyk, H., Yung, M.: Proactive public key and signature systems. In: R. Graveman, P.A. Janson, C. Neuman, L. Gong (eds.) CCS 1997, pp. 100–110. ACM (1997)
60. Hofheinz, D., Jager, T.: Tightly secure signatures and public-key encryption. In: R. Safavi-Naini, R. Canetti (eds.) CRYPTO 2012, LNCS, vol. 7417, pp. 590–607. Springer (2012)
61. Hohenberger, S., Waters, B.: Realizing hash-and-sign signatures under standard assumptions. In: A. Joux (ed.) EUROCRYPT 2009, LNCS, vol. 5479, pp. 333–350. Springer (2009)
62. Itkis, G., Reyzin, L.: Sibir: Signer-base intrusion-resilient signatures. In: M. Yung (ed.) CRYPTO 2002, LNCS, vol. 2442, pp. 499–514. Springer (2002)

63. Kachisa, E.J.: Constructing suitable ordinary pairing-friendly curves: A case of elliptic curves and genus two hyperelliptic curves. Ph.D. thesis, Dublin City University (2011)

64. Katz, J.: Digital Signatures. Springer (2010)

65. Katz, J., Wang, N.: Efficiency improvements for signature schemes with tight security reductions. In: S. Jajodia, V. Atluri, T. Jaeger (eds.) CCS 2003, pp. 155–164. ACM (2003)

66. Kleinjung, T.: The Certicom ECC Challenge. Available at: https://listserv.nodak.edu/cgi-bin/wa.exe?A2=NMBRTHRY;256db68e.1410 (2014)

67. Kleinjung, T., Diem, C., Lenstra, A.K., Priplata, C., Stahlke, C.: Computation of a 768-bit prime field discrete logarithm. In: J. Coron, J.B. Nielsen (eds.) EUROCRYPT 2017, LNCS, vol. 10210, pp. 185–201 (2017)

68. Knuth, D.E.: The art of computer programming. Vol.2. Seminumerical algorithms. Addison-Wesley (1997)

69. Koblitz, N.: Elliptic curve cryptosystems. Mathematics of Computation 48(177), 203–209 (1987)

70. Koblitz, N., Menezes, A.: Pairing-based cryptography at high security levels. In: N.P. Smart (ed.) IMA International Conference on Cryptography and Coding, LNCS, vol. 3796, pp. 13–36. Springer (2005)

71. Lamport, L.: Constructing digital signatures from a one-way function. Tech. rep., Technical Report CSL-98, SRI International Palo Alto (1979)

72. Lenstra, A.K., Lenstra, H.W.: Algorithms in number theory. In: Handbook of Theoretical Computer Science, Volume A: Algorithms and Complexity (A), pp. 673–716 (1990)

73. Lenstra, A.K., Verheul, E.R.: Selecting cryptographic key sizes. J. Cryptology 14(4), 255–293 (2001)

74. Lidl, R., Niederreiter, H.: Finite Fields (2nd Edition). Encyclopedia of Mathematics and its Applications. Cambridge University Press (1997)

75. Lim, C.H., Lee, P.J.: A key recovery attack on discrete log-based schemes using a prime order subgroupp. In: B.S. Kaliski Jr. (ed.) CRYPTO 1997, LNCS, vol. 1294, pp. 249–263. Springer (1997)

76. Lynn, B.: On the implementation of pairing-based cryptosystems. Ph.D. thesis, Stanford University (2007)

77. Lysyanskaya, A.: Unique signatures and verifiable random functions from the DH-DDH separation. In: M. Yung (ed.) CRYPTO 2002, LNCS, vol. 2442, pp. 597–612. Springer (2002)

78. McCurley, K.S.: The discrete logarithm problem. Cryptology and computational number theory 42, 49 (1990)

79. McEliece, R.J.: Finite Fields for Computer Scientists and Engineers. The Kluwer International Series in Engineering and Computer Science. Springer (1987)

80. Menezes, A., Okamoto, T., Vanstone, S.A.: Reducing elliptic curve logarithms to logarithms in a finite field. IEEE Trans. Information Theory 39(5), 1639–1646 (1993)

81. Menezes, A., van Oorschot, P., Vanstone, S.: Handbook of applied cryptography. Discrete Mathematics and Its Applications. CRC Press (1996)

82. Menezes, A., Smart, N.P.: Security of signature schemes in a multi-user setting. Des. Codes Cryptography 33(3), 261–274 (2004)

83. Miller, V.S.: Use of elliptic curves in cryptography. In: H.C. Williams (ed.) CRYPTO 1985, LNCS, vol. 218, pp. 417–426. Springer (1985)

84. Naor, M., Yung, M.: Public-key cryptosystems provably secure against chosen ciphertext attacks. In: H. Ortiz (ed.) ACM STOC, pp. 427–437. ACM (1990)

85. Nielsen, J.B.: Separating random oracle proofs from complexity theoretic proofs: The non-committing encryption case. In: M. Yung (ed.) CRYPTO 2002, LNCS, vol. 2442, pp. 111–126. Springer (2002)

86. Park, J.H., Lee, D.H.: An efficient IBE scheme with tight security reduction in the random oracle model. Des. Codes Cryptography 79(1), 63–85 (2016)

87. Pollard, J.M.: Monte Carlo methods for index computation (mod p). Mathematics of computation 32(143), 918–924 (1978)

88. Rackoff, C., Simon, D.R.: Non-interactive zero-knowledge proof of knowledge and chosen ciphertext attack. In: J. Feigenbaum (ed.) CRYPTO 1991, LNCS, vol. 576, pp. 433–444. Springer (1991)
89. Rosen, K.H.: Elementary Number Theory and Its Applications (5th Edition). Addison-Wesley (2004)
90. Rotman, J.J.: An Introduction to the Theory of Groups. Graduate Texts in Mathematics. Springer (1995)
91. Sakai, R., Kasahara, M.: ID based cryptosystems with pairing on elliptic curve. IACR Cryptology ePrint Archive **2003**, 54 (2003)
92. Shacham, H.: New paradigms in signature schemes. Ph.D. thesis, Stanford University (2006)
93. Shamir, A.: Identity-based cryptosystems and signature schemes. In: G.R. Blakley, D. Chaum (eds.) CRYPTO 1984, LNCS, vol. 196, pp. 47–53. Springer (1984)
94. Shamir, A., Tauman, Y.: Improved online/offline signature schemes. In: J. Kilian (ed.) CRYPTO 2001, LNCS, vol. 2139, pp. 355–367. Springer (2001)
95. Shanks, D.: Class number, a theory of factorization and genera. In: Proc. Symp. Pure Math, vol. 20, pp. 415–440 (1971)
96. Shoup, V.: A computational introduction to number theory and algebra (2nd Edition). Cambridge University Press (2009)
97. Silverman, J.H.: The Arithmetic of Elliptic Curves (2nd Edition). Graduate Texts in Mathematics. Springer (2009)
98. Vasco, M.I., Magliveras, S., Steinwandt, R.: Group Theoretic Cryptography. Cryptography and Network Security Series. CRC Press (2015)
99. Washington, L.C.: Elliptic Curves: Number Theory and Cryptography (2nd Edition). Discrete Mathematics and Its Applications. CRC Press (2008)
100. Watanabe, Y., Shikata, J., Imai, H.: Equivalence between semantic security and indistinguishability against chosen ciphertext attacks. In: Y. Desmedt (ed.) PKC 2003, LNCS, vol. 2567, pp. 71–84. Springer (2003)
101. Waters, B.: Efficient identity-based encryption without random oracles. In: R. Cramer (ed.) EUROCRYPT 2005, LNCS, vol. 3494, pp. 114–127. Springer (2005)
102. Wenger, E., Wolfger, P.: Solving the discrete logarithm of a 113-bit Koblitz curve with an FPGA cluster. In: A. Joux, A.M. Youssef (eds.) SAC 2014, LNCS, vol. 8781, pp. 363–379. Springer (2014)
103. Yao, D., Fazio, N., Dodis, Y., Lysyanskaya, A.: ID-based encryption for complex hierarchies with applications to forward security and broadcast encryption. In: V. Atluri, B. Pfitzmann, P.D. McDaniel (eds.) CCS 2004, pp. 354–363. ACM (2004)
104. Zhang, F., Safavi-Naini, R., Susilo, W.: An efficient signature scheme from bilinear pairings and its applications. In: F. Bao, R.H. Deng, J. Zhou (eds.) PKC 2004, LNCS, vol. 2947, pp. 277–290. Springer (2004)

Printed in the United States
By Bookmasters